END OF A JOURNEY

END of a JOURNEY

AN AUTOBIOGRAPHICAL JOURNAL 1979-81

—

PHILIP TOYNBEE

Edited by John Bullimore

BLOOMSBURY

First published 1988
Copyright © 1988 by Philip Toynbee
Introduction copyright © 1988 by John Bullimore

Bloomsbury Publishing Ltd, 2 Soho Square, London W1V 5DE

British Library Cataloguing in Publication Data
Toynbee, Philip
End of a journey: an autobiographical
journal 1979–81.
1. Toynbee, Philip – Biography
2. Authors, English – 20th century –
Biography
I. Title   II. Bullimore, John
823'.912   PR6039.08Z7/

ISBN 0-7475-0132-7

Phototypeset by Rowland Phototypesetting Ltd
Bury St Edmunds, Suffolk
Printed in Great Britain by Butler & Tanner Ltd
Frome and London

Contents

Acknowledgements

I should like to thank the Provost of Southwark, the Very Reverend David L. Edwards, and Terence Kilmartin, CBE, former Literary Editor of the *Observer*, for their reading of the typescript and for their helpful comments and advice.

The final text was read by Dr Graeme J. Watson – who patiently supplied answers to many queries and offered solutions to several textual problems.

I should also like to thank Sally Toynbee for inviting me to edit *End of a Journey*; Liz Calder for her belief in the book; Peter Leek for his indispensable professional advice and for his sensitive and scrupulous preparation of the book for publication; and Sarah-Jane Forder for her extremely efficient organisation of the book's production.

An excerpt from one of Philip Toynbee's reviews is included by kind permission of the *Observer*.

I am grateful to the following for permission to reproduce copyright material: Bocu Music Ltd (UK and Eire) for lyrics from 'I have a dream' by Abba, copyright © 1979 the World Union Songs AB; T & T Clark Ltd for extracts from *I and Thou* by Martin Buber, translated by Walter Kaufmann, 1970; Faber and Faber Ltd for quotations from W. H. Auden's 'Out on the lawn I lie in bed' and 'As I walked out one evening' from *The English Auden: Poems, Essays and Dramatic Writings 1927–1939* by W. H. Auden, edited by Edward Mendelson; also for quotations from T. S. Eliot's *Ash-Wednesday* and *Four Quartets* from *Collected Poems 1909–1962* by T. S. Eliot; and finally for extracts from *Markings* by Dag Hammarskjöld, translated by Leif Sjöberg and W. H. Auden; George Sassoon for 'Faith Unfaithful' from *Collected Poems 1908–1956* by Siegfried Sassoon, published by Faber and Faber Ltd; and Sheldon Press for extracts from *Love and Living* by Thomas Merton.

John Bullimore

Introduction

'And now to begin the filling-out and re-creation of the bare notes I have been keeping since last April, and all the earlier material which I accumulated before that. To be writing carefully and thoughtfully again! A great satisfaction; particularly as this long period of casual and clumsy writing has had a most depleting effect on my precarious self-respect. This must have been at least a contributory cause of my recent dejection, that bruising awkwardness of mind and spirit which I know so well.'

When Philip Toynbee wrote these words on 20 January 1979 he was beginning the process of transforming the brief entries in his pocket notebooks into a full and coherent journal. Although he had written entries in his notebooks for many years, he had decided to develop the record of a particularly significant period in his life in an attempt to communicate a new direction in thought, feeling and experience. This first journal was published in April 1981 as *Part of a Journey: An Autobiographical Journal 1977–1979*. By the time of publication Philip Toynbee was seriously ill; he died two months later, on 15 June, in his home, Woodroyd Cottage, in St Briavels in the Wye Valley, just ten days short of his sixty-fifth birthday and no more than a day or two after writing his last journal entry.

The present volume is a continuation of *Part of a Journey*, which was a record of Toynbee's life and thoughts from 1 August 1977 to 4 October 1979 – two years that had seen profound changes in his life. That first journal described in detail his emergence from severe depression, the final year of the organic farming community that he had founded, his love and concern for his wife, children and friends, and his constant and passionate desire for self-improvement. Above all, it recorded the new direction and meaning given to his life by his search for spiritual truth.

Shortly before his death Philip Toynbee had completed a roughly typed draft of *End of a Journey* (the title is not his – when he died, he had not decided on a title), with many handwritten additions and amendments, covering the eighteen months from 5 October 1979 to 27 March 1981. The record of the remaining months is taken directly from his notebooks and a series of numbered and dated loose sheets, which have been transcribed by Mrs Sally Toynbee with the assistance of her daughter Lucy and David Lambourn.

Some omissions have necessarily been made. These are generally entries which are too fragmentary to have any meaning for the reader; others are partly illegible (particularly towards the end of the journal) and too uncertain in transcription. Some sections have been reduced to achieve an economy in the length of the text, but these reductions are mainly in the quotations from other authors.

A few repetitions have been retained in the text when these seem to be themes or ideas of recurring significance.

During the course of the journal Toynbee frequently mentions *Pantaloon*, his twelve-volume tragi-comic verse epic, which he regarded as his most important literary work. It remains unpublished in its final, complete form, but the reader will find four self-contained extracts, which Toynbee submitted for the Arvon poetry competition in August 1980, reproduced as an Appendix to this book.

The best introduction to Philip Toynbee's method and purpose in writing and revising his journal is his own unpublished account of the process, written in January 1979. This was originally a journal entry, but was deleted by Toynbee from the main text of *Part of a Journey* and re-incorporated to some extent in the Preface. It follows in a shortened version:

The question of tenses already begins to set me the problems I anticipated; and the question of 'cheating' confronts me from the start: from the start, I mean, of this 'filling-out and re-creation' on which I now begin. I have always known, of course, that all writing is a form of cheating; that the process of translating some vague and half-formed thought or feeling into words *must* involve a tidying-up which domesticates, and therefore falsifies, whatever rough beast was stumbling about in the murky caves of the half-conscious mind. (Already I contrive the kind of metaphor which seldom if ever appears in those 'bare notes' on which I must soon begin to work.)

But the notion of being strictly honest with the reader – of which that parenthesis might pass for an attempt – is a chimaera which has led to a good deal of brutishly disingenuous writing in our time. To write at all, to write for publication most conspicuously, is always a self-conscious and contriving business. To pretend that this is not so is simply a further degree of self-consciousness – and of dishonesty: the salesman's appalling, 'Now I'll be perfectly frank with you,' which always heralds, to the wary, the opening of a major 'play' . . .

Ever since the three conventional novels which I wrote in my twenties I have felt a growing distaste for any form of narrative. I am not a story-teller, and what I have increasingly aimed at in my work has been an arrangement of illuminating moments, strung together by the barest minimum of chronological thread or explanation.

It might seem odd, then, that I should have written that journal of last winter and spring with so much enthusiasm; for surely of all literary forms the journal is the most strictly bound by passing time. But in fact the sequence of entries proved to be as arbitrary, or as orderly, as I wished to make them: I found that on some days I wanted to pursue an idea or an experience which I had been writing about in previous entries, but that on other days I had something altogether new and different in mind. In fact the journal form now seemed to be exactly what I wanted; though I have always known that I totally lack that casual, spontaneous fluency which gives the daily jottings of the great diarists so much power and charm. (I am fluent only in writing book-reviews, which I do with a professional briskness which still surprises me, after forty years in the trade.)

In April of last year, then, I gave up all attempts to compose an orderly book and started to keep notes which I thought of from the start as only the rough material for a journal which I would reconstruct at some future time. And yesterday's little surge of renewed hope and vitality coincided with the calculation that I now had enough material, of very different kinds, from which to construct a book which would say what I wanted. That journal is now to begin in September 1977, since this was a month of a certain significance in my life, and the earliest entries will be refashioned from the notes and the diary-of-ideas which I was writing at that time . . .

Here begins, then, a journal which will be carefully concocted from separate blocks of material, but one which will truly convey, as best I can make it, my hesitant and clumsy journey of the last sixteen months. It will not be a record of my daily life, though I shall use that material whenever it seems to be relevant. It will be an attempt to record a journey in the mind and heart – perhaps, though I still find the words alarming, part of the soul's unending journey in search of God.

5 OCTOBER

The still, small voice which Elijah heard. And isn't God's true voice *always* still and small; never to be heard in the thunder, or even in the mass revivalist meeting? 'My power is made perfect in weakness' – which means, for me, that the power of God can act only in the perfect weakness of love, which is also its perfect strength. Physical weakness – spiritual strength.

All forms of material power tend to repel all forms of love; even the infinitely persistent love of God.

'The irredeemable in a man of power: vice versa, the power of the redeemed.' Hammarskjöld, *Markings*.

And this too from *Markings*: '[to be] absolutely faithful to a divined possibility'. To divine = to make a holy guess. More strongly – to perceive by means which we can neither explain nor understand.

◆ ◆ ◆

My rash letter to X warning him against a fault which seems to be destroying his family life. Is it great love or great conceit which enables me to write such letters?

◆ ◆ ◆

Almost any venturing into strange and alien ideas is worthwhile so long as you have the faculty of *lending your credulity*. 'Let's suppose . . . What if it *were* so?' Even if you come back unconvinced, you may have seen things within that space which you'd never seen before; seen things, perhaps, which the propagators of the ideas never meant you to see in them.

◆ ◆ ◆

St John-Stevas, Minister of the Arts: 'We shall all have to suffer.' How dare such people say such things! Many will have to suffer from this government's wretched policies, and some will have to suffer very much. But, in the foreseeable future, Norman St John-Stevas will continue to live just as comfortably as he's living now. And so, of course, will Philip and Sally Toynbee.

◆ ◆ ◆

Regret for all the fine schemes I've thought and talked about, but never had quite the zest or energy to execute. For example, the plan to load up a lorry with hundreds of garden gnomes, drive down to

Sissinghurst one dark night and plant them all over the famous and much-viewed garden of Ben's formidable mother.*

6 OCTOBER

A bad hypnogogic last night. This time I knew that I was in bed, but I also seemed to be just outside a strange, narrow, very long church with an open door. If I could speak the word 'Annunciation' I would be able to get into the church and be at once released from that deathly-terrifying constriction of chest and heart. But I couldn't move my mouth to utter the word; and eventually I surrendered to what always seems like certain death by implosion of the lungs. And this apparent surrender proved, as it always does, to be the only way back to waking life.

◆ ◆ ◆

The Pope in Galway. Addressing that huge crowd in the open air, he spoke the extraordinary words, 'Young people of Ireland, I love you.' It was impossible not to believe him, and I was almost as moved by his words as the Irish listeners were. A brave, truthful and loving man.

Alas, this very fact may make him the most disastrous pope of our time. For it's plain by now that he's an extreme conservative in everything to do with discipline and doctrine: not an inch to be given even on contraception. The result of this good man's bad words will be that much of his unfortunate flock will continue to breed them-selves into stupefying misery; some will cheat, and suffer all the penalties of hypocrisy; some will despair of their church; some will even despair of religion itself.

10 OCTOBER

To Coventry for Saturday night with Jason and Chrissie;† and the D A [Depressives Anonymous] committee meeting on Sunday. As we were driving there I suddenly felt an idiotic but overwhelming fear that the house would burn down in our absence, and the only copy of Part of a Journey would be destroyed. I even tried, unsuccessfully, to telephone our neighbour, Nasi Hammond,‡ from a call-box and ask her to take the typescript into their house until we came back on Sunday evening. This made me realise for the first time how much I've

*Vita Sackville-West. Her son, Benedict Nicolson ('Ben'), the art historian and Editor of the Burlington Magazine, who died in 1978, was one of P T's oldest friends.

†P T's son and daughter-in-law.

‡More properly 'Nazi', though P T preferred not to use this transliteration of her (abbreviated) Persian name.

come to value this journal – which I began so casually and with such dubious expectations in August 1977.

A long and good talk with Jase, in which I agreed with almost everything he had to say against the right of anyone ever to exercise authority over anyone else. Though I did think he was going a bit far when he told me that he was determined never to have children for fear of being unable to avoid giving them orders; if only 'Don't touch the stove or you'll hurt yourself!' I couldn't help thinking of the X children as they used to be; the least ordered, the most disordered and the most discontented that I've ever known.

(Later – Christmas – J and I agreed that there are indeed certain people to whom we gladly *accord* authority; but these are never, of course, the kind of people who try to exert it.)

Half-way through that delightful evening I realised to my horror that I'd forgotten to bring my Ativan (tranquillisers) with me. The result – either of the fact itself or of my knowing it – was not only that I had a ghastly and entirely sleepless night but also, since we were sharing a bed, that I imposed my sleeplessness on S. Yet in the morning she was perfectly calm, while I was in a state of physical and mental desperation. The thought of the D A meeting appalled me: any thought of moving from that bed appalled me.

I did just manage to get to the meeting, stay there half an hour to register my goodwill, then tell the others that I was in too bad a state to stay any longer. They were very understanding, of course, as indeed they should have been, and so we drove off to pay a quick call on Lucy and Bernard* in their farmhouse near Rugby. This, too, was an act of some heroism, and every moment of that visit was a painful attempt to keep up appearances. S's loving and unremitting support on the long, long journey home. And as soon as we got here I gulped down three of my pills, and felt almost fully recovered within half an hour. A terrifying dependence, whether physical or psychological.

12 OCTOBER
During meditation try to be simply *a* man; *any* man; *man itself* before God . . . Try to strip away everything which makes me a character; gives me a temperament; distinguishes me from others.

◆ ◆ ◆

Respect the demolition-men: Freddie;† Zen; Krishnamurti; Eckhart . . . But I know that my own job is to try to build things up

---

*PT's daughter and son-in-law.
† A. J. Ayer, an old friend of PT's.

again, however rickety and short-lived these constructions may turn out to be. Provisional habitations for the Spirit: well, for a few spirits, anyway.

♦ ♦ ♦

Now Jim's face, after his latest season in hell, is *radiant* with recovered faith in the love of God.

♦ ♦ ♦

Here is a fine and important passage from Butterfield's *Christianity and History*:

> We have seen how those who once reflected upon God in history were wiser than those who worshipped the gods in nature . . . It may be true that nature and history are not separable in the last resort, but at the level at which we do most of our ordinary thinking it is important to separate them, important not to synthesise them too easily and too soon, important above all not thoughtlessly to assume that nature, instead of being the substructure, is the whole edifice or the crown. The thing which we have come to regard as history would disappear if students of the past ceased to regard the world of men as a thing apart – ceased to envisage a world of human relations set up against nature and the animal kingdom. In such circumstances the high valuation that has long been set upon human personality would speedily decline.

Essentially, this is the same point that Schumacher was making in that admirable little book, *A Guide for the Perplexed*; what might at first seem like a wise and humble acceptance of ourselves as part of nature can easily lead to a gross reduction of man's true dignity by the abolition of all vertical levels. Hitler was one of the end-products of those man–in–nature, natural man theories which began, apparently as a great act of liberation, with the prophetic works of Rousseau.

Butterfield goes on to insist that all men are sinners; and this, of course, is a corollary to separating the human species from the rest of nature. 'All men are naked apes' is the very opposite of 'All men are sinners'. Sinners can repent; can be redeemed; can sin less and love more. Naked apes are condemned by 'nature' itself to be what they are and never to be anything better or worse.

Berdyaev says it very tidily: 'The entire world is nothing in comparison with human personality.'

Yet the ecologists are surely right when they reproach man for his proud claim to be master of nature, with absolute rights to exploit the natural world in his own (apparent) interests.

Yes, but the attitude which is being attacked here is one which *too*

4

readily sees man as part of nature; as that part which is the supreme and natural bully over all the rest; the toughest boy in the class.

In order to safeguard and cherish the natural world man must be aware (*a*) that he is truly part of it, by evolutionary inheritance, and (*b*) that he has been raised above it by act of God; that he is not only natural but more than natural; that he is far holier than the holiest rock or shrine or image.

15 OCTOBER
From *Observer* review* of *The View in Winter: Reflections on Old Age* by Ronald Blythe:

Ronald Blythe's *Akenfield* is a modern classic which might be described, I suppose, as a work of amateur sociology. But the act of giving it this description, instead of reducing the work to something which lacks the true force of academic expertise, immediately makes one question the whole role of the professional. For Blythe wrote his book not only out of deep knowledge – he had known Suffolk villagers all his life – but also from a deep respect, rising at times to an apparent (though unstated) love, for the people he was writing about.

The village was a composite construction, but its inhabitants were real people. They must have remained real in the minds of many readers long after the book had been put down. It was certainly as vivid and memorable a work as Mrs Gaskell's *Cranford*, with the advantage over that fictionalised and rather idealised classic that Blythe had a thoroughly modern wish to see and report things as accurately as he could. One good legacy of the scientific method is that truth seems more important to us than the painting of pretty and charming pictures. But it is a much older legacy which insists that the best way of seeing people truly is by seeing them as individual persons, each of them unique and unrepeatable, each of them worthy of respect, most of them accessible to the discerning eye of true affection.

It is the failure of most professional sociologists to take account of the second of these truths which makes them fail so abysmally in their ostensible devotion to the first. It may be necessary in a so-called 'mass-society' for statisticians to supply government departments with information about how people behave when they are regarded as members of certain income-groups, of certain age-groups, of certain belief-groups. The fearful error of our time is the assumption that when a person has been cross-categorised in

* By PT.

every conceivable way he has been adequately described. The fact is that the *person* has not been described at all.

17 OCTOBER

I am a far more seriously handicapped man than our friend Wilson,★ who is twelve years older than me and suffers from crippling and often agonising arthritis. I am so pathologically unsociable that I cannot lead a normal social life, as Wilson heroically yet joyously contrives to do. And I know that for the time being I must accept this limitation, if possible without self-reproach. I must make the most of it.

In fact so far as my individual working function is concerned – as opposed to my function as a man under God, which I share with everyone else – I become more and more convinced that the current journal should be my main concern. This is partly because *Part of a Journey* was received with such enthusiasm at Collins; but it is also because I have come to recognise that my mind in its present state is better at receiving and expressing these disparate thoughts about God, Man and Myself than it would be at constructing some more formal and elaborate literary work. Is there even, perhaps, a certain humility in retreating from the grand manner and high expectations of *Pantaloon*† to the comparative directness and informality of this journal?

Probably not. For I detect the malign growth of new vanities to take the place of the old ones.

◆ ◆ ◆

I am still looking for The Book; the one which will tell me all that I need and want to know. A hopeless quest, of course. (But it may be that one of our motives for writing is to create that book, which nobody else can create for us.)

Prayer also seems rather hopeless these days; such empty repetitions. Only the long preparatory breathing-exercise seems to be any good: at least it calms me down a bit after the various strains and tensions of the day.

◆ ◆ ◆

Not a hermit but a hermit-crab. That fearfully soft and vulnerable tail, wound into the shell, behind a menacing but rather feeble claw.

★ Wilson Plant – Monmouth neighbour and close friend.
† PT's twelve-volume tragi-comic verse epic. (See Introduction.)

Lawrence (Gowing) telephoned to say that Julia★ has died at last. Many sad reflections on the saddest life I have ever known. What love and wit, what a strange and rich personality, were slowly corroded in her.

♦ ♦ ♦

Anthropologists say – or used to say – that primitive man is filled with terror because the natural world around him is an unremitting threat to his survival. Therefore this poor, cowering creature made trees and animals into gods so that those imagined beings would protect him from the real threats of wild beasts, storms, disease, etc.

This seems a very odd process of thought. I find it much easier to believe in God's progressive revelation of himself to man according to man's capacity to receive him. And when people attack this belief for being 'naively progressive' it's well to remember that there can be, and has been, some progress in the quality of faith. Many thoughtful and good-hearted Christians still believed in eternal hellfire at least until the turn of this century. And we know better? Yes, we know better.

But the other and complementary truth which is now better understood than ever before – for example in Bishop Taylor's *The Primal Vision* – is that there has been loss as well as gain in the religious journey from primitive man to ourselves. Loss of intensity: loss, above all, of a numinous awareness in all our daily actions; the perception of the sacramental everywhere around us.

♦ ♦ ♦

The great fault of Francis Bacon (the artist), Samuel Beckett, etc., is that they are naively representational. We *all* know that hellish inner state, and if we had the technical means we could all depict it. For the state of hell is actually *simpler* than that Middle Earth which we normally inhabit.

Heaven, on the other hand, is a domain which is *beyond* the understanding of ordinary men and women; seen only by the Blessed; and by them only in their rare moments of enlightenment.

It seems to me that all the painters I love most have had at least some glimpse of heaven, glorifying the visible world. From Piero to Vermeer and Chardin: from Bellini to Rembrandt, to Watteau, to Pissarro and Monet.

'Significant Form' indeed! And to think that so many of us fell for that dry, pontificated nonsense forty years ago, and were willing to

★Julia Strachey, author of *Cheerful Weather for the Wedding* and *An Integrated Man*. (See *Part of a Journey*, pp. 174–5.)

believe that the subject of a picture – 'mere iconography' – counts for nothing; that the shape is everything.

• • •

Fear is never far:
Mother of Heaven,
Keep me in hope.

22 OCTOBER

Lying in bed and looking through the middle window of my room I saw the red leaves of *another* cherry tree: i.e. not the one at the north side of the house which first came to my attention two years ago. Yet this is our fifth autumn at Woodroyd! I am still a very unobservant man; except on the rare occasions when I set out to be observant.

Yet I believe that my eye for falsity in the written word is sharper than it's ever been. The least tinge of affectation makes me give up that piece of writing at once. Clumsiness, on the other hand, is no deterrent: and this may well be reflected in the clumsiness of my own writing in this journal.

26 OCTOBER

Here on earth there is no 'bourgeois happiness' for the Christian, except for that of a relative lull in the struggle, and of those hours of quiet introspection (which, indeed, are integrally necessary) and peaceful concentration in which we draw on all of God's holy sources (on the revelations of nature, of art, of humanity, of the Prophets, and, finally, of the beloved Son, our Lord), and from which we draw strength for the final struggle, in which the Lord can waste and expend us for the honour of his holy name . . . The higher we climb, and the harder we fight, the more grace, light, illumination, and strength and promise do we draw upon ourselves – yes, draw down forcibly, especially the grace of the Cross and the grace of Pentecost, in other words, grace born of the suffering of redemption and of the struggle for fulfilment. 'Draw down forcibly,' I say. 'And from the days of John the Baptist until now the kingdom of heaven suffereth violence, and the violent take it by force,' says the Lord. Thus every struggle does indeed lead to greater bliss, to increase of love through increase of suffering, and in truth to eternal consummation.

Part of a farewell letter from the young Austrian poet, Hannsgeorg von Heintschel-Heinegg, just before his execution by the Nazis in

December 1944. How it brims over with Christian passion, saying more, perhaps, in its urgent clumsiness, than he could ever have said if he'd been quietly writing about his faith in a normal 'bourgeois' situation.

Dr Johnson's brutal remark about impending execution concentrating the mind wonderfully is proved true in an extraordinary and blessed way throughout this modern martyrology, *Dying We Live*, in which the letter appears. Almost every one of those Christian witnesses ended his life in a state of *joy*.

To which it might be said that their faith gave them some extraordinary psychological support; even a kind of pathological exaltation. But I find it much easier to believe that their faith, intensified by their extreme situation, enabled God to infuse them with his joy more fully than ever before in their lives.

◆ ◆ ◆

And this from Hammarskjöld, a man apparently on the very pinnacle of benign worldly success: 'The more God demands of us, the more dangerous are the raw materials He has given us for our achievement. Thank Him then – His gift is also the keys to the Gates of Hell.'

Well, yes; but though I made an approving note of this, I now begin to feel a bit uneasy about it. Isn't there a blare of melodrama in that last sentence? And melodrama, so I've long believed, is one of the most dangerous pits into which Christian intellectuals are liable to fall – e.g. Graham Greene, Simone Weil and Léon Bloy at their worst.

◆ ◆ ◆

Krishnamurti and Buber. Both drive us back to the barest and most rock-like essentials of I-IT and I-YOU. That is, to the field of right action. But for the believer the ground of all fruitful right action can only be the unseen God of Love – with whom neither K nor B seems to be concerned. So their writing is honourable but arid.

◆ ◆ ◆

Realm after realm, and all overlapping each other. Or many different planes intersecting at many different angles. The notion that what we happen to be able to apprehend directly with our five senses is all the reality there is now seems to me to be almost grotesquely parochial. And this conviction is the bedrock of whatever religious faith I have. THERE MUST BE MORE THAN THIS.

◆ ◆ ◆

Julia. Lawrence telephones to tell us that she left her body to University College Hospital, but they refused it. She also left a mass of

9

manuscripts, mostly ruined by dotty revisions made after her dementia set in. So she is pursued with ignominy even after her death. Just as some seem to be chosen by God for his special favour, others seem to be singled out for cruel rejection.

Yet I am sure that this can't be true.

• • •

I believe that God's total understanding implies – demands – his total forgiveness of every single person. Yet it must also be true that each of us has *some* area, however narrow, in which it is possible to exercise the will; and to do better or worse. So it must be at this narrow area of free choice in the Self/Soul that God's light is directed, willing us to will the best. Willing us to will the best we are capable of willing.

But many of us, perhaps most of us, are such botched jobs by the time we come to 'years of discretion' – botched by heredity; botched by early environment; botched by our own ignorance and stupidity – that the area left for God to work in is very narrow indeed.

And what we shall need after serving our time here is certainly not punishment, which would simply fortify our present sense of being hopelessly put upon and confined by circumstances, but a greater area of true freedom – and heavenly instruction on how to become free and willing lovers of God's will.

Perhaps a period of co-counselling with an angel. Ah!

• • •

Judge not: particularly in situations which I can see only from a distance. I now remember with real horror the easy, cruel, self-destructive malice which used to be the very air I breathed at Oxford and after.

28 OCTOBER

I get better and better at accepting these days in bed without either guilt or complaint. At their best they are probably the best days I have; the nearest I come to serenity. Quiet reading; taking notes for this journal; attempted prayer.

• • •

Religious experience. If I have had any at all, it seems to have been a kind of happy guessing which was somehow *assented to*.

But there have also been moments when an old and 'known' truth has suddenly come back into the mind with a new force; lit by a brighter light.

And moments – but these are very rare – when the outer world is seen with an almost pristine wonder. (Though God knows I am no nature mystic, nor anything like one.)

◆ ◆ ◆

From Ego to Self to Person to Soul. This is the right and proper progression for all of us. But in a sense it is also a description of how things really *are* for all of us. Even the biggest ego conceals a soul; and even the holiest soul is bothered by a persisting ego.

◆ ◆ ◆

Survival after bodily death. It would seem that nothing is more important than to make up our minds about this, one way or the other. Yet in the actual business of living we are far more preoccupied with our daily bothers and pleasures than with speculations about an after-life. This is said to be a sign of our deplorable shallowness and triviality. But perhaps there is more wisdom in it than folly; the wisdom of respecting the present moment; of knowing – without needing to be told – that we have to deal with what is on the plate immediately in front of us.

The rest is silence. (Well, perhaps not quite.)

2 NOVEMBER
Dead days: little pain; little pleasure. And miles away from any joy or anguish. Prayer seems like trying to push into a sodden mass of grey cotton-wool. (And sometimes the uneasy feeling that if something *did* give way in there I might push through into anguish rather than joy. 'Below, Below there is always Below.')

◆ ◆ ◆

Moody's *Life after Life*; and other current books of the same kind. I find them very convincing on the whole, these reports from those who have returned from near-death. But there is one appalling anomaly. They all seem to be agreed that would-be suicides are the only people who have experienced something like hell. It is suggested that they have committed the terrible offence of spoiling the plans laid down for their lives; of prematurely depriving themselves of the chance to do what is expected of them on earth.

This seems to me to be stupid and cruel nonsense. I have known many suicides very well, including my brother Tony; and they are far, far from being the most lost and God-deprived people I've known. All of them died fairly young: all of them died in a state of pitiful disturbance and pain. What they must have needed most of all after

11

death is just that loving illumination which is provided, it seems, for the rest of us. To suppose that those shining angels, or 'helpers', who meet so many at the moment of death are out to punish those who are driven by life to a final act of desperation is surely a crass negation not only of love but also of justice.

◆ ◆ ◆

Nobody deserves posthumous punishment: but a great many of us may be incapable of receiving heavenly love and knowledge after getting so hopelessly buggered up over here. Purgatory as a period of blessed instruction.

◆ ◆ ◆

A rare good dream; a wonderful dream. I was turning and twisting in the air with a beautiful girl; the movements of aerial otters. I lightly touched her shining bush, at which she sang with unearthly joy and a golden liquid poured out of the point that I had touched and turned into a stream of stars.

Woke in a state of unusual refreshment.

10 NOVEMBER

I recognise that this perpetual, jabbing dissatisfaction will almost certainly be my condition until I die. But I have the right to accept this only if I believe that it is accompanied by a continuing process of amendment, however slight, weird and virtually imperceptible. If there is to be any divinity in our discontent we must be really struggling to get out of it. A discontent in which we wallow, stagnate and groan aloud is anything but divine. (Yet how hard it is, at times, to know the difference.)

◆ ◆ ◆

Looking down from my west window at the much-looked-at valley. A sudden slight change of vision, and what had been well known was instantly better known; and differently known. So change is always possible and hope should never be abandoned.

Yet I am increasingly aware that the depression of 1974–7 has never entirely lifted; though even at its worst in these days it is immeasurably more tolerable than it used to be. My frequent, perhaps my usual state, is one of continuous strain, always verging on pain. Everything that I have to do throughout the day can be done only by a conscious effort of the will. And although I believe that the Heavenly Mother of my prayers is helping me as best she can, it *feels* as if I can keep myself upright and in motion only by a heroic effort of my own will, constantly renewed. Gravity against Grace. Gravity often crushing Grace out of all sight or apprehension.

Holy levitation is the perfect symbol – as well as the occasional reality – of those who have overcome the deadly and deadening pull of gravity. No wonder such illuminated, such *enlightened* figures as Saint Theresa float free from the dragging of this dark earth.

◆ ◆ ◆

But I sometimes hope that this persistent affliction may be a democratic gift from heaven. Apparently in a condition of the utmost good fortune, I am afflicted in order that I may never have to feel myself utterly removed from the vast ranks of the world's suffering masses.

'All right, Brother Indian, so you're suffering from starvation and the deaths of your children. Well, *I'm* suffering from endogenous depression and psychosomatic aches in all my limbs.'

It doesn't sound quite enough for true brotherhood!

◆ ◆ ◆

'The purer the eye of her attention, the more power the soul finds within herself. But it is very rare to find a soul who is entirely free, whose purity is not soiled by the stain of some secret desire of her own. Strive, then, constantly to purify the eye of your attention until it becomes utterly simple and direct.' Hammarskjöld.

But I wonder if it is wise to aim so high.

◆ ◆ ◆

I note a new and crafty form of self-satisfaction. Thus: I suffer, no doubt, mainly through my own follies and weaknesses; but in confessedly doing this very thing I may surely claim the title of a Suffering Servant. In fact to suffer ignobly, and then record these ignoble sufferings for others might be even more serviceable than to suffer nobly, but remotely, in a noble cause.

Heady stuff!

And this would always depend, of course, on never resigning myself to these painful ignobilities. It would depend on implying something like this: 'Look! Even this querulous and undignified man is still determined, under God, that he will complain less and direct more of his concern at others. You, who may well have far greater spiritual advantages than he has, ought to be making the fullest possible use of them. Surely the spectacle of this deplorable but still hopeful man will inspire you to rise higher than he ever can.'

Too heady? Probably; for I don't really feel that I am cut out to be a preacher.

13

12 November

Admitted that this present moment is the only one that matters. But it is also true that this moment has *no pre-eminence whatever* over any other present moment, past or future. So the real value of *this* moment lies in its absolute equality with every moment of present time. And seeing that this is so, one may catch a glimpse, perhaps, of what is meant by the Eternal Moment.

♦ ♦ ♦

Laura★ in a very bad way; unhappy almost to desperation. 'You *can't* be so upset,' I said, 'it must simply be the boredom of your job!' But just after I'd delivered this commonsensical harangue I was sharply reminded – it felt like a real nudge from the angel – of my own hysterical state in 1941–3, wildly complaining, in the middle of a war which was killing millions, about the insufferable horror of having to work every day at the Ministry of Economic Warfare!

15 November

A glimpse of the crescent moon just now, which didn't exactly bring any blessing or relief but reminded me that blessing and relief are somewhere about, even if not available to this man at this moment.

♦ ♦ ♦

'How could the moral sense of Reason – and of Society – have evolved without the martyrs to the faith? Indeed how could this moral sense have escaped withering away had it not been constantly watered by the feeder-stream of power which issues from those who have forgotten themselves in God? The rope over the abyss is held taut by those who, faithful to a faith which is the perpetual, ultimate sacrifice, give it anchorage in Heaven.' Hammarskjöld.

♦ ♦ ♦

'The tree is no impression, no play of my imagination, no aspect of a mood; it confronts me bodily and has to deal with me as I have to deal with it – only differently.

'One should not try to dilute the meaning of the relation: relation is reciprocity.

'Does the tree, then, have consciousness, similar to our own? I have no knowledge of that . . . What I encounter is neither the soul of a tree nor a dryad, but the tree itself.' Buber, *I and Thou*.

★ PT's youngest daughter.

A very exact description of my own feelings when I first confronted a tree, only just over two years ago.

◆ ◆ ◆

The great importance for me, now, of making a *decorative* garden again. I feel a certain defiance about this, defying that mixture of personal fear and puritanical self-righteousness which so much possessed me four or five years ago. At that time every scrap of available garden land had to be put down to vegetables, both to keep ourselves from imminent starvation and also to ensure my own ecological purity.

'Self-sufficiency!' I still believe, of course, that we should all be as independent as we can be, both of the State and of the tigerish bosses. (Though it is in the very nature of our unjust societies that it is only their beneficiaries who have any hope of escaping from them. How can an unemployed council house tenant 'get away from it all'?) In any case a multitude of sins were covered by that alluring term, self-sufficiency. It has, now I come to think of it, the most lamentable theological implications. And even in physical terms it was always a *reciprocal* sufficiency which we should have been aiming at, rather than little narcissistic units, closed in on themselves and their own survival.

◆ ◆ ◆

Mute, with signs I speak:
Blind, by groping seek:
Heed; yet nothing hear:
Feel; find no one near.

Deaf, eclipsed and dumb,
Through this gloom I come
On the time-path trod
Towards ungranted God.

Carnal, can I claim
Only his known name.
Dying, can but be
One with him in me.

A very fine late poem by Sassoon. But there is a sort of willed optimism about the last couplet which doesn't ring quite true to me. We know that there *is* always hope, but this is not to say that we can always feel it. I think this was probably an occasion when Sassoon felt hopeless, and that the poem began as a true account – a true *celebration* – of that dark night. In the last couplet he seems to be trying to cheer himself up.

◆ ◆ ◆

The sure sign of true depression is the utter *unaccountability* both of its coming and its going.

◆ ◆ ◆

'I will never again', I resolved – for the thousandth time, 'give way to such a shaming and undignified reaction.' What I minded was partly that I should act rightly before God, but far more that I should keep up appearances before my family. (Not that there's really so much to choose between those two: in fact to try to look well in God's eyes is even more absurd than to try to look well in S's eyes; for it is just possible that I might deceive S about my true feelings, but we know that God is never mocked in that way – 'Unto whom all hearts are open . . . ')

◆ ◆ ◆

Extreme brightness and variegation of the dying beech leaves. At least this autumn is forcing my eyes half-way open again.

◆ ◆ ◆

'God desires our independence – which we attain when, ceasing to strive for it ourselves, we "fall" back into God.' Hammarskjöld.

This is the kind of specifically Christian statement which cannot be paraphrased in humanist terms. And I sometimes suspect that all the most significant Christian statements are of that order – to Wilson or Freddie tiresome, pretentious and meaningless paradoxes: to the wise Christian, confirmations of his own experience: to a bemused traveller like myself, enigmatic but pregnant encouragements; half-perceived truths which make me long to see them more clearly.

Ruskin's famous piece of pious back-tracking seems to me a flat denial of all the subtlest and greatest religious perceptions: 'Nothing is ever done so as really to please our Great Father, unless we would also have done it, though we had no Father to know of it.' This is simply a polite way of saying 'Great Father, you may leave us now, for we have no further need of you.' At about the same time, Nietzsche was saying this much more dramatically and abruptly when he announced that God is dead.

What is needed now is certainly not a dogged restatement of Christian orthodoxy, but a far deeper exposition of just what it is that so profoundly separates faith from humanism. This is something I would dearly like to attempt, but I know only too well that I haven't the equipment for doing it.

◆ ◆ ◆

One of the faults of Buber, and of many other religious writers, is that they never make it plain what sort of language they are using. Thus they can move from the literal to the metaphorical to the poetical and back again without ever declaring which mode they are in at any given moment. This seems to give them the best of several worlds, but in fact it leads to a damaging confusion. Heavy abstractions are used as if they were concrete entities: a metaphor comes in handy for skipping over a difficult gap in the argument . . . A self-indulgent language.

◆ ◆ ◆

When praying just now I had a strange semi-vision of a small parrot-like bird pushing its egg towards me with its beak, in a mute request that I should hatch out the egg myself. I was deeply touched by this act of trust in me.

◆ ◆ ◆

Reflections on Bim's rough figure, sculpted out of Barn House★ sandstone: a little-old-baby-man, sitting and leaning forward to clutch his legs. Wisdom and innocence; wonder, peace and sorrow. I turn to him now at the end of my watching prayer, repeating the climax – 'The Love of God' – ten times, with ten long breaths, to the last decade of the rosary.

◆ ◆ ◆

The angel-spirit to whom I often pray, and who is far more real to me than Jesus has ever been, is, of course, a being on a far higher plane than mine. But I can share all my lacks and failures with him in the conviction that he may have a few himself. Yet he also receives his light directly from God, and longs – for this is at least one of his functions – to pass that light on to me.

(One of the oddest of Christian notions is that men are superior to the angels; and a very early notion, too, as I remember.)

17 NOVEMBER
'O death in life, the days that are no more.'
    The easiest and most flaccidly 'poetical' of attitudes to the past. It is true that the past haunts us all, and sometimes torments us with the most poignant nostalgia. But surely we should try to reanimate it and

---

★House near Woodroyd Cottage where Philip and Sally Toynbee lived before they moved to Woodroyd. PT's organic farming community was based there until its dissolution in 1978; Bim was a member of the community. (See *Part of a Journey*.)

repossess it, rather than sentimentalising it and pushing it mournfully away from us.

18 NOVEMBER

Phine's wedding.* I want to thank God for the joy of this; and I know that thanksgiving must be a part of worship. Yet there is a certain thoughtless facility about this element in much orthodox praying, for if we praise God for all the good that happens to us we cannot possibly absolve him from all the evil. The usual practice is to thank him for the good, and explain away the evil as being also good, but inscrutably so: a holy mystery. This seems to me to be cheating.

I can fervently join in that famous collect which praises God 'from whom all holy desires, all good counsels, and all just works do proceed' – in fact, with 'Heavenly Mother' for the opening, I use this splendid prayer every evening. I believe that all positive goodness in man does indeed proceed from God and in no way from our natural selves. And thus I can thank God for Phine's marriage to David in the belief that this is a great good which he has brought about by working within them both. But I would not dream of thanking him if it turns out that they have good weather for their honeymoon in Italy. For I do not believe that he is a weather God.

◆ ◆ ◆

While in London I collected the Verlaine bust which Ben [Nicolson] bequeathed to me. I thought at first that it was a Rodin, and fell into base speculations about its value – though never, of course, with an eye to selling it except when starvation (or beer-deprivation) really threatens. However, it turns out to be by an obscure – but obviously very good – sculptor called Auguste de Niederhausen.

Anyway, I've now set it up in the left-hand corner of my frame/ shrine – and what a difference that grim and battered fawn has made to the whole arrangement there. Now in my prayers he represents 'The Pain of the World' (to which ten breaths and one decade of the rosary), and comes immediately before my eyes move up to the towering trees and cliffs of *Icarus*† for 'The Hope of God'.

But the pain is doubly sanctified; first by the fact that this is Verlaine, who made such fine poetry out of his suffering and humiliation; secondly by the sculptor's marvellous dignifying of his most undignified subject.

(And Ben, dear donor, are you here as well; hovering benignly in

*Josephine, PT's eldest daughter.
†Bruegel's painting, *The Fall of Icarus*.

18

my room, yet another agent of the Lord? How surprised you must still be by it all!)

20 NOVEMBER
'The knowledge and love of God . . . ' This seems to be asking a great deal: perhaps it is saying that there can be no knowledge of God without love of him. (But then how can there be love without knowledge: alas!)

◆ ◆ ◆

'What is sad is to see reason identified with a kind of dissociation, almost a kind of alienation, as though nothing but contamination could result from any identification with the object of study.' Edward Robinson, in *Living the Questions*.

◆ ◆ ◆

Only God understands the individual obstacle-course over which every one of us has to scramble and tumble as best he can.

X, watching the antics of Y, as Y tries desperately to surmount those uniquely Y-shaped obstacles which X can scarcely see: 'How very odd Y's behaviour is!' And Y, of course, feels just the same as he watches X's strange capers and tumbles. But God not only sees each person's obstacles with perfect clarity; he also helps him to get over them with all the power of his love.

◆ ◆ ◆

From a *Guardian* review of a book called *The Mighty Micro*: 'He sweeps aside, in a dazzlingly persuasive chapter, such semantic irrelevancies as souls and emotion and creativity.'

At first I thought there was ironical intent behind this apparent praise; but no such luck. And these astonishing words made me realise how easy it is to slumber pleasantly in a dormouse nest of one's own chosen reading. Being a near-recluse here makes it all the easier to forget that the majority of my fellow-countrymen – certainly the majority of my intellectual fellow-countrymen – consider my faith to be the most ludicrous and pitiable mumbo-jumbo.

◆ ◆ ◆

The hostility of both Buber and Krishnamurti to *experience*. I find this very odd indeed. I know that we all tend to interpret our experience according to a whole conglomeration of unconsidered preconceptions; and I see that we should be continually doing our best to clear our eyes and minds of the distortions which result from this. But what

19

can there ever *be* in any mind or eye except what experience puts there?

One supremely important task is to choose the reports of others with the utmost care and discrimination. I know that I shall never share the experience of the saintly mystics, but I may be able to let what they have seen and known shine a true light on my own comparative darkness. In the light of what they tell me, my own muddled and obscure experience does in fact become half-way intelligible.

◆ ◆ ◆

Reading a life of Dick Sheppard. To my shame, I had always treated him with a certain contempt. This was partly due to my mother's triumphalist scorn for the poor little simple-minded do-gooder, whose sermons we used to hear at St Martin's during her brief transitional period in the C of E. But it was due much more to my later sense of superiority as a Communist and a 'realist' over the 'sloppy idealism' of the Peace Pledge Union.

I now discover that Sheppard was a true saint; a far deeper, broader, braver, more tragic figure than I'd ever imagined: a man who spent himself completely for love of God and man.

◆ ◆ ◆

'The artist does not reproduce the visible: rather he makes things visible.' Klee.

◆ ◆ ◆

'Be patient towards all that is unsolved in your heart and try to love the questions themselves like locked rooms . . . Do not now seek the answers, which cannot be given you because you would not be able to live with them. And the point is, to live everything. Live the questions now. Perhaps you will then gradually, without noticing it, live along some distant day into the answer.'

Rilke, at his most marvellous, quoted by Edward Robinson in *Living the Questions*.

◆ ◆ ◆

Yes, dear Lord and Mother, in this darkness of my room I *believe* that you are here. But I am not *aware* of your presence; I am never aware of your presence.

◆ ◆ ◆

I talk with a certain complacency, about my 'appalling memory'. But what this really means is that I have gone through much of life in a self-absorbed daze, paying far too little attention either to people or to things.

♦ ♦ ♦

A splendid dream. David Lusk, my good angel at Rugby, Christian and Classical scholar, killed in the war. He and I were jumping about together on a stormy and wave-tossed shore; huge boulders were crashing down all round us, even on top of us, out of a wild sky. But we knew they couldn't harm us, and we rejoiced in the whole scene and situation. I felt great love for this long-dead friend.

♦ ♦ ♦

Here I am, I thought this morning, driving along this particular road, at this particular time, within this particular domain of reality. But I might perhaps – by the will of God or by sheer chance – be suddenly transferred into an inconceivably different scheme of things, related to this one only as some very remote key is related to the tonic.

♦ ♦ ♦

I prefer Bim's little old man – who is both God and a worshipper of God – to the Verlaine bust. But in saying this I am making no artistic judgement between them; I am only saying that I seem to derive more love and truth from the first than from the second. (But what 'artistic judgement' *is* there other than this?)

♦ ♦ ♦

> The secret waits for the insight
> Of eyes unclouded by longing;
> Those who are bound by desire
> See only the outward shell.
>   Lao-tzu

He is saying, I suppose, much what Rilke was saying about living the questions. And what Simone Weil meant by 'waiting on God'. And no doubt my temptation is to try to assault the citadel; but perhaps this too is a way – to go on assaulting and assaulting and falling back, without resentment or even discouragement.

♦ ♦ ♦

Father Philip tells me that he feels great satisfaction in belonging to the (disestablished) Church in Wales. And since Tymawr★ is our place of

---

★ Anglican convent near Monmouth.

worship, I suppose S and I can make the same claim. And I like it too – the sense of smallness, oddity and some slight independence.

◆ ◆ ◆

Krishnamurti, Buber, etc., are trying to persuade us to strip ourselves of all the beliefs that we've blindly and unthinkingly acquired simply by belonging to a certain time and a certain place.

But there are times when I feel that the more we can acquire the better – 'compel them to come in . . . '; this may lead to confusion, but I think I prefer a rich confusion to a bare cell.

26 NOVEMBER

Present order of Meditation and Prayer

I. Reading (just now, NT, Kierkegaard's *Journals*, Buber, Hammarskjöld, Krishnamurti).

II. Sixty slow breaths, with a formal pattern of pauses.

III. The Rosary (a breath for each bead). Holding the crucifix – 'Holy Brother and Bringer of Light.' Lowest bead – 'May I see by the light you brought into the world.' Next three beads – 'Heavenly Mother. Heavenly Mother. Heavenly Mother.' Top bead – 'Thy Will be Done.' Coin of Virgin and Child – 'Heavenly Mother, Thy Will be Done.' First decade, staring at the Verlaine bust – 'The Pain of the World.' Single bead (and every succeeding single bead) – 'Thy Will be Done.' Second decade, staring at tree-tops and white cliff in the top left corner of *The Fall of Icarus* – 'The Hope of God.' Third decade, eyes on the furrowing plough – 'The Work of God.' Fourth decade, eyes on Simon's bowl under the picture – 'The Light of God.' Fifth decade, eyes on Anne's angel – 'The Peace of God.' Descent from Virgin to Crucifix, eyes on Bim's figure – 'The Love of God.'

IV. Criss-crossing the whole Bruegel, with the shepherd's raised head as the recurring centre, the intersection:

> 'Heavenly Mother
> Light of the World,
> Have Mercy upon Us.'

(This is a *very* formal pattern, with a strict and unvarying selection of objects; first vertically crossed, then horizontally, then down each diagonal in turn.)

22

V. Another breathing exercise, in sets of ten, with extreme concentration on the air entering and leaving the nostrils.

VI. Recollection of the last twenty-four hours, and the simplest sort of I-to-Thou praying for amendment.

VII. Intercessions. (But not always, and seldom with any real conviction.)

I don't find this very satisfactory; but I doubt whether I could devise another which would be more so.

◆ ◆ ◆

Toothache: so, many aspirins and a heavy dose of Ativan, followed by a dopey and very pleasant day in bed. Warmth, generosity, serene goodwill. Thanks be to aspirin and Ativan!

◆ ◆ ◆

'And as thy days, so shall thy strength be . . . and underneath the everlasting arms.'

◆ ◆ ◆

'Every developing human child rests, like all developing beings, in the womb of the great mother – the undifferentiated, not yet formed primal world. From this it detaches itself to enter a personal life, and it is only in dark hours when we slip out of this again . . . that we are close to her again.' Buber.

But surely when we slip back it is not into the same primal dark from which we came? Surely there must now be some sort of awareness, in that *living* dark, which we never had in the womb, or in infancy?

◆ ◆ ◆

Monet's *Gare Saint-Lazare*. Did he really believe that he was making an advance in realism; in more perfect representation of the world as it is? What he has done is a great feat of glorification: a grimy railway station has been transported into heaven.

29 NOVEMBER
Father Philip in a sad state; depression and physical discomfort; another epileptic fit last week. I not only feel great pity and affection for him; I also see my own early future in his condition.

Also visited Tom in his Cardiff hospital. An obscure but terrible collapse, due, so it seems, mainly to his despairing inability to adapt himself to the new home that has been found for him. I doubt if I could have saved him from this misery and prostration, *but I might at least have tried.*

◆ ◆ ◆

'The man who possesses that light which is the Hidden God is in a tragic situation – he is no longer able to live by the golden mean, but must live without rest in the tension between mutually exclusive demands.' Julien Gracq, quoted by Hammarskjöld.

But this is just as true of those who are very far from possessing that light, but who know that it is there and know that the only thing which *ought to* matter is their continued search for it.

◆ ◆ ◆

Reading a life of Thomas More. A true saint; and why be nervous of adding that part of his sanctity lay in his being morally ahead of his time? There has been so much complacency about our modern wisdom, and also so much abuse of the age, that one is chary of suggesting that there is now an *available* moral sensitivity of great delicacy, even if it seldom has the strength of its convictions.

◆ ◆ ◆

It is our unconsidered priorities which are often so desperately wrong and stupid. Tonight, for example, Tom's sister telephoning to tell us how he is getting on in hospital, and my nagging irritation that this was interrupting that silly TV programme called 'Mastermind'.

(Yes; but the other day I was in the kitchen talking to S and Laura about L's current problem when I was interrupted by a telephone call from Lady Collins to tell me, with many regrets, that they couldn't afford to publish *Pantaloon*. I went straight back to join the conversation in the kitchen, and didn't even think to mention this further bad news until S asked me what the call had been about. This was just as unconsidered as the other case, though I did feel an unregenerate pleasure afterwards when I recognised that my priorities had been right this time.)

◆ ◆ ◆

How hard the conviction dies that in old age there must come at last a closing stage of hard-won peace and calm. But I don't see the faintest sign of its approach.

◆ ◆ ◆

'That which you cannot turn to good so to order that it be not very bad.' Thus Thomas More shows the never-to-be-neglected note of

24

dry moral common sense. (But even the admirable More was far more concerned about his king's heresies than about his wife-murdering.)

◆ ◆ ◆

The saddest mistake made by the Roman Catholic Church was its own self-santification; making a human-all-too-human institution into the Bride of Christ, Body of Christ, etc. Once an institution is elevated in this way – Communist Party, National Socialist Party, etc. – there is no crime which may not be committed in its name.

◆ ◆ ◆

The news now is that Tom will certainly survive; though I have never seen anyone so close to death as on our last visit to the Cardiff hospital. Apart from my straightforward relief for his own sake and for the sake of all who love him, I feel that this gives me another chance to give him the help I never gave him over the last year.

◆ ◆ ◆

Abandoned Krishnamurti as part of my meditation reading. It is all so desperately dry and passionless; even deathly. I wouldn't at all enjoy the company of K's ideal man. (Whereas Buber becomes deeper and wiser the more I read him.)

4 December
Lady Collins agreed, with apparent enthusiasm, that I should send her *Part of a Journey* – this journal up to October 4th last year – and she seemed to think that it might well be possible to come to an arrangement about *Pantaloon* as well.

But who knows whether they will *like* the journal? Nobody has read it yet, except S.

◆ ◆ ◆

A vague plan to make a personal anthology of selections from the New Testament. It would, of course, be very misleading as an epitome of the whole thing. But I don't think it would be an emasculation. A concentration, rather, of what seems to me the enduring and ever-living truths of love, light, life, rebirth, liberty . . .

◆ ◆ ◆

Gerry★ and I have been writing to each other about 'expanding awareness'. But I don't see *into what space* he believes that this

★ Gerald Richards, Quaker correspondent and friend.

awareness can expand. If it is a purely inner space – as he implies – then he and those like him simply become depth psychologists, vaguely of the school of Jung. But if the mind simply apprehends the outer physical universe more sharply than before, then Gerry joins the physicists – who wouldn't have him at any price!

Where else can the mind expand – except into some order of reality which is neither psychological nor physical but transcendental? (Later, Gerry more or less conceded this.)

In fact, 'Enlarge my heart, O Lord, that thou mayest enter in.' And Evelyn Underhill – to whom all praise and honour – writes that even our spirits are finite while we are on earth. And this is a healthy corrective to all this dangerous talk about our being part of the Infinite, the Absolute, etc.

◆ ◆ ◆

Thinking about my lifelong search for a beloved Hero; from school-days on. Auden's Truly Wise Man. I still have hopes, though I now look in a rather different direction. (And begin to suspect that the Truly Wise Woman might suit me better.)

◆ ◆ ◆

I spent this morning listening very carefully to a new recording of *The Messiah* which Laura has given us. Following the text for the first time I not only heard the words and music wonderfully well, but was amazed to find that two-thirds of the libretto is from the Old Testament; only a third from the New. Natural enough, I suppose, since the whole justification for Jesus as Messiah comes from the OT. A useful reminder of how much there is to find there, when I get round to it.

I thought of all that had entered into this single occasion of myself listening to that recording. All my own past and present circum-stances: the Old Testament: the New Testament: all Christianity from the NT to Handel, and from Handel to now: Handel himself: Jennens (librettist): Basil Lam (editor of this performance): Charles Mackerras (conductor): the recording technicians . . . Extend the list to the lives and experiences of all these people and you realise that what has contributed to the single occasion of my listening is an infinite recession. Which applies, of course, though in a much less compelling form, to every moment of every human life.

And if we extend the chain of causes to heaven . . .

◆ ◆ ◆

'You must have an exalted mind and a *burning* heart in which, nevertheless, reign silence and stillness.' Eckhart, quoted by

Hammarskjöld. It is that burning heart which seems to be too often neglected by Buddhists and Hindus.

9 DECEMBER

Kerry and Mary were married in their local Hereford church. The first church wedding I've attended for thirty years or more – though so many funerals. What a pleasure it was to see nearly all the Barn House old-timers again, and to be reminded of how much they still keep in touch with each other. A little network of good friends surviving that close concentration of strangers which began the community in 1974. And that in itself is surely justification enough?

♦ ♦ ♦

Whatever may be said about the benefits of pain, to oneself and therefore to others, I cannot believe that this applies to *acute* pain while it is being suffered. A man racked by toothache is very unlikely to be a wisely benevolent man so long as the toothache lasts.

10 DECEMBER

I woke to that aching lassitude which is the physical aspect of depression. So I stayed in bed all day, and without guilt, as S had urged me. I know by now, though I always find it hard to remember, that such days in bed can be the most fruitful of all, *provided that I accept them thankfully*.

♦ ♦ ♦

In our efforts to help Laura it often seems very sad that we can never use what we both believe would help her most: our faith in the ever-present love of God (for all the lurches and wobblings of that faith). But at this point it would be a fearful mistake even to mention it, so little could it possibly mean to her.

And now I remember, with great gratitude, that when I stayed with my mother in the first anguish of Anne's★ decision to leave me she spoke only in terms that were appropriate to me; never of her own religious beliefs.

But when we talk with Jim, or Tom, about their troubles and ours what a mercy it is to be able to talk freely of the faith we share with them.

♦ ♦ ♦

★P T's first wife, to whom he was married from 1939 to 1949.

'The inner light which shines in the heart of man is sent by God. But it is actually the same as reason purified and disciplined.' Dean Inge.

Is this true? In what sense might it be true?

Berkeley's contribution, or addendum: 'Rational happiness is not to be had in this world.' If happiness is taken to mean joy, not pleasure, then this is surely true. For joy comes from God alone, and God can never be rationally understood by anyone.

◆ ◆ ◆

If Jesus said 'Abba' to God, why is it impossible for us to call him 'Daddy'? The implications of the two words must be very different after all. (Did they have any sugar-abbas in Palestine, I wonder?)

◆ ◆ ◆

Rochefoucauld has always disturbed me. His perceptions of how human beings think, feel and behave have a deadly accuracy. But if this were the whole truth about us – which he strongly implies – then indeed we would be living in hell.

◆ ◆ ◆

'Spirit is not in the I but between I and You. It is not like the blood that circulates in you but like the air in which you breathe. Man lives in the spirit when he is able to respond to his You. He is able to do this when he enters into this relation with his whole being. It is solely by virtue of his power to relate that man is able to live in the spirit.' Buber.

In other words, Love thy neighbour as thyself.

◆ ◆ ◆

Isn't there, perhaps, a certain false grandeur about the claim that our afflictions are sent by God? Or even in the claim that they are due to some deep and interesting psychological malaise? Many depressions, after all, are cured by pills; that is, by correcting some purely chemical malfunction in the body.

◆ ◆ ◆

Brown folds on the backs of my hands. The hands of an old man. But I don't find this at all disturbing.

◆ ◆ ◆

Evelyn Underhill's *Man and the Supernatural*. I must have read this book, without being much impressed by it, during the worst years of my depression. It now seems to me the best and most concise explanation of religious faith that I have ever read. Not at all in the modern mode, but just what we need to get back to. So I have cut out the first chapter and shall get it photocopied to use as a broadsheet whenever opportunity arises. This paragraph, for example:

> The word 'supernatural' is now out of fashion, having been cheapened by careless use; and modern thought is hostile to the dualism that it suggests. But those who dislike this antithesis of nature and supernature must still concede that in all its permutations, growth, rising and falling, even in its worst corruptions and extravagances, religion does maintain one fundamental character; that of witnessing to a living and abiding Reality which is distinct from and beyond the world. It cannot be set aside as one of the devices by which the abstraction called Nature bribes or frightens man into becoming his natural best: *for it often enters into sharpest conflict with that natural best.* Nor can it be explained as a consoling fantasy; for its ultimate demands are the hardest that humanity has to meet. (My italics.)

◆ ◆ ◆

One gift of faith is that it profoundly alters one's sense of the past: *respect.*

11 DECEMBER
Simplicity! E.g., if I could honestly and constantly desire above everything to be useful to God and man.

◆ ◆ ◆

'The soul's dark cottage, batter'd and decay'd
Lets in new light through chinks that time has made.' Waller.

◆ ◆ ◆

Something heavy and poignant oppresses me – to do with a vague yet painful pity for Laura and S. Almost as if some sad ghost/psyche/spirit were hanging about me.
But how much more freely I can talk to Laura now, and this is due at least as much to a change in me as in her (naturally – lovingly).

◆ ◆ ◆

Nature mysticism springs from our own 'internal' bond with the material world, but this bond is sanctified by God. God (again) is in the relationship – *I–Thou.*
All very well, but there does seem to be a whole range of religious experience ('cosmic') which my theology has to strain very hard to embrace.

◆ ◆ ◆

29

What I live in much of the time is a state of noisy (i.e. protesting) desperation.

♦ ♦ ♦

To repent is to retrieve the past. Now the Gargoyle* has a new meaning for me: I can repossess what I lost there.

♦ ♦ ♦

We have to protest all the time, 'Let me in! Show me! Tell me! Change me!' Yet we have to accept all the time – 'Yet not my will but thine.' Hard!

♦ ♦ ♦

Joel Goldsmith – the businessman's mystic; Jacob Boehme – the cosmic visionary. But both saw and proclaimed something of God.

12 DECEMBER
'We have to acquire a peace and balance of mind such that we can give every word of criticism its due weight, and humble ourselves before every word of praise.' Hammarskjöld.

♦ ♦ ♦

And now, just as I've decided that my letters are important, an old correspondent, J.F., rings up to ask if he can resume the correspondence he left off two or three years ago.

I *welcome* him back. Joke uneasily to myself about my correspondence course; former pupils, etc. But the fact is I do this well: have helped several people: should be pleased – as I am.

♦ ♦ ♦

I *knew* the penalty would follow. N telephones: S answers: I am in a state because he's said that he may ring back. 'Why didn't you ask him *to write?*'

14 DECEMBER
Josephine brought David again; and we soon found that we were very much at ease with him. He was a curate many years ago, and still retains, to me, a rather daunting technical knowledge of theology, which makes me feel very amateurish when talking to him.

♦ ♦ ♦

* The Gargoyle Club. (See *Part of a Journey*, p. 43.)

D A meeting at Coventry. S and I were in a sad, sour state when we got there, and found that communication with the others actually did us good – although the main topic was still the desperately boring one of another application to the Charity Commission.

◆ ◆ ◆

David gave me a bestseller paperback on 'the evolution of human intelligence'. Another reminder of the amazingly bland complacency of the dominant modern attitude. The American author, Carl Sagan, casually announces that there is no adequate evidence for telepathy; and he is capable of such crude philosophical naivety as this: 'My fundamental premise about the brain is that its workings – what we sometimes call "mind" – are a consequence of its anatomy and physiology, and nothing more.'

Later Sagan argues that because every 'brain state' is unique 'the sanctity of individual human lives is a plausible ethical consequence'. What a rubbishy confusion of categories this is! No two grains of sand are identical, but who would dream of talking about the 'sanctity' of each individual grain?

17 DECEMBER

There are two distinct lines which the ecologically-minded may take: (a) put man back into nature; (b) put man back under the love of God. Both demand humility of a kind, but the first has certain great and obvious dangers. Man must remember, so this argument runs, that he is himself a part of nature, and, remembering this, he will not want to ruthlessly exploit the rest of the natural order. But in fact it is the essence of all merely natural life to extend itself as far as it can. We have to rise *above* the natural level, not by the unconsidered exercise of our power over it, which is the 'natural' thing to do, but by cherishing the rest of nature – a most 'unnatural' attitude and activity. No red tooth or claw for us!

◆ ◆ ◆

As I clean my nails after gardening and before meditation, I sit up in bed and repeat 'Cleanse the thoughts of our hearts by the inspiration of thy holy spirit.' Even such childish symbolism gives me pleasure.

In fact for me the primary impulse to purify the mind is not to rid it of prurient thoughts; or even of malicious ones. Purification means trying to clear the mind of all the nondescript rubbish with which it is habitually cluttered up.

Purification = Simplification = Emptying . . .

The A A [Alcoholics Anonymous] book which we are reading aloud over our morning coffee is a series of short accounts by alcoholics of how they came to God through the A A programme. Most of these stories have a significance far outside alcoholism: they are stories of despair and new hope; apparently irreversible degradation followed by regeneration. Accounts of rebirth, in fact.

◆ ◆ ◆

Perhaps the worst of my many bad habits is this continual taking of my own pulse: 'Am I happy? Well, how unhappy am I, then? Am I more or less unhappy than I was this time yesterday?' This all comes from the wrong-headed assumption that happiness is the proper state of man; and that unhappiness is an unjust denial of his rights. Happiness is a good, and that must never be doubted. But it is a lesser good: an incidental good; a contingent good.

◆ ◆ ◆

'Reverence' is a good word. But no better than 'irreverence'. How necessary they both are! How appalling when the wrong people – and *any* institution – is revered! Idolatry is far more dangerous and widespread than too little respect.

◆ ◆ ◆

The Logical Positivism and Linguistic Analysis schools have done a great deal of good, forcing us to think harder about the words we use and what we really mean by them. But they have also led to a fearful triviality; as in a book called *Religion and the Scientific Outlook* lent to me by my new son-in-law. The author – T. R. Miles – 'demonstrates' that to talk about the existence or non-existence of God is without meaning; a piece of utterly futile verbal dexterity; a linguistic game. 'But wait,' he assures us throughout, 'I am a religious man myself, and I mean, in the end, to give back to you saddened believers all that I seem to be taking away from you.' What he gives us back is the whole of orthodox Christianity seen as *parabolically* true. Talk of asking for bread and being given a stone!

My rare expeditions into modern atheistic thinking – however disguised – do more to strengthen my faith than many a work which was written with that intention.

◆ ◆ ◆

Far from being the friend of religion, as so many in our time have supposed, Jung has done far more harm than Freud to a true faith in the objective reality of heaven. He was the greatest blurrer of our age;

continually playing with the language of myth and symbol; 'defending' religion because of its 'psychological truth'; finding that 'God'
does indeed exist – in the fascinating depths of the 'collective
unconscious'.

Freud's crudities have done far less harm than all this waffle. God is
there, whether we believe in him or not; whether we are all obliterated
or not: whether or not the whole physical universe disappears. To
believe less than this is not to believe in God at all; and great harm has
been done by all those people who have tried to cling to the word –
and to much of the traditional religious vocabulary – while allowing
its meaning to slip away into something utterly subjective and
amorphous.

♦ ♦ ♦

Christ's 'life in more abundance' surely means both more intensity of
living and also more variety of experience? What it *doesn't* mean
is Freud's 'oceanic feeling' – cosmic consciousness and all the
rest of it.

♦ ♦ ♦

A delightful inscription to some unknown Christian of the Dark Ages,
quoted by Evelyn Underhill:

> *Amavit Deus Comgilum*
> *Bene, et ipse Dominum.*

Lucky Comgilus!

♦ ♦ ♦

'God . . . who is Light, *and in whom is no darkness at all.*' Right! So
where does this darkness come from? It comes from the inevitable
anguish of our hybrid state – belonging to earth by long inheritance;
to heaven by our dawning apprehension of that heavenly, or divine,
light.

♦ ♦ ♦

It is considered very naive to believe in the Rise, rather than the Fall, of
man. But I believe in it most firmly. God's progressive self-revelation
to man, as man has become increasingly capable of receiving it.

19 DECEMBER
Third visit to Tom in his Cardiff hospital. He is now much 'better', in
that he is no longer being drip-fed; is sitting up and fully conscious.
But I have never seen a human being in such a terrifying state of

33

embitterment. His mouth a thin, hard line; his eyes as cold as hell . . . His whole person clenched against God and the world. I felt that here was someone who had simply been given too much to bear; with the result that he is now alone in his hell of despairing hatred where nobody can reach him. Or I knew, at least, that any offer of help from me would have been absurd; worse than absurd – a vulgar failure to accept the situation; a fatuous pretence that my words could reach and help him . . .

Only a saint might have reached him.

◆ ◆ ◆

Wesley. He is treated with great respect. But *the greater part* of his preaching seems to have been warnings about hellfire.

21 December

Found myself lecturing Laura on the absolute necessity of absolute truthfulness! But how I lied and lied my way through life all through my youth and well beyond it! And no doubt I would lie now if I felt the 'need'.

What I meant is that I truly respect those who are always true to the truth.

◆ ◆ ◆

What is one *to do* with the Nativity? That the beautiful story is not literally true must surely be plain to any honest enquirer. But to scrap the whole thing – Annunciation, Shepherds, Magi and all – would seem an abominable deprivation. The problem is, how to treat sacred and life-giving myth with true reverence and delight; and this is particularly difficult when for two thousand years the myth has been masquerading as historical truth.

But the best liturgy, like the best painting, does make one feel the great truth behind the story: new light born into the always darkening world . . .

Certainly I am trying to feel the reality of Christmas this time as never before. Trying to *honour the mystery*, and to perceive that the light of Bethlehem is still shining into the world as brightly as ever.

◆ ◆ ◆

'Of course, nobody thinks of God any more as an old man with a beard up in the sky . . . ' Followed by the knowing little chortle of the modern cleric who is well-versed in the mighty abstractions; from whose lips the words 'Infinite Being' fall with the ripest satisfaction.

I am being unfair, of course. But it does seem to me that the old man in the sky is really far more helpful and revealing than any of the abstractions. That old man means human wisdom to most of us; and human wisdom, after all, is a little step towards the wisdom of God. Just as a human person is a little step towards the supreme personality of God.

◆ ◆ ◆

Reading the extraordinary, moving, infuriating journals of Ida Friederike Görres, *Broken Lights*. She belongs so deeply to that ruthless yet horribly soft-centred period of the R C Church which lasted from about 1870 almost up to Good Pope John. There is a sort of cosy superiority and a proud delight in accepting all that is most provocatively superstitious in the dogmas of the Church. This is combined with a sadly chiding attitude to the Church – showing superiority even there – yet a total 'ecclesiolatry' behind it all.

But out of all that garish confusion wonderful perceptions do emerge, at least in the case of this lady. And I doubt whether they could have emerged from anything less extravagant than this particular ripe and steamy stewpot.

For example, I had been thinking hard, but not to much avail, about the Transfiguration, when I came on this from *Broken Lights*:

> Christ never went about 'transfigured' during his earthly life. Even as the Risen Lord he was 'disguised', as gardener, pilgrim, etc. Only the three apostles saw him transfigured, and then only for a single brief hour on Mount Tabor. Yet what they beheld was neither symbol, nor idea, nor promise, but reality irrupting from the world above, from the background of eternity into the earthly foreground. The transfiguration was never repeated and never again 'confirmed', but it had given them a key to what was to come. And later on Paul knows that we should grow from light to light through the vision of his splendour, 'and so we become transfigured into the same likeness, borrowing glory from that glory'.

So I must admit that sometimes, when reading Ida Friederike Görres, I begin to envy the R Cs their piled-up wealth of contraptions. But I have never for a moment contemplated deserting this equally faulty church of ours.

◆ ◆ ◆

On TV splendid celebrations at Winchester Cathedral, with a lot of 'Glorious Heritage' talk-over in a particularly fruity BBC voice. Then they allowed a parson from Basingstoke to appear, with his angry, ungentlemanly voice, telling us that the cathedral meant nothing at all to him or any of his parishioners: 'worse than nothing'.

35

Of course I am on his side – yet how bitterly I would regret it if the cathedrals were allowed to collapse.

♦ ♦ ♦

Moments when I really *fear* the Fool of the House, with his endless, mindless, egotistical inner chatter. He might almost be a real envoy of the Devil himself.

What *is* Evil – if it is anything at all? I have always tended to avoid this question. Why?

Partly because I hate all religious melodrama. But also because my own cosmology simply doesn't allow for it or account for it. I tend to say that evil is only the remnant of the fierce animal in man; but this won't do.

'There is moral evil and mystical evil,' says Ida F. G. 'The first is merely a negation of good – the second its reversal, its perversion, and has the same fascination as a reflection in a mirror.' I would be reluctant to accept this; but I may be driven to. (Perhaps; but I shall never accept the Devil, evil spirits, etc., which reek in my nostrils of abysmal superstition. What Ida calls 'mystical evil' I'd rather ascribe to strange and dreadful twists in the human mind.)

♦ ♦ ♦

Yet I do see that what I like to think of as common sense in my approach to religion may have an element in it of philistinism; even of intellectual butchery. The fact is that I fear falsity much more than I fear naivety and crudity.

But oh for this dry heart to expand; this tiny flame of the spirit to flare up; this stale mind's-eye to be dazzled by glory! So *niggling* a daily life!

♦ ♦ ♦

Thanksgiving: so important but so mysterious. For what category of benefits should we give thanks? Only, surely, for some godward sign in ourselves or in others. Certainly not for the happy accidents of a fine day, a beautiful tree, etc.

♦ ♦ ♦

Ida calls artificial insemination a 'blasphemy'. To me it is a near-blasphemy on her part to say such a thing – not because I am so keen on A I, but because I think the word 'blasphemy' should be very carefully reserved for words and actions which are directly and obviously against the love of God and man. (If the Pope said O K to A I, as well he might, Ida, like the rest, would soon come round. But if he recommended that heretics should again, where possible, be

36

burned at the stake, I hope and believe that she would tear herself out of her beloved Church.)

24 DECEMBER

Yet Ida rightly insists that it is a terrible thing to 'seek for excitement, drama and sensation in religion'.

But how she goes on about sex; against, that is, all forms of it except within sacramental marriage. I think it's high time somebody undertook the demythologisation of sex. Try to treat it as the greatest of pleasures; get rid of all that terrible 'dark mystery' stuff; D. H. Lawrence . . .

♦ ♦ ♦

When I was speaking to Sister Mary Eleanor of our friend M – who had found prayer almost impossible when she was in hospital and in great physical discomfort – she said: 'The Lord is surely pleased even with the least attempt.' And I thought how easily and naturally the Sisters use such language: I wish I could do so too, but my background and human environment make it virtually impossible.

♦ ♦ ♦

Ida says we cannot in Christian logic pray for release from pain, because pain is 'precious'. Well, that depends on whether you are capable of taking it as precious on any given occasion. In any case, I think one can legitimately YELL FOR HELP on *any* occasion.

♦ ♦ ♦

Dionysius the Areopagite, so Ida tells me, called angels 'messengers of divine silence'. Wonderful!

♦ ♦ ♦

Asked to list the right-wing virtues – on TV – Philip Larkin mentions 'thrift' as one of them. But I cannot see that thrift is in any sense a virtue – saving up for a rainy day is mere caution; due to fear and anxiety. The real virtue here is *frugality*; a very different thing. 'Take no heed of the morrow.'

♦ ♦ ♦

Ida is very good on the need for local, as opposed to universal saints. How I wish St Briavel were a real and known historical person, instead of a complete enigma. Then I might make a shrine to him in the new garden.

♦ ♦ ♦

37

The Desire to Please. This is usually considered a sorry weakness; but, *other things being equal*, it must surely be a virtue: even a great virtue.

26 DECEMBER

The best Christmas I can remember. Mass at Tymawr; Kerry, Mary and Richard at breakfast. Then driving to Monmouth to fetch Jack; and when we came to the edge of the valley, above Mitchell Troy, the whole valley was a shining sea of mist, with the hill-tops like little islands. Japanese. An otherworldly beauty.

Strong family feeling, in which Jack was warmly and truly included. (The test of real love in any group of people must be, I suppose, just that it is *not* exclusive; that it happily welcomes anyone in from the outside.) Gave Jack the crucifix which Bim carved for me, and without any regrets, since I can't think of any better use I could have put it to.

When Lucy and Bernard were driving Jack back to Monmouth in the evening, he told them how S had lifted him out of despair a few months ago. She has done this for several people, including her husband, on many, many occasions.

I gave her an opal ring, and at our evening prayer she said, to my great surprise, that she had always wanted me to give her a ring. (Well, I did buy her a wedding ring in Tehran, thirty years ago; but I see that that doesn't count. Still, how odd that all these years should have passed with this unspoken desire lying quietly between us. Obtuse of me? Perhaps.)

◆ ◆ ◆

Jason spoke very movingly in the pub about his real wish for poverty; real shame at having more than he absolutely needs. And this is a holy wish, though he'd never use such a word. (But it would not be a holy act to try to impose his poverty on an unwilling Chrissie.)

◆ ◆ ◆

Ida finds subtle and deep reasons for admiring *The Fountain*. I quickly suppressed my almost pavlovian sneer at Charles Morgan, and realised that what *she found* in that book is the thing that matters. (Not that this alters my opinion of Charles Morgan, but it made me a bit dubious about the whole business of literary criticism. I remember my passionate admiration for two novels by Pierre-Jean Jouve, and how this disgusted Michel almost to the point of nausea.)

◆ ◆ ◆

38

Ida's belief that we are less receptive nowadays to 'finer, more subtle impressions' not so much because we've become insensitive as becaue our minds are so crammed full with inessentials that there simply isn't room for anything new. Much in this. Modern life is a frightful bombardment of the mind: surely worse, more meaningless, hetero-geneous and violent, than ever before.

◆ ◆ ◆

So racked with tiredness that even to wash my face and hands is a task for which I have to consciously summon the will.

◆ ◆ ◆

'John [the Baptist] is the greatest of those born of woman.' This is the kind of thing that Ida slips out, more or less *en passant*. I find such obiter dicta *intensely* irritating. Who says so? How do they know? What do you mean by 'great'? (Well, Jesus says so in the Gospels; but what did he know of Plato or of Buddha?)

28 DECEMBER

Present prayer procedure: ten beads and ten breaths, as follows:

> With eyes on the Verlaine bust – saying, 'The Pain of the World.'
> Tree-tops and mountain-tops in the Bruegel – 'The Hope of God.'
> Plough-furrows in the Bruegel – 'The Strength of God.'
> Simon's pot – 'The Light of God.'
> Anne's angel – 'The Peace of God.'
> Bim's figure – 'The Love of God.'

Thoughts on these.

◆ ◆ ◆

This, in a letter from a stranger, lifts my spirits out of the dark: 'I thought I'd write to say how much I like and feel stimulated and comforted by nearly all you write . . . and I am sure there are lots like me who are moved by your words, and would like you to know.'

◆ ◆ ◆

'Wealth is a virtue which has to be practised, really learnt, if it is to be of any real value to its "owner", turned to good account, giving him confidence, freedom, power and independence – not enervating him, making him dependent, stingy, soft and vain.'

This is Ida at her most perniciously absurd. The *only* Christian use for wealth, as Jesus made very plain, is to give it away as wisely as one can. And those of us who are wealthy and cannot do what we know

39

we should do must at least avoid high-flown trumpery of this kind.

♦ ♦ ♦

But I shall part with her when she's at her best.

'I don't see growing old as something negative, not as descent into the dark valley, but rather as the climb to the last peak – before which one must rid oneself of all superfluous baggage, discarding all hampering equipment. The armour, the skins and wrappings the soul has laid upon itself for its own security would seem to be falling away, so that it must meet what is to come at last directly, naked.'

If only I could manage it!

Final feelings about this close companion of the last few days: a very clever mind and a passionate spirit, but terribly bound by the thongs of her Church. She goes through all sorts of dramatic contortions, but is never allowed to escape – however often she says the *permissible* things against the Church, e.g. that it is narrow, tired, stupid, etc. So there are far too many seemingly interesting 'hard sayings' and paradoxes which really spring from a naturally free mind writhing in its bonds.

♦ ♦ ♦

Hope is the best gift God has given me; never quite suppressed even by the worst dooms and glooms, or even by the daily, demeaning indignities of life.

♦ ♦ ♦

Strange conjunctions! I find this in my daily reading of Hammarskjöld: 'Do not seek death. Death will find you. But seek the road which makes death a fulfilment.'*

♦ ♦ ♦

Buber's endless abstractions make him very hard to read, even in these short, pre-meditation spells. One longs for the beautiful clarity of the very best parable: that of the New Testament.

♦ ♦ ♦

House arrest. This would be very little of a hardship *to me*.

♦ ♦ ♦

When I was at last able to admit that I, too, was angry, there was that breakthrough for which both of us were inwardly praying.

---

* Ah! 12 May 1981 (PT).

29 December

We must get closer and closer; but this can only be done by some means which allows us to approach each other. My temptation is to *push my way towards her*, brusquely brushing away the branches etc. which separate us.

◆ ◆ ◆

Yes, I do believe that we are partially but vitally responsible for what we do and say. But I also believe that total forgiveness is the only true justice. Punishment as such is always wrong; human-all-too-human; no conceivable part of God. But *teaching* is God's part; and endless learning is ours.

◆ ◆ ◆

Of Christina Rossetti I read that she was 'a disciplined Christian'. A good term: all I could never be.

Yet I find her almost total concentration on the person of Jesus very alien indeed.

◆ ◆ ◆

'With Thee is the well of life, and in Thy light shall we see light.'

30 December

Taking the New Testament as a whole, it would seem that the *principal* enemy is the Law. Naturally so, because the Law, at that time and at many others, is the greatest single obstacle to new light. Resting in self-righteousness and a false notion of the truth – that is, a static, uncreative notion of truth.

Jesus spoke very little about the obvious sins because he knew that none of them was so hard to penetrate as the sin of believing oneself without sin. He died in the single cause of LOVE OVER LAW – which is not at all the same thing as antinomianism.

◆ ◆ ◆

The Abject Army of the Self-conscious. My brothers-in-arms.

◆ ◆ ◆

Historical judgement of Christianity. Nobody can say that it has or hasn't added to the sum total of human happiness, virtue, etc. But what Christians can say is that it has provided a new way of under-standing ourselves and the world; of apprehending reality and acting truly within it.

◆ ◆ ◆

41

That rare pity tonight which is acute pain: even anguish.

◆ ◆ ◆

'Only in man has the evolution of the creation reached the point where reality encounters itself in judgement and choice. Outside of man the creation is neither good nor evil.' Hammarskjöld.

◆ ◆ ◆

To write a creed. What ambition! What impertinence! What a strong temptation!

◆ ◆ ◆

Far from leading to simplicity fundamentalism is the most complex, contradictory and disputatious of all Christian attitudes. The interpretation of twits!

◆ ◆ ◆

'I hope by my writings to have achieved this much: to have left behind me so exact a description of Christianity and its relation to the world that a young man with enthusiasm and nobility of mind will be able to find in it a map of the conditions, as accurate as any topographical map by one of the well-known institutes.' Kierkegaard, *Journals*.

So what Kierkegaard wanted to do was to create his own straitjacket for posterity to wear. Such arrogance; and such a fearfully false understanding of what religious truth is, and how it must grow and change. The new Law, laid down by K. (As if we hadn't enough of them already!)

◆ ◆ ◆

The word 'temperament' is not much used nowadays, but it is a useful one, and its meaning should be distinguished from those other words which seem to resemble it. It is not so inherent as 'nature', nor yet so accessible as 'character'. We are born with a nature which will be ours for life – tone-deafness, for example; or an athlete's body; or a mathematical mind. As for character, if we acquire a bad one and take to lying and thieving more than the average it is quite possible that bitter experience will correct this.

But 'temperament' includes such heavy burdens as a strong tendency to sloth and gluttony; impatience and ill-temper. Or there are some who seem to be extraordinarily lucky in their temperaments, being temperamentally cheerful and kind; even self-sacrificing. For those with unfortunate temperaments, which means, I suppose, the majority of us, this is the heaviest and most intractable material with which we have to deal.

When we come to our senses and long for repentance and change we are like people confronted with great lumps of cold and crumbling clay. And we know that this is the material out of which we must try to make figures which can be presented to God without abject shame and disgust. A fearful task. But an inescapable one.

31 DECEMBER

The last day of the seventies. Russia has invaded Afghanistan. The Cambodian refugees continue to starve. The USA plans to spend an extra 20 millions, or billions, on chemical warfare. A gigantic steel strike looms in Britain . . .

In bed I feel that sick terror for myself and the world which I haven't felt on anything like this scale since the Bay of Pigs: which I felt for months on end in 1956/7.

I know what my simple duty is, which is to show no sign of this to S or Laura; to continue to act normally day after day. And if the worst happens – if this country is bombed, but we are left alive to die slowly of radiation – then I must concern myself *only* with helping others to endure the horror. But, as for achieving that, I was never so conscious of how impossible it will be for me unless I am *really* filled with the love of God and man.

Yet at this moment even the prospect of having to go out into the cold night fills me with dismay, and a fearful sense of the deep inner softness produced by a lifetime of self-indulgence.

I had a grim vision of every human being moving about like a robot, controlled by his own fear and hunger, the centre of his own private universe . . .

O Lord, this lump of fear and self-distrust is all that I have to work with. Enlarge my heart, O Lord, that you may enter in. Use me, O Merciful Mother, as well as I *can* be used.

To say that one will need courage in order to make effective use of one's love is a wrong way of putting it. Real love creates its own courage. Love without courage is not love at all.

Fear casteth out Love.

The point, now and always, is not simply to act with love but to act with so much love that it breeds more love in others. Love as a culture of yeast, which the saints can distribute and which can then be indefinitely distributed, forever growing and spreading and raising the dough of the world.

'Not where I breathe, but where I love, I live.' Robert Southwell.

And although this is so far from being true of me – worried just now about a power-cut depriving me of my electric blanket! – I can surely find some godly use to be extracted from this terror. Act, if I can, as if my own death were about to overtake me at any moment. (It is not the mind but the heart which is wonderfully concentrated by imminent death, *pace* Dr Johnson and see the Christian testimonies of *Dying We Live*.)

Yet how much this corporeal, this animal me is dependent on warmth, enough food, even – not even but *especially* – my evening ration of beer. *After* getting these it can comfortably contemplate the exercise of a little loving-kindness. Without them it is too preoccupied with itself to think of anyone or anything else.

But if the ultimate disaster comes, without killing us at once, the soul will have to triumph over this abominably demanding body. For there will be many and terrible hardships as we all wait for death. So ill-equipped: so soft and spoilt!

Melodramatic? It certainly seems so when I look about me at all the loved images that guard this room. But why, in justice as well as in reason, should we *not* suffer as so many millions have been suffering all over the world, all through my life? This ludicrous, protected life can't last till the end, surely?

O blessed Lord and Mother, Holy Angel,
Square my trial to my proportioned strength.

❦ I · 9 · 8 · O ❧

1 JANUARY
Yet a glorious dream last night, after waking horrors and prayers until three o'clock. I was a young postulant, with many others whom I loved, waiting in the anteroom of some great Benedictine monastery. The monastery was enormous, and it was partly the size of it that gave me such happy confidence. I woke in a state of JOY.

◆ ◆ ◆

I can never say with utter confidence – here is an act of God. But I can say with utter confidence, here is an act, or event, which is plainly contrary to the will of God

◆ ◆ ◆

In one of the letters from *Dying We Live* the condemned man assures his wife that 'no man is tried beyond his strength'.

Alas, this isn't true: think only of all the intending martyrs who recanted. But what does seem to be true, judging from the evidence of this wonderful book, is that if a man can reach God and God can reach him he will be given a strength, a love and a faith which far surpass his normal strength.

◆ ◆ ◆

Alles vergängliche
Ist nur ein Gleichnis. ★

I have known this line for at least the last forty years; but it was only just now that I understood it. Yes; everything that I see *could* be a sign of heaven. Not because it was 'created' to be that, but because God has made it possible for my mind to use it in that way. (In fact the *'nur'* – 'only' – is a mistake: the emphasis should be on *'alles'*. *Every single* transitory object may be used as a sacrament.)

◆ ◆ ◆

'The Pharisee's fault was not that he felt himself to be better; it was true, humanly speaking, that he was better than the sinner. But the fault lay in his doing so in God's house, before God. Among men it easily becomes an exaggerated fear and trembling to use God's standard; there I speak as a man; and when others deliberately seek only worldly advantages and impertinently, under cover of goodness, then I say, no, that I do not do: in that sense at least I am better. But I do not presume to approach God with such nonsense.'

This is how Kierkegaard justifies to himself his arrogant contempt for nearly all the other inhabitants of Copenhagen. It is a most inadequate justification. For how easy it is to be humble 'before God': how very hard to be humble towards that insufferable, loud-mouthed man in the pub. Yet to the reader of K's *Journals* it is plain that he is racked with scorn, spite, envy and malice; very likely a worse man, for all his intellectual brilliance and even spiritual perception, than the man in the Copenhagen street.

◆ ◆ ◆

Now that I have put an earthenware pot beside Bim's little stone figure I see that he is *a beggar* – though I'm sure that wasn't Bim's intention. A holy beggar, both needing love and giving it.

◆ ◆ ◆

Justification by faith alone. An absurd and monstrous doctrine, of course, if taken in its strict Calvinist sense – namely that the great majority have been irretrievably damned by God even before they were born. But if it were to be put a little differently – 'No

★ From Goethe's *Faust* (Part II). 'All that is transient is only a metaphor.'

45

justification without faith' – then it begins to make sense. I would modify even this and say, 'Life cannot be fully lived without faith.'

For if God is indeed the supreme reality, how can any life which is lived in denial of him be anything but deprived; impoverished; dimmed . . . ?

◆ ◆ ◆

A model. A thin rectangle of cardboard, in principle strictly two-dimensional. Around it a mesh of gold wire, some of the wires penetrating the cardboard. Beyond the bright mesh of wire a great space of pure golden light – which interpenetrates the wire mesh so that each strand of wire is shining with this light. Beyond that space . . . inconceivable other orders.

The two-dimensional cardboard is earth, of course. The gold mesh is heaven, peopled by 'all the company of heaven'. The lighted space outside the mesh is the habitation of the unseen God. And who are we to say that even that 'God' of whom we can occasionally catch uncertain and indirect glimpses may not be in a state of humble adoration towards something unimaginably beyond and above him? For ever and ever and ever, Amen.

◆ ◆ ◆

It is easy to say that St Paul was in some ways jealous; hectoring; self-righteous; even perverse. But we must love and respect his passion and force; the massive solidity of his whole scheme of things. And if we have to reject much of that scheme, we must be sure that what we put in place of the rejected parts is not just a feeble attenuation of Paul's great vision.

True we cannot, in our time, have Paul's confidence in the possibility of putting the truth about God and man into words. But out of that humility and inarticulacy we must build our strength. The peculiar strength we need in our time is the strength to construct models; tell stories; set up symbols; discover signs – and use all these as a means of worship and understanding without ever forgetting that they are *only* models; stories; symbols; signs. (Though we must indeed hope that God has been working with us when we created these new means of approaching him.)

◆ ◆ ◆

'A sheer conundrum is not mysterious, nor is a blank wall; but forests are mysterious, in which at first you observe but little, yet in which, with time, you see more and more, although never the whole; and the starry heavens are thus mysterious, and the spirit of man, and, above all, God, our origin and home.' Von Hügel.

46

And what could be a better example than that of enlightened model-building of the kind we need now?

And these words, too, from John S. Dunne's *A Search for God in Time and Memory*: ' . . . a "mystery", meaning by that term not unintelligibility but inexhaustible intelligibility . . . '

3 JANUARY

Today Laura said, 'Isn't it better that I should be furious than just bloody miserable?' And the answer we gave was firmly *yes*; though qualified, of course, by the exhortation that the sooner she can get through her fury the better. For it is simply *no good* recommending love on every occasion; or pointing out that misery is less of an offence than anger. The anger does give her at least a temporary strength – and it can be a means of tiding her over until her feelings for Paul are at worst non-existent; at best pleasantly and distantly affectionate.

◆ ◆ ◆

What is a prig? The term must imply self-righteousness; but also a person who inappropriately and in all circumstances applies a moral judgement. (I sometimes fear that my reviews get more priggish year by year.)

◆ ◆ ◆

O Lord, let me see with pure eyes. (Restoration of a lost vision.)

O Lord, let me think holy thoughts. (By purifying – that is, by emptying and scouring the mind.)

◆ ◆ ◆

Blessed angel, help me to keep the threatening horror clearly in mind without being disabled by my fear.

◆ ◆ ◆

How much, when I think of nuclear catastrophe again, do I fear for my own skin? How much for my loved family? How much for humanity? Something of all three. But I was relieved to find that when I envisaged, instead of this universal horror, simply being told that I myself am to die of an inoperable cancer I felt that *most of* the weight would be lifted from my mind.

◆ ◆ ◆

47

'It is impossible to compromise on the Church of England; her sacraments are sacraments or they are not.'

This, by Charles Williams,* in 1942, is a very good example of that tone of defiant precision which was so much in vogue among many articulate Christians at that time. The pretence that religious statements are of the same order as scientific or common-sense ones. And how contemptuous those people were of the sloppy liberals who were saying that nothing is or is not a sacrament: that many things can be a sacrament according to the receiving mind and soul.

Error of the misplaced concrete.†

'Liberal Christianity' – still almost a term of contempt. And indeed it led to many a baby being thrown out with the bath-water. But our present (liberal) task is to make sure we know what the baby is; and then, if necessary, to fill his bath with clean water. The sparkling waters of life and light.

◆ ◆ ◆

But later, in the same introduction to Evelyn Underhill's *Letters*, Williams makes up for this by a splendid passage: ' . . . that great principle of grace by which we do not know what we are, what we achieve, or what we appear . . . '

The fault of all triumphalist Christians was a fearful lack of generosity; of magnanimity. A certain Lady Iddesleigh wrote in 1931 of 'that Catholic culture to which the wisest among us are seeking to return'. Also, 'Between the coming of the "White Christ" and the coming of the darkening Luther, the sun of Catholic culture shone in the North, and warmed with its glowing rays the Scandinavian character.'

Such smugness would be almost inconceivable today in any Christian quarter.

◆ ◆ ◆

Dante. Whenever I read the name I feel like that small boy who was left behind when all the other children followed the Pied Piper into the mountain – a part which I acted at one of my earliest prep schools, and which I have always felt to be an appropriate role for me. (As most of us do, no doubt.)

I read Carey's translation long ago, and derived absolutely nothing from it except the very small satisfaction of having at least read *that*. The *Divine Comedy* is obviously a rich treasure of strange and beautiful objects; but one which I shall never be able to explore.

◆ ◆ ◆

* Author of critical essays, plays and romantic thrillers – best known as an Anglican writer and for his association with Tolkien and C. S. Lewis.
† See *Part of a Journey*, p. 66.

Painters. Vermeer and Bellini were perhaps the most perfect glorifiers of Earth with Heaven's light. Veronese, Tintoretto, Rubens and Michelangelo were not glorifiers but vainglorifiers: boasters; magnifiers; triumphalists . . .

◆ ◆ ◆

'You will see that the material world, although of course an illusion in the form in which it appears to us, is an illusion which has strict relation with reality.'

'But don't worry and excite yourself or pull yourself up by the roots to see how you are getting on! That way lies spiritual insomnia, the most deadly disease in the world. Let yourself go more, and trust more: you will get in the end what you are meant to have.'

Both from Evelyn Underhill's *Letters*. The second is very apposite to my own condition. The first seems to me to be another way of saying what I have often written here, in different forms – that the material world is itself without meaning or virtue or purpose, but that God has enabled us to use this, our physical home and inheritance, as a means of finding him.

◆ ◆ ◆

Pride is really a false antidote to fear.

4 JANUARY
Isn't there something very childish in the longing to do exactly what we want? And isn't it equally childish to invent a God who has this enviable capacity which we would so much like to have ourselves? A more mature understanding recognises the need for tension; the creativity of opposing forces – ourselves and the natures we are born to: God and the intractable universe of cause and effect.

◆ ◆ ◆

The spirit is truly 'at home with itself' when it can confront the world that is opened up to it, give itself to the world, and redeem it and, through the world, also itself . . . But in sick ages it happens that the It-world, no longer irrigated and fertilised by the living currents of the You-world, severed and stagnant, becomes a gigantic swamp phantom and overpowers man. As he accommodates himself to a world of objects that no longer achieve any presence for him, he succumbs to it. Then common causality grows into an oppressive and crushing doom . . . When a culture is no longer centred in a living and renewed relational process, it freezes into the It-world which is broken only intermittently by the eruptive,

49

glowing deeds of solitary spirits. From that point on, common causality, which hitherto was never able to disturb the spiritual conception of the cosmos, grows into an oppressive and crushing doom. Wise, masterful fate which, as long as it was attuned to the abundance of meaning in the cosmos, held sway over all causality, has become transformed into demonic absurdity and has collapsed into causality.

Buber at his best; but I still find his terms unnecessarily awkward. Also I can't believe in his tenses. The frozen 'It-world' broken only intermittently . . . seems to be the permanent state of the universe; not an unnatural decline from a golden age when the spirit was perpetually operating here in all its fullness. The natural world has always been *resistant* to God: hence the creative situation in which we exist. When there is no more resistance, the (unimaginable) Kingdom of God will have come.

◆ ◆ ◆

Since the beginning of history – and *a fortiori* before history began – the great majority of mankind have lived in fear, pain, violence, sickness . . . Never forget your extraordinary good fortune in having inhabited this little patch of time and space where there has been almost complete external security.

But how can any Christian who has surplus money which he could give away to the starving not be ceaselessly aware that he is in a constant state of grave sin? (Reflections after sending grossly inadequate cheque to Oxfam.)

◆ ◆ ◆

As well as St Theresa's Fool of the House there is the Prig of the House congratulating himself whenever he's 'good'; the Bore of the House, forever worrying about the state of his soul . . .

◆ ◆ ◆

'I wonder if you idolise Corpus Christi day as much as I do? It is my "secret love" among all the feasts of the year I think . . .' This is Evelyn Underhill at her terrible, gushing worst; the mawkish and creepy side of Christianity. But she wrote this in that first stage of her extreme religiosity, and could never have been so appalling in her real maturity. The florid and decorative aspect.

◆ ◆ ◆

As a crude aid to my hope of making this garden for the glory of God I've decided to build a shrine to St Francis, as a culmination both in time and space, under the yew tree.

◆ ◆ ◆

The ex-colonel and his wife in the George. They are new arrivals and obviously longing to make friends. We are polite but fight off any suggestions of coming round for coffee, etc. How inhospitable and stand-offish this seems; indeed is. But there would be nothing in a closer relationship for either couple. Except, of course, on that deepest level where all human beings could meet: but to invite them to come down into *that* region with us would be regarded in our society as an intolerable and embarrassing affront.

◆ ◆ ◆

E.U. writes of 'our finite spirits'. I applaud this; if only because it gets away from what has become for me the almost hideous notion that our souls are part of God; are, as it were, of the same composition as God. (That they can *receive* God is a very different image, and much truer to what I feel.)

◆ ◆ ◆

'In religion our exclusions are nearly always wrong, and our inclusions, however inconsistent, nearly always right.' E.U. This is good, not because it should be followed, in any real sense, but because it corrects an imbalance; reminds us of a very important aspect of religious truth.

◆ ◆ ◆

A day of quiet love with S. I think there are more of them now . . .

◆ ◆ ◆

E. U., from Catherine of Siena, seeing Christ as a Bridge between the Divine and the Natural. That's more like it.

Also her excellent phrase 'spiritual self-seeking' – from which I never escape. The last, worst obstacle.

Then – and this is late in her life – she can be capable of this horror: 'All this is a great grace for which you must be very grateful, because it comes from the contrast between the great God deigning to touch you, and your own small soul.' Only humans, and humans of the worst type, are capable of 'deigning' – an abominable word. A repulsive image.

◆ ◆ ◆

O Lord, I will to will Thy will.

◆ ◆ ◆

E.U. She is continually reassuring her correspondents because they have fallen from states of blissful confidence in God's close presence into aridity and feelings of abandonment. But I have never had the first experience at all: *never*. At the very best a rare and dubious flash of warmth and light. So perhaps God can reach me only through the dry passages of the mind: perhaps the writing of this journal is my primary work for him; and perhaps the whole point of this journal will prove to be that it was written by a man who persevered to the end without receiving any overt sign at all.

This sounds like a piece of heroics. I don't think it is: I think it is a sensible act of resignation to a very real probability.

◆ ◆ ◆

Immediately there comes this from E.U., almost as if in direct answer to my resignation: ' . . . the blessed in the heaven of the moon – perfectly content to see God only by reflection, and not as those in the heaven of the sun, because it is His will for them and the fact that He *is* is enough.' Yes, and E.U. herself, who was often in the heaven of the sun, is one of my own most precious reflectors of that direct and holy light.

◆ ◆ ◆

Yet even she veers wildly about in this region where all we ever have is image and symbol. At one moment she is sternly insisting on the eternal, unchanging impassibility of God: at the next she writes about some action which would 'displease' him. How hard not to put him too far away or to bring him much too close; to depersonalise him, or to anthropomorphise him.

6 JANUARY
To S, as she was saying good night: 'I find it so hard to get my electric blanket properly adjusted. Ah, the crosses we have to bear!' Yes, but even self-ridicule has its dangers: of becoming a substitute for trying to cure the moral absurdity which one is ridiculing.

7 JANUARY
A wonderful telephone message from Lady Collins, to say that she and two other readers are very enthusiastic about *Part of a Journey*, and want to publish it at the same time as *Pantaloon*. This seems more like real business than ever before – re. *Pantaloon*. They are a huge firm; and I think it quite possible that the journal may succeed in dragging *Pantaloon* out into the light behind it.

◆ ◆ ◆

Cold, cold digging. This, surely my last garden, must be by far my best. As perfect as I can make it.

◆ ◆ ◆

Yes, there are certain public issues on which we have to be absolutely definite and clear. But I am very suspicious of anyone who is clear and definite about them all.

◆ ◆ ◆

A tentative sense that rather more of my daily life is now being lived in some awareness of God – or at least in the awareness that I should be aware of him. But the evening prayer remains as stiff as ever. I can't operate without a pattern; but I know so well what was meant by 'vain repetitions'.

◆ ◆ ◆

'Lord, teach me to seek Thee and show Thyself to me as I seek: for I cannot seek Thee unless Thou teach me, nor find Thee unless Thou show Thyself.' Anselm, quoted by E.U.

But this, from the Khonds, an aboriginal Indian tribe, is perhaps the most perfect prayer I've ever found: 'Lord, we know not what is good for us. Thou knowest what it is. For it we pray.' (From *God of a Hundred Names*, an anthology edited by Barbara Greene and Victor Gollancz.)

◆ ◆ ◆

'It was said unto me: "Take it generally."' Dame Julian of Norwich, quoted by E.U. I must read *Revelations of Divine Love* again: I feel sure that of all the great mystics she alone can speak to me directly.

◆ ◆ ◆

Very hard and cold work in the garden, rooting out frozen nettles. All this *has* to be done in this depth of winter, because only now will the garden keep still enough to let you work at it.

◆ ◆ ◆

Tonight, saddened by Laura's sadness, trembling at the reverberations of bad news (Afghanistan), I keep having to remind myself of yesterday's splendid message from Lady C. I am surprised at how little this helps. But I should know by now that God is indeed the *only* sure support; rock; fortress; etc.

◆ ◆ ◆

53

Von Hügel writes that 'even Jesus Christ does not exhaust the capacities of God'. How extraordinary that this should need to be said. Reading such things as this makes me realise how infinitely far I am from being an orthodox Christian.

◆ ◆ ◆

The sudden shock of realising that Jason will be twenty-seven in April. The flux of time seemed unbearable, and I almost wept to think of him as an eleven-year-old schoolboy; dead and gone. So we cling, perhaps, to belief in some other realm where 'time is no more'; where people aren't being continually seized away and changed . . . Though, God knows, I love this young man every bit as much as I loved the little boy.

10 JANUARY

As soon as I got into bed I started to read Kingsley Amis's latest novel, *Jake's Thing*, with much lip-smacking prospective enjoyment. Loud guffaws, but as I read on and on I found my spirits falling lower and lower; even the guffaws becoming rarer. The world he presents is indeed horrible, as he means it to be; but the real cause of my depression was that his self-representing hero is every bit as horrible as the people he is perpetually hating and sneering at. In fact, a horrible world judged and made still more horrible by a horrible judge.

I see more and more clearly that to sneer is *always* wrong; and always turns back against the sneerer.

11 JANUARY

One or two mildly self-sacrificing actions in the last few days, but in between a great deal of abysmal ill-temper; and one day-long, nagging row of the old type.

How we clutch at each other's hand when we pray each morning and evening: 'May we *love* each other; *trust* each other; and *honour* each other; *now* and *always*. Amen.' Clutching for dear life indeed; so that life may be dear to us both. My dear wife.

◆ ◆ ◆

'[Past theologians] have been concerned to produce a *better structure* of thought about the world. Our move to theology centred around relationship implies a descriptive metaphysic, where we are content to describe the *actual structure* of our thought about the world, and in particular a world related to God. This shifts issues from the realisation that Christian theology lives not in the pure spiritual world of Dr

54

Norman's Reith Lectures – but is instead oxidised by the air within which it lives, yet by such a process it never becomes inert. It is only by such reaction with the world that it retains comprehensibility and credibility. Sterile purity has never been an ingredient of the theological process and its inclusion would spell instant death. To look upon theology is to look upon a freshly washed beach – the landscape is continually formed anew. The moving hand of God works on, and that hand slips into the hand of man, carrying him forward, but giving no stereotype of the destination.' Stephen Platten, in *Theology* (January, 1980).

Yes; and this means that we can all make our tentative contributions; present, that is, our own images and symbols – without any intention that these should be incorporated in some great swelling mass of dogmas and assertions. Let them rest on the beach for others to look at if they like, until the next tide takes them away. Theology as a stream of prayerful images, stories, ideas, hopes . . . *offered*. And the only constant is that God/Heaven are real; are inconceivably above us, yet reach us with love. My present notion, for example, of heaven and a whole series of meta-heavens. A complete economy of exchange and transference, by which souls are moved from realm to realm . . .

◆ ◆ ◆

The famous Irenaeus prayer: 'The glory of God is a living man, and it is man's glory to see God.' But perhaps the first part is a bit presumptuous. We may, at our very best, be *one* of the glories of God; but how can we possibly know how many others he gives his light to?

◆ ◆ ◆

My evening prayer. It is absolutely right that one stage begins with the Verlaine bust, and the words 'The Pain of the World'. For first there is the plaster itself, the clay out of which it is formed. And being material means inevitable suffering. The hard clay of our suffering is the only possible ground from which we can reach towards 'The Hope of God' etc.

◆ ◆ ◆

'All truth is a Shadow except the last. But every Truth is Substance in its own place, though it be but a Shadow in another place. And the Shadow is a true Shadow, as the Substance is a true Substance.' Isaac Pennington.

12 JANUARY
We now take turns driving Laura to Lydney for an early morning

55

train. On my mornings I go straight back to bed when I get home – about 8 o'clock – and almost always enjoy a peculiar form of very light sleep, in which friendly and even comic dreams pass gently across my half-conscious mind. No wonder people are now so keen on 'altered states of consciousness'.

◆ ◆ ◆

I begin to see that what Buber calls 'It' is what most of us call Necessity; Causality; the Natural Order; the Material Universe . . . And what he calls 'You' and 'Relationship' is what I call 'Love of God and Man'.

◆ ◆ ◆

The greatest error and worst impertinence of the reductionist mind is daring to tell someone that when he says he believes X he *really* means that he believes Y. Or, alternatively, that he thinks he believes X for the reasons he gives, but the *real* reasons are quite different – and, of course, less creditable. Ugh!

13 JANUARY
Dream. All the substance is now forgotten, but how the *feeling* remains – of *dull* desolation; emptiness; futility; meaninglessness; pain and loss . . . As so often this was worse than anything I've ever known in waking life. Except, perhaps, for two or three moments of depressive anguish.

◆ ◆ ◆

So, remember – re. theology – that one should condemn somebody else's offering only when it directly conflicts with the single, central faith in the love of God/Heaven. I must recognise, for example, that all this unitive talk and writing is a real wisdom; a real symbol for a real experience. It is not so for me, but I must simply leave it alone: even honour it, if I can. But also I must not try to play with it, be tempted by it, or try to incorporate it in my own vision/guessing/ imagining . . . To try to hold incompatibles in the mind together is, surely, a quite unnecessary strain. Slowly build up your own outfit, giving it the consistency which the mind demands, yet always re-membering that there are quite different outfits which deserve at least equal respect . . .

◆ ◆ ◆

'What Christ did was of decisive and final significance for our relationship to God.'

56

Why 'final'? So many Christian writers feel they *have* to say things like this: perhaps they feel that it makes them sound tough and certain of themselves. But this, of all areas, is the one where we have the least right to be certain of ourselves or of anything else.

14 JANUARY

It is widely assumed in the Christian tradition that the concepts of sin and evil are what give depth to the whole faith. But Dame Julian almost brushes sin aside; and if we've learned one solid fact from Marx, Freud, etc., it is that the area of our freedom – the area, that is, where we can choose whether to sin or not – is far narrower than used to be supposed.

And yet one might say, of course, that just by the very fact of this narrowing the free-space becomes even more important; more concentrated.

Every day I realise more and more clearly that I understand almost nothing about evil. The only thing to do is to pray for some enlightenment here.

Puzzling, puzzling, puzzling . . . Then: 'But I don't, I *can't* understand!' Immense relief. Ignorance acknowledged becomes a blessed ignorance.

◆ ◆ ◆

St Birgitta. Again the old problem of the disturbing mixture of what she 'received from God'. Much holy and loving wisdom. But also foretellings of bloody death to those who opposed her; and the authentication of apostles' tombs in Italy which few modern biblical experts would accept as authentic.

I can't for a moment doubt that she was a true saint and mystic; even a particularly sympathetic one, in view of her human kindness, warmth, and unwillingness to condemn. But she belonged as much to the fourteenth century as I do to the twentieth; and what she was able to receive from God was all within the framework of her time and place. It would be absurd to say that God deceived her; better to say that all of us can receive God only through the filter of our circumstances and environment. With saints the filter is less opaque; but not even Jesus could escape being a first-century Jew: in fact 'escape' would simply mean dehumanisation.

17 JANUARY

Up to London to meet Lady Collins; first in the office, then for lunch in her magnificent flat overlooking Green Park. David Edwards, the present Archdeacon of Norwich, was there too; and both seemed enthusiastic at the idea of publishing the two books together. A *very* charming old lady, and shrewd as well. I don't think that I could be in better hands: and now I must simply wait while they set about raising money to help them with the large expense of *Pantaloon*. (I don't like to make too much of what seems a real possibility to me – that *Part of a Journey* will be a real commercial success and more than pay for *Pantaloon*.)

Alas, we dallied at the Orepool on our way home, after I'd drunk a great deal throughout the day. 'Ah me!', as I lie in bed this morning – and S away at her Citizens' Advice Bureau. And I thought how exactly right that is – ah ME, the unteachable self-punisher.

18 JANUARY

My growing belief in angels, and dependence on my own. But this is matched by a well-retained conviction that the whole idea of 'angelology' is absurd to the point of the ludicrous. What great spiritual lepidopterist has captured large numbers of the Host of Heaven; named them, numbered them and classified them? The same old human inability to rest quietly in ignorance and humble uncertainty. Negative Capability.

Tell me, Angelologist, what *precisely* distinguishes a Dominion from a Power?

19 JANUARY

Fear like a hollowing-out of the chest; but a filling of the mind with dreadful phantoms. 'The surest and safest method of conquest is simply to turn away from the evil, and draw yet nearer and closer to our Safe Refuge: a little child, on perceiving a monster, does not wait to fight with it, and will scarcely turn his eyes towards it; but quickly shrinks into the bosom of its mother, in total confidence of safety: so, likewise, should the soul turn from the dangers of temptation to its God. "God is in the midst of her," saith the Psalmist, "she shall not be moved; God shall help her, and that right early." "The name of the Lord is a strong tower, to which the righteous flee and are safe."' Molinos (?).

My 'temptation' is fear itself; to give way to it. And stubbornly to remember how many appalling things have happened and continue to happen in spite of God. He is a curious kind of fortress. Once inside it, we are in no way protected from the things we fear – e.g. nuclear war, deaths of children, economic ruin – but it is said that we are protected from succumbing to them: protected, while still in this world, from simply dissolving into helpless and useless victims of affliction. And I try to believe this; thinking of *Dying We Live*, I do believe it.

Not that grief and horror would be removed if, for example, Lu were to be killed in an accident. But in that case, I would hope to be, under God, a steadfast tower for S, however great my own suffering; instead of an extra burden on her in her misery.

◆ ◆ ◆

I see more clearly what Buber means in that long passage I wrote out last week. That in 'good' times there is a tolerable – in fact a fruitful – tension between Heaven and Earth; an effective striving of God to enter and enlighten the world; a struggle of Grace to infuse Necessity . . . In 'bad' times 'we feel whatever we do the compulsion of relentless fate, a stranger to spirit which bends every neck with the entire burden of the dead mass of the world.'

If I transpose the notion of historical good and bad times to good and bad periods in each human life, then this makes very good sense. There are times – very rare in my case – when I do seem able to rise above causality (fear) on the wings of the Spirit. Sanctity is liberation – or at least partial liberation – from the terrible chain of cause and effect. Which is why 'freedom' and 'liberty' appear so often in the NT as accompaniments of grace and salvation.

◆ ◆ ◆

Reading the good but quite unknown verse sent me by a stranger in Westmorland, I am shocked to realise that I never read poetry now. But this, as Harold Morland's verse-letters remind me, was once the best way in I knew. (Walking the streets of Oxford, at least a year before I went up, *transported* by my first and totally uncomprehending reading of *The Waste Land*. Leaning over Magdalen Bridge in the dark, and feeling that life was beginning again; that a whole new world of experience was opening out before me. And this, I suppose, is what I crave for now but seldom glimpse. This is the bliss of youth; the intimation of immortality. At least one can do one's best *not to forget it*.)

◆ ◆ ◆

The Crucifixion. I still cannot approach it. I am strongly aware of the mystery; but it remains almost impenetrable.

◆ ◆ ◆

At first I was so put off by the simple-sweet style of this life of St Birgitta (written by a nun of her order, published in 1931) that I thought I'd have to give it up. But perseverance has been richly rewarded. I find I can easily ride over the *bondieuserie* and concentrate

59

on the true devotion with which the book is written: in fact 'receive' this great saint, in a much thinner version of the way she received the love and truth of God. How strange the route from St B, in Rome, across six hundred years to me, sick of a lingering hangover in my bedroom here! God's mysterious ways.

Without the saints the Hobbes/Gibbon view of human life and history would be nearly true. It is these rare, strange, illuminated/ illuminating lives which save history, as even ten good men would have saved Sodom and Gomorrah: it is they who make it possible for us to understand the most that human nature is capable of. Yet how many of our modern historians or psychologists have studied the lives of the saints? The omission is amazing. It is essential for every one of us to be aware of these brothers and sisters; otherwise our view of humanity is confined to a view only of the vast more or less benighted majority. A very false view indeed, since this is in no way a statistical matter but an affair of the observable limits. Great attention, after all, has been paid to the opposite extreme (e.g. Himmler) – and many large conclusions have been drawn from it, both by historians, psychologists and ordinary observers of events. *Dying We Live* should be essential reading; at least as much so as *Mein Kampf.*

◆ ◆ ◆

Garden again, after a week away from it through snow, absence and depletion. Pulling out of this depletion seems a longer and harder process every time. I don't mean that it is so on this occasion, but that it *always* seems so; it is in the nature of the whole disease that it seems worse each time.

◆ ◆ ◆

How vividly I remember Elizabeth Bowen's words to me when I was leaving her house after dinner there in that ghastly year, 1949: 'Philip, I pray that you will be given fortitude.' I was deeply moved; and I am deeply moved again whenever her words come back to mind. How unerringly she saw what it was I most lacked; most needed. Still lack; still desperately need; now pray for on my own account.

◆ ◆ ◆

The sudden shock of realising, as I looked back quite complacently on the past day, that I expect and receive far more attentive care from S than I give her: that I still make too many of the traditional male demands on her.

A firm resolution *simply to be more tender; really* thoughtful – that is, trying to think, at any moment, what it is to be her; how she is feeling; what she would like to do . . .

60

How vulnerable we both are! But each can surely provide a unique protection for the other.

21 JANUARY

We are told over and over again not to try to force ourselves; to let go; to hand over to God . . . But perhaps we must also act on the principle of Beerbohm's Happy Hypocrite. (He concealed his evil face in a mask of loving-kindness the better to carry out his seductions etc. But the mask defeated the man: he became what he was masquerading as.) Or the principle of artificial respiration. Act *as if* you are impelled by gentle and loving emotions – even though your real ones may be very different – and perhaps the gentle love may slowly come, just as real breathing may gradually begin again because the lungs have been artificially compressed and inflated.

◆ ◆ ◆

Of course love always fails. Jesus was crucified: St Francis saw his order corrupted even before he died . . . But their love flows on through history, like a subterranean river of light.

◆ ◆ ◆

Excellent book – *The Drama and the Symbols* – by a Swedish theologian called Gustaf Aulén. 'It is faith in God which is the subject of theology.' He sharply distinguishes this 'Image of God' theology from the false 'Concept of God' theology which supposes that its subject is God himself.

Also very good against all the 'Ground of Our Being' theology of Tillich and others, which is so sharply in contrast to the N T God who is living, active, and constantly at war with evil.

I have felt this more and more; that if you try to comprehend and define God – e.g. by a massive battery of abstract, and preferably Sanskrit, terms – you will surely find that he simply evaporates into thin air. Or even that the effort to grasp these impossible concepts is driving you crazy.

The task, then, is to speak simply and intelligibly to God as if he were indeed a great, good and loving father – but to keep quietly *at the back of the mind* the awareness that he is truly this, but also unimaginably more than this.

◆ ◆ ◆

The 'great' theologians have been great misleaders far more than great enlighteners, simply because they were all trying to be systematic and exhaustive.

◆ ◆ ◆

Dream. That I was in the civil service after hopelessly disgracing myself in the Army – which was more or less my true situation in 1941. But here too, in this office, I was being disastrously incompetent. But for once my wretchedness was more than atoned for by the extreme kindness of the men and women who were supposed to be directing me. I awoke almost in tears, being so touched by their patient sweetness.

◆ ◆ ◆

Two men are sitting together in a train. A is constantly asking after B's comfort; would he like to shift a little in his seat; pull down the blind against the sun; go along to the restaurant car for a drink or a coffee; which then, drink or coffee, would B prefer? And what exactly will it be most convenient for B to do when he arrives in London: take a taxi; or a tube; how long will the taxi-queue be, does B suppose; where would he have to get off if he takes the tube? Would B now like to take his book out of his case? Or read a bit more of the paper? Which page of the paper would he prefer? And is he perhaps getting too hot? Should he ask the other passengers whether they'd mind if he turns down the heat a little? Or is this too much trouble? A notices, now, that B's shoes could perhaps do with a polishing before he goes for that interview. Shall he get them polished at the station? And what are his plans for lunch? What would he fancy for lunch? And would it be a good idea to telephone B's old friend C and suggest that they meet for lunch . . . ?

If we heard one man being so ceaselessly solicitous towards another, we would think that there must be something badly wrong with both of them. Yet this is in fact a perfectly normal stream of consciousness *within B's mind.* We are endlessly concerned with our own comfort and our own concerns; and this stream of self-solicitude is only rarely interrupted by the intrusion of someone else's interests. B, for example, may briefly wonder whether his wife is enjoying her day with her mother. Hope it all goes well . . . Then, must remember to buy myself that book. Nose needs blowing? Right, then. Pretty legs! Imagine what it's like higher up – if only . . . ! House for sale out of train window – reminds me of our mortgage payments, bank balance very low now. Worry . . . worry . . . worry . . .

Both desolating and absurd. How *on earth* can we ever squeeze ourselves out from under this constant heavy weight of self-concern? God alone knows.

◆ ◆ ◆

'Behold the heaven *and heaven of heavens* cannot contain this.' Solomon dedicating the temple. The notion, again, of realm after realm after realm, and each one inconceivable within all the lesser ones which it contains.

◆ ◆ ◆

In the NT, I learn from Aulén, the word 'almighty' is applied to God only once outside *Revelation*. (And somehow I find it impossible to include that vicious and extravagant book in the true canon.)

◆ ◆ ◆

Am I doing my best? It's clearly impossible for me to know; by its very nature an unanswerable question. I assume that God must know – 'unto whom all hearts are open . . .' But if I can never know what my best is, does it even make any sense to wonder whether I am doing it or not?

◆ ◆ ◆

It is *possible*, of course, that God has a *higher* opinion of us than we have of ourselves.

◆ ◆ ◆

Theology. Every guess or wild idea should be humbly laid on the altar, like a bright but dubious flower. Which will, in any case, fade before long.

22 JANUARY
Aulén. He asks the very pertinent question: why did so many of the disciples fail to recognise Jesus after the resurrection? His answer: this was not a resurrected body, but a new body, transformed and glorified. '[They could not have had] the naked idea that a dead person had become living, but the conviction that Christ as the Living One had taken up again and was continuing his unique life's work.'

This accords very well with my present utterly fascinated study of modern life-after-death experiences and theories. Yet there is a weakness here: surely if the body had been transfigured, *this* would have been observed and recorded; as it was at the Transfiguration itself? Whereas (e.g.) the stranger on the road to Emmaus seems a grey and almost spectral figure, who has to be rather comically and absurdly brought to life by being made to eat a meal!

◆ ◆ ◆

So many books, now, on the experiences of those who've returned from clinical death. So much agreement on the inexpressible joy of the experience . . . For the first time I begin to think it *as least as likely as not* that we do survive death, and that there is a further work for us to do. Watch out, though! My wish to believe this has always been very strong; my horror at the prospect of being snuffed out, equally great.

◆ ◆ ◆

Who was it, what brave young man, of whom that splendid story is told? X was dining, in the company of his F O boss, with the Bishop of Gibraltar. The topic of V D was raised, and the Bishop announced that he regarded syphilis as the Finger of God. 'Well,' said X, 'if that's his finger I wonder what the rest of him is like?' The story goes on that he was immediately sent out of the room, and subsequently lost his job. Well worth it!

◆ ◆ ◆

I heard of a little magazine called the *Christian Parapsychologist*; immediately wrote off, not only to subscribe but to order all the back numbers. I have been browsing through these with immense fascination, but also a persistent sense of slight uneasiness and shame.

This must be subdued – exorcised. For this is a field of research every bit as legitimate as any other – provided, as in any other, the proper cautions are observed.

◆ ◆ ◆

Prayer. Eyes on the ploughed furrows in *The Fall of Icarus* – for 'The Strength of God'. Marvellously more apt than I'd realised when I first began this: the perfect image of God working at, and in a sense *against*, the substance of the material world.

23 JANUARY

Running round the loop-road in the rain; and that most tantalising and exhilarating of all the sights we ever see – a slash of pale green sky between the wide darkness of surrounding clouds. But this time the feeling that the great and joyful new experience which this suggested (an image of swooping down into the valley with wings two hundred feet across, then up through the slash and OUT) was not something impossible, or lost for ever, but, quite to the contrary, something promised and certain.

There was also, of course, that half-awareness of not-quite-attainable memories: of incredible happiness long, long ago. But even this was no longer melancholy. On the contrary, an assurance that everything of value would be restored; somehow; some time, or out of time.

Is this the effect of devouring so many copies of the *Christian*

Parapsychologist? (The title, so far as I'm concerned, almost too good to be true; I see myself caricatured there.) Perhaps it is. But in a mood like today's it seems absurd and impossible that all my experiencing is soon about to end for ever and ever. And yet so little is known: only a fragment glimpsed, and misunderstood. Ah, there *must* be more to unfold; to flower; to open . . . (But all this very faint – either like a faded photograph, or like the first faint appearance of a print in solution.)

◆ ◆ ◆

'When self is annihilated, there is nothing left for the tempter to act upon. Oh, how resigned, naked, denied, annihilated ought the soul to be, that would not hinder the entrance of the divine Lord, nor his continual communion with it!' Molinos.

Yes; but it seems to me now that this can be carried too far: that *too much* might be destroyed, leaving nothing for God to enter or inhabit.

But this from the same little book of devotion which Gerry sent me – selections from Fénelon, Mme Guyon and Molinos – *seems beautifully apt and right: 'All endeavours merely to rectify the exterior impel the soul yet farther outward into that about which it is so warmly and zealously engaged; and thus its powers are diffused and scattered abroad; for its application being immediately directed to externals, it thus invigorates those very senses which it is aiming to subdue.'

Easy to see why the Church condemned quietism – both for bad reasons and good.

◆ ◆ ◆

When have I experienced *joy*? I think, always, of a certain moment in Paris, in 1946, sitting in a sunny café over a Pernod, waiting for a girl to join me and knowing that we would be going to Fontainebleau to spend the night together there. A secular, and worse than secular, occasion. Present euphoria of booze; ecstatic prospect of future adultery. So this can hardly be what they mean – yet how well I remember saying to myself, as I sat there looking at the Luxembourg Gardens across the street: 'This is happiness. *Now* I am happy. Remember it all the rest of your life!'

◆ ◆ ◆

Reading and reading about life after death – if any. I remember holding forth at an *Observer* lunch many years ago, with my usual

A Guide to True Peace – or the Excellency of Inward and Spiritual Prayer, edited by William Backhouse and James Janson.

exuberance, on my total conviction that death is annihilation. Charles Davie, an older and wiser colleague, was sitting next to me – and, when I'd finished, he said very quietly, almost in my ear: 'I do advise you, Philip, not to close your mind to the possibility of survival. Otherwise, you might find yourself very shocked and disorientated.' I was much taken aback: and much impressed, though not persuaded.

◆ ◆ ◆

Dreamed of death and woke to an agonising consciousness of Tom and his wretched state. Or rather, to an agonising consciousness of how little we have been able to do for him. Or rather, how little we have done for him.

◆ ◆ ◆

Reading now, 3.30 a.m., about the earliest Benedictine monasteries; heavenly refuges in a falling world. How envious I feel of those monks; yet also know that I could never pay the necessary price – in prayer, obedience, poverty, chastity.

24 JANUARY

The Christian view, I suppose, is that to cause anger in someone else is a worse offence than to cause grief or even misery. For anger is a sin, whereas grief and misery are God's opportunity. I see that this makes a sort of sense; but it doesn't correspond to anything I really feel.

25 JANUARY

To refuse belief in, at the minimum, telepathy, clairvoyance and poltergeists has become as black a form of obscurantism as the worst that Christianity has ever shown. But there are many who steadily refuse to examine the evidence, and commit themselves to disbelief just as blindly as so many Christians have committed themselves to the beliefs ordained for them by their Churches.

When I showed Bill* the opening pages of Evelyn Underhill's *Man and the Supernatural* (which I've now had photocopied) he sent me a postcard, as follows: '50 million years ago, a group of hairy primates suffered a genetic mutation which gave them an itch to find Order in the world around them. This itch made them find ways of:

a) clobbering their neighbours more effectively
b) explaining earthquakes
c) writing fugues

* Bill Bayley – Monmouth neighbour and close friend.

d) transliterating Linear B
e) seeking an Ultimate Reality
f) inventing the Queen's Pawn Gambit.'

In the Punch-house, in Monmouth, the following Thursday I suggested that this explained nothing; and after some vigorous and enjoyable argument – of a kind which I have only with Bill, in the Punch-house, on Thursdays between 12.00 and 1.00 – he agreed that E.U.'s supernatural was, after all, a reasonable explanation; though it was not one that he shared. I was almost taken aback by such good sense – being accustomed since I first met Freddie, forty-five years ago, to non-believing friends who treat all religious speculation as 'literal nonsense'. Bill's is a more old-fashioned and more intellectually courteous attitude. And perhaps this kind of rational and respectful disagreement may come back again after all those old bruisers have had their long say.

◆ ◆ ◆

Studying Bubbles as she lay on the sofa beside me I felt the *warmest* feelings, not of love but of *appreciation*. Pleased to have found the right word, my mind curvetted onwards to ask, 'Why should I not become a genuine cat-fancier; buy a cat-book and then, perhaps, a Burmese or a Siamese?' So typical of my eagerly, naively acquisitive way of thinking. (Not just a desire to acquire another cat, or cats, but the desire to acquire a new role/activity/interest. Folly! The old folly of at least half-believing that such fancies are part of the Great Way Forward.)

◆ ◆ ◆

'The Holy Spirit is that divine discontent that drives all creative persons on to their full stature as sons of God.' Martin Israel.

◆ ◆ ◆

Bubbles again. Looking into those yellow eyes: 'How much we share, being contemporaries at this particular moment in the great stream of time and evolution. Yet how mysterious each of us is to the other! What is it that you know which I can never know?

◆ ◆ ◆

I see from a review in the *Christian Parapsychologist* – now easily my favourite periodical – that Edward Lucie-Smith has written a book about Joan of Arc, explaining her visions, life, and death in Freudian terms. How easily one forgets that such crass idiocies are still perpetrated!

Or, to put it a bit more humbly, how deeply buried I am these days in books which approximately share my general outlook. This is inevitable, for I simply haven't time to study such works, from which I *know* that I could derive nothing but boredom and irritation. At my stage of life the mind cannot, of course, be wide open – if ever it was. The major decision has been taken; and this decision includes the absolute conviction that Lucie-Smith's treatment of Joan *must be* preposterous.

(In 1949, after four years of Labour government and of meeting scarcely anyone who didn't support it, I went with the Campbells to the horse trials at Badminton. And I was naively amazed to find the whole world of upper-class thuggery still alive and kicking, and just waiting for their come-back. Somehow I'd been assuming through all those years that they had simply shrunk away for ever into their gilded holes; for ever thwarted and defeated.)

26 JANUARY

Lu telephoned in a strange state of exaltation and distress. When S suggested that we should drive over to Rugby at once, she said, 'But do you really *mean* it? Would you *really* come all this way?' A poignant reminder that she's always believed herself the least loved of the three; or half-believed it, anyway – and so wrongly. It was only when we were in the car and half-way to St Briavels that I realised, with great satisfaction, that I had taken it as much for granted as S had that since Lu needed us we would go to her at once, and without question.

We found her very distracted; mainly about the dreary nastiness of the hospital where she's now working. They insist on keeping the ward-doors locked, as Pen-y-Fal never did. But when Lu is in charge of a ward she opens the doors and lets all the patients know that they are open. She has the right to do this, but also the heavy responsibility. If one of the patients ran out and was hurt, Lu would of course be blamed.

And now, at twenty-four, she has decided that she wants to become a psychiatrist. Which means seven years' training ahead, with A-levels in chemistry, biology and physics for a start. But she *will* do it, even easily, now that she has set her mind to it.

How insane that all this should be necessary. For to my mind psychiatrists are made in heaven, not on earth; and once a heaven-made psychiatrist like Lu – or S – has learned a little pharmacology, they are better qualified than the most expert practitioner who lacks wisdom, love, understanding . . .

Through her recent interest in my books on survival Lu seems to be making her own approach to God. We were very pleased by this, of

68

course, but very anxious, too, not to take advantage of her present weakness: not to put any pressure on her at all, and yet to be *available* with our beliefs: with our uncertainties . . .

◆ ◆ ◆

Prayer. Now, moving my eyes to the plough and its furrows, I say 'The Work of God' instead of 'The Strength of God'. It is a beautiful and traditional image; God tilling the soul as a ploughman tills the soil.

27 JANUARY
There must be a perpetual striving towards simplicity. But the simplicity must be, *for me*, a new one: which probably means an old one suddenly come alight for me. The worst thing we can do is to retreat into the harsh, black cave of an old and discredited simplicity – e.g. fundamentalism; hellfire; unthinking acceptance of ecclesiastical authority.

◆ ◆ ◆

'The person becomes conscious of himself as participating in being, as being-with, and thus as a being. The ego becomes conscious of himself as being this way and not that. The person says, "I am"; the ego says, "That is how I am." "Know thyself" means to the person: know yourself as being. To the ego it means: know your being-that-way. By setting himself apart from others, the ego moves away from being.'

Buber, at his very best. And how grossly adolescent it seems that at sixty-three I should still be toiling and moiling with the ego; forever trying to find out what I am *like*, instead of what, underneath all that trivial differentiation, I *am*.

But the catch is that so long as one remains utterly flawed, mis-shapen, contorted, one must still continue the wearisome (endless?) task of diagnosis with a view to cure; or, at least, to improvement. If not for one's own sake, then for the sake of those others who suffer from the effects of all our egoistic failings.

Oh, I know the answer – which is to cease to be an ego and to become a person. But how to do that is the unremitting and often so disheartening problem.

'The spirit-life is not evolved out of ourselves, as a tree from the seed, but is offered to us for our appropriation.' George Tyrrell. And the work of appropriation is life-long for most of us.

◆ ◆ ◆

'I have been made a laughing-stock, that is the martyrdom I have suffered.' Poor Kierkegaard at his preposterous worst. (But is this really much worse than my own device of escaping ridicule by self-ridicule? Yes, it *is* worse; for the clowning, however devious its unconscious purpose, is surely better than false dignity.)

◆ ◆ ◆

Well then, if it is true that we have a soul, or spirit, which survives death and enters a higher realm of endeavour, at what point in evolution did we acquire this splendid attribute? The only possible answer is: 'When it was possible, and as much as possible.' Perhaps Bill's hypothetical mutation was in fact a change which enabled the heavenly powers to implant a soul in that mutated man.

Absurd speculations, I suppose, but my irredeemably literal and pedestrian mind is bound to ask such questions.

◆ ◆ ◆

I have at last got George Tyrrell's (uncompleted) *Autobiography* and the continued *Life* by Maud Petre from Tymawr. For a long time this figure has been hanging about at the edge of my attention. What *a writer*, to start with. So far the autobiography reads like a dry appendage and corrective to Newman's *Apologia*; but for me it is a far more entrancing book because of Tyrrell's rich irony towards himself as well as towards his opponents and persecutors.

◆ ◆ ◆

Laura for the weekend with her new boyfriend. He seems a very likeable young man; kind, forthright and humorous. Also, she's now been moved to a different department at her office and seems to be enjoying this much more than the last one.

29 JANUARY

But bad news from Laura at midday, that A hadn't rung her up yesterday evening as he'd promised. S told her not to be so distracted; there were so many perfectly good reasons why this might have happened. But both of us felt almost sick with anxiety, so much it seemed a repetition of all the bad times with Paul. Had the young man taken fright – although he'd seemed to enjoy the weekend with us, and had been very loving when they'd last been together?

In S's case this sickness is almost entirely on Laura's behalf; a maternal pity and deep concern. In my case that selfless sorrow is also mixed with a heavy sense of burden and weariness. Oh God, is there no end to this pain? Whose pain, though, yours or Laura's? Well, it isn't always easy to separate them; but certainly part of it is for myself.

S said that all we could do was pray; and so we did. But it's hard to say just what we were asking God to do, if anything. All we could legitimately ask, according to our belief, is that he would give us the strength, the wisdom, the loving patience to help Laura as best we possibly could if she was indeed in trouble again.

So today poor old Verlaine was loaded with Laura's pain, as well as with all his own and all of mine. A sort of Christ-role, perhaps, for that sad bust. And indeed he had more to bear than this, for when S beat me at chess this afternoon for the third time running I behaved like a spoilt child; amazed, even as I spoke them, at my sour, resentful words. And forty years ago, when I taught Anne to play and she began to beat me, my reaction was exactly the same. Bad enough at twenty-three: at sixty-three obscene.

And then, to complete this wretched day of pain, fear, anger and humiliation, one of my semi-anonymous telephone callers rang at 11.30 to propose himself for a call. 'Or are you', he asked through his resentful booziness, 'still *incommunicado*?' Oh, I was civil, certainly, but ruthlessly refused his suggestion. 'Why not *write*?' A despairing wail.

Others seem to suffer noble pains, but mine are so wretchedly ignoble; grating; disconsolate; petty . . . like a blade scraping the skin rough and raw instead of cutting cleanly into the flesh.

◆ ◆ ◆

We help each other out of our respective scrapes. Would it be better if there were no scrapes and no positive help? It would surely be better if there were no scrapes but always the kind of unspoken, loving help which the Good give to each other without so much as a thought of what they are giving.

The trouble is this seemingly unbreakable ding-dong, or tit-for-tat, of pain which each causes the other. No good trying to trace it back and allot responsibility from the past: though certainly the obvious early 'fault' was mine. In fact the whole question of blame is a monstrous absurdity, because there's no way out like that. The only way out is love: or even, more modestly, by simple affection. (I think we use this good and modest word much too little; the all-demanding, extravagant 'love' much too much. Failing miserably in love, we feel that all is lost; the quieter word might be a better bet.)

◆ ◆ ◆

To you, Heavenly Mother, in the argot of our time, 'Be my guest!'

◆ ◆ ◆

71

Tyrrell, a much finer and braver man than me. But how deeply sympathetic I find him in his proud but self-mocking honesty; his passionate irony; the deep confusion of his faith.

30 JANUARY

But over breakfast we talked calmly and truthfully about ourselves, without any anger. A dividing of the spoils; the spoilings.

◆ ◆ ◆

Must abandon even the last wisp of the fantasy that *one* day there will be such a radical change that S and I will often be sitting with dear friends in the perfected garden, listening to Haydn and sipping a light Moselle.

◆ ◆ ◆

'Every virtue is a victory over fear.' Lanza del Vasto.

◆ ◆ ◆

'Just be still, and let God do with you what he wills.' *Just! Only!* The simplest and the hardest thing in the world.

◆ ◆ ◆

I've listened to no music at all for many weeks; and *know* that this is a period of inevitable deafness and deprivation.

◆ ◆ ◆

How grotesque that the figure I find hardest to grasp, love or understand in the whole wide-ranging Christian pantheon is – Jesus Christ!

◆ ◆ ◆

I contemplated a radical change in my room, so that I could stare from my pillow straight out of the best of my three windows – over the valley; wide sky above the far trees. I told S, and she said, 'But surely you don't mean to spend all *that* much time in bed during the day!' No; but I do now accept the systole and diastole of my life – that every outward effort, to other places and people or even to people coming here, will be followed by a more or less exhausted retreat up here.

Accept this, and with serenity. But never, never accept yesterday's childish ill-temper; or any of my other daily sins.

◆ ◆ ◆

Though I could never be any kind of evangelical, I do begin to understand the value of 'the Scriptures'. At least they are *there*, however uncertain their meaning – real words on real paper, really composed by real people and of real long-proven value. Tyrrell, himself certainly no evangelical, writes of 'the strong meat of the word of God' as against 'abstract theology'.

♦ ♦ ♦

'God knows that I am not bloodthirsty and I think I have in a terrible degree a sense of my responsibility to God; but, nevertheless, I should be ready to take the responsibility upon me, in God's name, of giving the order to fire if I could first make absolutely and conscientiously sure that there was not a single man standing in front of the rifles, not a single creature, who was not – a journalist.'

We are accustomed to hard words, of course, but these from Kierkegaard do seem a little extreme.

♦ ♦ ♦

Praying. 'The Hope of God' (with eyes on the tree-tops and high sky of *Icarus*). But perhaps it is simply that you have put yourself in a position where you have deprived yourself of any other source of hope. It is God or nothing, now: that's sure enough.

♦ ♦ ♦

Life after Death. I suspect that what I want most of all is simply to be able to think it possible by the time I reach my death-bed. Annihilation still appals me.

♦ ♦ ♦

Trust in God!
    To do what?
To give you trust in God.

Have faith!
    In what?
In faith.

These are the monstrous tautologies of our religion, rich with meaning or harshly derisive according to mood.

♦ ♦ ♦

Maud Petre on Tyrrell: 'His life was a continual struggle with temperamental difficulties.' *That* helps to explain my strong sense of affinity – though he was a man on an altogether different scale from me: a giant.

73

His constant prayer for 'the poor in every sense, physical, mental, moral, spiritual . . . their title is their poverty'. A real joy to know that I am truly one of the poor, in the fullest sense.

31 JANUARY
But shopping in Monmouth this morning has restored my sense of virtue – so meticulous; so courteous; so friendly; so patient. A model shopper.

◆ ◆ ◆

Why this strange pride among the most orthodox Christians in their ability to accept the whole caboodle? I imagine myself setting down large and bony morsels of food in front of a plump cat. 'The Incarnation?' Down it goes, with a licking of lips and a smug wiping of whiskers. 'The Virgin Birth?' 'The Atonement?' 'The Trinity?' As if the very fact that these morsels are hard to swallow makes this prompt dispatch – with scarcely a gulp or a belch – something amazingly virtuous and creditable.

(On the other hand, the tone of the modernisers can be equally boastful, in its brash defiance: 'Guess what *I* don't believe any more!')

◆ ◆ ◆

Which is worse, then – the misery and shame of having done an injury, or the misery, fear and anger of being the injured party? Both are very damaging to the unregenerate soul. But this ray of light from Tyrrell: 'The pains of growth, which some mistake for the pangs of death.'

He also has a certain bitter toughness, which I sometimes share.

◆ ◆ ◆

I ought to think more about duty – the bitter, unfeeling, necessary master which compels us to do approximately the right thing even when no better motive can be found. The hardest and worst master.

1 FEBRUARY
A beautiful and happy day, after the later wretchedness and harshness of yesterday. Even after so many experiences of ups-and-downs I wouldn't have believed, in the thick of yesterday, that such a recovery – restoration – would be possible for either of us.

2 FEBRUARY
David and Phine for the weekend. At supper tonight I persuaded

74

David to tell us the full story of how he came to leave his job as a C of E curate. A bitter tale, and told with a good deal of bitterness. On a smaller and less public scale, the same old story of Erasmus, Tyrrell, Küng . . .

3 FEBRUARY

Tyrrell. But what a terrible burden a wronged man has to bear. That bitter self-absorption is the added injury which they did him. As he knew so well, and expressed so much better than I have: 'The appetite for personal justification grows tyrannical with indulgence.' (Warning another priest from an act of intended martyrdom.)

All this – Tyrrell, Küng, etc. – reminds me again of how very little part 'the Church' plays in my life, either as a concept or as a force. I suppose these monstrous organisations are necessary, do more good than harm; but how much trouble they've caused throughout the Christian centuries!

◆ ◆ ◆

Almost superhuman energy of Tyrrell, as in all great men. Apart from all his books and declarations, the long letters written almost daily; the journeys; the talk; as well as his priestly duties until near the end of his life. (And I find it a heavy burden, therefore cause for self-congratulation, that I spend one morning a week on my letters!) What a writer, too! This, for example, when charged with being too little concerned with social problems: 'By faith man walks consciously in the light of eternity, and sees earth and its burdens as from a distant planet, a speck in immensity. And yet he labours for the alleviation of its sorrows *as they can never labour who need the assurance of success.* (My italics.)

4 FEBRUARY

Letter from Oxfam this morning: 'Dear Mr and Mrs Toynbee, I would like to express our deep-felt gratitude for the very generous aid to our work overseas . . . ' In fact what we gave is about five per cent of our present capital! (Yet neither of us could quite avoid the glow of self-congratulation which this letter produced.)

Afterwards I thought, 'But why not have given to some *Christian* charity?' I suppose because I dislike the idea of any good work labelling itself in this way – as if hoping to benefit itself, by self-advertisement, from doing what should be done quietly and without ostentation. But this is very unfair; for if the charities didn't announce themselves as Christian, many ill-wishers would be asking why

Christians are doing nothing. A harsh world. A very ungenerous, envious, back-biting world – now as always.

◆ ◆ ◆

Kierkegaard verges on paranoia all through his *Journals*. Sometimes he goes over the verge: 'Should my journals be published after my death it might be done under the title: *The Book of the Judge.*'

Yet to see oneself as a judge is so directly contrary to true Christianity that I am amazed at the presumption which allows any to accept the legal and professional role.

◆ ◆ ◆

The beginning of all religious faith is to admit the concept of the inconceivable. First of all, no more than the recognition that there *may be* aspects of reality which cannot be grasped by the limited human equipment of mind and senses.

But we now know from the physicists that even within the physical world there are indeed observed phenomena which make nonsense of the very basis of traditional thinking and understanding.

So is it not *probable* that there are whole realms, domains, orders of reality which are far beyond our powers of conception? And in fact there is a great cloud of witnesses to testify that they have had some experience of such ineffable but realer-than-real domains. These witnesses agree on much, etc., etc.

If one must go in for apologetics, this seems to me by far the best approach.

◆ ◆ ◆

No, I don't tell lies any more, except out of politeness or amiability – and I have come to feel a deep abhorrence of lying. Yet I have been a Great Liar in my time – I even used to maintain indignantly to Anne that an undetected lie must be accepted as the truth by the recipient. In other words, what couldn't be disproved is as good as true. And perhaps I would be just as ready to lie again now if I had real occasion to do so – say a love affair with some beautiful lady in St Briavels. (Though how *that* would be conducted under our present regime only God could advise and contrive. It is assumed that he would refuse to do so; but what on earth do we know of God's attitude to individual acts of love/adultery?)

◆ ◆ ◆

A snobbish reluctance, here in bed at night, to turn straight from the tragic magnificence of Tyrrell to Rose Macaulay's *Letters to a Friend*. Yet I knew her quite well; liked and respected her very much. She had, among other things, the right – and rare – kind of dignity. (How comically and well she put Evelyn Waugh in his place at that party long ago. He'd armed himself with an ear-trumpet which he pointed at anyone who spoke to him, to the old fogey accompaniment of 'Eh? Eh? Eh? Speak up! Can't *hear* you . . . ' S and I had been somewhat victimised by this, but when Waugh tried it on Rose she simply gabbled calmly on in her ordinary, rather inaudible voice. In the end he grumpily lowered his instrument of mockery.)

First impression: how terribly strong was her sense of past sin – alarming, somehow. (I am much more bothered by present sin.)

Her almost gushing enthusiasm for liturgy, and defiant triumphalism about the C of E. She turns the Church into something all too like a cosy London club. What about the deprived millions of the industrial cities, and the brave defeated parsons of *those* parishes? Not that I give much thought to them either, alas.

It occurs to me that if Rose had talked about the C of E to Dick Sheppard, her friend and fellow-pacifist of the ten years before these letters were written, she would have learned something of its smug, backward and authoritarian prelacy. That wasn't the whole truth either, but it was, and is, too much of the truth.

◆ ◆ ◆

Oh midnight fear! The wilderness again.

Dear God, let me out of here! (And yet I see no glimpse of anywhere else.)

The only recognised duty now, to *hold out* until death without too badly damaging those I love by my dangerous weaknesses and incapacities.

For years now, we've had to live without a future; without any confidence that the human race will survive us. A blank of possible nothingness ahead, instead of a great living expanse of infinite possibilities – for a few. For the rich and established, a confidence that everything would go on exactly as now – heir and heir after heir – and for those on the make . . . But perhaps for the poor the future *of the world* has never had any meaning . . .

But why should this be so fearfully mutilating? Surely it should make us all the more aware that the present moment demands our fullest attention, and that true depth of feeling and knowledge comes entirely from the past, never from foolish invented futures.

Yes, but this heavy concentration on the present makes me even more aware of past and present failure . . .

Out of the increasing tushery of Rose's letters, flashes of pain and insight. Now this: ' . . . the kind of unhappiness that must be a shadow of what one will feel after death – the misuse of life, the missing of its meaning, and now too late, life never turns back.' How strikingly apt that was; the true consolation of fellow-suffering.

◆ ◆ ◆

But I had to abandon Rose's letters at 1 a.m. And it has been a relief to turn back to Evelyn Underhill's *The Life of the Spirit and the Life of Today*. The required astringency: 'The sense that we are not yet full-grown has always haunted the race. "I am the Food of the full-grown. *Grow*, and thou shalt feed on me!" said the voice of Supreme Reality to St Augustine.'

This may be true of the race; it must certainly be true of many, many Christian individuals. Perhaps the word 'immaturity' has been over-used in our time; but it is this, above all, which I feel in myself as the worst barrier between God and myself. (A far worse barrier than those past sins which troubled Rose so terribly.)

5 FEBRUARY

After that long, hard night – the inevitable result of a new policy of pill-reduction – I spent rather a bleary day. Yet worked away at the garden in quite heavy rain, ever-conscious of the April deadline for sowing grass. My enthusiasm is very high just now; and I feel sure that this will be the best garden I've ever made; better, even, than the Barn House water-garden.

Tried Runciman's *Crusades* again; and failed for the third time. Why? Partly because I am still so heavily hooked on religious works; but also because this kind of largely narrative history – political and military – doesn't much appeal to me any more. Also, of course, no individuals emerge plainly at this period. What I need when reading history now is a great deal about how people thought and felt – as well as can be guessed; how they lived; what they wrote and painted . . . all with an absolute minimum of economic information. In other words, social, cultural and religious history enlivened by biography. Morris Bishop's *Pelican Book of the Middle Ages* is proving much more acceptable.

6 FEBRUARY

So I took three bold Ativan last night, slept like a log and woke with a rare enthusiasm for the day ahead. I started an article on the Devil; harder garden work in even heavier rain; lively prayers; chess in the Orepool with S. Such abounding energy and good spirits!

Which has not been at all a common condition during the last few months.

✦ ✦ ✦

As for cigarettes I shall never mention them here again. I made a tremendous resolution for the opening of the new decade – no more till death us do part – but fell at Lucy's under heavy temptation. So I imagine that I will go on resolving and failing for the rest of my life; which seems to mean about twice as many days when I don't smoke as when I do. Lung cancer would be a bit hard after such a comparatively abstemious regime.

✦ ✦ ✦

A letter from my correspondent, F.J., who has been moving about the Highlands ever since he first wrote to me about two years ago. He wants me to find somewhere for him to live in this area; is broke, and sounds desperate: 'This is an S O S.'

It was, of course, an impossible request, for how can I possibly know what sort of place would suit him? But I wrote at once – to explain why I was bound to fail him; could not, as he clearly would have liked, invite him to stay here while he looks for a place in the neighbourhood. This is the second reminder within a few days of how *evanescent* I am as a helper to anyone: I can so seldom be anything better than a letter-writer, always refuse them when they try to get closer.

But I shan't feel guilty this time. There are a very few whom I do occasionally see and talk to. And as for the others, I write often and I write as well as I can.

✦ ✦ ✦

Is 'God' simply another name for 'all the company of Heaven'; Heaven seen in its aspect as one powerful and united will? Or is there an order, which we call 'God', which is at least as high above the angelic order as that is high above the order of nature?

Not exactly verifiable or falsifiable propositions, either one of them. But I find that such ideas as these do at least stretch the mind; make it more aware of how little we know yet and how much there is which we can never know.

✦ ✦ ✦

Even now, twelve years after his death, a 'new' book by Merton has been brought out. They have called it *Love and Living*, and so far it doesn't read at all like barrel-scraping – e.g. this succession all on the same page:

79

Whether or not you claim to be interested in it, from the moment you are alive you are bound to be concerned with love, because love is not just something that happens to you: *it is a certain special way of being alive.*

Love is, in fact, an intensification of life, a completeness, a fullness, a wholeness of life.

The meaning of our life is a secret that has to be revealed to us in love, *by the one we love.* And if this love is unreal, the secret will not be found, the meaning will never reveal itself, the message will never be decoded.

Yes; and it is just because the secret remains almost entirely a secret to me that I know my love is inadequate.

7 FEBRUARY
Not only music but all beauty seems to have retreated from me. But I have a strong feeling that this is quite all right; that, *for the time being*, I have to concern myself with other things; that when I come back to music, art and poetry I shall do so with a new kind of understanding; and advantage.

♦ ♦ ♦

A book called *To Die is Gain* by a German Lutheran pastor called Johann Christoph Hampe. This is much more 'respectable' than most of the works I've been reading with this sort of title; his preliminary chapters on the way we view death now are very good indeed. As opposed to our usual furtiveness about death, and refusal to speak about it even – no, *especially* – with the dying, he writes: 'It used to be continually maintained that the final hour was life's most important hour. To take it away from someone is therefore as good as robbing him of the fulfilment of his life's significance. In the framework of this thinking, to call dying a process seems too colourless. Is dying not more an activity on the part of the dying person? Language indicates this as well. It uses an active verb: I die, not I am died. It can even use a transitive verb: I die my own death.'

About ten years ago S and I agreed that if either of us is told that the other has a terminal disease he/she will not conceal this from the other. But on my part, *not* on hers, this agreement was made with fear and trembling. I made it chiefly because I know that if I didn't do so I would be suspecting the worst every time I became even trivially unwell. In other words, I was simply using fear against itself.

But now – and not *only* because I more than half believe in survival – I would want to be told for the kind of reasons that Hampe is writing about. How trifling it would be to die in a state of deception and self-deception; surrounded by the general pretence that 'you'll soon be up and about again'!

8 FEBRUARY
Yesterday morning, at our weekly meeting in Monmouth, Father Philip told me what is, I take it, the classical order or organisation of Christian prayer; namely:

> Adoration
> Contrition
> Thanksgiving
> Supplication.

I realise that almost all my prayer probably comes under the last heading: supplication for more light; hope; love . . . also for others to be helped (intercession) but not *nearly* so much of that. There is quite a lot of contrition as well, but this tends to be outside my formal praying. As for adoration, I scarcely even know what it means. And though I would like to give thanks, I find it hard to know what I can legitimately give thanks *for* – i.e. how many of the good things are really gifts from God and not just lucky breaks.

But I shall certainly see what I can do with Father Philip's plan.

◆ ◆ ◆

Have at last got up a bit of speed with my piece on the Devil. I start by presenting the case for his active existence; and have found this dreadfully convincing. However, I have succeeded in preserving my incredulity.

◆ ◆ ◆

I had forgotten the absurdity of the introduction to my edition of Dame Julian – whom I mean to read, this time, with the greatest possible attention; in fact making her my only devotional reading before my evening prayers. The editor keeps reproving her, like an affectionate but irritated schoolmaster, for her sad lapses from ortho-doxy: 'Her subsequent meditations [on the uniting of the soul to God] bring her back to her besetting problem, how to reconcile the judge-ment of Holy Church on sin, with the love of God who can never be angry . . . Behind this picture lies the persistent refusal to come to terms with the biblical concept of wrath as part of divine love.' And so on. Sweet, well-meaning, but *naughty* Dame Julian, to believe that God is Love!

◆ ◆ ◆

Praying. Criss-crossing the shepherd's upturned face, and dwelling on it at each passage.

◆ ◆ ◆

The Peace of God. We usually think of this as the final state achieved by wisdom and sanctity. But for those of us who know that they will never get there it is surely best to resign ourselves to – or rather, try to rejoice in – the fruitful Turmoil of God; the struggle which he won't allow us to relinquish.

◆ ◆ ◆

The sudden desire – largely induced by my recent reading about survival – to put a wreath on my mother's poor, bare grave in that Cumberland village. Not for any superstitious reasons; but because I believe that this would be a symbol of reconciliation. Ask Bun* whether he'd like to do it with me. I've visited the grave only once since the funeral thirteen years ago – casually, when we just happened to be passing.

9 FEBRUARY
How garrulous I have been in this present notebook! Better be quiet?
   No, not yet.

◆ ◆ ◆

'Death is necessary so that we may become conscious of the reality that we are'; 'Death's meaning and its reality is an expansion of our existence.' Hampe.
   But if I have really come to believe in all this, how amazing that it hasn't instantly and radically changed every moment and aspect of my life. Particularly after a lifetime of the most violent *timor mortis*.
   Perhaps it *has* made some change of this sort, but subterraneously. And perhaps it will gradually rise to the surface and flood the whole of my conscious mind.

◆ ◆ ◆

Delighted to find that I have read Len Deighton's book about the Battle of Britain with almost complete attention and fascination. These pilots remain, for me, the supreme heroes of my own gener-ation. (And the one I knew best, my Oxford friend John D, seemed when I knew him to be such a *silly* and even snobbish man, though clever and always most engaging. I'd have expected him to join the

---

*Nickname of PT's younger brother, Lawrence.

Guards and then get himself a cushy job as ADC. But he joined the RAF at once, and was himself shot down just after shooting down one of the German aces.)

By strange chance an occasional correspondent of many years, S.F., wrote me a letter about Christian pacifism which arrived this morning: 'My own position is based on my commitment to Christ, as I understand him, not to pragmatism.'

I do not understand the Christ of the New Testament as being totally opposed to war in all circumstances; and, even if he had been expressly so, this wouldn't be a *compelling* reason for me to become a pacifist. I cannot believe, from my study of history, that violence has never done any good. But perhaps S.F. is right, and pragmatism is of no use here: perhaps war is simply wrong in itself, whatever the good result of a 'just war' may be. I come nearer and nearer to that position.

◆ ◆ ◆

A Spy for God, by Pierre Joffroy. The extraordinary life of Kurt Gerstein, who joined the SS, and even helped to make gas for the death camps, because he believed he could serve God best by 'keeping all these things in his heart'. Well, not only that; he also did all he could to let the Allies know what was going on. A noble, brilliant, deeply touching man; one of God's fools, in the best sense (how I love him for looking grotesquely untidy in his SS uniform, and for raising his uniform hat to ladies instead of saluting them).

But the point here is that Gerstein chose the pragmatic and not the purist course. He was even able to watch Jews being whipped into the ovens at Belzec – shattered to his depths, but refusing to make what he would have regarded as a useless and self-indulgent protest. The role – and think of having to live with those associates for four years! – wrecked him physically; and who can say that he chose wrongly? It would have been easier, without a doubt, to have walked into the gas-chamber with the others.

In the end he killed himself while waiting to be tried by the Allies as a major war-criminal. His story only emerged afterwards, bit by bit, largely through the efforts of the French author of this book.

I am haunted by Gerstein.

11 FEBRUARY
Resting, between bouts of hard digging, on a provisional stone seat which I've set against the upper garden wall, I was looking down at the well-known wedge of fields running away from me between the woods. It seemed as if hope was almost something tangible, breathed up at me from the valley: not the faintest tinge of melancholy or regret.

The sense that whatever lies ahead, after death as well as before it, must transcend this moment, and therefore include it. Nothing is ever lost.

◆ ◆ ◆

My present near-belief that we not only survive death but shall *all* receive a loving illumination, and further work to do in a higher realm, might seem to trivialise what we do on earth. This is rubbish, of course, for the whole notion of reward and punishment is pathetically human, and in no way divine. To live well here matters intensely; (*a*) for its own sake, and (*b*) because it is bound to have some effect in the other world, if only that of presenting us there in a rather more *useful* condition.

◆ ◆ ◆

Gerstein. I still don't understand how he was *able* to stand there, giving none of his horror away, while the Jewish mother held out her child to him outside the gas-chamber and implored him to save it. Was this heroism of a very extreme order? Certainly, he was weeping helplessly next day in front of that Swedish diplomat in the train. But had he, in spite of his genuinely tender heart, been somehow toughened and hardened as well simply by his constant association with the S S?

◆ ◆ ◆

True praise of God is quite unlike praising a powerful human being. Far from abasing ourselves in order to flatter the emperor by proclaiming how high he is above us, our adoration of God should be a means of bringing us closer to him. The purer our praise the more we ourselves are filled with the God we are praising.

◆ ◆ ◆

I dislike Kierkegaard more and more: an arrogant, sneering, whining man, alas. Here he is trying to be humble: 'Profoundly humbled before God I have felt myself to be less than ordinary men. That is also the reason why, as I know before God, I broke off my engagement. As a penitent I have thanked God for giving me the opportunity of serving the truth so extensively and in pure idealism. And I have learnt what this means in the eyes of the world, and I have learnt to bear witness to Christianity, but not in the same way as all the parsons' trash does.' Not a very successful attempt at humility!

◆ ◆ ◆

Thoughts of heavenly happiness are closely associated with such earthly joys as walking or bicycling through beautiful country with S, on our way to a delightful, constantly anticipated pub-hotel; good beer and a good dinner and up to a great big bed together.

How base? Or a legitimate sacrament?

◆ ◆ ◆

'Man may, indeed, open the window; but it is the Sun himself that must give the light.'

This, from the little Molinos-Fénelon-Guyon collection. But there are other passages which make it easy to understand why quietism was treated with suspicion – 'He who rests in the divine will, and is exempt from (even the holiest) desires, is infinitely more peaceful and glorifies God more.' I doubt whether anyone, except, perhaps, real contemplative saints, can ever achieve a state in which we cease to desire to be closer to God. There would be a terrible spiritual smugness in that. The fault is to put the Peace of God above the Love of God, and therefore of man.

◆ ◆ ◆

'Heaven-sent opportunity.' A cliché which, like 'Godsend', has come to mean the opposite of what it seems to be saying. What this foolish phrase now means is a piece of utterly fortuitous good luck.

13 FEBRUARY
Two very nice Boston girls in the George last night, one of them doing research on the role of women in the German Lutheran, Anglican and Irish R C Churches. They had been trying to get into the youth hostel in the Castle since 4 o'clock; couldn't afford the price of a bed and breakfast. S whispered to me, suggesting that we ask them back for the night. Horrified refusal. But, after a struggle, I did the right thing and told S to make the invitation. But by then S had heard another offer being made, and refused because there was a cat in the house and one of the girls was allergic to cats. Good old Bubbles! A rare case of managing to make the right gesture without having to suffer the result.

Yet how absurd! How *unpleasant*, to be so crabbishly inhospitable. (And in the pub, full of the most voluble goodwill.)

14 FEBRUARY
Two excellent encouragements given me by Father Philip in Monmouth this morning. 'Trust the past to the mercy of God, the present to his love and the future to his providence.' St Augustine. (But I would put 'hope' for 'providence'.)

85

And this, by somebody called René Voillaume: 'All these contradictions should not shock or discourage us. They belong to the human condition. We bear within us a conflict that will go on all our lives [*cf.* Molinos *et al.*]. We cannot escape from the cross of our humanity, with all its weaknesses.'

15 FEBRUARY
Now, as I dig, the tits on the bird-table are as intensely *there* to me as trees have been to me (periodically) over the last two years. But their charm interferes a little with this sharpness of being-themselves. As perhaps it should.

Am I, then, moving up the scale – vegetable to animal, to human, to divine? Or would such a way of regarding another human be to treat him as Buber's It? I believe it would.

♦ ♦ ♦

And the birdsong as I was at my prayers. Full of the promise of heaven. *Can* this really be so? Or have I, as I often suspect, forced my way towards this reaction only because I have wanted it so much?

16 FEBRUARY
England-Wales match this afternoon. How much I still mind; and particularly, of course, after England's splendid victories over Ireland and France.

Childish? Certainly.

Ignoble? Perhaps.

♦ ♦ ♦

After a hard morning's work at my desk, followed by a vigorous hour and a half on the middle level of the garden, I settled down with beer and sandwiches to watch the match. A sense of extreme contentment – which was utterly shattered by the ferocious first few minutes of play. Growing tension right up to the end of England's hair-raising victory; so that when we got to Ledbury to meet Keith and Sheila★ I was so tired that depression seemed to be surging up from the depths. Nor are things all they might be with D A: will we ever be able to make the really *united* effort which will be needed if we're ever to get this awkward machine into the air?

★ Keith Middleton (a founder of Depressives Anonymous) and his wife.

Today Kerry and Mary came to lunch; also Dave with delightful second daughter, Tara – Michele kept at home by Joanna's illness. A delightful occasion, starting with mass at Tymawr for Kerry, Mary and me; plenty of beer and wine, though this means little to them, and a superb cassoulet by S. Much talk, of course, about old Barn House days; all of it very friendly. Both Kerry and Dave said that those years had meant a great deal to them, that they would never forget . . .

Kerry's Mary is a splendid person; and I've seldom seen a newly married couple whose future looked so good. They are working together with a mentally-handicapped group in Hereford; and I can see how much each would be able to give. Dave now so much calmer, and his natural sweetness able to show itself very clearly.

◆ ◆ ◆

All prayer should be a form of acknowledgement, to be followed by thanksgiving. Thus:

'Help us to . . . ' means 'We know that you are helping us to . . . '
'Grant that we . . . ' means 'You have granted . . . '
'Forgive us for . . . ' means 'You have forgiven us for . . . '

(Though the first two always include the proviso 'if it be your will for us'.)

◆ ◆ ◆

An interesting book by Father Martin Thornton, *Prayer: A New Encounter*, based on Macquarrie's existentialist theology. Yet this shifting about of words often leaves me dissatisfied. He claims that he really and truly believes in the creed; then proceeds to interpret it in a way which would be utterly incomprehensible to those who sweated it out word by word at Nicea. I don't really approve of this desperate clinging to old bottles: the new wine will either break them, or simply fail to ferment at all.

No, I don't find 'Holy Being' a usable substitute for 'God'.

Another common habit among modernisers is to reject some old simplicity as being too naive for words, only to repeat it in a far more complex and less effective form. 'That "marriages are made in heaven" is profound theology by this interpretation; it only becomes trite when God the Father is turned into a benevolent match-maker. Can there be a genuine faith-commitment in the transcendent initiation of this proposed union?' How on earth does that last sentence differ in meaning from seeing God the Father as match-maker? And why not keep to the simplest model?

Theology has always tended to be complex; even contorted. But, unless simplicity can be drawn out of it, I cannot see that it will be much use to anyone outside the charmed circle of theologians.

Also, I am bothered by a kind of persuasive evasion which is so often practised by modern religious thinkers. For example, it is often said that creation is a continuing process; that it's very naive to see it as a single event in time. But this slides past the hard challenge of evolution, which even now, after a hundred and twenty years, plays all too little part in Christian thinking. (Unlike the 'challenges' of Marx and Freud, which are all-too-eagerly accepted, evolution is not a speculative theory but an undeniable reality.) Is God responsible for the whole evolutionary process? If so, why such a long and agonising method of creation? If – as I strongly believe – God was increasingly able to intervene in the evolutionary process as the human mind became capable of receiving him, then when was he able to start this intervention? How hairy was the first 'man' who received a soul?

It is just such naive questions as these which have to be faced, but so seldom are.

18 FEBRUARY

A day in bed after the various exhaustions of company, work and the Welsh match. The returning sense of my really *burdensome* unaware-ness; and the outward signs of this are (*a*) that I order books with a sort of frenzy, still hoping to find the ultimate eye-opener; and (*b*) that I have speeded myself up again, rushing through my day and somehow including even my full hour of meditation/prayer as part of what has to be done; got through; achieved . . .

And as for all the folly of grabbing at books without knowing whether they'll be any good to me or not, I'll never deny that they have been my only royal road towards God. And just after I'd written the passage about unawareness I came on this in Renée Haynes's excellent *The Seeing Eye, the Seeing I*:

> On this analogy one might well speak of a general awareness threshold. No doubt this is in part genetic, in that some people inherit keener senses, or a wider range of them, than others; but it is also, I suggest, closely connected with the ability to accept the unexpected and the apparently irrelevant; an ability inhibited by the overmastering desire prematurely to rationalise experience, to make immediate sense of things . . . [Those with a low awareness threshold] will perceive much more than the rest, whether by sensory or by extra-sensory perception, because that awareness is diffuse. It is not sharply focused on a single object to the exclusion of everything else.

For all my *intellectual* readiness to perceive the utterly unexpected; to accept the wildly improbable, I'm afraid that my mind/senses are united in a sort of extreme conservatism. (Yet how I long to penetrate what I increasingly recognise as the thick screen of mere physical appearances.)

◆ ◆ ◆

Grave temptation to buy very expensive new computer chess-player. Half-way through my prayer-time found it irresistible to re-read fascinating information sent me by the importers. Mammon intruding, hand in hand with Frivolity.

20 FEBRUARY
'The Church becomes necessary to me because man is social and faith must be shared, or I as should prefer to put it, existence is always being-with-others.' This, from Martin Thornton's book seems to me a really deplorable example of wantonly sacrificing old and valid words for new, fashionable and useless ones. The fashion in this case being existentialism. Indeed the whole book, though full of good incidental perceptions, seems to me a typically modernist disaster.

21 FEBRUARY
When, in her asthmatic attack, S needed all the help I could give her, I again gave it willingly, even lovingly, yet had to make one small, fatal remark which nearly undid all the good I'd been able to do her.

22 FEBRUARY
Anne's visit. Such ancient, deep, unalterable affection. Once a wife always a wife. Those ten years, for all the horrors I did her, can never be forgotten; I mean the constant thread of unbreakable love underneath the horrors.

23 FEBRUARY
Arrival of Sargon! Got Jeffrey over to help us get it going. *Sick* excitement for fear of its failing. But calmed by prayer; even the stomach. Shame and delight in this outrageous toy.

◆ ◆ ◆

'Character *can* change, desires *can* be modified. We are not stuck for all eternity with the characters and desires we now have. It is perfectly

89

possible to have what Professor Price calls "second-order desire, a desire that some of one's own desires should be altered."' This from Michael Perry's excellent paper on 'Spiritual Implications of Survival' – a plea for a *working* purgatory, which is just what I've been arriving at by my own path. It is, as he says, a long, long business, this attempt to change one's own desires. I pray, hope and largely believe that this task will be still available in the next realm.

✦ ✦ ✦

There should be no prayer of petition; only of acceptance.

24 FEBRUARY

And, having written that, I find this in Dame Julian: 'And so our customary practice of prayer was brought to mind: how through our ignorance and inexperience in the ways of love we spend so much time on petition. I saw that it is indeed more worthy of God and more truly pleasing to him that through his goodness we should pray with full confidence, and by his grace cling to him with real understanding and unshakeable love, than that we should go on making as many petitions as our souls are capable of.'

What a writer! What a woman! Of all the Christian classics, *Revelations of Divine Love* means the most to me. (Yet when I read it before, deep in the blue years, it only just reached me through the gloom.)

✦ ✦ ✦

'One does not find God if one remains in the world; one does not find God if one leaves the world. Whoever goes forth to his You with his whole being, and carries to it all the being of the world, finds him whom one cannot seek.' Buber.

Too dogmatic. There are other ways; though I do believe that this is the royal road – the road of love for the dearest people.

✦ ✦ ✦

Even Merton, towards the end, was slipping dangerously into that new-fangled language which tries to use human terms instead of heavenly ones: 'Love, then, is a transforming power of almost mystical intensity which endows the lovers with qualities and capacities they never dreamed they could possess. Where do these qualities come from? From the enhancement of life itself, deepened, intensified, elevated, strengthened and spiritualised by love.' Why not say, from God?

90

Cigarettes. Like a child (*a*) playing with matches, and (*b*) eating too many sweets. But more absurd than either, embracing the follies of both. They actually do make me feel ill, almost at the first puff.

Ativan also on the new Good-Resolution Programme. Oh to be rid of all pills altogether; and all drugs except for dear alcohol in its present form of *almost* perpetual moderation.

◆ ◆ ◆

There may perhaps be three orders of 'miracle': (*a*) natural laws operating but not yet recognised or understood – telepathy? (*b*) direct divine intervention, and the contravention of all natural laws by some rarely exercised capacity of Heaven; (*c*) divine use of (*a*).

◆ ◆ ◆

They all seem to shudder, these days, at the term 'liberal Christianity' – as if it were a mere historical phenomenon which belongs essentially to the naive, pre-Great War past. But the task of recognising what must be discarded still goes on; must go on. We must find at least a temporary resting-place, where faith is real and deep and doesn't scratch at us with some infamous contradiction.

◆ ◆ ◆

What amazing happiness this afternoon and evening! Heaven knows why, but everything – gardening, prayers, pub, telly, supper – seemed very good; and S, of course, the best of all.

But as I was saying the Mother prayer across *The Fall of Icarus*, the words 'Have mercy on us!' suddenly shone with a real and dire meaning. Have mercy on us who can be happy in such a world as this: have mercy on our culpable and almost perpetual blindness to the sufferings of others, neglecting, in the fruitful order of our lives, the enforced and agonised disorder in e.g. Cambodia.

27 FEBRUARY
Only one Ativan last night! Woke regularly every hour – instead of every two, as normally – but got plenty of sleep and felt very confident today.

◆ ◆ ◆

'Yes, in the pure relationship you felt altogether dependent, as you could never possibly feel in any other – and yet also altogether free as never and nowhere else; created – and creative. You no longer felt the

one, limited by the other; you felt both without bounds, both at once.'
Buber.

Somewhere this is true of S and me: it must surely be. But have we ever – since our earliest love in Tel Aviv – really *felt* it? We ought to penetrate our love, and learn to dwell in it. Without self-consciousness. Ah!

♦ ♦ ♦

In a very good book on the Great War which I read a few months ago this story was told. After many terrible days at the front, a battalion was to attack at dawn the next day. They all knew that perhaps half of them would be killed. A new and very young recruit suddenly lay down in the mud and sobbed. His platoon sergeant lay down beside him, took him in his arms and kissed him: without a word. I'm haunted by this; the glory of love suddenly revealing itself. *The love which is always there*, but so seldom seen; or even felt.

♦ ♦ ♦

The American hostages in Iran. Of course it is true that their suffering is nothing compared with that of those tortured by the Shah. Yet I feel for them far more deeply and constantly. Because they are people like myself in their expectations of normal and comfortable life. Because I would crack hopelessly under the agonising strain of their – by world standards – trivial ordeal.

♦ ♦ ♦

But if at death we enter that realm immediately above our own, it cannot be so totally, incomprehensibly different from this one or we would be utterly lost and bewildered there. For it is inconceivable – and somehow quite *wrong* – to imagine that we ourselves are totally changed 'in the twinkling of an eye', to make us fit inhabitants of the next stage. Such violent discontinuity of self would be moral non-sense. Therefore the next realm up must be accessible to us as we are, here and now – however strange and different and glorious it may seem. Aim *there* – and not beyond. (Beyond – i.e. God – is only for the spiritual astronauts.)

♦ ♦ ♦

'Simply because we are human persons, we receive that outpouring, that self-giving of love, in a personal guise. Within the deep centre of the soul, Deity-as-It-is-in-Itself is transformed into God-for-us; the ineffable, non-personal Godhead reveals Itself as personal, the It becomes a He, an intimate Thou.' F. C. Happold, *The Journey Inwards*.

This is a good way of putting it, and yet deeply wrong, surely, in its implication that God is *really* 'non-personal' and only, as it were, puts on personal clothes for our benefit. Of course he must be far more than *merely* personal in our ordinary sense of the word – which means one person among many – but our apprehension of him as loving Friend and Father is a true apprehension; absolutely though not comprehensively true.

But at another point in this useful little book Happold goes badly wrong. He says that prayer is 'a way of overcoming the division between the conscious and the unconscious'. My long and deep suspicion of Jung comes, I now see, from what I take to be his romanticisation of the unconscious; making it the Collective Unconscious, full of marvellous mysteries and their beautiful symbols . . . Freud also elevates the unconscious, though in quite a different way: the Freudian implication is that to reveal an unconscious motive or fear is to reveal something which is *more real* than the lies we tell ourselves in our conscious thinking.

My own belief, these days, is that the primary function of the unconscious is sanitary; to drain away the worst and most useless of our emotions – as in my meagre, dreary yet horrifying dreams.

Perhaps we do have to sink deep into our own minds in order to pray properly, but I don't believe that we are sinking a shaft into the unconscious mind. In fact, I would rather say that we are so quieting the mind, and laying it trustfully open, that God is able to enter it. That is, I still feel that the God-Within model is a very dangerous one, particularly in our time; and that opening the soul to God-Without is a far better image. A far *humbler* image, to start with.

28 FEBRUARY

But last night, trying for a second Ativan withdrawal, I was still awake at 4 o'clock, and beginning to panic – the panic being increased by that hateful state when I can find nothing that I want to read. (What an addiction *reading* is! My worst, by far.) So I took a second pill; and managed to calm myself to sleep by about 5.

Result, a slightly airy condition in Monmouth; the way lack of sleep can, very occasionally, make one high instead of heavily weighted down. Showed Bill our new friend Sargon in the Punch-house; and, as I rather suspected, he strongly disapproved, feeling that this was the dehumanisation of his favourite game. True, in a way, I suppose – except that it was some very clever American humans who made Sargon.

◆ ◆ ◆

Over to Jeffrey and Nasi for chess this evening, to learn the very bad news that they are going to sell their house and move. He is – in a sense – at my Yafford★ stage; the premature settling down into country bliss. I was kicked out of this illusory world by Anne; or rather by my own inability to deal with it. Jeffrey is being kicked out by the urgent needs of his painting, which make the big house and garden an intolerable responsibility. How close I felt to him as – abandoning chess – we talked and talked! I said, what I have long felt, that his way of not drinking – with total, fanatical aversion – is very like my way of drinking.

He and Nasi are the only close neighbours we have ever made real friends with since Brian and Dorothy at Barn House fifteen years ago. Just because we see so few people, and because Jeffrey and Nasi are every bit as unsocial as we are, their loss will be all the sadder. And when we talk of 'certainly keeping in touch', how strongly all four secretly suspect that we shall, on the contrary, drift quickly if regretfully apart.

29 FEBRUARY

I'd written to Gerry (Richards) suggesting that, if we talk about expanded awareness etc., we must decide *into what* the mind is able to expand. It seems to me that the possibilities are: (*a*) deeper into one's one mind – which means that all religious endeavour is simply a sort of metapsychology; (*b*) into a better apprehension of the material universe – which makes the process into either art or physics; (*c*) into another and higher (deeper, wider) realm.

Today came a warming card from Gerry: 'I'm having a correspondence with Arthur Peacock about "transcendence" and have been triggered by that into looking again at your "triad of alternatives". I'd settle for your (*c*) if you phrased it this way: "It (the mind) apprehends that aspect of reality not known to us empirically, which we categorise as distinct from the empirical world, but which interpenetrates it." You win?'

I wrote back that I prefer 'all the company of heaven' to his philosophical lingo, but that I'm sure we mean the same thing.

2 MARCH

A night with Jason and Chrissie in Coventry, for DA meeting in Rugby on Sunday. The four of us drove to a country pub to meet Lucy and Bernard. One of those very good family evenings; love and good

★Country house in the Isle of Wight where PT and Anne Wollheim lived.

94

talk. And the DA committee meeting, where I'd dreaded tension, turned out to be one of the best we've ever had.

4 MARCH

Two very hard afternoons in the garden; real construction work. Too hard; felt old and a little sick. But I tell myself, with some truth, that there really is a deadline. I must get the upper lawn levelled in time for sowing in April; and there's a lot of earth still to be shifted. But in fact a longer and slower pace would be just as good for getting the work done; and far better for my health.

The same old trouble – still rushing at too many things; but on the whole I think I *have* slowed down my tempo a bit in the last three years.

◆ ◆ ◆

Jean Sidgwick – translator of Lanza del Vasto – with whom I've been in correspondence for a few months. Father Geoffrey (Curtis) wrote so warmly both of her and of me – 'two of the people I value most in the world'. So she came to Tymawr, and S and I took her out to lunch at the Gocket.

Instant recognition of holiness. Instant and loving understanding between her and Tymawr. But, though I appreciate both so much, I *know* that I am not of their company, as Father Geoffrey imagines. He told Jean S that I am a very good Christian, whatever I may think: and this accords with the judgement of others that I *give the impression* of loving well and widely. It isn't so, alas. They mistake friendliness and openness for something better. I am neither malicious nor arrogant; but I am still pitifully selfish and self-centred.

Or does God, perhaps, work through me in a way which I don't even feel? How strange a vehicle!

◆ ◆ ◆

Help me to love! You, 'from whom no secrets are hid', are well aware of how grossly I fail in this; this which is everything. You know how *laboured* I am in the few good works I ever do: how conscious of the effort. Whereas S, for example, acts at once and unthinkingly and unselfconsciously. For me the consciousness of obligation is, alas, my sad, dry substitute for the spontaneity of love.

5 MARCH

There is only *one* prayer, after all – Thy Will be Done. Everything else is only a variation on that.

◆ ◆ ◆

Dame Julian describes God as 'utterly kind and *unassuming*'! What a strange and wonderful word!

◆ ◆ ◆

That very expensive computerised chess-player has gone wrong already. How calmly I took this, much to my own surprise. (And firmly intend, of course, to get a replacement.) This made me realise that these have been very calm weeks, on the whole; quiet, rational, affectionate. But it is just in such a period that I realise how far our love still has to grow; that all real love must be always growing – or fading.

◆ ◆ ◆

Reading Lanza del Vasto's book, *Return to the Source*, about his journey to Gandhi at the age of thirty-five. A fine writer – beautifully translated by Jean S – and already at that age a wise and learned man. The book makes me acutely aware again of how much I have missed in this life. 'A man is a fool if he does not understand that the things that happen to him are signs, and makes no attempt to read them.' I have felt this during the last few years; but I don't know whether these signs are indeed 'sent' or whether we are supposed to discover signs in whatever happens to happen. Does it matter? In fact, though this is in some ways contrary to my articulated theology, I cannot help feeling that some of these signs have been directly worked for me by . . . God? Heaven? My angel? (Increasingly, now, I find that the notion of heaven means more to me than 'God'.)

◆ ◆ ◆

Looking at the lampshade beside my bed, a dull yellow, stained with scorch marks. I held my hand underneath it to hide the bright bulb; and this seemed a very perfect model of our normal vision. Some – but not I – can take their hands away and see the fullness of the light which shines so inadequately through the palms, the dull fabric, and the little gashes surrounded by black scorching.

◆ ◆ ◆

'Honesty is a certain equality between what one takes and what one gives.' Lanza del Vasto. Yes, and it is no use cheating here; saying, for example, that what one gives is the work of the mind, etc. He means that one must make the gifts with one's hands; and live with great simplicity in order not to consume more than those gifts are worth. He is right; and we are people who take grossly more than we give.

6 March

A particularly jolly Thursday. But after it I began to feel that desolate 'expense of spirit': until I sharply reminded myself that the sacrament of friendship is one of the most important of all; that to talk well and drink happily with friends is a great good, and anything but a waste of spirit. (I probably waste far more of my spirit up here alone in my room, trying to pray and meditate.)

◆ ◆ ◆

Tea with Norman and Jean Hughes (my old Rugby schoolmaster and his wife); Annette Sinker there too. All those three are nearing eighty now. All are ageing 'well' – and yet I did feel a certain melancholy among them. 'This isn't good country to age in,' said Annette as we drove her home. But it is also very painful for any of us to leave this lovely valley, in order to end our days on some dull plain or other.

◆ ◆ ◆

Why should I not feel that my writing has *sometimes* been inspired? Indeed I must think this, for how can I take sole credit for what is really good, knowing that the light of Heaven is the real source of *everything* in us and from us which is really good?

◆ ◆ ◆

'Man has places in his heart which do not yet exist, and into them enters suffering in order that they may have existence.' Léon Bloy.

Dare I send this to Tom – who is suffering more brutally than I've ever suffered? Has one the right to proffer consolation to those in a worse state than any one has known oneself? I feel dumb in this situation: yet dumbness may be a form of timidity; a way of avoiding responsibility.

◆ ◆ ◆

Elbows bent; hands cupped; fingers curled a little upwards. Then 'Thy will be done', for an outward breath felt at each finger and thumb tip in turn. This is a good new prayer; easy to do anywhere, at any time.

◆ ◆ ◆

7 March

But I do, now, have moments *of total faith*. 'All shall be well.' For all of us. Here and hereafter.

◆ ◆ ◆

97

Merton warns against our falsely simple 'God' whose 'chief function is to protect us against a deep encounter with our true inner self and with the true God'. Perhaps; but another way of hiding from the true God may be by forever seeking in the depths and coming up with more and more negations; or abstractions. Better, I feel now, to make a simple image and worship it in the full knowledge that it is too simple; that God lies well behind every image that we make. There is, after all, a true simplicity, which doesn't falsify; as well as a lazy or stubborn oversimplification which allows us to believe that we have *got* the truth of God.

◆ ◆ ◆

S's breathlessness again. Laura was angry with me for not having *made* her see the doctor sooner. I suppose I could have pressed her even harder. If so, why didn't I? Fear? Laziness? Knowledge of how deeply she hates both pressure and visits to the doctor? None of these seems adequate, nor all of them together.

◆ ◆ ◆

Reading Rosalind Heywood and Renée Haynes. I entirely believe all the psychic wonders of which both these honest women tell: I also believe that their friends and acquaintances also have these visionary powers. But I have virtually no such experience myself; nor have I ever known people who have. How thick and solid and stubbornly resistant the outer world appears to me! How much I wish I had these ladies' capacity to pierce its hide!

But at least I am now constantly aware that there *is* another reality which interpenetrates our own. Turn but a stone and start a wing. Yes, the valley out there thronged with angels. Or filled with the presence of a single angel.

8 MARCH

At least I got up this morning and made sure that S went to the doctor with me. At least, though feeling worse and worse, I wrote the letters I'd meant to write. But as I waited for Steve and Adima (old Barn House friends from early community days) I felt so sick with apprehension that I really thought I might have to retire as soon as they came, making my abject, useless apologies. Prayed *hard* for strength, drinking Sam Smith's, deeply inhaling one of Laura's cigarettes.

One or all of these remedies worked well. It was a delightful visit.

◆ ◆ ◆

Rosalind Heywood ends her book, *The Infinite Hive*, with a mescaline experience. '[The Divine Mother] was like a pearl coming into a world of diamonds . . . I saw that spirit could shine through form, however humble, but to equate the two would be idolatrous.' As if all those strange powers which had been rather trivially used for most of her life except when she was a V A D in the Great War had been fully released into their proper function by that drug. Mere strangeness was transformed into holiness.

9 MARCH
And a wonderful dream of Rosalind Heywood, as I remember her at my grandfather's house when I was about twelve. A handsome blonde lady in the dream, whose face suddenly began to unfold into a rose, receiving celestial light and transmitting it to me in the Yatscombe★ garden, down by the bamboos and the azaleas.

◆ ◆ ◆

Sudden longing for music this morning. I carefully dusted the very dusty music-centre and played Beethoven's Mass in C. Rusted-up ears penetrated only by occasional passages. Now I must scour them out by *careful* listening.

◆ ◆ ◆

Dame Julian's disturbing visions of Christ's blood streaming from all his wounds and filling the whole world. This too is all right. Of course it is. She transforms it into joy.

◆ ◆ ◆

Do the 'unique Incarnationists' (i.e. orthodox Christians) believe that God intervened in Palestine, in 4 BC, in order to redeem the whole 'created' universe? If so, how pitifully parochial, both in time and space. But if the Incarnation was only *for us*, on this planet, how much less it seems than they claim!

◆ ◆ ◆

'Help me, dear Mother, to grow towards my death.'

10 MARCH
The humour of angels must be *unimaginably* funny. But what do they laugh *about*?

◆ ◆ ◆

★Name of the house belonging to Gilbert Murray (PT's grandfather) on Boar's Hill, Oxford.

After getting D's scrawled poem, I rang up G and learned that he'd had to commit her to a mental hospital. Horror, and a sense of *total impotence*. I am not a wise man, and a deep crisis of this sort makes me fearfully aware of my ignorance and folly.

◆ ◆ ◆

Today I have felt like an old, furred-up pipe in limestone country: nothing can flow through me any longer. How I long to shed this body; but is there such a thing as a separate 'I' to do the shedding?

Then I had my small, fleeting vision – of S as a little tender bud, half enclosed in leaves. A bud which I can still help to flower.

Or is this just the florid effect of my present reading? I don't think so. Whenever I've received anything like a message, it has almost always had to do with S.

◆ ◆ ◆

'The thought came to me that little boys play with wooden swords and will be soldiers when they grow up, and little girls play with dolls and will be mothers tomorrow. And we humans cherish certain images and with them play at religion, but when we have grown, what shall we have become?' Lanza del Vasto.

◆ ◆ ◆

Yes; what I lack so much (furred-up pipe) is *openness*: I feel that my soul has been narrowed and shrivelled by too much thinking. (And yet I know that I must go on plodding away with the mind; that this is what I *am to do*.)

Then comes this: 'The function of thought is to unify the multiple. Faced with the *one*, it has nothing to do. It can only try to break it up. But the purpose of meditation is knowledge of the one, of the inner one, of the self. Thought cannot therefore force its way in there. The very nature of thought, and not a failing of thought, prevents it from penetrating the mystery.' Lanza del Vasto.

◆ ◆ ◆

Longing for a purely physical escape – which symbolises every other – I look in all directions and find them blocked. My comfort; my habits; my drink . . . (On an ordinary day I now drink exactly two pints of Guinness each evening, between 6.00 and 7.30. This seems moderate indeed; but it is profoundly *immoderate*, in that I *must* have just *that* much at *that* time. I am no less the slave of my two pints than more sensational cases are of their two bottles of whisky.)

◆ ◆ ◆

100

'The pure scientist ignores God. "He does not need that hypothesis." Likewise the pure yogi does not need what men call God. But the man who is not journeying towards God has made some false semblance of God his goal.' Lanza del Vasto.

♦ ♦ ♦

No doubt my dualism of Heaven and Earth is a philosophy/theology for amateurs: at any rate for those with no deep spiritual experience. But how much better to accept this elementary status than to try to stretch out and embrace THE WHOLE! I am all for partial truths, well known to be partial.

♦ ♦ ♦

As for the old fault of self-consciousness, introspection and so on, the only question to ask oneself is 'Am I as available to God as I can be?' The answer is always no, of course; but it is the right question all the same. Keeps one heading the right way.

And it may be that my task is to show that God can use even this conglomeration of follies and weaknesses. (Provided, of course, that I go on trying to get rid of them!)

♦ ♦ ♦

'God and man . . . are actually and for ever Two, the two partners of the primal relationship that, from God to man, is called mission and commandment; from man to God seeing and hearing; between both, knowledge and love. And in this relationship the son, although the father dwells and works in him, bows before him that is "greater" and prays to him. All modern attempts to reinterpret this primal actuality of dialogue and to make of it a relationship of the I to the self or something of that sort, as if it were a process confined to man's self-sufficient inwardness, are vain and belong to the abysmal history of deactualisation.' Buber.

In spite of that terrible last word this is a master-passage; true dualism preserved; and by one of the great mystics of our time.

♦ ♦ ♦

'For the letter killeth, but the spirit giveth life.' But I think the letter killeth only if it is taken as an adequate substitute for the spirit; or a verbal cage in which the spirit can be enclosed. Sometimes – as in this famous passage! – the spirit lights up the letter; reveals itself through inspired words.

♦ ♦ ♦

11 March

As I was praying for D, sitting down on the stone between bouts of hard digging this afternoon, I felt for the very first time that this intercessionary prayer was somehow meshing; connecting; even *working*. This was partly, perhaps, because of a new method, in which I use my hands with my breathing and praying. But whether it worked to her direct benefit I can't know or even guess.

◆ ◆ ◆

Sudden horrid memory of those Barn House humiliations in the very early months of the community, when I was summoned to a court of loved-ones and strangers! What fearful injuries S and I did to each other at that bad time!

14 March

How charming and delightful Lu's company is! But suddenly, after a few too many drinks, she was paranoiacally shouting at S and me, 'Don't whisper about me! All my childhood you were whispering about me.' And many of us feel like this at certain times – and at any age – that the *others* – the grown-ups; the sober ones; the sane ones – are whispering terrible things about us.

◆ ◆ ◆

But I now find that prayer for D, or Tom, is better if it takes the old form:

> 'Heavenly Mother,
> Light of the World,
> Have Mercy on us.'

On *us* – rather than on *him* or on *her*. True prayer for another should never be *de haut en bas*, from my comparatively all-right state to your misery: it should involve the one who is praying in his own prayer; perhaps – for saints only? – the whole of humanity, past, present and future, should be involved.

◆ ◆ ◆

The biography of that weird semi-saint Caryll Houselander by Maisie Ward, which I first read in 1976 and have therefore largely forgotten. Again, the horror of the specifically R C world: they always talk about 'the Catholic . . . For us Catholics . . . ', but why not 'Christian'? I'd like to say why not 'Human'? And how revolting I find the jargon, and much of the specific imagery. Yet I partly envy them for having all that imagery and all those things to do. I have had to start from a complete denuding; a bare cupboard: and even now there are not many bones in it.

◆ ◆ ◆

'Christ's Passion'. This is normally the elevation of a special case – as if the death by crucifixion of Jesus of Nazareth was actually an agony which weighs as heavy as, or heavier than, all the agony suffered by all the rest of the human race. This is horrible. And the make-believe that the dead Jesus still suffers the same agony whenever we commit a sin is one of the most revolting bits of Christian nonsense.

But if 'Christ's Passion' *stands for* all human pain, then it is a rich and living symbol at the very least.

Caryll Houselander: 'It's only when we try *not* to accept our special suffering that it can really break us.' Yes; for the luxurious suffering of those who are able to stand back and look at their pain. But most of the world's suffering is utterly crushing, brutalising, deadening. Simone Weil is at her least convincing when she tries to make this worst affliction a way towards God: *the* way towards God.

◆ ◆ ◆

How on earth did I manage to write that perfectly adequate review of six books in OUP's *Past Masters* series today – on Jesus; Marx; Aquinas; Dante; Pascal; and Hume? I felt utterly dry and weary as I dragged the typewriter across my desk to me. Is this just extreme professionalism? Or by your help, my blessed angel? Both, perhaps.

◆ ◆ ◆

Laura said, when I was trying to comfort her yesterday, 'It's strange, Papa, that you don't lose your temper now.' This isn't true, of course; but it must be partly true. Pleasure in this, of course; but also dismay at the thought of the monster I must have been.

◆ ◆ ◆

Where does sacramental vision end and idolatry begin?

◆ ◆ ◆

Yes: it really is possible, however odd, to will that one would will otherwise than one does will. In fact one of the most fundamental prayers is 'Change my will, O Lord.' In other words, '*Thy* will be done.'

15 MARCH
England's victory (over Scotland) – something of an anticlimax after

all. Also, I was saddened to find that Wales's defeat gave me almost as much pleasure. *Not* Ireland's victory, but Wales's near-humiliation. Mean-minded in the extreme, particularly in the hour of England's triumph after so many years.

◆ ◆ ◆

Now that I've finished reading *True Peace* – as part of my pre-meditation reading – I realise that this little collection of quietist direction* does suffer from a terrible lack. Not a word about love of others; let alone about actively helping others. This utter concentration on self-perfection is a real heresy; and the Church was right to condemn it. (Though probably for the wrong reasons – i.e. the quietist self-perfecter has no great need of the Church.)

◆ ◆ ◆

Buber is bold enough to say that Buddhism is inadequate. '[The Buddhist's] inmost decision seems to aim at the annulment of the ability to say You.' Or, in simpler terms, Buddhism is *essentially* an atheist religion, as it was quite openly so in its early and pure form. The Buddhist and the quietist have much in common; as have all those forms of religion which concentrate on the self at the expense of God and Neighbour.

◆ ◆ ◆

I am finding much of this latest posthumous Merton collection (*Love and Living*) a disappointment; and worse. He should not write about 'the fuzz'. Not only is this a piece of sycophancy towards the estranged youth of the sixties; it is also an unchristian dehumanisation, like any other comprehensively abusive label.

And this is unpleasant too: 'Celebration is crazy: the craziness of not submitting even though "they", "the others", the ones who make life impossible, seem to have all the power.' But in so far as that splendid counter-culture failed, it did so because so many of its members saw themselves as already perfected; the forces of light opposed to the ('straight') forces of evil. One of the oldest religious errors. For this is where the message of the quietists is really necessary and important; seek ye first the 'they' who are within. And in the 'they' whom you see over there, seek the seed of love which is in everyone.

◆ ◆ ◆

*Quietism was originally the attitude of extreme asceticism, contemplation and total self-surrender to the will of God advocated by the seventeenth-century Spanish priest Miguel de Molinos. Today the term is often used to describe the practice of withdrawal from worldly affairs into a spiritual and contemplative life.

The weakness of God. If there were no weakness in him, how would he communicate with all the weakness in us?

But also his strength: the strength of unqualified love. And strength is a much better word than power, which has too many odious associations.

16 MARCH
A heartfelt, unspiritual cry:

> 'There's always my own BED
> Ahead!'

◆ ◆ ◆

'All doctrines of immersion are based on the gigantic delusion of a human spirit bent back into itself – the delusion that spirit occurs [of its own accord] in man.' Underneath the subtlety and complexity of his language Buber remains a believing Jew; and reminds us of the immense value of that faith – its refusal ever to forget or neglect the profound difference between man and God.

◆ ◆ ◆

Does the virtue/strength of one spouse rise as that of the other falls? A ludicrous idea, like the man and woman of the nursery barometer who come in and go out alternately, but are never in or out together. A tempting idea at times. Ghastly, the rare occasions when S and I have been down in the lower depths together. (For there is no companionship there.)

17 MARCH
For some incomprehensible reason the Australian Broadcasting Company wanted me to read out the review I wrote of Broch's *Death of Virgil* in 1978. So off we went to Bristol, where I was put in a little room by myself, instructed only through earphones, and solemnly read out what I had written with so much confidence eighteen months ago. It sounded frightful: as heavy and turgid as I was accusing Broch of being. (Not that I feel that I've been cured of that since then. Far from it; that is a permanent tendency of mine in all my writing.)

But at least I was able, on this Bristol expedition, to give much-needed strength to S and Laura. Thank heaven!

◆ ◆ ◆

'The only cure for worrying about our own sins is to concentrate not on self-perfection but on the love and tenderness of God . . . Even ignore your own soul: keep your mind on God and on His love. For prayer imagine (only it is not imagining, but true) that at every second of the day about four Masses are being said, and that you, your life, yourself as you are, now in this second, are your offering for the Mass, and offer yourself as you are in union with Our Lord's offering at Mass.' This passage from Caryll Houselander is a very complete example of what I take to be deep spiritual wisdom attached to utter gibberish. For let's suppose that those masses were suddenly said no longer. Would this mean that 'God and His love' would no longer be there? Such superstition appals me. For God is not helped, so I believe, even by the most time-honoured magic, but by the exercise of love and honest prayer.

'[My vision] was simply an almost unbelievable showing of the heart of the Mystical Body of Christ literally bleeding before God with the wounds of the world.' Caryll H again; but this time the terrible gibberish without the wisdom. The image is revolting: but she will not even have it – 'literally' – that it is an image.

But here she is at her best: 'Psychiatry has a humble yet magnificent service to offer in simplifying man's response to grace.' And this: 'Sanctity is the only cure for the vast unhappiness of our universal failure as human beings.'

18 MARCH
A major absurdity. I detect that my recent and tentative belief in a beneficent purgatory after death has slightly but definitely reduced the strength of my private sanction against smoking!

◆ ◆ ◆

We are told that it is a Platonist error to think of the body as a prison in which the soul is held captive. But with increasing age this becomes a more and more tempting image. Though I still greatly enjoy the works of the body – from digging to beer, from bed with S to bed alone in exhaustion after work – I clearly foresee that next stage in which the body will be nothing but a hateful burden. And how delightful, if I reach that stage, to imagine the captive bird within, who will fly free as soon as the dreadful old body lets it go!

◆ ◆ ◆

What are these 'needs' which burden and limit me so? They are simply long-accumulated habits, attached by claws which have dug deeper and deeper through a lifetime of self-indulgence. No wonder the great religious figures have stripped themselves of nearly all such 'needs'. Even of food itself – e.g. St Catherine of Siena.

◆ ◆ ◆

The extreme – e.g. de Caussade – concentration on the present moment has always seemed right to me. But in that case present sin and present pain are of absolute and eternal significance just as much as present depth of prayer. So any notion of post-mortem rectification is frivolous and vulgar.

Jesus was dying in anguish for only a few hours; but Christians are quite right to treat the Crucifixion as a symbol of all human pain since time began. At least they are right to do this provided they mean the Crucifixion according to Matthew and Mark; where Jesus dies in despair, crying, 'My God, my God, why hast Thou forsaken me!' How smug and diminishing are the additions in Luke and John – e.g. 'Father forgive them for they know not what they do.' (Nor is this at all in keeping with Jesus's usual attitude to his enemies.)

◆ ◆ ◆

Struggle! Struggle! Struggle! Struggle! Struggle! To stay in the same place. The Red Queen syndrome.

◆ ◆ ◆

Now our third chess computer has collapsed. But after the first two or three minutes of despairing rage I was able to see it as funny; or at least as funny *too*. Thanks be to God! A proper punishment for my childish folly and greed. £300 perhaps wasted. (And in any case, playing it proved to be strangely boring. It could usually beat us even on its lowest level, but this was partly, I'm sure, because one simply can't put one's heart into playing against a machine.)

Still trying to *buy* the Holy Grail!

◆ ◆ ◆

A fine baptismal prayer from the Free Church of Berkeley, USA (1971): 'By your life-giving Spirit, O God, bless these waters as the means of our union with Jesus our Brother, the vanguard of our new creation.'

Well, I cheated a little there, so anxious am I to find true allies: after 'O God' come the words 'which at the beginning hovered over the deep', with their implication of God as Creator of the Universe. But still, in this strange field one has a perfect right to take what one can from anywhere, and not necessarily to take it whole.

19 MARCH
An odd situation. I'm sitting in the pub near Parkway station, waiting for the girl from the *Observer* to arrive and interview me in the context

of the republication of *Friends Apart*.* Reading extracts from Eckhart and Tauler in Kenneth Leech's new book *True Prayer*, but half listening to one old woman and two old men talking about all the ills that their flesh is heir to.

Leech speaks of the necessary experience of God's darkness within us; and this is fine, but what is usually within *me* is trivial and self-concerned anxiety. This must be the worst material of all for God to work on. But perhaps even this . . .

The great thing about the splendour and immediate relevance of these ancient prayers is that they leap across the centuries and abolish time. Reading secular history hardly ever does this; nor should it. For in most fields the more we suppose that our predecessors thought or felt like ourselves the more we fail to understand them; the more we traduce them.

◆ ◆ ◆

The interview in the George. That charming girl, Janet Watts, taking notes and encouraging me with her smile as I talked and talked about ME; and our old friend Jane Bown leaning this way and that to take hundreds of photographs. How much I tried to please; and yet to be honest too. That stuttering self-correction was the fruit of both impulses.

Yes, but what about *her* charm? Of course she must have been just as conscious of using it as I was conscious of using mine. (And I know, of course, that mine is still in good working order when needed; though not very often needed now.)

20 MARCH
Deeply tired today, after nine days of almost continuous company. Most of it very welcome company; some of it loved. Must overcome my deep impulse to consider all talking an expense of spirit. Both the company and the exhaustion are an opportunity: for me: for God. And in the apparent confusion of these days – i.e. my routine was badly broken! – there must be a fruitful order hidden somewhere. Waves and troughs. And in each trough I ought to be quietly absorbing all that I saw on the crest of the last wave.

◆ ◆ ◆

Abba's 'I Have a Dream'. *Very* seductive, but would become insufferable if I had to hear it many more times.

◆ ◆ ◆

* A memoir of two friends of P T's, Jasper Ridley and Esmond Romilly, killed in the last war.

A day in bed. Trying ten minutes of prayer at ten minutes to every hour. Feeling quite pleased about this, when the bombshell exploded of an unavoidable social obligation – a neighbour's real and urgent need. How *instantly* my smooth, calm day was disrupted by gloomy anticipations.

◆ ◆ ◆

Comte's three historical stages: Childhood – Theological; Early Manhood – Philosophical; Maturity – Scientific.

This makes very little historical sense; but it is useful as a model. Provided one adds: Wisdom – Theological. (A resurrected and re-constituted faith. A second childhood, but in the very best sense; childhood recaptured, but 'changed, changed utterly' by all that has intervened since the first childhood.)

◆ ◆ ◆

A really terrible book called *Beyond Belief*, by an American 'sociologist of religion' called Robert N. Bellah. This writer, a clever and thought-ful man, would certainly regard himself as a sort of religious fellow-traveller; as someone who has risen well above the crudities of scientific materialism and naive disbelief. For him – as for Jung in psychology – religion is not only a very interesting phenomenon but also a very useful one. Belief does a great service to man, both as an individual and as a social animal. 'I expect traditional religious sym-bolism to be maintained and developed in new directions, but with growing awareness that it is symbolism and that man in the last analysis is responsible for the choice of his symbolism.' This would be fine, of course, if the writer believed that the symbolism we use and change is an attempt to express our beliefs about a reality outside ourselves. But Bellah makes it plain over and over again that he believes nothing of the kind. For example: 'These feelings are handled initially by the development of protective symbols, which are redolent with the mysterious potency of the unconscious feelings; that is, they are highly magical and sacred.'

These people are the most dangerous of all; the supreme patronisers who understand nothing about the true nature of faith. How absurd and naive – for all their apparent sophistication – to think that men and women are going to preserve the socially or psychologically 'useful' elements of religious belief while discarding all its depth, passion and substance. 'Let's go on pretending to believe, although we know quite well that there is nothing really there.'

◆ ◆ ◆

Usually, now, I seem to receive the strength for an encounter/ordeal; but usually only just enough.

◆ ◆ ◆

Yesterday I had asked myself, rather uneasily, why God, or the angel, seems to make so little of the opportunity surely offered by dreams. The mind must then be far more accessible than during the long waking hours of endless mental scurrying. Today came a letter from Richard Mackie, saying that he had been 'short of' about a hundred dreams; had now managed to dream eighty of them. I also found in Laura's room a book called *The Dream Game* by Ann Faraday, and began to read it. Coming downstairs after my prayers, I picked up the telephone book and found lying under it another book called *Dreams and Dreaming* (left there by Laura's present boyfriend on his last visit). We went out to the pub, and this time were sitting close to the speaker when the Abba song was playing:

> I have a dream,
> A song to sing,
> To help me cope
> With anything . . .

> I have a dream,
> A fantasy
> To help me through
> Reality . . .

> I believe in angels . . .

In bed I felt a strong impulse to read *Ash-Wednesday*, knowing that it was Eliot's first specifically Christian poem and that I hadn't read it for at least thirty years. I came on this:

> . . . Redeem
> The unread vision in the higher dream.

Reading the Leech book on prayer just before turning out the light I found the famous quotation, 'Young men shall see visions and old men shall dream dreams.'

I can't remember ever having such a succession of clear and insistent messages.

The Faraday book is appallingly written – 'Basically this is what it's all about' – but interesting and thought-provoking. She insists that our dreams are wise and that they are always telling us something which our waking minds need to know. For the time being I accept this; I plan to write down my dreams as best I can, and see whether I can make any sense of them.

One of the major con-tricks of recent history has been the appropriation of the past by the Right. In fact the official Right and the official Left have vied with each other in trampling on everything in the past which is of true and lasting value. The so-called Conservatives, with Labour periodically lending a hand, have thundered down the Gadarene slope of industrial growth and technological development, utterly heedless of where this mad rush was leading us. And both sides, of course, have had the poor deluded people behind them in this.

Yes, yes, I know that there were no good old days. But what has been needed, and utterly lacking, was a true, wise, life-enhancing conservatism, ready for change but always considering the loss as well as the gain.

♦ ♦ ♦

What are the main surviving obstacles to my faith? First, the long Confucian era, when men lived, thought, felt and acted at least no worse than in most Christian ages; yet believed in neither God nor heaven but only in a decorous and decent life on earth. Second, diabolical/demoniac visions, felt by those who experienced them to be just as real as their angelic/divine visions. Third, the existence of such people as W. M. and George P: the first a savagely sour peasant-farmer, who ended his life on speaking terms with nobody, not even the brother and sister who shared his house; the second a gross, bullying yet obsequious Guards officer; a monster of vulgarity and egotism.

These obstacles are not insuperable, of course, but they are awkward. For I disbelieve in demons and Devil quite as strongly as I believe in angels and in God. And though I know that there is the seed of a soul in everyone, both W. M. and George P died without showing the faintest sign theirs had ever sprouted.

♦ ♦ ♦

'Essentially since Kant,' writes Bellah, 'the attempt to anchor theism in metaphysics, in any kind of cognitive statement about the structure of the cosmos, has been exposed as hopelessly delusory.' Thus he shows his true colours in the end. All one need ask him is to replace the word 'theism' with the word 'atheism' and then tell us whether that statement is any more true than the other.

Surely we know by now that both belief and disbelief are acts of faith; metaphysical assumptions which depend, not on any possible proof, but on the whole nature, experience and inclination of the individual.

♦ ♦ ♦

Back to Blake, for another true dualist:

> Twofold always, May God us keep
> From single vision and Newton's sleep.

◆ ◆ ◆

My most immediate need is for the *peace* of God; but I can think of it only as the distant, eventual, uncertain reward for a kind of hard spiritual work which may well be beyond me to accomplish. Yet how can I know God's love, or feel real love for him, until I can escape from this frightened, anxious, self-assertive, insatiable ego? In fact it seems that there can be no peace without love, no love without peace. I think this is called a double-bind.

◆ ◆ ◆

Alas, Radley, not God, filled my mind as I was levelling the garden this afternoon. That TV programme yesterday; the dreadful essence of public school, sharpened by a strong aroma of the second-rate and pretentious. Yet not quite deplorable or ridiculous enough to come into the category of Very Bad School, of which Paddy★ and I are such delighted connoisseurs.

Is it childish of me to retain this profound antipathy? I don't think so. Loveless; arrogant; stupid – a dreadful concatenation of false values.

◆ ◆ ◆

Meanwhile this levelling of the garden is the hardest job of this kind I've ever done. Not that the physical work is too hard, but the estimation of what soil should come out of where, and where it should go to. But I *shall* get it done before the deadline for sowing grass next month.

◆ ◆ ◆

'This language [of animals] is the stammering of nature under the initial grasp of spirit, before language yields to spirit's cosmic risk which we call man.' Buber.

'Spirit's cosmic risk' is splendid.

◆ ◆ ◆

A hundred slow breaths without distraction – easily a record – except, of course, for the *underlying* awareness that I was beating all my previous records. A naive procedure indeed; but such is my lot.

◆ ◆ ◆

★ Patrick Leigh Fermor.

A second reflection on that dream about B; how I compelled her, after just a fortnight's marriage to me, to move out of Castle Howard★ into a small cottage on the estate. Perhaps B was standing in for S! And perhaps it is true that I've confined S here, gradually imposing on her not only my secluded way of life but also her very *need* of such a life.

But what can I do?

I have tried to persuade her to do more voluntary work; to get away from our closed-in way here, and lead a life of her own. But once again it was I who was doing the persuading; putting on the pressure. Putting the pressure on her to remove herself from the pressure I put on her. Another double-bind. They must be God's favourite jokes against us. Or are they his *koans* – the real chances he gives us?

Love, as usual, is the only way: and how much I have loved her during the last few weeks! More deeply, I truly believe, than ever before.

◆ ◆ ◆

Anyway, I have become very doubtful about the rather slick assumption, in *The Dream Game*, that there is one true interpretation of every dream. What carefully remembered dreams may do for us is simply to shake up the waking mind, and lead it into wider and wilder speculations.

22 MARCH

But here is Merton at his very best again: '[It may well be] that the reason God has ceased to be present to man (therefore "dead") is that man has ceased to be present to himself, and that consequently the true significance of the statement "God is dead" is really "MAN is dead".'

◆ ◆ ◆

How vividly, this evening, I saw The Pain of the World, as I repeated those words yet again while staring into the poor, fawn-like but hollowed-out eyes of Verlaine!

◆ ◆ ◆

'Loving myself as I was as a child is absolutely the crossroads of personality development. If I can't find love, compassion, acceptance, understanding for that early self, then I sentence myself to travel a lonely road, destination perpetual loneliness, emptiness. We are so limited in our powers as children, so totally at the shifting mercies of

★P T's maternal grandmother was a member of the Howard family, and as a child he spent part of each summer at Castle Howard. (See *Part of a Journey*, pp. 89–90.)

powers beyond our control. We take the words we hear so absolutely literally. As adults we often wrap ourselves in the symbols of power, money, position, connections, and despise those persons without power; we also despise ourselves when powerless, when helpless children, we despise our inner self, our child, still present, still hungry, still suffering, still afraid. "Unless you become as a little child, you cannot enter the Kingdom of Heaven." That "little child" is *you*, your own inner self, your child.' Jack Downing.

Wonderful! And I vividly remember, at the age of ten, imploring my future grown-up self not to disown or despise this ten year old. And I come back again to the great and loving service Connie★ did me by redeeming my childhood; telling me, against all the family witness, that I had been 'a delightful child, mischievous, imaginative and affectionate'. So not after all – at least not exclusively – the monster so often recalled to me by my mother. (And why did she treat me as a monster if not because something had half-killed the child in *her*!)

◆ ◆ ◆

I dislike this dream book more and more. That fatal, ultra-modern conviction that every difficulty or problem we meet must be due to some sort of 'hang-up'. That all we need do is relax and be our 'natural selves'. Of course it is true that old Nobodaddy-Superego can be a fearful tyrant whom we must overcome. But only so as better to face the enduring, real and unavoidable challenges – the challenges, above all, presented by other people and their needs. And if we *cannot* love X, who demands something of us which we find hard to give (e.g. time and close attention), *then we must act as we would if love were really there.*

To equate the right course with the easy course is a horrible and sloppy error. At least as bad as to assume that the most difficult and painful course must be the right one.

24 MARCH
Up to London to return the now much-hated chess-machine (money readily refunded); to talk to Louise, my fellow literary-executor, about my father's affairs; to talk to Lady Collins about the progress of those two books. Real worries about both the last two; but for the moment, here in bed, I have prayed for relief from worry, and relief has come.

★ Constance Hellins – long-lost childhood guardian fortuitously refound by P T in 1976 after fifty years' separation. (See *Part of a Journey*, pp. 108–110.)

25 MARCH

'Whereof we cannot speak, thereof we must be silent.' This is all very well; but there is a false notion that ordinary language evolved as a means of ordinary communication; and is therefore quite unsuited for describing a spiritual experience. In fact, of course, language was evolved by spiritually-conscious beings; not by linguistic philosophers.

26 MARCH

Reading *Four Quartets* again; after many years. I realise that though the words are still very familiar I never had the least idea what they meant until now; nor did I care! I don't think the poem seems *better* for this greater understanding, but certainly more accessible; amenable; even lovable. A contrived clumsiness – which is quite a cunning and successful device.

28 MARCH

So Paul has turned up in Gloucester again, and Laura has immediately gone back to him! This is a dire bombshell, after all the suffering they have caused each other in the past, and our long conviction that she can never be happy with him. But, as always, we can give her nothing but our love and support; though we also, I'm afraid, gave her a good deal of anger when she first broke the news to us.

In a time of crisis like this I find that crafty and extravagantly self-indulgent manipulation may be just the thing – e.g. yesterday evening's six fierce cigarettes, two large whiskies and an extra Ativan. With this support I survived quite well, and was even able to offer myself as a temporary pillar of wisdom to S as well as Laura.

◆ ◆ ◆

So I kept records of my dreams for a week; but have now decided to abandon the whole project. I don't believe that they all have some subtle and beneficent meaning which we can discover by patient examination. I think they probably serve many purposes, and that perhaps the primary one is a psychological drainage system.

Last night, for example, I was back in the Army again, as I often am in dreams, and the horror was very great. But no doubt this released some sharp anxiety of my waking life, and did me less of an injury because it was all muffled up in a dream.

Not that they don't sometimes leave me washed out and distressed when I wake up for the last time of the night. My dreams are seldom good; usually neutral and grey; quite often painful.

◆ ◆ ◆

I notice that when talking aloud to myself, which happens more and more often, I seem to adopt the role of a very simple, almost childish character. This afternoon, for example; discussing every move I was making in the process of levelling that upper lawn – or bowling-green. As if I could reassure myself by my own stolid innocence. Curious. *Not* false: a real release of the simple child within.

◆ ◆ ◆

The Budget. How much more bitterly the rich hate the poor than vice versa. Their suppressed guilt poisons their minds and forces them to think of the poor as nothing but feckless layabouts, dishonest scroungers, disloyal 'commies', etc.

29 MARCH
Dreams again. The attempt to describe them never really succeeds. They are indescribable because of their strange and, in every case, utterly unique atmosphere. Yet they are also much simpler in ostensible events than waking life: they lack all detail. I am not even sure that they can truly be called visual: conceptual, rather?

◆ ◆ ◆

'Whether one speaks of God as He or It, this is never more than allegory. But when we say You to him, the unbroken truth of the world has been made word by mortal sense.'
Buber gets better and better, as if straining to release himself from his earlier verbal contortions; and saying the same thing with a hard-won simplicity.
And this: 'Our knowledge of duality is reduced to silence by the paradox of the primal mystery.' Which is one of the ideas I was trying to express in my paper on Evil: for us there must be a dualist model; for God, and perhaps for some of the mystics, there may well be a unity which most of us can't even glimpse.

30 MARCH
We had decided against going to Tymawr; but I woke at 7 o'clock with a strong urge to go; flew out of bed for quick shave and coffee; then down the valley and over the river in a beautiful morning of bright sun and very clean white mist. Our little Palm Sunday procession from the library to the chapel. Such warm feelings!

◆ ◆ ◆

Memories of the past suddenly pierce me: shafts of pain. For I am still so very time-bound; so conscious of time lost and gone for ever, instead of seeing it wisely, as an eternal present. The face of Isaiah Berlin suddenly appearing to me behind closed lids. And shall I ever see that dear old friend again? (How shocked *he* would be if he found angels attending him after death!)

◆ ◆ ◆

I see now, as I never quite saw in the early days of the Barn House community, that real privacy is as necessary as real community. A human being has equal need of both. (And now, alas, I almost completely lack the communal, the social, the sense of belonging to a group, or even to a neighbourhood. My privacy has become so obsessional that it denies me the other half of life.)

◆ ◆ ◆

Suddenly, in Coleford, I bought three science-fiction novels; and read them one after the other without a pause. All three were good, and reading them gave me a very pleasant feeling of release. Release from the thrall of earnest and holy reading.

31 MARCH

Of course, I believe that nearly all the governments of the world are set on courses which are as mad as they are bad. And this, on the whole, with the agreement of their own peoples. Yet I take full advantage of the material advantages which this kind of policy provides: a car, a telly, superfluous and luxury food.

But supposing that I could follow in practice what I so deeply believe in theory – live a really frugal and simple life. Wouldn't I be so puffed up with spiritual pride that my last state would be worse than my first? A facile and false way out; for the frugality and simplicity would be wholly directed towards a prayerful love of God and neighbour: they would be a means, not an end.

◆ ◆ ◆

In Galatians Paul shows himself quite aware that Jesus used to say, 'Abba! Father!' But this was one of the most idiosyncratic things recorded in the Gospels and must have sounded very odd, even repulsive, in the ears of a well brought up Pharisee like Paul: something like how 'O God, our dear Daddy' would sound in the ears of an intellectual Roman Catholic of our own time.

What a great pity it is that Paul, who knew some of the original disciples quite well, was so determined to prove the equality of his own apostleship that he never asked them about, or at least never wrote about, the life, sayings and personality of Jesus.

◆ ◆ ◆

Now and again an oasis in the long desert of Kierkegaard's whining, vicious and paranoiac *Journals*: 'The creation was really only completed when God included himself in it. Before the coming of Christ God was certainly in the creation, but as an invisible sign, like the watermark in paper. But the creation was completed by the incarnation because God thereby included himself in it.'

I would say that God has always entered the material universe as far as he could – even, perhaps, before the evolution of man; drawing evolution towards the point of a spiritual being. But what orthodox Christians see as the Incarnation was certainly a major new step in heaven's infusion of the earth; in divine penetration of the material universe.

◆ ◆ ◆

I've sometimes had an uneasy feeling that I ought still to be reading works by the humanist opposition; a legacy of my liberal inheritance, I suppose. But the truth, as I see it, is that books by people who are spiritually ignorant are worse than useless to me now. For example, I no more want to read Freddie on God than he would have the least interest in reading me on epistemology.

◆ ◆ ◆

Three per cent increase in our already vast defence budget. Like a little boy waving a revolver about as a sign of his manhood. The trouble is that the revolver in the childish hands of our rulers is a loaded one.

◆ ◆ ◆

TV programme on the USA. Not so much love-hatred as love-fear.

◆ ◆ ◆

Reading a long life of St Hugh of Lincoln, firmly based on the biography written by his own chaplain in the early thirteenth century. Though the original has been rather irritatingly touched up by triumphalist (French) RC hands in the nineteenth century, and though some of Hugh's own words and actions seem very remote, how amazingly close I feel to him most of the time! Across eight hundred years – Renaissance, Reformation, Industrial and Scientific Revolutions – he speaks directly to my heart and even to my faith.

◆ ◆ ◆

A recent resolution has been to read Shakespeare as soon as I get to bed. Started on *Hamlet* just now, and was appalled to find it utterly *preposterous*. It was as if I had simply lost touch with this most familiar of all literary conventions. Alas for me!

◆ ◆ ◆

What is the primal religious statement of our time? Surely it should be something like this: 'There is more than we can know.'

4 APRIL
The crowded market in Agincourt Square today; bright spring sunshine; a sense of real joy and companionship. Which led us to go up in a body to Wilson's hillside cottage after closing-time in the Beaufort, and drink bottle after bottle of wine on his little lawn. An idyll? Nearly, but not quite, for there were too many currents of deep disagreement; in fact irreconcilable differences of value. Yet how many happy memories of W's 'hovel'! How sad that it now seems to belong so much to the past!

◆ ◆ ◆

Today I have valiantly overcome my first real hangover for several months: worked on letters in the morning; heroic earth-levelling after lunch. Well propped and upheld, now, by self-satisfaction.

5 APRIL
The most exciting boat-race I've seen since 1952 – when S and I watched the actual finish from our friend F's house on the river at Mortlake. Satisfied by Oxford's narrow squeak; but glad to find that the more atavistic emotions have almost melted away.

◆ ◆ ◆

How splendid Dame Julian is once she has got through all the almost succulently gory visions of the Passion. 'It would be most improper for me therefore to blame or criticise God for my sin, since he does not blame me for it.' It is not a complete theodicy: but much better than many that we've been offered.

It is impossible for us to comprehend the completeness of God's understanding of our *inescapable* follies and misdoings. (Which doesn't mean, of course, that there are no escapable ones.)

◆ ◆ ◆

Well, after that remarkable day when the hope of Revelation through Dream was apparently being thrust at me time after time; after that week of recorded dreams; after concluding that the only possible message was the early (and rather far-fetched) interpretation which made me more aware than ever that I may be unconsciously oppressing and even imprisoning S – after all that, I have tried three times to tell her this, and each time I have said it so badly, even irritably, that it has come out as an act of aggression against her.

Instead of saying, 'If I am in any way on your back show me how to get off it,' I have been saying, 'I wish to God you'd get out from under.' Not 'in so many words' either, but in those very words. And she, of course, reacts with a pained and angry counter-attack.

> Do not let me hear
> Of the wisdom of old men, but rather of their folly . . .
> The only wisdom we can hope to acquire
> Is the wisdom of humility: humility is endless.
> T. S. Eliot, *Four Quartets*

◆ ◆ ◆

This evening we watched a Mozart Mass on the TV, and listened to the simultaneous broadcast on our speakers. Very, very beautiful, of course; yet I think I was more pleased by the occasion – Easter tomorrow, Worcester Cathedral, Worcester and Cardiff choirs, the BBC Welsh Orchestra – than by the music itself. (How maddening it is, listening to music, when one can clearly perceive that it is beautiful, yet know all too well that the beauty of the music is not really reaching one!)

Tried *Hamlet* again – most of Act II. Not much use. Then I looked at some Bellini madonnas (peace on earth!) and they did the trick at last. For it is these visual arts, which I have neglected most, which I now need the most. (Yet shall I ever summon up the strength and courage to go to Italy again, and see all that I've missed there on all my earlier visits?)

6 APRIL
Easter Day. And there are many millions of people all over the world who genuinely grieved for Jesus on Good Friday and rejoice with him today. How fortunate they are, for this is religion at its truest and best – the human symbol which is also more than human; the beloved man whose suffering and rising from the dead make him shine like God. Buber's I-Thou at its holiest and sweetest.

Why are S and I excluded? For the almost absurd reason that we cannot believe in the presence, now, of the man who was called Jesus of Nazareth two thousand years ago. Alas, a symbol does not work unless it is believed to be much more than a symbol.

So what does Easter mean to us? Chiefly – we agreed – an extra quality of happiness at Tymawr, both during and after mass; and loving cards from our best friends among the Sisters on the breakfast table.

* * *

Buber goes on getting better and better: 'But [this being alone] is the castle of separation where man conducts a dialogue with himself, not in order to test himself and master himself for what awaits him but in his enjoyment of the configuration of his own soul – that is the spirit's lapse into mere spirituality. And this becomes truly abysmal when self-deception reaches the point where one thinks that one has God within and speaks to him. But, as surely as God embraces us and dwells in us, we never have him within.'

He is a good Jew in the indignation he feels at every form of self-divinisation.

7 APRIL
After carefully studying the letter in which Lady Collins (now 'Pierre' to us both) makes the firm's proposals very clear, I realise that they are simply not going to publish *Pantaloon* unless they can raise enough money to do so. I tried to face them with the choice of taking both *Part of a Journey* and *Pantaloon* or of getting neither; and they are saying that they prefer neither to both. This is a blow, of course; but of a very familiar kind.

So I shall now write to Pierre and tell her to go ahead with *Part of a Journey* on the understanding that they go on doing their very best to raise enough money to publish *Pantaloon* as well. And my advance of £1,000 on *Part of a Journey* will be spent on the typing of a really good copy of *Pantaloon*. (My mess of print and bad typescript cannot have seemed a seductive object to any publisher.)

Of course it isn't an ideal arrangement. But at least *Part of a Journey* will appear quite soon; and perhaps its reception might help *Pantaloon* as well.

* * *

Yesterday Janet Watts's very friendly, even respectful interview with me appeared in the *Observer*. A rather sombre, but quite flattering photograph by Jane Bown; with Josephine's rose-twined putto on its pedestal just behind me. No doubt at all that my vanity was tickled by all this – and my hopes for the success of *Friends Apart* (due on Tuesday) slightly raised.

Could it possibly be that *Friends Apart* will give a helpful lift to *Part of a Journey*; and that *Part of a Journey*, making at least something of a hit, will actually get poor old *Pantaloon* into the air at last, to soar at once to the empyrean and there cavort with the *Divine Comedy*, *Faust* and *Paradise Lost* . . . ?

◆ ◆ ◆

It almost seems that I have begun to acquire a crafty *allergy* to cigarettes; certainly this last bout of smoking – and in particular the first cigarette of the day – has made me feel physically sick as well as morally disgusted. If only I could keep that physical and mental nausea fixed in the mind, as I now set off for the five-hundredth time on total and permanent abnegation.

8 APRIL

In the last dream of the night my whole house – though not a known one – was filled with human dung: and rats, gorged with it, were crawling across it to die, so fat that they kept splitting open down their bellies. What a fearful token of my imperishable self-disgust! How remote the horrified dreamer seems from the hero of last Sunday's interview – 'ragged, elegant and humane'.

◆ ◆ ◆

The London Region of the BBC telephoned to ask if I would come up and do an interview on *Friends Apart*; either tomorrow or on Thursday. Unthinkable at such short notice, so I turned it down. This shows that my aversion to making a sudden move is far stronger than my wish to sell more copies of *Friends Apart*. Or is it simply due to my childish inability to face a temporary unpleasantness for the sake of a later advantage?

◆ ◆ ◆

I've now been reading through *Part of a Journey* for what I hope will be the last time. It looks much better after this interval: it is, at the least, an unusual book.

And I cannot think that there is anything in any of this journal which will make anyone think the worse of S; quite the contrary. Even Anne, who tends to hate any writing of mine which is in the least 'confessional', has read about a third of *Part of a Journey*, likes it very much and assured S that it seems in no way embarrassing *to her*. (Though I do see, of course, that to be written about, however gently, is a very

122

different thing from writing about oneself, however harshly.) This was the book I *had* to write at this time – this book and no other – and to leave it unpublished until after our deaths is more than I can bear to do. This is not because I still crave for public acclaim – though I do – but because the book has a relevance at this time which it may well lose as the years pass.

◆ ◆ ◆

Thinking of the vast backward weight of our animal inheritance, it isn't surprising that we find it so hard to pray: that we find it such an *unnatural* thing to do.

◆ ◆ ◆

Dream of leading Tony★ around Castle Howard, as if he no longer knew his way there. '*Yes!*' I said to myself. 'This time he is really here; he is *really* here.' All I knew was he had been away for a long time, and that he needed help.

Very typical dream about him. It is more than forty years since his death, but that dreaming self still refuses to accept it. In those forty years I have certainly dreamed more about him than about anyone except my two wives; but he has not been dead for a single moment in a single dream.

◆ ◆ ◆

Dame Julian is surely the most radiantly cheerful of all the great Christians. Too resolutely, *almost* defiantly, cheerful ever to be canonised. '*All* shall be well, and *all manner of things* shall be well . . . ' Rank heresy, of course.

◆ ◆ ◆

'Woe unto the possessed who fancy that they possess God!' A fine bit of prophetic warning from Buber. But I must say that at least I have never been in danger of that exalted delusion.

◆ ◆ ◆

Again and again this latest barrel-scraping of Merton's makes me realise that he had gone dangerously far towards accepting the worst as well as the best in the spirit of that age – the late sixties. 'The "sacredness" of man consists precisely in the fact that the truth for which and by which he lives is primarily within himself . . . ' *Primarily!* Buber is the best possible corrective to this appalling anthropocentric fallacy.

★ P T's elder brother.

123

It was indeed wonderful that Merton could stretch his mind so widely; but sometimes this generosity of mind and heart led him to forget the *indispensable* theistic belief – that God is primarily outside man and beyond man, and is able to enter a human being only through a patient, reciprocal and ever attentive act of love.

• • •

Frequent indigestion late at night simply and solely because I will go on making fat sandwiches and eating them in bed. It is unbelievable how, even at my age, one can continue to forget – no, *over-ride* – even the most obvious and repeated lessons. 'Because I enjoy a sandwich now, I will take the high risk of pains in the stomach just when I'm trying to get to sleep.'

And if we can't even behave with the merest prudence in looking after our physical condition, how much less shall we be able to sacrifice material advantage for the sake of spiritual reward? (*Reward!* Oh, what a give-away!)

10 APRIL
Friends Apart's first review – by Emma Tennant in the *Guardian*. She is civil towards me – 'exemplary clarity and wit' – but finds it 'hard to decide which of the two [Esmond Romilly or Jasper Ridley] would have been the more unpleasant to know'. She takes a snooty and lefty view of them as two odious and dated 'charmers'; a type, she implies, which is mercifully as dead as the dodo.

Emma was once my niece, the eldest daughter of Anne's sister Elizabeth; and I suppose she was the first baby I was ever acquainted with. I remember playing pram-games with her, rolling her away from me in a Hertfordshire wood just before the war. I would have thought that she must have had many upper-class charmers among her friends: indeed that she might well be one herself . . .

But it is never any use trying to explain an annoying review away; and least of all for an old reviewing hand like me. How often I've told myself that if I dish it out I must also be able to take it!

The interesting question is this: would I have preferred a review which, instead of saying that this is a good book about two nasty people, had said exactly the opposite? Well, the truth is, I suppose, that since I meant the readers to like and respect my two dead friends the book *does* fail, however 'exemplary', if it fails in this.

Perhaps I should have capsized Emma's pram when I pushed it away from me up the hill, and should have really meant it when I kept telling her never to come back again.

• • •

In any case Ativan deprivation took up much more of my attention today than Emma's review. What a struggle it was to get the shopping done; and then to meet so many people with a more or less grinning face!

I am often tempted to condemn my many complaints as the moans of a spoiled old man who knows nothing about real hardship, etc. But the truth is that on many days I do find life *very* hard to live; simply to do the most ordinary things is often a heavy physical and mental strain. And it is no use adding to this the burden of self-disgust. Yes, I would indeed be much more unfortunate if I were a beggar in Calcutta. Yes, indeed, the difficulties that I have to face and resolve are much less severe than the difficulties that beggar has to face in getting enough to eat. But it is as useless and irrelevant for me to upbraid myself for finding life hard to live as it is for loved ones to tell a depressive to pull his socks up. What matters is not that others have far worse afflictions than I have ever had, but how I deal with my own lesser, but real and undeniable afflictions. 'Yes, but you have *so much* . . . ' – 'Too much, and too little . . . '

In other words, afflictions are true afflictions, no matter what human condition they spring from, or accompany. I knew a rich lady who *died* of her hypochondria in the end.

◆ ◆ ◆

I can remember only two trivial, but presumably memorable occasions, when my parents expressed open irritation with each other in front of me. Easy to say the conventions of their class and period restrained them; easy to say that this suppression of their true feelings probably contributed to the final and deeply embittered bust-up. But how I respect them both – from where I am now – for that surface dignity which they maintained! What a gross fault it has been in later generations to suppose that restraint must be equated with suppression; that there is something healthily honest, even admirable, about an immediate and public exhibition of angry feelings.

◆ ◆ ◆

'The world is there,' writes Robert White, 'whether we like it or not, and it follows laws of its own, whether we like them or not.' A most useful and timely reminder. What's more, I'd add that we are largely – almost entirely – the creatures of this world, and bound by its laws, whether we like them or not.

How bored God must get ('unto whom all hearts are open') by the dreary droning of our ego-centred minds. What heavenly patience our guardian angels must need to put up with these infinitely repetitious monologues! How they must weep for all the time we waste on our almost unrelieved concern for our own present and future well-being.

Ativan withdrawal symptoms worst so far. But I haven't taken so few tranquillisers for so long since Dr E first put me on them nearly twenty years ago. A certain pride in this achievement almost atones for the sharp discomfort.

Yes, but Lucy tells S – on the telephone – that they've proved, by the use of placebos, that these drugs lose all their effect after being taken for about six months. So it is very possible that all these symptoms are 'only in the head'; not directly physical at all. This may be so, but I cannot *sufficiently* believe it to stop Ativan altogether in the confident assurance that this would 'really' have no effect. (We get better and better at diagnosing our fallacies, but no better at getting rid of them.)

◆ ◆ ◆

Since writing last Sunday's review of *The Gnostic Gospels* by Elaine Pagels I think I've begun to have a better understanding of why early Christianity had begun to encrust itself with such a monstrous carapace of dogma and theological definition. Only within that carved and ornamental tortoise-shell of orthodoxy could the deep incarnational truth be preserved; the ever-living truth that man can be entered and transformed by God without ceasing to be man.

◆ ◆ ◆

Digging deeper, now, into the twelfth and thirteenth centuries. A very great age, in spite of the romantic sentimentalisation perpetrated against it by the Chesterbelloc, etc.

Shall I buy the whole *Cambridge Medieval History*? If I did, how much of it would I ever read?

I still have this hope of getting to know some period so well that I can virtually move into it at will and feel truly at home there. In the forties I bought a whole library of books about, or written during, the French nineteenth century. But at least three-quarters of them remained unread until I sold the lot in 1978.

◆ ◆ ◆

The Hasidim. The splendid humour of those great rabbis of the Pale; too rare in Christianity.

◆ ◆ ◆

Red Queen syndrome again: the need to run and run, gasping for breath, in order to stay in the same place. This seems to get worse with age – and in spite of constant self-assurances that we must, after all, be moving infinitesimally forward.

Better, perhaps, to see ourselves as swimming against a current or a tide; and if you watch the bank *closely* you will see that the tree which was once level with your eyes has, after all, moved back a yard or two.

◆ ◆ ◆

'Rejoice!' This is not an injunction; let alone a command. It is a declaration of joy already achieved. When I tried it out, rather tentatively, in the garden yesterday I did feel a sudden flicker in the heart.

◆ ◆ ◆

We are unadapted beings. Or rather disadapted. Disadapted in this world as soon as adopted by the other. A very good bargain, of course; but not always easy to appreciate.

◆ ◆ ◆

'Whoever knows the world as something to be utilised knows God the same way. His prayers are a way of unburdening himself – and fall into the ears of the void.' Buber.

True, true, *true*! But does anyone – even the greatest saint – ever get beyond some form of utilisation? Why do we long to love God and man? For their sake *only*? Who would dare to make such a claim!

◆ ◆ ◆

My four sacred objects, to be held in the hand while praying: the iron, the stone, the bone, the wood. I have used them for about four years now, and still, from time to time, draw something new out of them. This evening as I held the wood tight I thought of the Cross as a cruel symbol of the physical world onto which Christ was nailed, but also as his only support while he died; the living tree supporting the dying man.

12 APRIL
A most heart-warming letter from Pierre this morning: 'I am so very delighted with the wonderful news that you will allow us to publish *Part of a Journey* as soon as possible . . . I really cannot tell you how happy I am that things are at last getting on the move.' And 'I will do everything I possibly can about *Pantaloon*.' I'm sure she will.

◆ ◆ ◆

Ken Baker, that cheery, bucolic and boozy grave-digger, has been found bloodily dead in St Briavels. Rumours of murder appal and delight the village. His constant joke, perhaps his only one, was about measuring each one of us for our graves.

◆ ◆ ◆

The George: the Orepool: the (Monmouth) Beaufort. Without these places our lives would be monstrously and depletingly isolated. They provide, and represent, at least seventy per cent of our social life. Yet most of our London friends hardly use pubs at all; they see each other in their own houses; or go to concerts or the theatre together.

14 April

Meeting the Snowdon family in St Briavels, all three children, the youngest being wheeled in a pram by Dave; such warm feelings. Then Rose No. 1 ('Bim's Rose') came to lunch with us, having just stayed with Kerry and Mary, staying now with the Snowdons. And she said how much the old Barn House meant to her and to all of them. Warm, warm feelings – partly, of course, because my personal failure with the community seems to be largely atoned for by their enduring friendship with each other.

◆ ◆ ◆

The birds. Their perpetual song now, but how rarely I become actively conscious of it. Is the voice of God like that, always speaking, but hardly ever listened to and heard?

◆ ◆ ◆

'Panorama' on the tobacco industry's unrelenting attempts to spread their message into the Third World. The brazen wickedness shocks and astounds me. Why should I be astounded after all these years? And have I the right to be shocked?

◆ ◆ ◆

Poor Ken, whose death has still not been 'solved' by the police, has appeared on the front page of the *Western Daily Press* (Bristol). Little did he think that he'd ever have such fame.

15 April

A delightful expedition to Bristol. St Mary Redcliffe; George's second-hand religious books; pub and Indian restaurant. What a pleasure simply to walk about in this most elegant of all England's large cities. Yet ten days ago there were savage riots here – young people, mostly black, who have no jobs and who feel that they are being constantly harried by the police. So I walk through the wilderness of this world, but contriving never to meet the public horrors: walking, as it were, between the pleasant screens of a well-protected life, through which only the newspaper and the TV occasionally penetrate.

It's said that if 1,000,000 people are suffering X amount of pain this cannot be described as Pain 1,000,000 X. True. But if one's own family happens to be the millionth to be 'made redundant', how can one not feel that this is another lump of pain added to the total?

◆ ◆ ◆

I've never before heard the mating owls so loud, weird and urgent as they are tonight.

16 APRIL

These Life-after-Death books all agree that suicides are in for a bad time, because they have gone against the will of God: and this almost persuades me to reject the whole thing. For when I think of Tony, and of all the many friends who've killed themselves, I know that they, of all people, must have needed immediate love and understanding.

But of course the idea of a special punishment for suicides is utterly gross and absurd; a blank denial of the love and wisdom of God. Tormented souls to be tormented again as a punishment for their torment!

◆ ◆ ◆

The first article of my faith is this: 'There is more than we can know.' The second article is this: 'What we cannot know is better than anything that we can know.'

◆ ◆ ◆

Oh, this garden; this garden! As I work and work out there I feel all too little real joy, but often, by the end of the afternoon, a deathly exhaustion deep in the bones. It is so important to get the complex slopes of these future lawns exactly right; but this means constant changes; more earth here, less earth there. And raking, raking, raking, raking till I feel that I can hardly straighten my bent and locked back. Deadline for sowing – April 30th. But this is absurd, as I well know; perhaps an excuse, more than anything else, for giving in to that grotesque impulse of mine to work too hard, too fast and for too long. (Or else to collapse into the guilty luxury of a day in bed.)

◆ ◆ ◆

129

Laura gave us supper in her Gloucester flat to meet her friends the Ns. (It was he who spoke to her on the train when she was crying, gave her his card and offered his help and blessing.) He teaches at Aston University, and is a very lively, intelligent man. At first he seemed a little suspicious of me – and perhaps I was nervous with him – but as the evening passed we became very close. It's many years since I've so much enjoyed a conversation with a stranger. My life doesn't lend itself to such occasions, after all.

17 APRIL
The brightest and warmest morning of the year. I open my window and groan at it. A Scrooge of the Springtime.

Yes; but after prayer, rest, reading and beer I am partially restored to hope and curiosity. Looking into Bubbles's eyes, I see something so alien there that it almost frightens me.

◆ ◆ ◆

Is it true that St Francis supported the Children's Crusade? I must check on this. But if it is true, far from being shocked or disappointed, I would almost be *glad*: not, surely, from any envious wish to debunk a great saint, but because the full humanity of even the greatest saints is such a necessary part of them. And one which is so often obscured by the hagiographers.

In the same (slightly suspect) book I read that Merton suffered from bouts of severe depression. This would help to explain the depth of his understanding, but make it still harder to understand how he could have written so much while fulfilling his daily monastic obligations. God must have given him more time than he gives to most of us.

◆ ◆ ◆

How Dame Julian hates the whole concept of sin and punishment! How well she knows that her revelation denies them both! That God *denies* sin is surely a profound though very difficult apprehension.

The Light that shines *in* the Darkness. Not simply as a comfort and encouragement, but because the light can be best seen when we are in the dark.

◆ ◆ ◆

Pain and Fear. Coming and almost going; then coming again, like the worst undulations of toothache.

Let my cry come unto Thee!

Between us a dark fog through which we prod at each other with

130

fingers as sharp as knives. How else could either know that the other is still there?

19 APRIL
The charming skewbald horse in the field just below John Josephi's house has now entered the ritual scenario of our evening drive to village and pub. We stop the car; he walks vigorously across the field and puts his head over the hedge; we exchange a few friendly noises . . .

23 APRIL
A bold expedition to Bun and Jean, spending a night with Lucy and Bernard on the way, then a full Sunday in Nottingham for DA's AGM – very tiring; many stresses and strains – then two nights at Ganthorpe. With Bun's help I took off on a flight of comic fancy at dinner – Australian, Yorkshireman, German . . . At one awful point I felt as if my wings were failing me; were beating far too heavily to keep me aloft . . . I thought I saw a weary expression on the faces of my niece, Rachel, and her husband, Richard. But I *think* I managed a fairly graceful landing.

◆ ◆ ◆

The business of my father's literary estate. I have been a very idle and incompetent literary executor – one of three – but have now enlisted Bun to help. He will be far better at it than I have been; and it must be said that we share the same interest – namely in keeping the patrimony as unpecked-at as we can. (We've had many despicable rows about money in the past; mainly my fault, being envious of his better fortune which springs, in turn, from his generally better treatment by our mother. My God, what years it took me to recover from that childhood jealousy! But I do believe, I do honestly believe, that I no longer feel the very least trace of it. At sixty-three! Bravo!)

◆ ◆ ◆

A good review of *Friends Apart* in the *Observer* by an obviously perceptive young woman called Hilary Spurling. But with this book – written, after all, twenty-seven years ago – I am in the pleasant position of welcoming good reports without much dread of bad ones.

◆ ◆ ◆

The distance between what I think I am and what I would like to be remains as wide as ever. I would like to think that both have moved up

131

the scale together, but keeping their distance. Yet I can't honestly say that this seems to be the case. True, I reacted with novel calm to the faulty new lawn-mower, at which I would have raged and stamped only a few years ago. But when I look out at the landscape of my life I can't pretend that it looks any different. No change at all, then? Well, perhaps I see a little further into that unchanged scene: a very little further.

◆ ◆ ◆

The religious 'expert', I read somewhere, is not the professor of theology but the saint. Of course; but well said. And 'religion' is not a special subject at all, but everyone's subject in so far as he tries to put his faith into practice.

◆ ◆ ◆

'May God deny you peace and give you glory.' Unamuno. But glory, alas, is not the only alternative to peace.

◆ ◆ ◆

Ninety-four days without depression, as registered in my diary. This is the longest term since my ECT; ended this afternoon with what was, I suppose, a fairly mild attack. But I cannot feel much joy in my long exemption; for, although that specific horror hasn't been felt, these have been, on the whole, dour and ungracious days.

Who would believe, from the outside, that a life of such apparent privilege could be so hard to struggle through! There are so many days when everything that I do seems to require a little more strength than I really possess. The capital wasting away, as Fitzgerald put it, I seem to remember, in *The Crack-Up*. That journey north, for example, laid me out in bed for two whole days; utterly whacked not just by exorbitant drinking but by talking, by travelling – simply *by not being here.*

And yet I believe that there is rejuvenation ahead – for both of us. Rebirth; restoration; renewal . . . It *must* be so, for we cannot drag out the rest of our lives on these terms.

◆ ◆ ◆

Phine rang and asked if she and David could stay this weekend. I had to say no – to my own daughter and son-in-law; I had to say that I was too tired and bruised to receive even them. And this makes me a sort of invalid, doesn't it? I am, in a strange and unaccountable way, a man suffering from a chronic disease.

Yes; but if I simply accept that this is so, how shall I ever be cured?

Yes; but if I refuse to accept it, strain continually against it, won't the disease get worse and worse?

Oh Lord, give me that kind of love which would make me actually want to *meet* my fellow-men! *L'ermite malgré lui.*

◆ ◆ ◆

Merton very good on the symbol as a means of *communion* which is always in danger of collapsing into a mere means of *communication*. (Or of assertion, one might add.)

◆ ◆ ◆

Someone, a long time ago, addressed me by name: 'You! Yes, you; Philip!' Many years later I said, half-attentively: 'Well then, what?'

Since then there has been an implied answer that I may be spoken to again at any moment; that I must pay careful attention.

And the worry is that the answer may have been given – perhaps many times – but that I missed it, being so constantly preoccupied with the sound of my own trivial and trivialising thoughts.

◆ ◆ ◆

Well, at least I feel fairly certain now that this writing is what I should be doing. I even feel, at times, that I am truly *called* to keep this journal as best I can.

◆ ◆ ◆

How much of the N T was written under the firm belief that the world was just about to come to an end? Useless to deny that this is an immense barrier between us and the writers of the Gospels. (For our fears of the end of the world are very different from their joyful expectations of that event.)

The blackbird singing in the blossoming cherry tree. But this is transformed by present fear and horror over Iran. Instead of meditating on the eternal recurrence of spring, I try to understand that all this might be utterly and horribly destroyed.

Well, God, of course, will survive the worst we can do to ourselves. Heaven will not be radioactive after the Fall. So there will be renewal of some unimaginable kind.

Or perhaps we shall all be rescued from time at the last moment; and the blackbird will be singing in the cherry tree 'for ever'.

Whatever that may mean.

◆ ◆ ◆

For a very short moment, as I was looking out of my back window

133

and up the valley, I thought: 'Well, why not a revelation to me, now? Yes, and just because I am the most grotesquely unworthy recipient of any such thing.'

Common sense answers: 'You flatter yourself. You are not the most unworthy recipient, but simply one among a vast number of unworthy recipients.'

Kierkegaard's incessant self-awarded superlatives. He may have been a great thinker, but he was also an ass; an unpleasant, self-obsessed moral and intellectual snob.

Every form of snobbery is directly and grossly anti-Christian.

But we, deprived even of the negative superlatives, can always fall back at least on this: *that we shall never give up*.

♦ ♦ ♦

'Nothing is ever done so as to please our Great Father, unless we had also done it though we had no Father to know of it.' Ruskin. This sounds very fine at first, but I doubt if it's really true. A good action done without thought or knowledge of God is quite different in texture from the same action done in the consciousness that God is in the action. A good Christian is a different kind of person from a good humanist.

It is not arrogant to say this. We must believe that we can act deeply in this world only with some measure of the knowledge and love of God. (That God gives his love to humanists also is clearly true; but there must be conscious reciprocity for the action to be as deep and as full – *as abundant with life* – as it possibly can be.)

♦ ♦ ♦

St Paul's teaching of justification by faith was in opposition to justification by the law. And this was one of the greatest religious advances ever made. Taken out of its context and cruelly distorted into a doctrine, that wise teaching became a monstrosity.

♦ ♦ ♦

Another impulse towards faith: 'Things are so odd that they must be odder still.' That 'odder still' continues somewhere, well out of our normal sight.

♦ ♦ ♦

How often the only person who can help you is the one person who – in a self-defence as desperate as your own – is bent on doing you harm.

Yes, but this particular clinch led to a unique triumph; a beneficent

crow of peace suddenly separating Dum from Dee – who thereupon
fell into each other's arms to give and receive not injuries but love.

◆ ◆ ◆

Can God be surprised? If not, he cannot be a God of Love; for the only
love we can understand is constantly rejoicing in the unexpected.
The best love we have ever known is recurrent, almost vertiginous
renewal.

25 APRIL
Fully reorganised at last, and working quietly in the garden, when S
comes out to tell me of a newsflash about the American fiasco in Iran.
Fury. Horror, Terror.

◆ ◆ ◆

Absurd piece of dialogue in the evening:

    S: 'What's the matter?'
    P: 'I'm terrified.'
    S: 'Is that meant to be an attack on me?'
    P: 'No, no, *no*! I'm terrified about *Iran*.'

Immense relief felt by both. Ah, only a world crisis and the danger of
nuclear war; not, thank God, a resumption of Woodroyd Cottage
hostilities.
    Lunatics!

◆ ◆ ◆

True penitence is not an apology for any single deed, but a constant
awareness of all that one fails to be. Perhaps; but why, then, is this such
a crippling and disheartening emotion?
    Because true penitence must include a stalwart determination to do
better and to be better. True penitence should invigorate.

◆ ◆ ◆

One of my worst states in bed at night is being unable to find a book
that I can bear to read. Tonight I tried *Inquiring Man* by Bannister and
Fransella, an excellent psychological-philosophical Penguin; Dean
Stanley's *The Eastern Church* (third reading); a book by Erich Fromm;
Evelyn Underhill's *The Life of the Spirit and the Life of Today*; *True
Prayer* by Kenneth Leech. All these books seemed utterly impossible in
their different ways – dull, or wet, or opinionated, or too-clever-by-
half . . . I settled for Stanley, in the end, perhaps because it is so much
the best-written of the five, and buried myself in the Council of Nicaea
until sleep mercifully closed it down.

26 April

Anger is certainly stronger than fear just now; but I must never forget that fear is deeper. Some comfort!

◆ ◆ ◆

'Another idol that is not so obvious is that of supposed "spiritual experience" sought as an object and as an end in itself. Here, too, the temptation that offers itself is one of escape from anxiety and limitation, and an *affirmation of the individual self as object*, but as a special kind of object, *to be experienced as free from all limitations.*' Merton, at his very best.

◆ ◆ ◆

If I were asked now, today, 'What have you learned about God from your own direct experience?', I would answer, 'Nothing at all.' (But there might be other days when I would answer differently; when I would say that although I have had very little experience of God, what I have had is derived *from every moment of my life.*)

◆ ◆ ◆

The blackthorn blossom is very thick this year; another of our good signs on the way to St Briavels.

◆ ◆ ◆

Resolutions all undone, I lie smoking in bed, faintly dulled by last night's heavy dose of Ativan, feeling a melancholy resignation which is almost pleasant. 'There you are, then. beloved Mother, this is all there is of me after all.'

28 April

The 'official' last grass-sowing day – April 30th – looms terribly close. But each working afternoon on the huge scheme – 560 square yards to be shaped and sown – seems to increase rather than diminish the work ahead.

◆ ◆ ◆

My own form of heroism this morning in managing to review the second volume of my old friend Peter Quennell's autobiography. But after two painful and sticky false-starts the fingers soon begin to rattle over the keys, almost like someone writing in his sleep.

◆ ◆ ◆

When Josephine was born, and likely to die in the first two days, my then sister-in-law Elizabeth said: 'One of your troubles, Philip, is that you have no stamina.' And when that other Elizabeth (Bowen) clasped my hand so tightly at the door of her London house during the worst of 1949 and said, 'God give you fortitude, Philip,' she must have recognised that this was indeed what I most lacked and needed.

I haven't acquired much stamina or fortitude with all these years. No, but perhaps a little.

29 April
Laura wanted to spend one day of her precious annual holiday with us, knowing that we were in a bad way and wishing with all her heart to help us. We refused, of course, but were deeply touched by her concern. And even wisdom. It has often happened that we seem like the children; our son and daughters like the grown-ups.

30 April
But today I felt a sudden release into health and hope. They came back like half-forgotten friends after so many dark and broken days.

◆ ◆ ◆

A happy word with Sister Mary Eleanor at Tymawr; at eighty-one so cheerful and lovable, yet sharp as a knife.

And a fairly long talk with Sister Benedicta, mostly about the new chaplain. From all that she tells me about him, and all that I've felt from his sermons and a few words exchanged in the hall, I suspect that he may be the very person we need. Not, of course, to give us detailed advice on how to conduct our lives but simply to help us, by his own obvious openness to God, to open our own hearts and minds.

Sister B and I talked, as well, about the Peace of God: the mysterious fact that it is anything but immobile or quiescent; an active radiance . . .

◆ ◆ ◆

I always manage to have something ahead of me of which I can say, 'When once *that* is done, *then* I can start leading a sensible life and trying hard to pray.' Once I've got the garden sown; once I've persuaded S to accept the caravan–bicycle trip to Norfolk; once I've got this journal properly up to date; once I've received from Collins the fresh new copy of *Pantaloon* . . .

'There is no rest for us: the horizon will always recede . . . and our progress is like that of the imprisoned bee over the window-pane by which we learn that we cannot get through.' George Tyrrell.

Sally hoeing in the front garden, and I raking after her. To work *together* is real balm; and happiness.

4 MAY

Wittgenstein's most famous proposition can be reversed: 'Whereof one cannot be silent, thereof one must speak.' That is, speech is a necessity only for those who have never learnt how to be silent.

I jabber, therefore I am.

Somebody said that all art aspires towards the condition of music. I think that all language *should* aspire towards the condition of silence: that is, of prayer.

5 MAY

I live in a state of extreme physical withdrawal yet of unmitigated excess. Too much food; too much beer; too much work yet too much lying in bed; too much reading; writing; thinking; fearing . . .

◆ ◆ ◆

We are like a person's two hands clenched so tightly together that they can't be pulled apart; but clenched just a little wrong, as if the fingers were in the wrong order. So what is needed is relaxation; even withdrawal, if only for an instant, so that we can fit the hands together again with every finger in the right place.

6 MAY

Half the sowing done this afternoon. Immense satisfaction. And, if I can get the rest of it done tomorrow, I shall surely be able to relax a little.

And surely, when the grass grows, those subtle curves and slopes will look both strange and delightful.

◆ ◆ ◆

£5,000 poetry prize announced. I plan to select three bits of *Pantaloon*, cut them into shape and submit them under three different names. What a dream of glory and vindication if I got the prize! I have to remind myself vigorously that this is most improbable.

7 MAY

Sowing completed – but no sooner done, after hard work from 1.30 to 5.00, than I realised that one of the slopes rose much too sharply. So I trundled out first one, then two, then three barrowfuls of soil to make a gentler fall and rise. Everything depends in this garden on getting such things right.

But now I never want to see a rake again. I find that at my age I would rather dig for two hours than rake for one.

And, though I am a week late, it has been so cold and dry these last three weeks that the seed would never have germinated earlier.

◆ ◆ ◆

An Amended Prayer, with Breathing and Movements for Hands, Arms and Head

First stage Breathing out. Eyes closed; head bowed; palms together in front of chest: 'Peace.' Held for one, two, three or four further breathings in and out.

Second stage Breathing out. Eyes opened; head raised; hands lowered and cupped, elbows at right-angles: 'Heavenly Grace.' Breathings as before.

Third stage Breathing out. Eyes closed; head bowed; hands crossed over chest: 'God lives in me.' Breathings as before.

Fourth stage Breathing out. Eyes opened; head raised; arms extended with cupped hands: 'May I live in the knowledge and love of God.'

So far I have found it possible to do this very naturally, and with real satisfaction. (It gives me a certain formal pleasure that the stresses increase from one, to two, to three, to four.)

8 MAY

After nearly half a century of shaving I have adopted the habit of knocking my razor from time to time sharply on the basin, or bottom of the bath: this releases the solidifying soap from between the blade and the holder. What brilliant further discovery might I not make if I had another fifty years of shaving ahead of me!

◆ ◆ ◆

Lately, though (because?) my waking life has not been good, I have had many good dreams; kind, friendly, funny.

◆ ◆ ◆

Father Philip in Monmouth. I suddenly realised as we were talking that my affection for him is partly based on our shared – and perhaps rather unusual – combination of naivety and shrewdness.

♦ ♦ ♦

Woke to great happiness at 4 a.m., and as I was reading about St Anselm the birds began to sing and I had a rare sense of what might have been the closeness of God.

9 MAY
S had taken Laura up to London, to see *The Barber of Seville* with David and Josephine. And this must be the first twenty-four hours S and I have been apart since she went to America for her brother David's funeral in 1976. A weird feeling of exhilaration tinged with loneliness. Free! Free! Yes, but to do what? And as the afternoon wore away and I fiddled about in the garden or lay restlessly on my bed and tried to read, I felt a great urge *to pay a call*. So, with the excuse of a book to lend Bill and a garden gadget to learn about from Susie, I walked over to Birchfield at 6.30; stayed about an hour, drinking their Scotch and talking very pleasantly. But this was something I would *never* do if S were here.

When I got back, I watered the whole of the newly sown top lawn.

10 MAY
Reading Southern's *St Anselm* with a mixture of extreme fascination and extreme boredom. The philosophy is meaningless to me; though I find the description of the general intellectual climate very interesting and strange.

♦ ♦ ♦

St Anselm's proof of the Incarnation:

> Man cannot redeem himself.
> God should not redeem man.
> Therefore only a God–Man can redeem man.

The first proposition is the only one that makes sense to me; very good sense too; but the vital second line seems utterly meaningless. Beneath God's dignity to do so?

♦ ♦ ♦

Re-reading the penultimate, Inferno volume of *Pantaloon* (*Malcontenta*), I was amazed by its power and vividness. Startled and delighted, but also *appalled*, just as the reader is meant to be. I have taken out the 'Ode to Jenny' as my fourth entry for the poetry competition.

Polishing and reshaping these excerpts so as to make them presentable on their own, I am pleasantly surprised that I can get straight back to writing verse in the various manners required.

◆ ◆ ◆

After reading two very different accounts of the English fourteenth century, I recognise that all good history is the history of injustice; or must, at least, include a constant awareness of injustice. This has nothing to do with Marx; everything to do with Jesus. The anguish of the poor is the black thread that runs through almost the whole of history.

◆ ◆ ◆

Suggest a Christianity based not on Virgin Birth, Crucifixion, Resurrection; but on Baptism, Transfiguration, Crucifixion, Pentecost. Three great manifestations of the Holy Spirit: and the one terrible absence of the Spirit.

◆ ◆ ◆

Read of another scarifying American millionaire revivalist. These are among the most wicked men of our time, whatever they may think of themselves. In this case he collects his money from 4 million of the poorest of poor whites, assuring them of miraculous worldly success in exchange for their dollars. Which then go to buy him another house, two more Cadillacs . . .

Intelligent preachers of fundamentalism in our time are the very worst enemies of Christianity. There is an easy test of a man's faith: do you believe that everyone is damned except those who share your exact views of what is necessary for salvation? For if there is one thing which our age should and can teach us, it is a humble awareness of our own fallibility; a deep suspicion of self-righteousness.

The trouble with the Jesus of the Gospels is that he taught just this when he was speaking about the Pharisees, but taught quite the opposite lesson when he furiously denounced – and condemned to eternal fire – all those who would not or could not accept him as Master. So he left plenty of savage quotations for the only-we-are-saved-and-all-you-others-will-go-to-hell.

11 MAY
Two very good collects – for the Fourth and Fifth Sundays after Easter:

O Almighty God, who alone canst order the unruly wills and affections of sinful men: grant unto thy people, that they may love the thing which thou commandest, and desire that which thou dost promise; that so, among the sundry and manifold changes of the world, our hearts may surely there be fixed, where true joys are to be found; through Jesus Christ our Lord.

O Lord, from whom all good things do come: grant to us thy humble servants, that by thy holy inspiration we may think those things that be good, and by thy merciful guiding may perform the same; through our Lord Jesus Christ.

I would replace 'Almighty' with 'Merciful'; 'commandest' with 'desirest for us'. But otherwise neither of them offends my own heresies in the least. (The notion of God 'commanding' seems slightly absurd: to command so much and be obeyed so little surely makes him seem like a raging but impotent sergeant-major shouting drill instruction as the company drifts or scurries about at its own sweet will.)

◆ ◆ ◆

I believe that . . .

I am aware that . . .

The difference between faith in God and knowledge of God. Yes, but this is a strange kind of knowledge, which for all but a very few, is constantly failing, constantly having to fall back on faith. And faith itself is constantly failing too, and having to fall back on perseverance through the wide wastes of doubt.

◆ ◆ ◆

Honey sandwiches at midnight; my latest sin. A sin indeed, since they give me indigestion and mar the night and sometimes the whole of the next day. As stupid as the sickening cigarettes against which I continue to struggle.

◆ ◆ ◆

'Send in the Clowns', the beautiful pop tune of 1975 which Laura brought back from London. True melancholy and bitterness; a lovely and haunting tune.

She raved about the opera; and has suddenly opened up to classical music, after toying with it for the last two years. I love the expression on her face as she talks about music, the light on her face: 'It's like a sort of, opening up to *everything* – not just to music itself.' I was tempted to say, 'Yes; to the light and sound of Heaven,' but avoided this bad ploy; and simply said that I knew what she meant, and knew it very well indeed. Which indeed I do; though she, with her mother's ear, is far more likely to achieve this opening through music than any other way.

◆ ◆ ◆

Gardened for a full hour this afternoon with only a single thought of God (God wot!). I suppose this comment reveals a certain advance; and the shock I felt when I remembered to pray as I sat down between bouts of hoeing S's garden.

◆ ◆ ◆

'The same blessed love teaches us that we should hate sin for Love's sake alone.'
'The soul by its very nature can have no hell but sin.'
These two splendid and noble revelations sum up the whole of Dame Julian's message. How few Christians have listened to it!

◆ ◆ ◆

I do indeed hope and believe that this will be the best garden I've ever made; yet it is sad how little relish I have for it compared with my great enthusiasm for the four earlier ones. My real longing is not in it? My real longing is for God, but since I never find him, hardly ever have even the faintest sense of his presence, it is as if my longing were continually being sent out into a great empty space, and never returning to me with any twig from the Tree of Heaven.

And yet I *must* go on sending out these undespairing enquiries.

But know, at the same time, that the surer way is not into that open space at all, but through other people. Through S, of course, far more than through *everybody* else.

Yes, but to treat another person as a route towards God, a means of pushing oneself upwards towards heaven, is surely a grotesque abomination.

Ah, how *hard* it is! It is so desperately hard to *think* one's way into right feeling if one is not, by nature, a right-feeler at all.

12 MAY
This afternoon we manoeuvred the caravan up to the entrance to the field; succeeded, after much thought and trouble, in turning it round to face outwards. It is filthy, after a winter under the trees. But my spirits rose to see it there, ready for my cleaning operations tomorrow. They rose still higher when I persuaded S to get on her bike, and we went off for a short and wobbly spin together.

We plan – I plan, S conceding – to take caravan and bikes to

Norfolk at the end of the month for a week's 'chubbing'. (Church- and-pub-crawling.)

◆ ◆ ◆

Christ as Lucifer in his first role: the light-bringer. As Prometheus, but a Prometheus who brought holy fire to man *by the will* of Father Zeus, transforming the furious Sky-God into a God of Love.

◆ ◆ ◆

Tolerance implies indifference. Here is a word which needs to be rescued, or another word found instead. A vital, positive, loving, appreciating tolerance is the most important quality which our age supplies and which all good Christians must have.

Kierkegaard, of course, flatly and contemptuously denies this.

What we need is a few martyrs for tolerance: perhaps there may have been some already.

13 MAY
Beautiful, wide blue days, as hot as midsummer. But alas, a drought is now threatening. The art, as we told each other sitting in the garden, is to enjoy the sun without allowing our enjoyment to be spoiled by fear of the drought.

14 MAY
To Tymawr, to see our friend Marianne who is on a short retreat there. The new, and surely very late, leaves of ashes; little limp, olive-green hands. Apple blossom and lilac. (Do I mention such things to show that I am, after all, a genuine countryman of sorts? No. I mention them when they particularly attract my attention.)

Much the best was the horse's mane. On the way to Tymawr I saw the sun shining through the rough mane of a chestnut horse, like a blaze of golden fire along his neck. I thought we'd passed too quickly for S to look back at it, so said nothing about it. But it was what I think the Quakers call an 'opening'. And on the way back I asked her whether by chance she'd seen it too, in spite of driving. She had! And for a moment we rejoiced together in that memory of an illumination.

Days of love and peace, after so many hard days of *Sturm und Drang*.

15 MAY
I took the 'Ode to Jenny' out of the *Malcontenta* volume of *Pantaloon*; and have been working hard on these two and a half pages for the last

144

four mornings. I don't suppose I've ever worked quite so hard *and continuously* on a short poem. With what result? I haven't the least idea; but will know well enough, I suppose, when I get far enough away.

16 MAY

The first faint olive-green tinge on the lower, and sloping, lawn-to-be. Only nine days after sowing! The fastest lawn I've ever grown – out of about seven. This is accounted for by the hot sun and my very profuse watering.

A beautiful sight; and, as I was watering this evening, I could almost see the green stain spreading under the water of the hose.

◆ ◆ ◆

The Fall of Icarus. After looking at it hard for at least eighteen months, how much there is still to be discovered there! Chiefly, and suddenly, today how much it is a *constructed* picture; how totally unrealistic . . . I knew this before, of course, but see it now with a new and revealing clarity.

17 MAY

Resentment and pity are a real form of imprisonment; a treadmill.

Then the light came and showed me that there is only one kind of love which could get me out, and forward: get us out and forward. Thus ancient and familiar truths can suddenly come to life.

This was a perception, of course, and very far from being an attainment. But the perception was wonderful, and made the attainment seem almost possible.

◆ ◆ ◆

'I am sure that no one genuinely asks for mercy and grace without mercy and grace having been given him first.' Dame Julian.

Yes indeed; but the catch is in that 'genuinely'. How can we ever know whether our asking is genuine or not? Mine, I fear, is always self-interested: never a pure act of love towards God or another person.

◆ ◆ ◆

What awful frivolity there is in the widespread feeling among Christian intellectuals that 'Liberal Theology' is old-hat; unsmart; absurd. True liberality is the true way forward. To combine openness of mind with humbleness of heart.

18 MAY

I had asked Sister Benedicta whether S and I might be able to have a talk with the new chaplain (John Richardson); and after mass today he came up and suggested it himself. I have a great confidence in this young (35-year-old?) man. Could this be one of those meetings which are 'arranged'; which happen at the very moment when they are needed most? I pray so. I have so strong a feeling of our need for help from someone quite new and quite outside our clenched condition.

◆ ◆ ◆

David, Phine and Pip have just left, after a very loving and entertaining weekend. S and I sit in the garden playing chess and drinking beer, as the sun goes down and a dove coos from the wood. Acute melancholy: which is a very different thing from depression; at least has an element of beauty in it.

◆ ◆ ◆

Very good programme on Christian Aid and the Third World. Very good in making me feel like an unspeakable pig; pig and wolf combined. The man who makes little jokes about his sin of eating a honey sandwich at midnight! Truly sickening.

I know that I am imprisoned in the hideous myth of my time and place – the Society of Greed and Anger. Is it better or worse to be aware of this yet to do nothing about it? The old question.

20 MAY

Praying today – I was at the second stage of concentrated breathing – there *was* one of those rare flickers of the inconceivable. A way out and forward, almost physical, glimpsed with amazement and immediately withdrawn.

◆ ◆ ◆

As for that damned sin of the honey sandwich – which weighs on me, partly I suppose, through Rupert Brooke associations – this is what might be called the Walrus and the Carpenter syndrome. But why use that foolish, fashionable, evasive word?

Walrus and Carpenter behaviour – criminality – weeping over the delicate vice of slightly overeating at night, while millions are starving.

Or the Maria Theresa bestiality – *elle pleure et elle prend toujours* (after the second division of Poland).

We murder by our greed.

22 MAY

Grotesque *Daily Telegraph* headline seen in Monmouth today: THATCHER TO SET PAY EXAMPLE. Was she, then, going to reduce her own standard of living to that of the unemployed? No; she was going to make sure of holding down the wages and salaries of *others* in government employment. Granny, burn that!

But what an effect it would have, if a whole government decided to live in the way that the poorest people in their country are forced to live! Such a multitude of preachers who never even dream of trying to practise. And I am one of them. (Yes, but at least I don't preach forbearance to those who are poorer than I am.)

◆ ◆ ◆

Lust is not very often stirred now. Seeing again the dark girl at H's shop, I felt a sort of tender gratitude to her for being attractive in just that particular way. Thank you for maintaining the beloved type. (And not even a remote fantasy of possession.)

23 MAY

An entertaining lunch with Julian Mitchell to meet Sheila Cassidy. But I drank a little too much – only *a very little* too much – and have now begun what may be at least two days' punishment.

Yet if I had drunk *only a little less*, the afternoon would have been sharply and perpetually uncomfortable. The horns of a more-than-forty-year-old dilemma.

24 MAY

'. . . that we may perfectly love thee and worthily magnify thy holy name.' But as I spoke these familiar words I suddenly smelled pipe tobacco outside some headmaster's door.

◆ ◆ ◆

A coals of fire review for Gavin Ewart, who had gone out of his way to review and be crushing about the published bits of *Pantaloon*. He almost ordered me off the territory of verse; called me an 'amateur' and a bad one at that. Because I wrote no serious verse till I was forty.

Of course I was very angry at the time; but probably gave him a rather better review than he deserved in my effort to be just, magnanimous, etc. Better cause for self-congratulation than childishly getting my own back: but there are no good causes for self-congratulation, pleasant though it is.

◆ ◆ ◆

The blues are threatening heavily today. Heavenly Mother, keep the black dog off my shoulders!

◆ ◆ ◆

Yes; I know that God's forgiveness is perpetual; a fountain always full of water; not a tap which is turned on when the right words are spoken. But I can only reach the water of that fountain when I can approach it with calm; my mind stilled from this wild, self-abusive grunting and moaning.

◆ ◆ ◆

So strong a temptation tonight to allow – or engineer? – a state of total collapse. Announcing that I am truly in a condition of depression then I immediately receive the fitting treatment; I am *exonerated* from work, from company, even from going downstairs.

Isn't it the case that I have pretended to myself for many weeks – or at least for many days in those many weeks – that, whatever this strain and oppression may be, it must not be called by the dread word itself. And there comes a time when the strain of denying the name becomes intolerable.

25 MAY

So now, this morning, I broke down into tears at last. Depression had been recognised, in every sense; given *de facto*, if not *de jure* status. And the fear and torpor were so great that I couldn't even face the lunchtime picnic with Poll★ and the children.

Of course there is a strong element of relief in all this; but surely the relief is justified. As I lay on my bed, alone in the house, drinking beer and trying to read prayers during the picnic hours, I felt the indulgence towards myself which a sick man deserves. (But there is a price to pay, of course: once recognised, he may get a stronger hold and be much harder to dislodge again.)

◆ ◆ ◆

In this condition, for example, lying in bed is often no relief. I cannot relax either body or mind.

I wrote a bad poem; which was the only way I was able to pray.

◆ ◆ ◆

Beer is indeed the greatest help – apart from S. Perhaps my whole 'journey' has been to find a God who will be an adequate beer-substitute.

★ P T's daughter, Polly.

148

The Folly of Old Men. Each day we hang another foolish pendant round our necks, weighing down head, mind and soul.

◆ ◆ ◆

But idly turning on the TV earlier this evening, I found them half-way through the second act of *Hamlet*. How nobly he speaks to the condition of all tormented men. For though he is so great in words and in torment, he is not great in person. So he speaks to us as Lear, Othello, Antony and Macbeth never can.

Laura sat up with me and was as moved as I was.

Yet I wouldn't dream of going even to Bristol to watch a good *Hamlet*. Few men are more sunk in the torpor of their habits.

◆ ◆ ◆

Ann H★ sent us a book with the formidable title, *Power Through Constructive Thinking*. By an American (of course) called Emmet Fox. But it turns out to be full of very good things, in spite of Fox's appalling conviction that God also gives cash and advancement to those who think about him in the right way. 'God is only to be contacted within, and never without . . . ' This is an obvious enough truth, but one which has somehow been eluding me, so determined have I been to insist that God *exists* quite independently of us and our minds. He can *meet* us – it seems self-evident now – only by entering into our consciousness.

26 May

Tweedledum and Tweedledee again. A ridiculous charade between us. Yet none the less painful for its appalling absurdity.

Perhaps what God requires of us now is a certain dryness: even a retreat to affection and as much respect as possible. Leave the word 'love' alone for a bit: the word is perhaps too large for us in our present state. Whereas to be real *friends* at this late stage might be the best possible new beginning.

27 May

Off with caravan and bicycles, S driving all the way to a great Caravan Club park at Sandringham. Fearful late Bank Holiday traffic all the way, but worst of all from Peterborough on. And then, in the park, to find the caravans jammed together as they would never have been even two years ago. The number of caravans on the road has doubled

★Ann Horne, long-time correspondent.

149

since we bought ours at the end of 1977; no wonder, but it becomes that much harder to find any sort of parking privacy.

Perhaps the next fifteen years will be known as 'the Caravan Age' – before we are all driven back into our houses by the price of petrol. (No great hardship for me, I must say.)

But very friendly neighbours this morning; and a general warmth towards other 'vans' and their occupants.

28 MAY

Walsingham. A disappointment, of course; and the Anglican shrine even worse than that. But this counts as one of the 'holiest' places in Great Britain. What does that mean? The most extreme view is that it just *is* a holy place, and its holiness was discovered by man. More moderately, some might say that it has been made (objectively) holy by being treated as such for so long. But I can't really get further than saying that it is a holy place only because, and in so far as, we treat it as holy. Who knows?

Binham Priory. And our right decision to look over it first; then settle in the local (ruined) pub for drinks and snacks. In other words, there is still a faint feeling of obligation about sight-seeing, as there never could be about settling down in a pub.

Certainly, too, I am far more bothered – even indignant – about the horribly tarted-up pubs of rural England than about Victorian restorations in the churches. When I think of the White Rose at Lindsey in the fifties; an ale house with nothing but benches and a single old rough table; old rough Stan Partridge fetching out pints from cool barrels in the stone passage . . . And then our visit four years ago – to find the whole inside ripped out and turned into a place fit for city commuters. We talked to one of the old patrons, an abashed labourer sitting in the darkest corner he could find: a ghost. So pubs are simply stolen from the people they were meant for; just as grammar schools were stolen from the local people and turned into boarding schools.

Sentimentality? I don't think so. And when we got to Aylsham, settled the caravan on this pleasant farm and began to look around, it was a great joy to feel that this bit of England really is different from ours; not just in the lie of its land (which presumably they'll never quite be able to alter – except by the Bomb) but in the *feel* of its little towns and villages. As well, of course, as the immense difference in the churches. Great grey towers like splendid fortresses of God.

There is a rusty and rotting old elevator in the corner of the field; and I can remember the time when they were the wonder of the countryside. They must have had a fairly short life, before vanishing into Arcadia. I looked at it, and peed behind it, with great affection.

And in the middle of our field penned ewes are lambing. What a happy and lucky choice this was. Rain battering down in the night, and the bleating of ewes and lambs. A strange remedy – if that is what this is – that we should pen ourselves up together in this little box in the middle of strange country. But in fact I do have high hopes that we shall win some sort of renewal from this strange interlude.

29 MAY

Biked to North Walsham, and back by a different and longer route. I was last here in 1919, aged three, holidaying at Overstrand with my grandparents. But my only memory is of the single-track line – Great Northern and Great Eastern Joint? – and how my greatly admired Uncle Stephen, seven years older than I, was allowed to ride in the cab by Mr Peck, the engine-driver.

Fierce rain and wind on the way home, and when we put on our capes they became sails trying to drive us back. And I thought how very good it was of S to make no complaint about something so little to her taste. Gallant, without showing it: even unaffectedly merry.

Later in the afternoon the sun came out and I walked a little way along our narrow little road, finding six church towers, at varying distances, in the whole circle which I could survey from the top of a bank. According to the map – Banningham (our own village, quarter of a mile away); Colby; Suffield; Antingham; Erpingham; and Aylsham. Happiness.

Back in the caravan I held a skein of wool for S to roll (another nostalgic activity); S knitting a jersey for Nasi's baby-to-be. But on the news we heard that twenty men and women had been given eighty lashes each for drinking and 'fooling about' in Tehran. This was performed at a new institution known as the Centre for the Abolition of Sin. Should I go there for a short course – say, forty lashes and one hand off?

But it wouldn't be true to say that we drank and fooled about with any diminished pleasure that evening.

30 MAY

Made friends with the couple in the other caravan. Strong cockney voices, though they came from Newark: an overwhelming sense of gentleness, innocence, true virtue. And when I meet such people I always want to ask them how they do it: though the whole point is, of course, that they haven't the least idea that they are doing anything, or being anything out of the ordinary.

How strong a contrast to S and me in Norwich! After the hideous boredom of the Castle Museum, sudden violence over indecent red slabs of roast beef for lunch. Murderous in the cathedral. And so much, said I to myself, hardly able to see a thing, for my notion of a healing and purifying expedition!

Then what an afternoon in the caravan – of rain driving down on the thin roof above us while we went through the ancient charade of parry and defence! Physical nausea. Went out to vomit behind that rusty and now quite cheerless old grain-elevator.

But the arrival of a small troop of Boy Scouts to camp in another corner of the field gave us something else to think about. When the sun came out at last, they began to caper about; play rough cricket; try to light camp-fires . . . A pleasure to watch them.

The gift of tears.

31 MAY

What is needed is a great but *generous-hearted* charismatic movement. Why this terrible compulsion which drives nearly all Christian re-vivalists to revive the terrible narrowness of fundamentalism and the crippling malformation of ONLY-OUR-LOT-SAVED-AND-THE-REST-OF-YOU-DAMNED?

◆ ◆ ◆

We walked down the road this morning to look at Banningham church, and found a young art-historian there, busy with his camera. He is writing a great work on English church furniture; has published in the *Burlington*; had even met Ben . . . What a joy to meet somebody so familiar; to break, suddenly, into a language long unused. A more dubious joy was to reveal my own identity, and receive appropriate respect.

After driving off to two more churches, S and I had lunch with this young man and girl-friend in the pub by Blickling Hall.

Boredom through Blickling Hall, though everything magnificently managed by the National Trust. I fear that my newly acquired architectural interest is almost exclusively ecclesiological.

◆ ◆ ◆

The impulse to make this journal more brisk, exclamatory and precise: much less circumstantial and long-winded.

◆ ◆ ◆

Perhaps my very first statement of faith should be something like this: I believe that there have been many minds, every bit as human as mine, in which concern for and about the self has become genuinely secondary to an almost perpetual concern with God and other people. The existence of such people is the greatest of all religious witnesses; miracles.

◆ ◆ ◆

Bacon and eggs in the caravan this evening to a Mozart Quartet from the BBC. It is the quality of mastery, of masterliness which is the most easy to recognise and the hardest to define. I am tempted to think that there is an absolute and clear distinction between those works which have this and those which haven't. As I would say, the most complete possible entry of God into a human soul – and a partial entry. But I think this is altogether too absolutist an attitude.

Again, though, a certain sadness that my capacity really to hear such music is so limited.

Happiness; and perhaps all the more keenly felt after the shame and misery of Norwich yesterday.

I JUNE

The best day so far. To Aylsham for the *Observer*; then reading it together till 11 o'clock. Then a quiet stroll through the sun to Banningham church for a family service; about six young couples with very young children, and a young curate using an electric torch as a symbol for the invisible working of God in the world. But is it possible for a young child to have any sort of real faith in the unseen? We are told to become as little children; and I think I know very well what this means. But *real* little children are very different creatures from adults who have regained, or retained, certain childlike qualities.

Banningham pub – not a good one – for drinks; then back to the van for a cold lunch; then off on what should have been the longest ride so far. But after two churches and about six miles I had a puncture. I accepted this gracefully enough – *just* gracefully enough – then rode S's bike back to the caravan and brought the car back to where she was waiting.

So we made the best of it by a short walk through some delightful woods, still very fresh and spring-like in this delayed spring.

We were sorry to see the scouts packing up and leaving, after a weekend largely ruined, alas, by yesterday's dreadful weather. I feel the utmost benevolence nowadays for human beings who in no way encroach on my own life; or encroach on it only as much as *I* want. Easy to be contemptuous of this; but it is better than nothing. In fact it is possible that I feel more of this benevolence in these years of almost pathological withdrawal than I did in my years of free-and-easy sociability.

'Accept!' I said to myself, at the time of the puncture. 'Accept whatever comes'; if not *from* God – whom I cannot without a strong sense of absurdity hold responsible for the puncture – then *for* God. I begin to understand what is meant by offering *our* misfortunes to God, even the most trivial of them.

◆ ◆ ◆

> You shall love your crooked neighbour
> With your crooked heart.

I came on these lines of Auden's for the first time today; and felt that he could not have written them if he had not been, as I found him during our few meetings late in his life, a desperately twisted and disconsolate man. Wonderful lines.

2 JUNE

We took my bike to be mended in North Walsham, but it couldn't be done till late afternoon. So S went off to a hairdresser in Aylsham while I did the morning chores – emptying the lavatory, pouring out the waste water, collecting fresh water from the farm, cleaning out the van. Then I walked down to the church at an almost Buddhist pace, each step taken with the greatest care, attention, deliberation. Small, bright oak trees; larks; cow-parsley and mercifully small fields of gently waving green barley. Prayers in the church; and unusual peace. A *strong* peace.

Will it last? Both common sense and Christian realism say of course not. But Christian hope says it is *possible*. Any occasion, even as mild and undramatic as this, *might* be the moment of lasting change; of real renewal.

And a Christian must keep in mind both the large probability of the moment leaving nothing perceptible behind, and the minute possibility that this is at least the beginning of rebirth.

Penitence should be perpetual. But this doesn't mean beating the breast and moaning about one's past sins: it means a ceaseless awareness of the difference between what one is and what one might, and should be.

◆ ◆ ◆

Off in the car to go up the coast from Bacton to Cromer, churches all the way. Coming out of one of these I stumbled and turned my weak ankle, which immediately began to swell. In Cromer we bought an elastic bandage, and S bound up my ankle in the car. But I was almost sure that this had put an end to my bicycling for the rest of our stay here. Then indeed, though not complaining, I did feel rueful; melancholy; even resentful – but against who or what? It was almost as if my morning's peace were being deliberately tested. 'Right, then! Try it on *this*!'

But as I followed a plump lady up the steep steps of a windmill, hobbling gallantly, I observed her naked legs and pleasant bottom with at least a mild stirring of relish and appreciation.

♦ ♦ ♦

Reading something horrible in the paper about new effects of the government's appalling economic policy, it occurred to me that in *public* affairs we should never talk about love at all. For this greatest of all forces is quite outside the possible realm of public policy. What we must work for here is *justice*, which, though never achieved by any society anywhere, is at least a seamark by which a good government should steer. Justice can at least be discussed in public terms, and gross acts against it can be publicly and clearly exposed.

For we are not GOD, to be able to dispense with justice altogether, all justice transcended and over-ridden by holy love.

3 JUNE –
But to my joy and amazement I found this morning that I could cycle much better than I could walk; in fact almost without any inconvenience at all. So off we went, over this delightful rolling country – rolling quite enough for us to get quite familiar with these once-alarming gears – and arrived for lunch at a miraculous and quite unexpected village called Heydon. This was one of those places – like Bishop's Castle – which seemed to have almost succeeded in avoiding the passage of the last fifty years. The pub, for example, was 'unspoiled' – which meant, I realised as I keenly inspected it, simply that it resembled the pubs of my youth – late Victorian, with rather tatty thirties wallpaper. No matter. Beauty is in the eye of the elderly nostalgic, and I felt at home eating bread and cheese on those benches as I never could in the modernised pubs of *c.* 1960 onwards. And what a village green outside the window – with small, brick, eighteenth-century cottages all round it. (No doubt inhabited by commuters from Norwich – a class we strongly resent, until we remind ourselves that we would certainly try to be one of them if I had to work in Norwich.)

Then a great biking afternoon – Suffield, Antingham and distant Bradfield. How much I loved and admired S's plump and energetic pedalling as I rode behind her. (But sometimes I put my hands down to the dropped handle-bars, lowered my head and raced a few hundred yards ahead like a sprinter in the Tour de France.)

4 JUNE

We took the bikes to Blickling by car quite early in the morning, left the car in the pub park and set out from there for a full day's riding. First to Salle – pronounced 'Saul' – and one of the most famous churches in Norfolk: all perpendicular and all built at one go in the fifteenth century. Splendid. But marred by the fact that the window in the north transept had been walled up to make way for a preposterous Regency monument to a local squire. When we talked to the aged sexton, who was mowing the graveyard, he expressed his undying indignation at this piece of egomaniacal vandalism. He told us, too, that the 'village' (there can't have been more than eight or nine cottages) had just managed to keep their own parson so far – in fact, an old and retired one – but that he greatly feared that Salle would be attached to a local group of churches next year. How natural, the wish to remain on their own: how sadly inevitable the *Gleichschaltung*.

Then on to Reepham, as magical as Heydon, though a little bigger. We sat outside a pub watching a tiny market, eating a modest snack and drinking cold beer. A memorable moment.

But when I asked four different people in the market where I could find the church (in fact, two churches joined back to back), not one of them knew that it was just round the next corner of the square. The things we take no interest in become invisible to us – as churches were largely invisible to me for at least two-thirds of my adult life.

Back at the caravan – via Cawston church – we stood naked behind the elevator, soaped each other all over and poured cold water over each other. Much refreshed for beer and chess in the van, before setting out on our self-promised splurge – dinner in a fairly renowned restaurant at the bottom of an old mill. Disappointed by the food, as usual, and a little shocked at our gross extravagance. But happy to bed after this last and best day of all.

I had hoped for a purification by unalloyed love and happiness. But perhaps that wretched Friday played its necessary part; and this last day has been a triumph and a glory.

5 JUNE

On our way to Kersey a great new road swung us half over and across the village of Claydon, where there is a memorial to Bubbles* in the

*Jasper Ridley.

church. A mild sense of desecration, as I remembered our visits to his mother's house nearby, and its extraordinary name – Mockbeggars Hall. (How I used to long for Bubbles to invite me there; but he never did.) But I was also grateful, I must admit, for being taken so quickly past what used to be a formidable bottleneck.

Long, long journey home – and how much longer for S in the driving seat. But nothing except utter exhaustion ever persuades her to let me drive, for she is almost pathologically afraid of being driven *by anyone*. (I make the point that this is a rule from which I am not exempted, rather than one which applies only to me.)

As we sweltered round London on that dreadful North Circular Road, then lunged onto the endless motorway, I was trying to write a creed in my pocket notebook. As we reached the Severn Bridge, I had concocted this:

I believe in God the Holy Spirit whose love and wisdom are beyond all human understanding.

I believe that God loves every person on earth with an equal love.

But I believe that a person can best receive the love of God by himself loving others; by frequent, if possible by constant prayer; by a persevering faith in faith; and by hope for the grace of continued hope.

And I believe that a person can reject the love of God not only by closing his heart and mind against it but also by denying it to all those whose faith is different from his own.

Therefore I believe that I must pursue my own way towards the knowledge and love of God with whole-hearted devotion, but also with respect for the ways of others.

And I believe that to pursue a way towards the recognition and the returning of God's love is both the best justification and the supreme blessing of life on earth.

Yes, but as we got over the bridge into our own country I began to worry about what we'd find when we got home; the house burned down, or news of something much, much worse . . . And I'm afraid that I allowed this foolish anxiety to show all too plainly.

6 JUNE
'Struggle continually, but always with a reconciled heart.' From the Taizé community. This profoundly Christian counsel always sets one an almost impossible task.

◆ ◆ ◆

I did my first mowing of the new garden this afternoon, between heavy showers, and it has at last taken the shape that I had been dreaming of. It really is like a *sculptured* shape – and only the middle stretch still utterly untidy; an eyesore. But I shall work *slowly* on this through the summer; paving and making the pond. But I know now that I shan't be able to build the higher of the two walls myself: I daren't try to lift those heaviest stones.

◆ ◆ ◆

Thoughts on John Drury's *The Pot and the Knife*. This is a fine book, as I would expect it to be; but what interests me most is that although Drury, whether he likes the label or not, is just as much of a Liberal Christian as I am, my whole current of ideas seems to diverge quite widely from his. And this divergence seems to spring from the words 'myth' and 'symbol', on which Drury is heavily dependent but which I find less and less useful the more I think and pray about all these great Unthinkables/Unprayables. This, for example: 'Believers are being called to something trickier and more interesting than the outright championing or rejection of myths, or the entirely detached analysis of them, if that is possible. They are being called to evaluate and use them sensibly, whether they are their own or other people's, in the cause of human goodness which they believe to be God's cause.'

But this seems to be a quite impossible 'calling'. Myths have power only while they are still believed to be literal truth; a 'sensible' evaluation must reduce them to pleasant tales, at least; useful metaphors, at best. And a useful metaphor is good for communication, perhaps, but certainly no use for praying.

This passage in Drury's book is soon followed by a famous quotation from the *Four Quartets*:

> . . . You are not here to verify,
> Instruct yourself, or inform curiosity
> Or carry report. You are here to kneel
> Where prayer has been valid . . .

Drury comments: 'Now we have another basic duty, uncomfortably like that banned in Eliot's lines, to fit in with acceptance and wonder.' I agree that this is true of certain Christians during certain periods of their lives – I mean speculative, intellectual Christians during the period when they are trying to evolve for themselves a faith which they can fully accept, with both mind and heart. But this is not the condition of most Christians any of the time: it surely cannot be true even of speculative Christians all the time. Unless we can pray with simple hearts, we cannot pray at all.

It is worrying, but not altogether surprising, to find Drury writing about 'the divinity which is not exactly "us"'. And here, of course, I have to differ from him absolutely, and without reservation. For I do believe, with Barth and co., that God is 'wholly other'; though, unlike those austere and frightening theologians, I believe that God the Wholly Other chooses to enter us, by a billion incarnations, and thus to make it possible for us to know him, in part; to love him, and to do his will.

But I do agree with the most general of all Drury's theses – which is that this is the time for a great work of Christian reconstruction; an arduous co-operation between thinking Christians in an effort to re-create their faith in such a way that what has become (a) offensive, (b) incredible, and (c) superfluous shall be discarded *without depleting the faith that remains*. Demythologising was certainly a necessary process; but what is needed now is a passionate restatement of Christian truth in new and forceful, mind-and-heart-delighting terms.

Drury: 'People in pews are helped by the news that doctrines and images have not dropped out of the sky but, like the rest of the furniture, have been made by particular people's efforts to realise their ideas, and have intelligible histories.' I would put it differently – something like this: 'People who might sit in pews would be helped to do so by the admission that every attempt to express the inexpressible reality of God in words is useful only for a certain time; that the creeds which are still repeated in nearly all Christian churches are words which are no longer useful for most of us; and that we must find other words to express as best we can our enduring faith in the reality of God's love for us.'

I am also very much against Drury when he writes 'sensibly' about saints. 'The affecting power [of such modern figures as Bonhoeffer and Hammarskjöld] is the more striking for carrying through in an age when critical knowledge, being greater in extent if not in depth than ever before, makes impossible the allegations of faultless heroism or sanctity made on behalf of yesterday's worthies. This absence of pedestals has the daunting beneficial effect of making clear that such people are not magic but just people – and so something of their sort is possible for, and required of, us.'

In this passage it seems to me that Drury is resolutely sawing off one of the major branches on which Christians are precariously perched. It is not worthy to describe St Francis as one of 'yesterday's worthies' – and what has yesterday to do with it? Indeed I would use sanctity, and its real historical manifestation in this world, as the very basis of a renewed and reinvigorated faith.

Admitted, of course, that many canonised men and women never deserved the honour: some never existed to deserve it. Admitted that even the great saints, of whom we are reasonably well informed, were

159

not faultless. *Nevertheless* I firmly believe that sanctity is a real thing, possessed in varying degrees by real people. Drury's 'magic' is a dismissive word. But what if one says that God is in all of us; but in some men and women so much so that they are transformed by it into *perceptible* vessels of God's light and love? These people – in the Christian tradition from Jesus himself to such as Bonhoeffer and Mother Teresa – are the great witnesses; the most important demonstration we have of God and his work on earth. We may not be able to believe all that they have believed: we should be aware that saints in other traditions than the Christian have very different beliefs from ours. But this I take to be the minimal belief of all whom I would describe as saints – that there is a reality beyond this world perceived by the senses, and that this reality both contains and offers love, truth, freedom, beauty . . . beyond all normal human conception. (The saints are those who have come *markedly* closer to conceiving it than the rest of us are able to do.)

So I think it a really disastrous ploy of Drury's to try to cut the saints down to size. True, we should try to be as like them as we can: but no less true that the great majority of us will undoubtedly fail to be as they were. In fact our real task is not to try to imitate St Francis, but to learn all we can about him, to love and revere him and to see all we can of God through that man who was so greatly possessed by God.

Though this is far from his intention, I feel that Drury's book will have a reductive effect. We must retain the undimmed glory, whatever new words we use.

7 JUNE

Oh for the blessings of *frugality*! Which means, of course, the blessing of really desiring it.

◆ ◆ ◆

In grey or doubting times there is nobody better than Dame Julian: 'Truth sees God: wisdom gazes on God. And these two produce a third; a holy, wondering delight in God, which is love. Where there is indeed truth and wisdom, there too is love, springing from them both. And all of God's making . . . '

How much better she says it than I ever can. And the reason is simply that she was a saint, *and had herself perceived these truths*.

◆ ◆ ◆

What a lot of time is wasted on ecumenical strivings. In so far, that is, as they are aimed at the re-creation of a single Christian Church. Let all of us worship as we wish, in whatever Church we wish or in none. Let us respect each other's worship; freely exchange our differences of belief; worship together if and where and when we can. (But it would be pure hypocrisy for me to worship alongside someone who would believe, if he knew my own beliefs, that I am a black heretic and condemned to everlasting flames.)

8 JUNE

There was some tension and sadness at Tymawr today. I do suffer with them, though the purity of my sympathy is a little marred by a strong, unregenerate curiosity.

They will, of course, get over this. Because of what they are, they will probably be stronger in love and the truth for having suffered whatever it is.

◆ ◆ ◆

'And the more [we understand] the more will we long, both naturally and by grace, to be filled with eternal joy and happiness. We have been made for this . . . '

Reading this passage from Dame Julian in my prayer-time today, the words 'We have been made for this . . . ' suddenly shone from the page, almost literally. I can join readily now in the Christian faith that God 'made' man, for I believe that without what God has infused into us of himself we would not be recognisable as men. All that we value, in us and in the world around us, is from God. The valuing is from God.

◆ ◆ ◆

'My impression is that what I am writing is entirely my own. And then, a long or a short time after, I at last . . . see that I have been helped.' After this Kierkegaard is soon away again on some destructive and idiotic flight of angry egotism; but this is surely a real perception. I feel it too. (But what about the bad bits?)

◆ ◆ ◆

Laura spent the whole morning going through the libretto of *Tosca* (Italian and English): then she listened to it carefully in the afternoon. She is in a state of real radiance just now, in her great discovery of music. And she has, thank God, rid herself at last of that sad, impossible incubus. How life is opening out for her! And it suddenly occurred to me that perhaps our primary task has not been, as S and I have thought, with ourselves but with our youngest daughter. And perhaps, for all our faults in that field, too, we may have been serving God best in the help we've given her.

161

9 JUNE

In the George yesterday evening, Deidre (who owns the pub with her husband Roy) insisted that S, Laura and I should come up to her sitting-room and meet some American guests. My horror at this fearful compulsion quickly dissolved in the good company and bottle after bottle of champagne. We staggered away after about three hours of this – and all agreed this morning that we'd enjoyed ourselves immensely, in spite of present hangovers.

For me this is the best sort of social event – totally unexpected and therefore with no time for dread. And now we are spending a very pleasant day of restful idiocy.

10 JUNE

The notion of 'offering' a pain or distress to God is one which I don't really understand, but which appeals to me very much.

◆ ◆ ◆

Léon Bloy writes somewhere that personality is the unique vision which each soul has of God. One would have to add 'whether the individual mind is aware of this or not'. If we were all conscious of this, if all of us were becoming fuller and fuller persons – i.e. lesser and lesser egos – in the consciousness of God's light and love, *that* would be thy kingdom come.

◆ ◆ ◆

Every moment counts; or at least can be made to count.

◆ ◆ ◆

It is strange that although we must aim at our own *good*, as soon as we start trying to serve the good of others, and not their happiness, we shall almost certainly tumble into odious priggishness and presumption. The good of others is the business of themselves, of God, of their spiritual directors, and of any saints they may happen to know. Our part is to serve that (large) portion of their total good which is their happiness.

◆ ◆ ◆

There is no limit to the splendours of Dame Julian. Today, this: 'Our soul has a twofold duty: to wonder in all reverence, and to suffer in all humility, even while we always rejoice in God.'

◆ ◆ ◆

In no prayer do we really ask God to do something for us. Every prayer is an attempt, aided by God, to become more of what God is already and always doing for us.

◆ ◆ ◆

The little tin of 'Essential Balm' which Polly gave me. For me it is the scent of heaven: but really of my childhood – some delicious cough cure I sniffed or drank. Cinnamon? Camphor? Friar's Balsam? Eucalyptus? Celestial odours!

Yet something of heaven *is* to be found in childhood, even, perhaps, in the most terrible of childhoods. For there were moments then of absolute openness; joy; preparation for flight into an infinite sky . . .

◆ ◆ ◆

I have at last solved the difficult engineering problem of how to do the work – paving; walls; ponds – in the central strip of the garden. This is a great relief; it had been weighing on me more than I knew.

12 JUNE

Seeing someone fishing on our way to Monmouth. Usually this has no particular effect; but this time I felt such a yearning for all those joyful times, alone in beautiful places, from the age of eight (lake at Castle Howard) to the age of fifty-seven (end of last of twelve seasons on the Monnow). I gave it up at the start of the community, reckoning that I couldn't 'waste' either the time or the petrol on such a frivolous activity.

But perhaps I shall try to join that club again. I doubt if I've ever been so close to God as at certain great fishing moments.

◆ ◆ ◆

Father P in a very depressed state. I tried to help: he said that I had helped.

13 JUNE

A new and terrible affliction. The strong sensation, as I was waking in the night, that something – first S in minute shape, then a mouse, then a snake – was moving round and round inside the back of my head. Terror. Terror of madness. O God, have mercy!

◆ ◆ ◆

So one must feel pity for everyone except oneself. Not pity-condescension, of course, but pity-compassion. But here, too, there is a trap awaiting us; for how can we *feel with* someone else unless we first know what it is to feel with ourselves?

14 JUNE

No snake this morning, thanks be to God. But cringing fear of it much of today.

◆ ◆ ◆

Nowadays the window of the Coleford bookshop is chock-a-block with local history. When we first came to the area, I used to search everywhere for even a single dusty pamphlet. Does this mean that people are really beginning to take an interest in where they live?

◆ ◆ ◆

Muggy mist and drizzle. Should I (*a*) go to bed and read my review book on Ruskin; (*b*) go for a run; or (*c*) work on the garden?

Do what you *want* to do, for Heaven's sake! Ah, but it's not so simple; for what I want to do must include what I shall want *to have done* by 5 o'clock. (Therefore I worked on the garden.)

◆ ◆ ◆

Who was that elderly queer friend who once said to me, 'Life, my dear, is a mad scramble across no man's land from cradle to grave, with absolutely *no* cover and under fire from both sides at once'?

No, I never *quite* feel that. For me it has been more of a wild butterfly-hunt, through bog, scrub, nettles, wood and water, never quite making the catch.

15 JUNE

Snake again, but I was able to will and pray it away; and felt a certain pride in this act of exorcism.

◆ ◆ ◆

Sudden memory, for no perceptible reason, of getting the news of our Bedlington terrier's distemper from my mother when I was at the Dragon School. My misery *and terror* at the prospect of Tilda's death. Not, I think, mainly for Tilda's sake, but because such an event would have seemed a threat to that absolute security of the home which I have *always* needed.

I was twenty-eight when I first heard – quite casually, at a party –

that it was generally understood that my mother and father were going to be divorced. And though at the time I was on good terms with neither of them – perhaps scarcely even on genuine speaking terms – yet I was appalled, miserable, furious.

Yes; and I am still the most domestic of animals.

◆ ◆ ◆

Listening to the *Missa Solemnis* with Laura this morning; and as the single word CREDO burst out I felt, yes, that's *it* – and that's *enough!*

◆ ◆ ◆

Ram Dass interviewed last night on the TV. I still liked and respected him, certainly no less because he's abandoned his Indian robes and looks like a prosperous American executive. Memories of Kerry and me talking endlessly of his ideas, his book, his tapes, in the early days of the community. And then – to my joy! – Kerry himself ringing up to ask if we'd been watching.

But what I could never take, and can take even less now, is this line about everything being (a) absolutely as it should be, and (b) quite incapable of being changed by anything anyone does or says. Then why, *why*, WHY does dear Ram Dass still spend his time trying to make all this strange stuff clear to us?

Fight the good fight is much more my line.

16 JUNE
Reconstructed the very top of the garden in pouring rain this after-noon. Not for appearance's sake but to make a plateau for us to bowl on. My mind is now much taken up with the future delights of playing bowls – and even inviting the neighbours in for bowls and tea. Well, bowls and wine.

◆ ◆ ◆

I've now finally abandoned my four-month attempt to write out my deepest thoughts about EVIL – in the sense of human wrong-doing. The subject seemed to move further away every time I grabbed at it; and however stealthy my approach.

What remains of all that labour? Primarily, that I absolutely share Dame Julian's absolute faith that God is absolutely loving. Therefore, that he is in no way responsible for the appalling things that human beings do to themselves and to each other. Nor do I believe that these enormities are due to the machinations of a devil, or devils.

Fear is at the root of all evil (greed for money is simply one hopeless attempt to gain absolute security).

The evil which cannot be accounted for as some form of fairly direct self-interest – i.e. defence against the myriad causes of our fears – is due to some form of insanity. Psychopaths, sadists . . .

This, left by itself, is certainly a bit too glib. Why, when there is a social demand for monsters – e.g. in Nazi Germany – are so many men and women so ready to turn themselves into monsters? Neither fear nor madness explains *the whole of* that phenomenon. Unless one takes the easy, tautological way out of saying that all concentration camp guards were by definition mad.

So I am forced, perhaps, to a much-amended version of original sin – the Christian doctrine which I have always most detested and despised. Something on these lines: that when man's mind reached a certain degree of complexity it also suffered some sort of natural but calamitous warping; distortion; imbalance. Arthur Koestler has been saying something of this kind for many years – though I doubt whether his pharmacological solution is the right one.

Thus God enters the evolutionary scene not only in order to raise man from his natural development into no more than a highly intelligent animal, but also to save him, as part of this process, from a fearful perversion of his animal nature.

By far the greater part of 'sin' is simply the dark scurrying of minds hopelessly preoccupied with their own trivial anxieties; thus blinded to the light, deadened to the life of God. But within many of us – and we should never forget it – there is a capacity for wickedness of an altogether different order: for gratuitous wickedness; the warped enjoyment of doing harm; of deliberately opposing all the purposes of God . . .

17 JUNE

> *Humanism*: This is all there is.
> *Faith*: There must be more than this.

♦ ♦ ♦

Gabriel Marcel's word – *disponibilité*. Which John Hick describes as 'openness and availability to others'. Hick goes on: 'It is to be so liberated from self-importance, so unthreatened by the otherness of others, that one can respond to them freely and immediately. In Jesus's own mind it meant seeing people as children of God to whom he was seeking to give the quality of existence which the New Testament calls eternal life.'

In fact I now see Dame Julian as on a par with St Francis; in some ways speaking even more directly to our own time. If only the Church had taken her revelations to heart – but of course it could not even beatify her, so remote was she from all the harsh trappings and dogmas which had been interposed between man and the love of God.

If one excludes the morbid images of Christ's wounds, and the occasional quickly-bobbed curtsies to orthodoxy, I believe that we have in her book the purest revelation of God's true nature which is to be found anywhere; even in the N T.

A new Julianist Christianity for our time!

◆ ◆ ◆

Here are two passages from the Afterword to Buber's *I and Thou*. If his obscurity sometimes seems almost wilful in the text itself – but I am not at all sure that it is – he makes his meaning beautifully clear in this coda: 'The concept of personhood is, of course, utterly incapable of describing the nature of God; but it is permitted and necessary to say that God is *also* a person.'

'The existence of mutuality' – wouldn't 'reciprocity' be better? – 'between God and man cannot be proved any more than the existence of God. Anyone who dares nevertheless to speak of it bears witness and invokes the witness of those whom he addresses – present or future witness.'

As Dame Julian bears witness for me, six hundred years after the Revelations of Divine Love were made to her. I cannot believe that John Drury would really wish to treat her as a 'worthy of yesterday'.

In fact, far from cutting ourselves off from the Christian past, the more we can draw from it the deeper and richer will be our own faith.

Strange and sad that when we were in Norwich I was so far from being aware of the love of God that I never spared a thought for Dame Julian or her cell there.

◆ ◆ ◆

So great a relief to us that Jeffrey and Nasi are not going to leave their house after all. They are the best neighbours I've ever had; and it is almost comical how much Jeffrey and I share our frenetic fear of any intrusion on the fixed and regular order of our lives.

19 JUNE
In Monmouth I saw an elderly man who looked shabby, a bit weird,

and bore all the marks of heavy failure. I instantly and closely associated myself with him. This wasn't due, so far as I can tell, to sympathy, compassion or love: I certainly wasn't saying to myself, 'There but for the grace of God . . . ' No, I was saying, 'There *go* I' – and it was only afterwards that I added, 'Well, I am not quite so weird as he was; I am not, in the public and obvious sense, a failure. It must be that we are all weird in our own ways; all failures in our private lives.'

◆ ◆ ◆

Epitome of Jesus's message: 'Not Law but Love.'

◆ ◆ ◆

Seeing strangers in bars or in the street, I feel a much greater instinctive respect for them than I used to do. The weariness and resignation of so many elderly women.

20 JUNE
Cruise missiles cheerfully accepted by the government; and all my old CND horror, fear and indignation stir again. But I notice that when I am in the best of health I become quite incredulous about nuclear and other catastrophes. 'How could this ancient village and all its familiar ways be suddenly torn to bits for ever? It seems quite absurd.' But my mind still tells me that we are in for appalling social troubles, and *probably* for the nuclear horror as well.

I realised many years ago that extreme good health is a deceiving drug which induces a manic optimism. Probably we see and feel things most sanely when we are a little down, but not down too far.

21 JUNE
In the bad black days of upper-class 'conversions' – from about 1925 to 1955 – nobody ever said, 'I have become a Christian,' but nearly always, 'I have become a Catholic.' And indeed they felt much closer to their old upper-class non-believing friends than to a Methodist shopkeeper, or even a Quaker doctor. If pressed for an answer, they would have said, 'We are the only Christians. Better an honest non-believer than a heretic who blasphemes against The One True Church.'

And if I went to a Methodist service, would I feel closer to the rest of the congregation than to Anne or Terry or Martyn or Robert? Well, there is a sense – an important sense – in which I would. (Which doesn't mean that I would prefer their company to that of my old friends.)

◆ ◆ ◆

'It isn't *fair*!' In private life this is a childish cry. The child has a right to be treated fairly by his parents – and in particular to be treated no worse than a brother or sister. But an adult should have moved out of that sphere and into the sphere of *uncalculating* love.

So it is utterly foolish and childish for two adults to be forever weighing up the injuries and services that each has done to the other.

'Take up your cross and follow me.' To ask whether our own particular cross is 'fair'! A *monstrous* absurdity.

So, in public life make justice the aim and the guideline; in private life make love the aim and the guideline.

◆ ◆ ◆

Working away at my creed. 'I believe in God the Holy Spirit whose loving wisdom lightens the darkness of this world.' Then, *for Christians*, a second clause: 'And I believe in the godly message of Jesus Christ, who lived and died to show us that love is greater than any law or doctrine.'

◆ ◆ ◆

It isn't *happiness* which we should try to weigh against the suffering of this world. First, because the suffering so far outweighs the happiness in quantity; secondly, because the quality of mere happiness is not dense or intense enough to appear in the same category as the bitter pain and misery of the world. The only 'thing' in the world which can be placed beside all this pain and misery is human love and goodness. It is not that one can weigh the life of St Francis against what is happening now in Cambodia; though this is sometimes done in an absurd attempt to justify the ways of the creator-God to man. But this love and goodness is at least able to live in the company of extreme affliction. There isn't nearly enough of it, as we all know; but not only does it provide the only real alleviation of pain: it is also – in a way that I don't understand – on the same level as pain; the only human experience which can reach into the depths.

Happiness, though much to be valued, is too shallow to be matched with pain; joy, on the other hand, is of a kind with anguish. But then joy is not a high degree of happiness; it is different in kind from happiness and is the natural, though not invariable, associate of love and goodness.

◆ ◆ ◆

'I believe in God the Holy Spirit who sends the light of his loving wisdom into our darkness.'

◆ ◆ ◆

Fear almost cured today by looking at the reproduction of Pissarro's wonderful picture of Pontoise. The dark figures of the old man and the old woman shuffling along that winter road of dirty snow; and the light streaming through trees and houses on the left. Yes, like the light of God's loving wisdom. An almost transforming moment.

◆ ◆ ◆

'Grace does not overthrow nature, but fulfils and perfects it.' Canon Allchin. This comforting, seemingly very sane assurance springs from belief in a creator-God who made all things as seemed good to him. In fact it seems to me that grace is on a higher level than nature; not only transcends it, but also cuts straight across it. The very good natural man is not *nearly* a holy man.

23 JUNE
'I believe in God the Holy Spirit whose loving wisdom is the true light of the world, and the hope of grace.'

◆ ◆ ◆

A parable-dream – forgotten almost as soon as I woke up. But what was not forgotten was that the dream was not telling me to do anything, but was simply doing something in and to me. I woke in the certain knowledge that some small new light and strength had been given me.

> While I do rest my soul advance:
> Make my sleep an holy trance.

For once I believe that this nightly prayer had been answered.

◆ ◆ ◆

Went to Bristol and bought two of the cheapest possible sets of bowls; but still very expensive. During the last week I have thought far more about bowls – whether to extend the new lawn, whether to level a piece of the field – than about God, my soul, etc.

24 JUNE
'Christ is head of the Church.' An ecclesiastical commonplace, I suppose, but when this caught my attention in a book on holiness I

suddenly felt something close to annoyance that such wide, windy and empty statements should still be made. What would he think, Jesus of Nazareth, dead two thousand years, if he could see inside St Peter's; study the Vatican accounts; listen to the Curia in session?

♦ ♦ ♦

But reading about holiness – which means reading about saintly love – makes me realise all the more clearly that I know nothing about holiness and very little about love.

♦ ♦ ♦

Suffering. So many entirely different kinds. By far the commonest is the unchosen, cruel and demeaning pain of physical affliction, caused by brutishly hard work on too little food or by disease. There is the unchosen pain of bereavement. There is also the rare suffering of the severe ascetic, training himself for the service of God. There is the high and noble suffering of the man who has taken up his cross, and bears the suffering of others. Finally, there is the despicable suffering – more or less limited to those in comfortable circumstances – of the man who is morbidly preoccupied with his own ego.

The last of these is the only one I know well from personal experience. And I know that even this type of suffering may be a mortification of the self in the end; if only by sheer surfeit; self-disgust; self-boredom.

The first sort, which attracts less theological attention than any of the others, is by far the worst, as well as the commonest.

♦ ♦ ♦

Phine telephoned to tell us that she is to be confirmed. Such good news. And strangely she is the only one of my five children who was baptised in infancy. Why did Anne and I do that, having no faith whatever at the time?

25 JUNE
Sixty-fourth birthday. I begin to feel like a reckless spendthrift: 'All right! Let them all come! The more the merrier!'

♦ ♦ ♦

I do feel that on occasions something is shown to me: usually something very well known, but known afresh to me in something like a flash of grateful recognition. Usually these flashes are concerned with attitudes and action; and it is often said that unless they are

171

followed by personal change they are no use at all. I don't believe it. Even if I entirely fail to live what I have been shown, the showing itself is still of the greatest value; particularly if I can show it to other people. (Though I know, of course, that the best way of showing it is not in words but in living.)

27 JUNE

The dinner party. Our first dinner party for local friends for at least two years; and I feel in this aftermath that I never want to give or go to another. All our four friends were *good* friends of whom we are truly fond; but talking to them all together seemed more and more futile, even painful, as the evening passed. One comes down so often to the single common topic – which is political-social in some form or other – and this topic now fills me with boredom and disgust. I know our differences so well; and believe that nothing new or interesting can possibly emerge from airing them yet again. Apart from this, I am just not interested, now, in monetarism versus incomes policy, etc. – nor ever was, at this level, even in my most political years.

There is much pleasure to be had in talking to any one of these people, when things can be said more thoughtfully and more deeply. But gatherings of this sort, even as small as this one, seem to me a complete waste of spirit.

What's more, though none of us got the least bit worse for drink, great quantities of wine were consumed, and this has put me out of action for two days; two days of futile distress. (For those who are not suffering from acute physical want or pain, surely the word FUTILE is the most terrible in the language.)

♦ ♦ ♦

'Sin' to my mind could be defined as anything which one does, or thinks, or feels, which creates an obstacle between God and oneself. Yet this won't do as a definition, because the word has such heavy and inextractable moral implications. Yet merely foolish, idle thoughts can hardly be described as wicked.

There is need of a wider word. 'Darkenings' won't do. I must think about this.

♦ ♦ ♦

In 1680 the Orthodox Patriarch of Jerusalem formulated three conditions necessary for a canonisation:

1) Unquestionable orthodoxy of faith.
2) Holiness of life, and a confession of faith which would go as far as martyrdom if necessary.

172

3) Obvious manifestations of divine grace – miracles, healings, etc.

What an appalling reflection on the Christian religion! Correct belief first, and then again; one mention of holiness; none of love. (And if it is said that holiness includes love, then this should at least be made explicit.)

It is the old issue of Jesus against the Pharisees; Paul against Peter; Gandhi against the orthodox Hindus and the caste system. Law against Love.

And in our time, the same goes for those who believe in the necessity of priestly sacraments; the verbal correctness of the creeds *must* be opposed by the love which invites everyone who wants to do so to worship with us, in praise and love of the God of Love: '*Compel* them to come in.' (Which doesn't, of course, mean compulsion in our sense; but *urgently invite* them to come in – all those brothers and sisters in the street – to join in our feast of love and praise. But some would say, alas, they can't be asked in unless we've interrogated them first about whether they've been properly baptised and confirmed.)

◆ ◆ ◆

No; I hear *nothing*. Not a whisper; not a breath in this dark and empty night. A sign shall not be given . . .

◆ ◆ ◆

We talk a lot about the spiritual benefits of pain and so on; but the fact is that when pain – mental or physical – is acute only a saint can prevent his mind from being totally concentrated on the suffering and clamorous ego.

Well, getting nowhere without despair may be, for some of us, the only way of getting somewhere. (But how bleak and smug these little protective paradoxes sometimes seem! It is as if we resolute 'believers' can make *anything* serve our faith; including every strong and legitimate impulse to faithlessness.)

◆ ◆ ◆

Yet I know that there is a right way to live in this appalling world: I recognise that right way of living in others, and am all the more certain, in that act of recognition, that I shall never be able to live as they do.

28 JUNE

> When the Devil is ill the Devil a saint would be:
> When the Devil is well *the devil* a saint is he.

173

Much truth in this. When I am unwell, unhappy or both, I long with all my heart and mind for God. When I am healthy and cheerful, as I've been all day today, I am too busy with the happy details of this life to think of any other; too preoccupied with earth to think of heaven. Yet it is also true – as I noted yesterday – that though suffering may make us crave for God it also lies between God and us like a burning desert, and prevents him reaching us or us reaching him.

Is there then, O Lord, some precise intermediate state of health in which alone, if we seize it quickly enough, we may catch a glimpse of you?

◆ ◆ ◆

What is 'grace'? It is, I suppose, God's free gift of himself to man. The utterly unsolved mystery is why some receive it and some do not. (For Paul, Augustine, Calvin, Pascal, etc. are quite right in observing that there is no direct ratio of grace received to good actions done, or even prayers arduously said.)

Why did this sinner suddenly receive irresistible grace while that one received nothing and was left to die in his sins?

My answer must still be that God sends his grace *wherever he can*; and that we understand only very little about what helps and what hinders him in this. (Any more than we understand why some people should be 'psychic' and others not.) As for me, I feel that I am so thick-skinned and so earthy that it is an impossible task for God to reach me; or for any kind of spirit to reach me.

◆ ◆ ◆

Isherwood's *My Guru and His Disciple*. This fascinating book belongs, I suppose, to the same rare genre as this one – a journal which is intimate in every way, but which contains as its backbone an unconcluded (unconcludable) spiritual quest.

It would be foolish to think that my quest, or his, is an effort to believe *more*: as it were, morsel after morsel of some body of doctrine being swallowed, gagged on, swallowed again, until at last the whole thing has somehow been 'taken' without being vomited out again. I am certainly not in search of more propositions to accept, whether old ones or new ones of my own devising.

The quest is for fullness of life; for a lived and living faith; for love of God and man in every moment of every day . . .

◆ ◆ ◆

TV programme based on Sir Alister Hardy's Religious Experience Research Unit. I was deeply moved by the experiences described; particularly the least 'substantial'. The overwhelming sense (but not

174

conveyed by any of the senses) of a loving presence; and of words spoken – e.g. 'I am always with you' – but not heard by the outer ear. And at least thirty-three per cent of ordinary people seem to have had an experience of this kind.

One of the interviewers believes that man acquired a spiritual sense in the natural course of evolution. He believes that it has 'survival value'. I don't think this explains anything: and it is strongly contradicted by the total conviction of all the people interviewed that the power which confronted and helped them came from outside them.

30 JUNE
Unexpected guests! Horror of the three days stretching interminably ahead, filled with small-talk and grins.

◆ ◆ ◆

'Matter and Spirit are not divided; they are inter-related. The former is evolved from the latter, and the difference between them is only one of degree.'

From Isherwood's *Ramakrishna and His Disciples*, which I've been stimulated to read again by his Guru book. This is the kind of utterly metaphysical statement which both fascinates and disgusts me. The truth is that we can't even tell whether such an assertion has any meaning or not. And yet some minds – and my own is one of them – yearn to fly up into those great mysterious spaces and gabble about what they think they see there.

And his sharp division between the Psychic and the Spiritual. This is useful; but it may be just a device for removing from the Spiritual everything which we don't like to find there – e.g. evil spirits.

◆ ◆ ◆

One must see very clearly and constantly that in any set of circumstances there is (a) the best possible thing to do, which would almost certainly mean fundamentally changing the circumstances; and (b) the best thing to do within the given circumstances. Thus, in the *Gita*, Krishna is not telling Arjuna that the best thing *of all* for him to do is to fight the battle: he is telling him that within his circumstances as a warrior he should fight rather than avoid fighting. (At least I hope this is the right interpretation.)

The best thing for S and me to do is to give up four-fifths of our income to the starving; live with the utmost simplicity, combined with the most apparent love; *not* cut ourselves off from ordinary company, but bear quiet witness to our faith by what we have become and therefore are. But, within circumstances, we must entertain these

175

foreign guests with a will – worse for S because she has to do by far the most of the work; worse for me because I find the company more agonising than she does. It will be a small, ridiculous but real triumph if they leave on Friday believing that we were both delighted by their visit.

◆ ◆ ◆

Is it presumptuous of me to believe that I need as much courage to endure this company with smiles and chatter as the saints have ever needed to kiss their lepers? In fact they would not be proper saints unless they kissed their lepers with joy; with *real* joy. Imagine kissing a leper, but wrinkling up one's nose in disgust! Very much my style in too many of my efforts at amendment; trying, as I've put it before, to live far beyond my moral means.

2 July

There is, perhaps, more 'merit' – odious word! – in giving one's time and chat to ordinary people who are in no special need, rather than to desperate people who feel that I alone can help them. The mild but very important cause of courtesy.

◆ ◆ ◆

More thoughts on TV programme called 'Spiritual Experience'. The oddity of these breakthroughs surely lies in this: that they can some- times be won by arduous years of sanctification, yet sometimes they happen out of the blue to ordinary people in quite ordinary circumstances.

◆ ◆ ◆

Polytheism. There may be more to be said for this than we usually assume. Perhaps it makes more sense to say that God is both One and Many, rather than that he is only One or Many. Christians worship God in three forms, however much they may insist that all these three are really 'the same'. Why not, then, worship Krishna or Siva or Vishnu or Brahma or Kali . . . according to one's present inclination? One might regard them as different aspects of a single Godhead. Or one might regard them as genuinely separate – though never, in any rational pantheon, in conflict.

◆ ◆ ◆

When these instructions arrive from Amnesty International to send off express letters to some Minister for the Interior – copies to the Ambassador in London – I immediately do as I'm told. The cases are

176

always appalling; heart-rending. Yet I must admit that my first re-action to seeing the Amnesty envelope is not joy at the chance of help-ing fellow-creatures in great affliction, but dismay at the thought of an hour's complicated work, just when I wanted to be doing this or that.

◆ ◆ ◆

The latest fashion always takes the form of being against what is thought to be the current fashion. Thus hardly anybody now dares to call himself a Liberal Christian, for fear of being associated with all those musty old figures like Colenso, Bishop Barnes and the nineteenth-century German Protestant theologians. And it's true, of course, that this tradition ran right into the sand with the Death of God books of ten to fifteen years ago. Yet liberal is just what we have to go on being – tolerant, thoughtful, adventurous, but knowing the difference between baby and bath-water.

◆ ◆ ◆

Non-malicious conversation about people is the most tolerable form of small-talk. But it only really works with someone not seen for some time. 'Getting up to date on X, Y and Z . . .'

◆ ◆ ◆

'God speaks to man through the natural world and through that world in *all* its aspects or not at all.' David Cockerell, in *Theology*. Why on earth should this assumption be made? God does not speak to me through Himmler.

3 JULY
Two people are arguing fiercely and with personal venom. But just below that surface of self-righteous bluster each feels that he is really wrong: that he *must always* be wrong.

Just after writing this, a very good letter from Sister Benedicta saying that we should feel in the wrong as much as possible. That this may well be God's way of pushing us forward.

◆ ◆ ◆

We probably tend to know our own faults better than we know our virtues. But we never shall know either as God does.

4 JULY
Let us today be almost *preposterous* in our courtesy to one another.

◆ ◆ ◆

'To the superficial observer orthodoxy appears to be faith in the highest degree, but in reality it is only attachment to an institution . . . ' Père Comblin.

5 JULY
Jason and Chrissie for the weekend. It is strange and almost eerie how much the present tension between them resembles the tension between S and me at the time of the BH community. There is no doubt of their deep love for each other, but Jason longs to put his moral ideas into better practice; live a more co-operative and frugal life. Chrissie wants the normal freedom of a person living normally in our society; and believes, in any case, that Jason is incapable of living the way he claims to be longing for.

I felt much sympathy with both; but tried above all to tell Jase that there are never only two possible extremes; that the many ways in between do not have to be disreputable compromises but may be new openings to unimagined new ways of living, feeling, thinking and hoping.

How often it has seemed to me that life must be either this or that. But what emerged was not only neither of the two perceived alternatives; it wasn't even a mixture of the two. Thank God for the unexpected.

6 JULY
Terrifying reports from the USA in today's *Observer*: the Hawks rampant, and a growing belief that a nuclear war can be won. Also a rather lordly article by Conor Cruise [O'Brien] putting down the nuclear disarmers with the help of Simone Weil. I want to write an article in reply: or rather an article which will express my revived passion for the old CND line in its simplest and most extreme form; that is, total and unilateral nuclear disarmament by the UK, including, of course, the sending back of all American missiles.

I must get my ideas straight about this. Fundamentally they are the same as they were when I was – very inadequately – campaigning for CND in the late fifties. But I hope there is a stronger moral element now; a little less fear for my own skin. (Still plenty of that, though.)

◆ ◆ ◆

Perhaps the terrible doctrine of predestination is partly right after all: not that God wills some to receive his grace and some to be denied it; but that some are simply born accessible to grace and some born impervious to it. This would explain why some of the resuscitated have reported experiences of joy and glory, while others remember nothing at all. It would explain to me why I have never received a particle of grace, as reported so wonderfully by the fortunate ones.

So some really are saved – i.e. for a further life on a higher level; and others are really damned – i.e. to eternal oblivion at death. I have no doubt that I would be among the damned if this were true.

(But do I write that in the knowledge that if I believed myself to be saved I'd probably be damned for that alone? We are all publicans now, if we remember what the parable tells us about the two. 'I am damned – [*sotto voce*] which at least gives me a sporting chance of being saved.' Oh these toils of self-consciousness in which so many of us writhe and squirm!)

7 JULY

A day of many frustrations, but I kept my irritability almost entirely out of sight (one quick frenzy about posting letters).

For one thing, I realised this morning that the first twenty pages of my 'fair copy' were very bad; heavy, over-explanatory, solemnly egotistical. The process is that I write the original flash of inspiration in my pocket notebook; then type out a first version of this; finally retype and, in principle, perfect. There is a varying time-lag between these processes, and it was only two weeks ago that I began the fair copy of the journal for last October. There had been, I recognise now, that familiar growing discomfort, like a swelling boil or a groaning stomach: and then, this morning, the eruption at last. I knew that the whole of this new beginning would have to be ruthlessly slashed, changed and retyped.

This gives great relief, of course, but not on the first day. All I can feel just now is irritation with myself for wasting these two weeks on writing trash: and shame that I can still write so badly after all these years.

Yes, but by this evening relief has come. And I thank God that I saw how much was strong at such an early stage. To be, now, lighter in every sense – brisker, funnier (if possible), less repetitive, simpler yet more elegant. Yes, an *unobtrusive* elegance.

◆ ◆ ◆

I suddenly remember that this is the day when management and printers are settling the fate of the *Observer*.

◆ ◆ ◆

God and Pain. I believe that he tries to ease all pain except the pain that he can use. But the pain that he can use is only a very small proportion of all the pain there is in the world. Most of it springs from harsh physical privation, and is a stupefying, even brutalising affair which God can hardly ever pierce.

◆ ◆ ◆

Ramakrishna again. I see more than ever that the metaphysics don't matter. In fact my dislike of metaphysics has become almost as great as Freddie's – though we each direct our dislike from diametrically opposite metaphysical platforms. I was bothered the first time I read this book – ten or twelve years ago – by Mother Kali and all the rest of the pantheon. But I now see very clearly – so I believe – that these are simply forms of worship; good in so far as they help us to know the love of God, bad when they present themselves as savage destroyers etc.

As for the metaphysics – there may be Unity, Godhead, Brahma, the Absolute, etc. behind everything, but nearly all of us surely do best not to bother our heads about this. (I know from experience how my own head used to be bothered to frenzy by trying to meditate on this vast and impersonal abstracting.) Far better that we stick to the foreground of *obvious* dualism: God and Man, Heaven and Earth; that we worship our personal god or gods as beings of limited power but of unlimited love.

Ramakrishna could and did transfer his ecstatic love from Kali to Krishna, Ram, etc.; from Kali to Allah; from Kali to Jesus. But he always came back to Kali again. This is not artificial syncretism, but the natural generosity of heart and vision of a great saint. Very different from the Brahmo Somaj movement which tried to create and organise a new synthesis of Christianity and Hinduism – a hopeless enterprise.

◆ ◆ ◆

New arm movements at prayer now; wider, freer, happier. And the firm resolve to pray more – i.e. to make prayer more part of the substance of my life.

> Heavenly Mother,
> Light of the World,
> Help us to know your love.

8 JULY
Only just received Julian Mitchell's *New Statesman* review of *Friends Apart*, though I knew of its existence at least two weeks ago. It was very good, as Julian had told me it would be:

Friends Apart . . . is a classic account, in the form of a memoir of two friends, of the moral, political and amatory confusions of a young middle-class Communist in the thirties. It reminds us how very unstraightforward things actually were, how unsimple the issues . . .

One longs to hear more, for another version of those years, using, say, Castle Howard and Tonypandy as the poles; or the Liberal Girls of the great country houses and the international students he led on a delegation to Spain.*

However, he is quite wrong in thinking that I could go on exploiting that particular seam. God knows I've mulled over my own past more than enough already.

◆ ◆ ◆

Sheila Cassidy sent me her book *Prayer for Pilgrims*, which I've begun reading with great enjoyment. This, for example: 'We should think of prayer as an art which will only develop with care and perseverance and continued practice throughout our lifetime.'

9 JULY
How strange that the miracles of Jesus were once such a stumbling-block: and perhaps still are for some. How strong it must have been, that dogma of nature's 'immutable' laws.

I am sure that Jesus *could* have walked on the water quite easily, whether he did so or not. And that he would have regarded this feat as something of very little importance.

◆ ◆ ◆

In the middle of many good prayers I suddenly thought of Phine and her confirmation. True, I have thought about it with pleasure quite often in the last few days; but why did it never even occur to me that I should go up to London for it? Deep shame at my usual self-preoccupation. I shall ring her up tomorrow and find out when it is to be; or whether it has already happened.

But the prayers *are* good – wide and happy gestures.

Resolved, on Sheila Cassidy's advice, to make a real effort at continual prayer. So the happy thought came to me, why not buy an alarm watch and set it to go off as a reminder, say every half-hour! Any excuse for a new toy. Grotesque!

◆ ◆ ◆

*Excerpts from Julian Mitchell's review supplied by editor.

Deep in my re-reading of Isherwood's *Ramakrishna*. O you great lord and saviour, if only I had known you I might have learned how to love God. This book moves me even more deeply this time than when I first read it ten years ago. A true gospel of our time.

He told Vivekananda that 'religion is not for empty stomachs'. But Isherwood goes on to point out that he never exalted social service above spiritual training. 'The stomachs must be filled, certainly; but the fillers of the stomachs must first be trained to fill them, and trained spiritually as well as technically.'

What radiant charm and humour he had! How I would have loved him!

◆ ◆ ◆

A very kind and friendly review of *Friends Apart* in *Tribune*: 'Toynbee has written honestly and movingly of the passing, not only of dear friends, but of a space in our history which has gone for ever. As he writes in his Introduction, it is only possible to see this now that "the thirties" has acquired a special meaning and set of associations. The book was first published in 1954, but its focus is even sharper to us now in the eighties.'*

And a letter from dear Decca† to say that she has ordered many copies and is plugging it with a publisher friend.

10 JULY
I have to confess that I find the general tone of Ramakrishna more sympathetic than that of the N T Jesus. Certainly he never abused – let alone condemned to eternal flames – those who rejected and mocked him. On the other hand, that humour and playfulness and frequent lightness of touch are just what the evangelists might have left out.

In any case I would never dream of leaving my Church and becoming a Vedantist. My reason for staying has never been a personal loyalty to Jesus, but a strong association with the whole Christian tradition of thought and worship.

◆ ◆ ◆

Looking at my father's photograph: 'Either you know now, or you are in a blank of eternal ignorance. At least you no longer share our nagging uncertainty.'

◆ ◆ ◆

* Excerpt supplied by editor.
† Jessica Mitford, a close friend of Philip and Sally Toynbee and author of a memoir of PT, *Faces of Philip*, published by Heinemann in 1984.

Ygdael Yadin, alas! How much we admired, and almost loved him in Israel. But now he is a politician like the others, committing himself to the appalling policy of his Prime Minister; the brutal settling of the occupied Arab territories.

◆ ◆ ◆

Ramakrishna. That brilliant common sense which is one of the essential signs of a great master; the deep knowledge of what men are as well as of what they could be.

◆ ◆ ◆

So I telephoned Phine to ask whether she would like me to come to her confirmation. But it was done last Saturday. Alas – yet some base relief as well that, despite the shame, I would not have the journey to London.

11 July

I said to S, in the course of some quite innocuous conversation, that I thought our lives 'disgusting'. She was offended. But of course I think this of any rich people who live in a starving world and do virtually nothing about it. And, if I exempted her, that really would be patronising and self-righteous: *I* am aware of our moral obloquy, but you, poor unthinking little thing, how could anyone blame *you* for being so morally insensitive?

◆ ◆ ◆

Lost my false teeth again, but this time evidently for good. I became frantic and almost hysterical. Why? Partly the intolerable conundrum of where they could possibly be: then, secondly, the sense of that ever-threatening chaos sending a sudden tentacle into my carefully ordered life: only third, the bloody inconvenience of eating pap and having to pay several time-consuming visits to the dentist.

So much – yet again – for all my prayers; all my striving for the peace of God. How terribly easily I am thrown in this way.

◆ ◆ ◆

Proofs of a new book by Don Cupitt called *Taking Leave of God*. So these extraordinary parsons continue to abandon their faith: but instead of weeping for the loss and leaving the Church they seem to rejoice in their splendid freedom, and preach atheism from behind a dog-collar. Madness!

◆ ◆ ◆

This is what I would now say to the unbeliever: 'Take a hundred and one just men; honourable, thoughtful and trustworthy. Suppose you discover that a hundred say they've had no religious experience whatever; but the hundred-and-first says that he has what he can only describe as direct experience of God. Then the negative testimony weighs nothing against the positive. Any more than the millions who had never seen Australia weighed against Captain Cook and his crew.'

On the other hand, if many of the hundred, hearing the hundred-and-first's inevitably stuttering description, said, 'Ah, yes: we have had experiences like that, but we do not interpret them as experiences of God; only of something deep within ourselves', then things become much more difficult.

♦ ♦ ♦

Sheila Cassidy: 'We must make prayer our first priority and arrange the rest of our lives accordingly.' Right: yet even I, with so much time, it would seem, utterly fail to do this. Renewed resolutions.

♦ ♦ ♦

I've at last begun John Oman's *Grace and Personality*, long out of print but sent me from Collins by Pierre at my request. It is said to be the classic (1917) theological work which adopts my position of God's power being solely the power of love. So far I find it a difficult but rewarding book, but one which shows no sign of going so far as to strip God of all his imperial omnipotence.

From this book: 'The faith which does not rely wholly upon God, but partly on exciting or disciplining its own soul, lives in valetudinarian anxiety about its spiritual health.' Right on! Don't I know it!

And this: 'The supreme hindrance to the coming of God's kingdom is idolatry, not evil-doing.' Of course they are very often the same thing; but this is the right place to put the emphasis.

♦ ♦ ♦

I do see, after a day of such frustration and humiliation, that I am probably in need of being even more heavily crushed than I have been so far. Not that I want to beat my breast; but I may have to be brought not only to my knees but down to the ground with my face pressed into the dung.

How melodramatic this sounds; and perhaps false. Yet it is a real feeling for sure; a true sense that what is still unbearable in me is the cocky little ego, who seems to swing up again whenever he's knocked down, with the impudence of a weighted doll.

♦ ♦ ♦

The roses in front of the house, which I've tended with such care, must have been blooming for several weeks. Yet I *saw* them for the first time this evening, and then only because the weeds are now so intolerably high.

My mind is utterly concentrated on building the walls and laying the paving in the middle of the garden. And how easily I become blind like this to everything except the immediate object of my attention.

14 JULY
'All in all I do my best,' writes Sheila Cassidy in her book on prayer. This has come to seem a modest claim; and I'm sure she meant it to be that. In fact it is a tremendous assertion; for how can we ever know what our best might be? No one would say, 'I am as perfect as it is possible for me to be.'

♦ ♦ ♦

'Despite any feelings we may have of grief or pleasure, God wants us to realise by faith that we are in fact more in heaven than on earth. Our faith comes from the natural love of our soul, and the clear light of our reason, and the stability of our mind, given by God when he first made us. And when our soul was breathed into our body, and our senses began to work, at once mercy and grace began to work too, in pity and love caring for us and preserving us.' Dame Julian.

♦ ♦ ♦

'Religion [is not] a device for reinforcing morality . . . The Beatitudes take a different road. They start from the view that a good will is primarily of insight, not of effort.' Oman.

Compare the strong Buddhist insistence on overcoming ignorance; on achieving understanding; which is often neglected in Christianity. (And this doesn't, of course, mean intellectual understanding or insight.)

♦ ♦ ♦

It seems to me that glibness is one of the worst faults of religious writing; just because there can be no real verification in this sphere we should be extra careful not to flit away into airy nothings.

♦ ♦ ♦

Looking again at the reproductions of Caspar David Friedrich. How beautiful the best of them are; Romanticism at its undemonstrative, melancholy best. A world forever at twilight.

16 JULY

We learn from the news this morning that negotiations between management and printers have at last broken down; so it seems virtually certain that the *Observer* will fold at last. After how many years – perhaps as many as twelve – of teetering on the brink of disaster.

Of course my first thought is for myself – I mean, of course, alas, my first thought is for myself. Will I be able to get a job somewhere else; perhaps on the *Sunday Times*? How will we live if I can't? I shall presumably get my half-pay pension; and there is the capital we got from the sale of Barn House. So we will quite comfortably survive in any case, though I may have to start making my own beer again!

And I know that I am very lucky compared with most of the others. I was to retire next year in any case, though Terry★ and I had agreed that I would still do regular work for the paper after that. In fact I now know very few people personally who work for the *Observer*; so many of the old guard are dead or gone; and I cannot possibly feel the same warm emotions towards the paper as I did in the gallant fifties, when there were only a dozen of us on the editorial side, and we, together with the two or three porters and messengers, really were a band of brothers and sisters.

But this is the only institution to which I have ever given part of my heart and all of my loyalty. It is appalling for the hundreds who will lose their jobs. It is sad, if not worse, for the country that one of its few good newspapers should disappear.

But I suppose the blow hasn't hit me squarely yet. There is to be more news this afternoon; so perhaps there may be a last chance of survival.

17 JULY

I see no reason at all why traditional Christian faith should not be both broadened and deepened and intensified. That is the task.

◆ ◆ ◆

I am not sure – just now – that God exists: yet I have never been so sure that without faith in him we are done for.

◆ ◆ ◆

'As we do battle in our souls with some apparently unreasonable demand of God, we both weep at the unfairness of it and at the same

★ Terence Kilmartin, Literary Editor of the *Observer*.

time gain strength from the "certainty born of faith" that out of this pruning will certainly come new growth.'

This, from Sheila Cassidy, was just what I wanted to hear; urgently needed to hear.

◆ ◆ ◆

'Grace is grace precisely because, *though wholly concerned with moral goodness, it does not at all depend on how moral we are.*' Oman. This is almost that one book which I've been searching for so long.

◆ ◆ ◆

I once knew a scholar who was also a strong and triumphalist R C. He was the narrowest, most arrogantly intellectually snobbish man I've ever known. How far from God he seemed. (But this is not for us to say.)

◆ ◆ ◆

On certain days we are truly a microcosm of the terrible world outside. Lebanon, Cambodia, Iran, El Salvador, Russia, South Africa – they are all here, in this raging and God-forsaken cottage.

◆ ◆ ◆

How many occasions when it seems right – essential – for one person to make a humble apology to the other: but never quite right for the other person to receive it.

18 JULY
More and more convinced that justice is a human invention; a stop-gap which is necessary for us because we cannot love each other enough to do without it. Therefore it is anthropomorphic blasphemy to talk of the justice of God.

◆ ◆ ◆

The deep fault of Sheila Cassidy's in many ways excellent book is that she always assumes that prayer will at some time, or in the end, be rewarded by joy and true communication with God. For me prayer seems like an endless slog which must be slogged through to the very end. Perhaps this journal should be called *Red Queen Running*. And each new volume *Red Queen Still Running*.

19 JULY
Josephine, who read anthropology, suggested a brilliant image of

anthropologists at their fieldwork. A lot of people are sitting round a fire; some holding out their hands to it; some warming their backs; some just sitting and staring into it; some cooking on it; some poking it . . . The anthropologists report all these various postures and gestures, but never say a word about the fire. Excellent!

20 JULY
One of the sternest lessons of life and faith is that self-pity is *never* justified. (On the other hand, *if* one is ill it is mere stupidity to pretend that one is not.)

24 JULY
A very enjoyable visit to Lucy and Bernard. In spite of her decision to become a doctor – and that she's already begun working on her own for the three A-levels she will need before even starting her medical course – Lu is tormented by acute social guilt. She feels that she ought to go and work with Mother Teresa, or some equivalent, and her anguish about this is as genuine as Jason's is about the duty to live and work more co-operatively. I try to say that we mustn't try to live above our moral means, etc. – that it is humility, not cynicism, to accept the moral obligations of where we are. But I know that their moral means are considerably greater than mine.

In the local Dunchurch pub, the terrible faces of two prison officers from Olney. What horrors are going on behind walls all over this green and pleasant land through which we've been driving – Gloucester, Evesham, Stratford, Warwick . . .

25 JULY
'One must accept joyfully and with the whole will exactly the state of prayer which God makes possible for us here and now; we will have that and no other.' Dom John Chapman.

But perhaps he wills us to pray better, to come closer, and it is our failure – not his decision – which makes us pray our meagre prayers.

The most conspicuous fact about the world – now that we know so much about the horrors going on everywhere – is God's failure to reach the afflicted, try as he may; try, as my faith tells me, that he unceasingly does.

And after starting to read a history of Spain lent me by Bill, to prepare myself for our expedition to Seville in October, I am reminded again that history is an almost uninterrupted scream of pain.

◆ ◆ ◆

Now it seems that the *Observer* is really sunk at last. I might be able to board another ship; shall get a hand-out in any case; so I try, not very successfully, to think of all the others who have no such compensations.

28 JULY

Strange to learn that Benjamin Britten was never a believing Christian, considering how churchy he must have been; liturgically inclined, even.

◆ ◆ ◆

As I reached the (Bruegel) plough this evening, and my prayer to 'The Work of God', I suddenly saw the word as meaning his working like yeast rather than a plough: the little portion of yeast within, which can make the whole person ferment with love and joy. (But my yeast is almost entirely quiescent.)

Also at prayer I suddenly remembered that the test match was just reaching an exciting stage. Should I cut short my prayers to watch it? A sense that this 'temptation' was simply too childish and silly – as if this really mattered to anyone but me. In the event I compromised, shortening my prayer *a little* before watching the calamitous start of England's second innings. And as those four wickets fell for eighteen runs I was saying my most familiar prayer, with a comical and unexpected relevance:

> Heavenly Mother,
> Light of the world,
> Have Mercy on us.

◆ ◆ ◆

Reading a Dick Francis thriller till late at night; and how grateful I felt to that brilliant writer for taking me so firmly and engagingly away on a fantastic journey into his exotic world of jockeys and trainers, bloodstock, breeders and beautiful horses.

◆ ◆ ◆

If the widow's mite, then what about the millionaire miser's £1,000 which he forced himself, in a sweat of agony, to give to a good cause? Doesn't he deserve at least as much praise as she?

(Still suffering from the guilt renewed by our talk with Lu. She agreed with me that our lives are 'disgusting'. By any obvious standard all of us – all us reasonably well-heeled people in this world – are guilty of mortal sin every minute of our lives. For we are consciously allowing people to die rather than reduce our own comfort.)

Another magnificent passage from Oman: 'The supreme moral defect is not the lack of a good conscience, but the limitation of our insight which makes it so extremely easy to have a good conscience.' As Gerry said once, Buddhism is better than Christianity at least in this respect – its insistence on the importance of overcoming (spiritual) ignorance; on insight, true self-examination and understanding.

(But what if one has the insight to understand one's own perpetual sin, but not the strength to overcome it? I suppose this means that the 'insight' is a fake: real insight into the suffering in East Africa just now would *force* S and me to disgorge.)

29 JULY
Our good friend Jean M believes in transubstantiation. Was I shocked by this? Yes, a little; though I felt in no way divided from her.

◆ ◆ ◆

Married life: how little Christianity has had to say about the reality of this extraordinary institution.

◆ ◆ ◆

When S is angry with me, she says, among much else, that I give people who don't know me well a grossly false picture of myself as some sort of holy man. I know what she means. Talking to Jean M today, I detected a sort of earnest, honest, almost-stuttering *sincerity*. This is not in any sense deliberately put on; yet it may well give a false impression. I am more devious, and far more self-absorbed, than that.

◆ ◆ ◆

'Peace.
God lives in me.'

I mean 'in Heavenly Grace'!

◆ ◆ ◆

Two favourite proverbs of Newman's: 'Holiness rather than peace' and 'Growth is the only evidence of life'.

Archbishop Tait: 'The great evil is that the liberals are deficient in religion, and the religious are deficient in liberality.'

Just as true today as then. (All three from David L. Edwards's excellent book, *Leaders of the Church of England, 1828–1978*.)

31 JULY

In Monmouth: how prosaic but how real is that sadness of old age at the sight of a particularly attractive girl: 'Not for me! Never again for me!'

But the truth is that she would almost certainly have been just as inaccessible to me when I was in my roaring heyday. How seldom I ever dared to make a pass except when too plastered to make it with any real hope of success.

1 AUGUST

A very simple, very bright flash: 'It is impossible that we are the best there is.'

2 AUGUST

Utterly convinced that the world cannot be saved except by a wide acceptance of God's love. But almost everywhere the power of that love is blocked, denied, ignored.

◆ ◆ ◆

Showed S my much-revised 'Servant Cavalier', and she was so moved by it that I really did have a fantastic conviction that it will win the prize.

There is something almost paranoiac about the way I am hiding my traces as I send in my entries. The deep conviction that almost all poets are deeply hostile to my work: and indeed many of them reviewing the published volumes of *Pantaloon* more or less ordered me off their territory. What a triumph it would be to win that prize! (But how unlikely!)

6 AUGUST

Dame Julian: 'He kindles our understanding, he directs our paths, he eases our consciences, he comforts our soul, he lightens our heart.'

'[God's] love that cannot, will not, be broken by sin, is rock-like, and quite astonishing.'

7 AUGUST

Reflections on booze. Nowadays I seldom get drunk, except on rare and entirely suitable occasions. But I know very well how much drink still dominates my life. The need to avoid all situations where there might not be enough, and therefore all social contact would become like holding up a raw wound to the wind. The need, equally, to avoid all occasions where I might drink too much and the result would be humiliation, sickness, remorse.

Yet I know – admittedly from only about three months' experience – that any attempt to stop altogether would lead to even greater constriction; greater pain.

◆ ◆ ◆

On the telly: wild Iranian 'students' in the USA simply out to cause all the trouble they can; and a wild American crowd shouting back at them: 'NUKE I-RAN! NUKE I-RAN! NUKE I-RAN!' The terrible wide world from which I try to hide myself away here.

◆ ◆ ◆

Sometimes the sudden recognition of a fault committed during the day thuds in the stomach like a blow: 'Oh God, did I say *that*; think *that*; do *that!*' Not gross sins; but the usual acts of nasty querulousness; impatience; irritation. Yes, I am a querulous man; and this is gross enough when it colours large patches of our lives.

10 AUGUST
After yet another painful and shaming fracas I find myself almost shouting at the sky, 'Why can't you leave us *alone*? Why do you *keep on* rubbing our noses in the mess of our lives?' But this, of course, is quite contrary to my theology, such as it is. I do believe that it is our own ungodly natures which lead us to scrap and snarl and yap like wretched dogs; and I do believe that God alone can help us to live in loving peace together.

Oh but I do wish that he would/could help us *more*!

◆ ◆ ◆

Hard, dull, grinding garden work; dragging yet more earth down from under the yew to fill up the space all round the upper pond. At the moment there is no pleasure in this work; and the major technical difficulties seem more a threat than a challenge.

◆ ◆ ◆

'. . . a new beginning and an eternal one. To this new beginning all his blessed children born to him by nature shall be brought to him again by grace.' Dame Julian.

Yes, born in nature to be potentially channels and vehicles of his grace: born anew to receive his grace. But the normal state of the journeying man is surely the very wretched one of knowing that all

192

this is so, yet finding himself still incapable of making himself available to the grace of God.

She also writes that 'Neither grace nor nature work independently of each other, nor can they ever be separated.' If this is so, I have never been able to recognise that it is so. To me nature remains a possible field for the operation of God and man together; but *in itself* utterly godless, neutral, indifferent.

◆ ◆ ◆

'The Hope of God.' As I pray this prayer my eye is on the small bird against the far white pinnacle in *Icarus*. He is tiny in the picture, but only he can fly out of the picture if he wishes; and only by following him, with our eyes at least, can we follow him into that wider freedom of the spirit: of heaven.

◆ ◆ ◆

If only my life could flow more *sweetly*; instead of all this clambering and clawing. Each day I embark like a deep-sea fisherman, taking to the dangerous seas which lie all round the safety of my room. To any outside observer this would seem a preposterous thing to say; but I know what inner failings threaten me at every point.

Yet I still believe that each day should be glorious; and even more glorious than the day before.

11 AUGUST

I ran round the loop-road in very heavy rain, and remembered another run like this about two years ago. But then I was in a state of elation, almost joy: this time it was with the good but quieter sense of having managed at least to get a certain grip on the day's events; writing a difficult review, and now making use of the rain which had made all garden-making impossible. Of course, I know that we are never in control of circumstances; but sometimes a little more than others.

◆ ◆ ◆

Laura's T-shirt with VIVA ROSSINI! stuck all across her chest. Delightful. How she has come alive through her love of music; and of Rossini in particular. She gets tough biographies out of the Gloucester library and really reads them; devours them. It is an aesthetic and intellectual passion; and I must admit that I had not thought she would be capable of it.

◆ ◆ ◆

'It is the property of the eternal law of God that he who will not be ruled sweetly by him, shall be ruled as a punishment by himself; that he who, of his own will, throws off the sweet and light yoke of charity shall unwillingly suffer the insupportable burden of his own self-will.' St Bernard.

Wonderful! But I do not think this is God's law so much as the incomprehensible law of the way things happen to be. For I believe, with Dame Julian, that God would save and glorify every one of us if he could. And may do so yet!

12 AUGUST
So down come the grouse on all the moors of the North! But I dislike the people engaged in this sport more than I pity the birds: entirely the wrong way round.

◆ ◆ ◆

It seemed likely that there would be a major BBC programme about *Part of a Journey*; but this has fallen through. On the telephone Pierre suggests a reproduction of Michelangelo's *Creation of Adam* for the cover – which I use in that first volume as a symbol of man stretching towards God, God towards man, and the fingers just not touching.

◆ ◆ ◆

Appalled tonight at the oppression of our enormous ignorance. I felt closed in, blinded and deafened by ignorance. So much – I guess; I *know* – lies *through* those symbols on my shrine; through every material object that we see or feel. And this material world, which seems to block us everywhere, should be itself a way out of itself.

At least on that wet run I was looking again; looking, in particular, at the luxuriant hedges of this drenched summer, and resolving to keep my eyes more open and alert from now on.

13 AUGUST
TV programme on communications with composers. The admirable Rosemary Brown, whose sincerity is beyond doubt: the even more admirable John Lill, whose great intelligence and deep musical knowledge make his beliefs all the more convincing. But they ended with a wretched buffoon who talked about writing oratorios for Handel – of which they played an unspeakable specimen – and of all the great musicians inhabiting Jupiter. What a thud! But this is a world of loonies and dotties, with the light shining through it only in rare cases.

◆ ◆ ◆

Re-reading the *Gita*. I find it has a lulling effect. But when I do pay proper attention I am depressed by the whole doctrine of striving for honourable extinction.

♦ ♦ ♦

For the last few weeks I've been deeply preoccupied with the Arvon Poetry Prize – polishing and cutting my four fragments of *Pantaloon*. At times two of them seem so good to me that I cannot imagine them not winning prizes. At more rational times I recognise that the competition will be gigantic – this must be the biggest prize ever offered for poetry – and that even if my entries are good enough to get prizes they're all too likely to be lost in the rush.

Still, it is a good exercise. And I am glad to find that I can write in that way as well as ever.

And if I won – what a *colossal* triumph! Plus the certainty of *Pantaloon* getting eagerly published. Plus . . . HUSH!

14 AUGUST

Jean Hughes rang up S to tell us that Norman died on Tuesday.

When we arrived at Barn House in 1960 the visiting parson told me that a Rugby schoolmaster of mine was living just below us. I told him that we'd have to sell the house and move *at once*; really meant it too, for I have grim memories of nearly all of them. But when I heard it was Norman I was delighted; one of the two or three I had really liked. We differed deeply on politics, etc., but had many very enjoyable talks during the last twenty years about books, history, etc. A charming and amusing man.

But since we moved to Woodroyd we have seen much less of them. And when I heard of his death my immediate thought, after horror for poor Jean, was, 'Oh God, why didn't we see more of them! My wretched isolationism! And now it's too late for ever and ever . . .' (Very quick intrusion of the old EGO, as usual.)

Thinking of Norman tonight, and wondering whether he is not 'in the light', I suddenly found our ignorance quite maddening and terrible. Why? *Why*? WHY? Why life? Why death? Why anything?

Have faith! In what? In faith. But I also know that my faith is all take and virtually no give. I want so much from God; and feel that until he gives me something I shall have nothing whatever to give him.

♦ ♦ ♦

Dentist's waiting rooms. Quite long periods in ours for S and myself. At least I now make some positive use of such occasions; never reading; trying hard to pray.

♦ ♦ ♦

How did I live so long without faith; or at least without this constant worrying at faith, as dog with bone? Because I was still able to put my hope in worldly success: fame and acclamation. Above all, in the eventual triumph of *Pantaloon*. But suppose, now, that I win the Arvon prize; that *Part of a Journey* is a wild success; that *Pantaloon* is published and adulated: all that would be dust and ashes. *Delicious* dust and ashes, of course, but no more sustaining for that.

Or am I fooling myself about this? Do I crave the literary recognition I believe I deserve; and do I feel held back by this unfinished business? I sometimes imagine that if I could once get all that behind me, *then* I could really concentrate on the Spirit.

Illusion upon illusion, I dare say.

16 AUGUST
The concentration on ethics – on 'being good' – leads, says Bonhoeffer (Merton quoting and agreeing), to our being forced to live 'in the glaring and fatiguing light of incessant consciousness'.

Yes, that is the horror: the self-reformer is, alas, often more bound up with his own self than the sinner. It is possible, after all, to be an *innocent* sinner; a happy-go-lucky, thoughtless, agreeable, selfish bastard. I imagine that God is even more bored with us self-tormenting self-reformers than with those light-weight rascals.

◆ ◆ ◆

Norman's funeral, in the little Tintern church; his grave almost on the river bank. And beautiful weather, for a rare change. Jean obviously in great grief, but she is very brave and stoical. Odd to think that I was probably his only ex-pupil there: the sole representative of generations of Rugby boys!

As poor old M.W. said not long before *his* death earlier this year, 'We are all in the funeral belt now.' But he, the biggest hypochondriac in Monmouth, had suffered many agreeable deaths before the final one took him.

And do I really believe that Norman and M.W. are now in a realm of light? I believe it as much and as little as I can believe that they have been extinguished.

◆ ◆ ◆

Making use of the fine evening, we invited Jeffrey and Nasi over for bowls. It was the greatest fun; certainly far more fun than our long and serious chess evenings used to be.

◆ ◆ ◆

News tonight that the *Observer* is definitely saved at last. Immense relief.

17 AUGUST

Getting to my bedroom tonight after a certain amount of biting and scratching during the day, I began to abuse S in the most violent terms as I walked up and down. I knew at the time that these terms wouldn't do; but the free use of them did me a great deal of good. Dear old Phil's Primal Scream Therapy, I suppose. Having given her hell, I went on to give myself hell too; but not mournfully; with just the same gusto and enjoyment as I'd felt when going for her. Positive exhilaration.

I am both ill-tempered and self-pitying. She is both resentful and implacable. What a combination of combinations! What a nest of two vipers!

Then a wonderful dream in which Steve and other old Barn House friends were inducting me into a new course of the most benign therapy: there was to be a long dancing journey; there were to be girls – many of these were already making themselves available to me; there was to be glorious dope . . . And something of the Spirit as well; as if to make the whole affair utterly guiltless.

This is classic escapism, no doubt; but what a blissful way to escape!

18 AUGUST

God and the World. What I have left out of my 'theology' is God's contemplation of the uncreated, natural, neutral and non-human world. No wonder I left it out, since I can't possibly have the faintest notion of what it even means. But it does bear trying to contemplate.

On the other hand, the danger of pantheism is very real to me: a sloppy and ultimately a useless faith. For, if God is in all things, then all things are of equal value: there is no discrimination: there is no point in choosing or striving. A general mess, in fact.

◆ ◆ ◆

The Hasidim. *Must* make a proper study of them. Meanwhile, my reading of medieval history is gathering real pace and interest. If only I could submerge myself in that: another hide-out, but a richly decorated one.

19 AUGUST

S's sister Susie came yesterday for a three-week visit – her first time out of America. I have always liked her very much, and the fact that

197

we have little obviously in common doesn't matter in the least. She is bright and funny and warm-hearted. Also I enjoy her excited curiosity, and begin to look around me as if with her wondering eyes.

◆ ◆ ◆

'There is a communion with God, and a communion with earth, and a communion with God through earth.' Teilhard de Chardin. And the first is the best, but by far the hardest.

The danger in Teilhard is pantheism – to my mind a far worse mistake than polytheism. To me, at least, it makes sense to suppose that God may be many as well as one: why not?

20 AUGUST

There are times when the best hope for S and me is a common recognition that we both belong to the Community of Fools.

God loves *us*! If this is so then he can only be loving something in us which we are quite incapable of seeing in and for ourselves. (But less incapable of seeing it in others.)

◆ ◆ ◆

The Confucian centuries must surely be very worrying to a thoughtful believer in God. For such a long time so many people lived a worthy and dignified life without the faintest conception of a God of Love.

Yes – we have to say – but they were not living the fullest life available to man. Faith is that extra dimension which makes it possible for a believer to use all his potentialities.

◆ ◆ ◆

The following passage issued by Vatican II is quoted by Merton in *Love and Living*: 'Any act of war aimed indiscriminately at the destruction of entire cities or extensive areas along with their population is a crime against God and man himself. It merits unequivocal and unhesitating condemnation.'

Fine: but if that is what the R C Church really believes, why aren't all its individual members in all countries unilateral disarmers?

Alas, large religious bodies can make admirable statements but seldom feel the need to follow them through.

23 AUGUST

Over-worked in the garden – and at my desk – until I now feel sick with exhaustion. Why? What against? The shame of non-achievement, I suppose. But now I feel a better-deserved shame at giving way again to that utterly destructive inner demon.

Serenity. For me the most inaccessible of all the virtues.

And all this endless self-examination! The young are justifiably introspective, being fascinated by themselves just as they are fascinated by everything else. But I am bored almost to tears by my own person; and regard it far more often as an obstacle between myself and God than a means of reaching God.

◆ ◆ ◆

'All fanaticism is a strategy to prevent doubt from becoming conscious.' Harry Williams, in *The True Wilderness*. I woke at 3.30 a.m. and found myself precisely in that wilderness; found this book a real help in trouble. More so than when I first read it, and felt, for some reason, a bit snooty about it. The point is that he really knows what it is – the dreariness, the self-disgust, the terrible triviality of one's own mind and heart . . .

25 AUGUST

To dinner at Wilson's, with S and Susie. A delightful evening, but for the fact that by the end of it I was stricken dumb, half-oblivious and incapable of self-propulsion by drink. I must have taken secret swigs from one of our host's bottles in the kitchen; for what he served was good drink in sensible amounts.

So I spent the night in his 'hovel', being – I learned next morning – quite unable to negotiate his perilous little path up to the road.

The first gross occasion for many months; but all the old shame and distress. I still find this occasional compulsion very strange.

27 AUGUST

Now I have done all I can to 'In Memoriam: England 1946', the last of the four poems I am submitting for the Arvon Prize. I have improved the original from *Pantaloon* more than I'd thought possible: and I guess that this is the poem they will like best; or dislike least. But my own order would be:

'A Servant Cavalier'
'An Invitation to the Shade of William Butler Yeats'
'In Memoriam: England 1946'
'Possession'.★

★ All four poems are included in the Appendix at the end of this book.

The last, though so very carefully worked, is really a bit too rich a mixture.

◆ ◆ ◆

How far is it possible, or even right, to extend the practice of Christian hope to the social sphere? There is sometimes a dangerous fatuity about social and political optimism – after so many dire lessons in the recent past. Therefore I try to keep down my spirits when I read these intensely exciting reports of the Polish workers' strike.

28 AUGUST

Saints seem to benefit from ill-health – perhaps because they are able to treat it as an additional means of subduing and depleting the ego. But most of us are spiritually as well as physically depleted by constant illness; it horribly concentrates our attention precisely on the suffering and complaining ego.

◆ ◆ ◆

Increasing urge to visit John R, the Tymawr chaplain. I am in no doubt at all that I need help; that my spiritual stagnation is a condition which can only be altered by the Spirit working more effectively through another person.

Physically, psychologically I am a leaky old tub wallowing through the endless sameness of these grey seas. The Spirit is the wind, of which my sails catch scarcely a breath – *kaum einen Hauch*.

◆ ◆ ◆

Perhaps the doctrine of the Incarnation is simply the strongest possible way of saying that God is able to reach man: that heaven does make real contact with earth.

29 AUGUST

W, who used to be a much-admired Dominican, used to say that he drank in order to attain, or at least reach towards, a state of ecstasy. I find, on the other hand, that beer-drinking tends to bind me more firmly to this world. It mildly muffles whatever mild spirituality I may possess, and gives me a very welcome sense of greater security in this fearsome realm of earthly reality.

◆ ◆ ◆

There are times when a book is the only effective anaesthetic. And what a panic I get into – as tonight – when I desperately try one book after another and find that none of them is doing the trick. Tried science-fiction, NT scholarship, medieval history . . . finally lighted on Blessed Symons's *The Quest for Corvo*, which I haven't read for forty years and which was just what I needed.

◆ ◆ ◆

At last I've completed the paved surrounding of the pond, raised a good two feet above its natural level. That central stretch of the garden begins to take shape at last, particularly from my own window. But I cannot say that it has been a labour of love. An anaesthetic element here as well – a warding-off of the afternoon devil: a real grind.

◆ ◆ ◆

Had to do my review of Evelyn Waugh's letters twice over: very rare. An unusually difficult task; chiefly, I suppose, because he has always fascinated me as well as appalled me.

30 AUGUST

> The Lord is everywhere
> And always perfect:
> What does he care for man's sin
> Or the righteousness of man?

This, from the *Gita*, is the absolute contradiction of the whole Judaeo-Christian tradition. How much I prefer this from the *First Letter of John*: 'God is light and in him is no darkness at all. If we say we have fellowship with him while we walk in darkness, we lie and do not live according to the truth; and if we walk in the light, as he is in the light, we have fellowship with one another . . . '

31 AUGUST
At last some sense from Kierkegaard: 'The most tremendous thing which has been granted to man is: the choice, freedom. And if you desire to save it and preserve it there is only one way: in the very same second unconditionally and in complete resignation to give it back to God, and yourself with it.'

   This is the kind of 'hard saying' which reminds us that those who try to reduce Christianity to a form of high-minded humanism are very far from the mark.

◆ ◆ ◆

Jase and Chrissie here to meet Susie. A delightful weekend, though Lucy and Bernard sadly missed. When J was a little boy I used to wonder how I could ever love a full-grown man *as a son*. No difficulty at all, of course.

And it seems – I hardly dare to write it – that the Polish government really has accepted the full demands of the strikers. I haven't felt such exhilaration about a public issue since Dubček – and what happened then!

2 SEPTEMBER

A grotesque situation! At 10 p.m. this evening I realise, with the usual shock, that I haven't given a thought to God or any spiritual matters since the last pause in my garden work at 3.30. But why the hell should it be that way round all the time? What have you done, dear Lord and Mother, to remind me of your ever-loving care and presence?

The task we are set is preposterous. Our lives are crammed with diversions of every kind; physical objects constantly intrude on our attention; there are people to speak to; anxieties to assuage . . . But it is demanded of us that we surmount all these obstacles and live in a state of unremitting worship!

Yes, a preposterous task; but the only one which now seems to me to be worth attempting: and with the full knowledge of almost certain failure.

And certainly the alternative tasks – e.g. to become famous, rich, admired, etc. – seem even more absurd.

3 SEPTEMBER

According to the doctrine of the Atonement the human race was very much in the situation of Lear's Young Lady of Smyrna, whose grandmother threatened to burn her: 'But she seized of the cat, and said, "Granny, burn that! You incongruous old woman of Smyrna."' 'Incongruous' is a good Lear word, but hardly strong enough to describe the savage God of the Atonement.

◆ ◆ ◆

Why do I so much dislike the word 'Christology'? I suppose I feel that so much time and paper has been wasted on these infinitely complex, utterly unrewarding speculations. But some of my recent reading has made me recognise that I have never really faced the problem of Jesus; which must involve, of course, the problem of whether or not I have the right to call myself a Christian. I think I shall have to try to get my ideas a bit more straight; become, in fact, a temporary, crude and blundering Christologist.

5 SEPTEMBER

On my obstacle course it would seem that the major obstacles are Meetings with Other People. But perhaps these should be seen not as obstacles but as special opportunities. An Opportunity Course! If only I could see this life in such heroic and cheerful terms!

◆ ◆ ◆

So the crucifix is the principal symbol of the Polish revolutionaries. I wonder just what it represents for them – the old rock-like Church of Rome as a strange symbol both of their nationhood and of their independence from the Communist state? Or readiness to die for love of God and man?

◆ ◆ ◆

My long deadness to music has now turned into a positive aversion. I cannot bear to listen properly: feel threatened by the sheer boredom of trying to do so. I suppose this will change.

◆ ◆ ◆

A comic and poignant view of human beings. A street-scene viewed from high above, revealing that each person is the centre of a circle of attention which moves about him wherever he goes. In fact each person is the centre of a whole world, his private circle of attention never circumscribed but simply fading away into vaguer and vaguer degrees of consciousness.

◆ ◆ ◆

A very good day of solitude. No doubt we both need them, at regular intervals.

6 SEPTEMBER

But the tap that refused to be turned off instantly released the underlying hysteria of my long exhaustion. I need at least a week's retreat for the peace to sink in any distance below the surface. O Blessed Solitude! (Yes, but what if S were *not* coming back on Monday afternoon? What if she were never coming back? Terror as well as misery, of course.)

◆ ◆ ◆

I decided, in any case, that I would be better at Tymawr than here; so I rang up Sister Paula and was lucky enough to get myself a room for tonight. And now I lie in this very comfortable Michaelgarth bedroom, having done my best to make it resemble my own room at home – tin of cold beans eaten out of the tin with a teaspoon (for I didn't want to face the company of high tea); cans of Newcastle Brown; watch and notebook by my bed; Bisodol and aspirins by the wash-basin . . .

Evensong was good, but Compline was better. A real sense of loving fellowship as we prayed for protection against all the perils of the night. How much I need the united *endorsement* of the Sisters for my peculiar faith!

7 SEPTEMBER

To believe in a God of absolute and unqualified love is not to believe in something less than an omnipotent creator-God but in something very much more. We can quite easily conceive of some huge version of *Homo faber* and *Homo regnens*; but we constantly fail to conceive of a being so unlike ourselves that he creates nothing but love and rules by nothing except the power of love.

◆ ◆ ◆

Who knows how many Christians were martyred under Stalin – i.e. preferred death to giving up their faith. Perhaps more than in all Christian history until then. (For how can we count as Christian martyrs those who were killed by fellow-Christians? And even if we did count that multitude would it equal the perhaps several millions who died unknown and unsung in Russia between, say, 1925 and 1953?)

◆ ◆ ◆

Sister Paula and I were discussing the Pope's proposed visit to England; and thence to the limits of ecumenicism. She said that she could not meaningfully worship with a unitarian, since all her prayer is directed at God through his divine Son. 'But I am a unitarian!' I said. 'And so are half the most thoughtful priests of our Church!' She shrugged, a little sadly. But this did lead me to think about the problem.

To say I will pray with anyone who will pray with me is altogether too sloppy. Should I, could I, pray with the bloodthirsty ayatollahs of Iran? What sense would there be in my 'praying with' a genuinely atheist Buddhist? Needs to be thought very hard about.

◆ ◆ ◆

Sister Paula talked about the Bomb as well; and wondered if I knew of any way to protect cows from radiation. 'More important to protect nuns!' I said. (She was thinking of Tymawr as a place of refuge after the Bomb falls; and of how to feed their refugees.)

How I love that place! How refreshed I felt when I came back here this morning! Then delightful bowls and supper with Jeffrey and Nasi. And so to my quiet bed.

And I have arranged with John Richardson to see him after Evensong on Tuesday – fourth anniversary of my being made an Associate: of my being raised to the status of Brotherhood. ('Brother Philip' still at my place in chapel and in the breakfast room.)

10 SEPTEMBER

To worship Jesus as the (almost invisible) seed of light, whose wonderful though imperfect flower is (*a*) the New Testament, (*b*) all the great Christians ever since, known and unknown.

◆ ◆ ◆

Strange effect of reading Dame Julian immediately followed by a verse or two of the *Gita*. Walking in Monmouth today, in a slight stupor from a bad night, I suddenly felt very *Gita*-like: calm, harmonious, controlled and in order, but without strain. Dame Julian in no way contradicts any of this, but adds the fire of a deeply personal devotion to God; the fire of holy love.

How marvellous to live a *Gita*-like life, but suddenly burn, from time to time, with a Julian-like adoration.

◆ ◆ ◆

Reflections on Susie. A very warm and radically democratic character. No respecter or disrespecter of persons. Yet she is totally non-political, which means that she will vote for Reagan. How much does that matter? A little, I think; though, God knows, the Thoroughly-Politicised Man is a fearsome being indeed!

11 SEPTEMBER

Learned only today that Mrs A's son had a fearful motor-bike accident six weeks ago and has been lying in hospital between life and death ever since. Also, that Ruth P's husband has cancer of the prostate gland. As usual, other people's frightful miseries shame one's own.

12 SEPTEMBER

A hard, tense day. I had a terrible time writing the review of the Schumacher essays, feeling that I was somehow sheering off from what I really wanted to say – namely, WHAT ABOUT GOD? Somehow it seems crude to be so frank; also likely to cause more annoyance than sympathy with his cause.

Then great dissatisfaction with the final (cemented) stones of my largest garden wall. Very uneven, both vertically and horizontally. Trailing flowers will cover this; but I hate to feel that it is so crudely done, even if hardly anyone will be aware of it.

Also, gave Wilson another poem to read; and his obvious evasiveness shows that he hates it. Why did I break my almost invariable practice of keeping such things to myself until publication, if ever? A great mistake, for I now feel deeply discouraged about that bloody prize. *Of course* I won't be one of the winners: must accept that fully before judgement day.

But a very good first meeting with John R. He is open-minded as well as open-hearted. I look forward with great hope to the fortnightly talks we've agreed to have.

13 SEPTEMBER

'C. S. Lewis was a thoroughgoing supernaturalist, believing in the Creation, the Fall, the Incarnation, the Resurrection, the Second Coming, and the Four Last Things.'

Sharply held up by this sentence in the introduction to *Christian Reflections*, I gave up what must be my fourth or fifth attempt to read Lewis. I can't agree that these beliefs are the sign of a thoroughgoing supernaturalist. On the contrary, they represent for me an attempt to domesticate the supernatural. They are like an old map of unexplored regions where guesswork is boldly used: 'Here be monsters' – and Lewis, like all strictly orthodox Christians, is actually prepared to describe the monsters in considerable detail.

The more thoroughgoing a supernaturalist is, the less he finds possible to say about that ineffable domain.

◆ ◆ ◆

Re. our busy mythologisers – a myth is as good as a mile. They mean to use myth as a means of preserving such beliefs as Lewis held, but transforming them all into 'as if'. I'm sure this won't work, tempting though it is.

14 SEPTEMBER

Holy Cross Day, and therefore a very special Sunday for Tymawr (the Society of the Sacred Cross). John R rose to this splendidly with a magnificent sermon. I feel more and more drawn to him, but at the

same time very much aware that he can move in regions which I can
hardly even glimpse.

◆ ◆ ◆

I think I now know what the 'freedom' and 'liberty' of the NT mean.
Oh to be free of this ever-frightened, ever-demanding, habit-
imprisoned self!
  Heavenly Mother, help me to shed it. ('To shed' is a valuable verb.)

◆ ◆ ◆

In David Edwards's lively and stimulating book, *Religion and Change*,
there is one sentence which I cannot swallow at all: 'It is crucial for the
future of religion that its defenders should see that the main weight of
their case can no longer rest on the weakness of man.' What *I* see, with
more and more clarity, is that our devastating weakness is the
strongest of all impulsions towards God. And not just a psychological
need either. *Why* are we so weak? So appallingly self-destructive? If we
were nothing but the products of evolution, one would expect of man
the sort of strength-through-adaptation which all wild animals possess. But God's entry into man has made man-without-God into a
wretched contradiction; a being estranged from the fullness of his
nature; a flying fish which is not aware of the wing-like possibilities of
its fins.

◆ ◆ ◆

'The most painful thing a soul can do is to turn from God through sin.'
Dame Julian. And the second most painful thing a soul can do is to turn
from sin to God.

◆ ◆ ◆

The Pilgrim's Progress. I plough along it at meditation time, with
admiration but without finding myself very deeply involved. But the
Key of Promise which Christian uses to free himself and Hopeful from
Doubting Castle did strike a chord. Do I really believe in the promise
of the NT? After all, Jesus promised very specifically indeed that the
Kingdom would come in the lifetime of his disciples – and he was
utterly wrong.
  But this is not the whole point. There is a real promise in the
NT – that God really does reveal himself to men and through men.

◆ ◆ ◆

Why did I watch the whole two and a quarter hours of that film *The
Battle of Britain*? Partly because I still hero-worship the fighter pilots.
But nearly all the film was very realistic shots of people killing and

207

being killed. 'Seductive', as Jason said, but a horrible seduction. (And reading Len Deighton's brilliant novel about the world of film-makers inflicts the same sort of seduction. An insidious writer – for he is, of course, half in love with what he shows to be so hateful. And I am too. Looking up from this book and trying to say a prayer, I realised that it had moved me miles away from any such possibility. It really is dangerous to immerse ourselves in evil, however remote and exotic a particular form of it may seem.)

◆ ◆ ◆

Even so wise a man as C. H. Dodd can write with a terrible glibness when defending his faith: ' . . . the death and resurrection of Jesus Christ had the character of a decisive conflict in which the powers of evil did their worst and the sovereignty of God was conclusively asserted for the salvation of mankind.'

Conclusively asserted! But think of the horrors of the last two thousand years; and how undiminished they are in our own time. Cambodia alone is enough to show that God has no such sovereignty on earth.

What can be said is that a new seed of light was sown in the N T; that a new possibility for man was presented. But there was no decisive conflict – the conflict goes on and on and on, within each one of us and all around us. A horrible and devastating conflict; not a joyful call to arms. So many millions who have died since the Crucifixion in utter misery, loss, futility.

15 September
Prayers much better than usual; perhaps through something imparted to me by John R. In what way better? More searching: managing to mean more of what I say.

◆ ◆ ◆

Dodd's very good point that Jesus doesn't say, 'Thou shalt love God' – which would be an impossible, even a ridiculous command. He says, 'God is your Father; become what you are, his child.' In other words a sense of total dependence must come first, pace David Edwards.

17 September
I had asked Connie whether she would allow me to dedicate Part of a Journey to her, and had left it with her when we saw her in August. Today came a wonderful letter; very affectionate and explaining her

own religious attitude – very independent, of course – for the first time. Talking of myself as a ten year old, she now adds the adjectives 'lovable' and 'adventurous' to the 'mischievous, imaginative and affectionate' of three years ago.

It is very odd, for, after all, it wasn't only my mother who thought me an impossible monster. I was much disliked and despised at all my schools – until I became a football hero at Rugby.

◆ ◆ ◆

The *Gita* is at least as contradictory as the NT. For example:

> Self-controlled,
> Cut free from desire,
> Curbing the heart
> And knowing the Atman,
> Man finds Nirvana . . .

but:

> Their every action
> Is wed to the welfare
> Of fellow-creatures . . .

and:

> His mind is dead
> To the touch of the external:
> It is alive to the bliss of Atman . . .

but:

> Who burns with the bliss
> And suffers the sorrow
> Of every creature
> Within his own heart . . .
> Him I hold highest
> Of all the yogis.

It almost seems as if the high and frigid doctrine of calm indifference to the world is constantly broken into by the truth of compassion.

◆ ◆ ◆

Why will no Christian face the savage and vindictive fits of rage into which the New Testament Jesus so often fell, promising eternal torment to all who rejected him? Here are some of Dodd's euphemisms:

It is this that gives point to the *tremendous warnings* that Jesus is reported to have uttered about the consequences of rejection . . .

He criticised [the Scribes and the Pharisees], and sometimes in *trenchant terms* . . .

The strictures are *severe enough* . . .

(My italics.)

17 SEPTEMBER

Just now, being in a hurry, I found myself sitting on my bed, smoking, drinking a cup of coffee and trying to cram in my usual prayers. Grotesque! And yet, I thought, if we didn't know that tobacco is a poison, smoking would be a fine sacramental device – as it once was among the American Indians. And no doubt the coffee bean was sacred somewhere or other.

Yes, but in any case the smoking would have not been done with great *empressement*; the coffee drunk was part of a careful ritual. My attempt to have a quick cup, a quick cigarette and a quick prayer all at the same time remains an absurdity; if not an enormity.

18 SEPTEMBER

As I did my shopping in Monmouth today I realised that I was playing the part of a man of almost insistent harmlessness; a man of resounding moderation, good humour and modesty. But later in the afternoon I proved to be not harmless at all, once I was taken out of that public context and returned to the nest. A nasty display of ill-temper, with the usual cat-and-dog as a result.

No! The yoke is not easy and the burden is not light. Or rather, the task of accepting the yoke and lifting the burden is not light but the very hardest that we can be set. *Anima naturaliter Christiana!* On the contrary, the good Christian is a fantastic rarity; a prize specimen. And we ordinary, difficult, inadequate, remorseful men and women are constantly tormented by our inability to resemble these born freaks.

19 SEPTEMBER

I am now as sure as I can be that this constantly recurring lassitude, depletion, exhaustion, is the current form that my depression takes. Yet I must fight against it; for, if I don't, I feel the danger of falling right back again into that pit of four years ago.

◆ ◆ ◆

I wonder if my endless and ludicrous struggle against smoking is a sort of mock-battle; a way of avoiding some far more important demand which is being insistently made on me and which I am consistently avoiding? S says that I am not half so knowledgeable about myself as I suppose, and she may well be right. Yet this accusation pains and annoys me, for self-knowledge is one of the few good qualities which I have always claimed. God alone knows! is probably the answer.

20 SEPTEMBER

Sudden wild nostalgia for my very earliest, cloudiest Communist days; the pamphlet John Cornford sent me at Rugby, a black silhouette of Lenin with arm outstretched against a field of deep maroon; the Parton Street bookshop; my first meeting of the October Club at Oxford . . . How clearly it all comes back to me now, those passionate longings for brotherhood with the whole world and the conviction that my own emancipation, freedom, growth were directly dependent on working for that glorious fraternity. What worlds unfolding! What wild and confident happiness!

Never for a moment have I felt this kind of ecstasy from any of my religious aspirations. And although it is true, of course, that Communism was a god that failed, the *hope* was real enough. Bliss was it in that dawn to be alive – however false the dawn.

And now I feel again the ancient, visionary hope, as my body aches, rumbles and belches, of the freed soul winging away from this gross prison and joining all the company of heaven.

Is this just as great an illusion as the other? Well, it has better credentials at least.

23 SEPTEMBER

Richard Mackie – a much valued correspondent, who knows much more than I do about the Church and its ways (liturgies, festivals, doctrines, etc.) – has sent me a strange little book, *Letters of Direction* by the Abbé de Tourville (1842–1903), from which I take this slab of flattering unction: 'Most people are like sheep and follow, without much satisfaction to themselves, the lines of past tradition. A very small minority emerges, with great hesitation and amidst endless discussion, to be faced by troublesome and pressing contradictions. It is, however, of that minority that you must be, when God has put you there by interior vocation and natural aptitude.'

Dare I believe myself to be a member of that strenuous, over-strained, exultant yet tormented band? *How* dare I believe it when I remain so deeply in the dark; so heavily and blindly unenlightened!

◆ ◆ ◆

'The purification and slow constitution of the Individual into a Person, by means of the Thing-element, the apparently blind Determinism of Natural Law and Natural Happenings . . . Nothing can be more certain than that we must admit and place this undeniable, increasingly obtrusive, element and power *somewhere* in our lives: if we will not own it as means, it will grip us as our end.' Von Hügel – who else? – quoted by Graham Greene.

And how does this 'Thing-element' represent itself most cogently, solidly and vividly for me? Why in beer, of course.

◆ ◆ ◆

The bar of the Green Dragon, Hereford; surrounded by rather noisy *souls*.

But now, waiting for S, I've crossed to the little working-class pub across the road. And it is *true* – no affectation whatever – to say that I feel far more at home here than in that county hotel. By what right? It isn't a question of right at all.

Conversation between two fuddled old men beside me:

'You must agree with me always.'
'*Always?*'
'Yes, *a*lways!'
'All right then, always.'

◆ ◆ ◆

But, alas, this Tourville moves into just the kind of preposterous arrogance which I feared. 'We are as it were the first proofs of an edition printed only for connoisseurs but destined later on to be given to the world at large. It is good to be among God's experiments for the future; only we must realise that we do belong to the future.' Ugh!

This was written in the nineties, I suppose: and now, nearly a century later, what has become of all that brave new Christian thought? We are still floundering and foundering in the same old mire of complexities and contradictions.

25 SEPTEMBER

The round glass paperweight whorled with green, yellow and white, which Susie brought us from Arkansas, has now replaced Simon's pot on my sacred shelf. It seems a gross interloper there; but perhaps it too can become the Light of God for me. It is an 'object of vertu' after all, however strange, and could perhaps become an object of virtue, too.

◆ ◆ ◆

How close we are today in our shared depletion; in our shared resolve to entertain K in her misery at lunch tomorrow and to endure the Spanish holiday with Laura and Anne which is now looming so desperately close.

◆ ◆ ◆

I have begun reading Schillebeeckx's enormous *Jesus* – to be followed by his enormous *Christ*. Complete fascination. But why does he have to make *so many* conventional genuflections to official faith? This, for example: 'One is a Christian if one is persuaded that final salvation-from-God is disclosed in the person of Jesus and that this basic conviction gives rise to the community or fellowship of grace . . . I believe in Jesus as that definitive saving reality which gives point and final purpose to my life.' Why 'final' salvation-from-God? Why 'the' (not 'a') community of grace? Why 'that definitive' (not 'a true') saving reality?

What orthodox Christians proudly call 'the scandal of particularity' is a real scandal in our time. For how dare we so limit God's action either in place or time? Who can tell what new light and hope may be prepared for us – a light which could never contradict the light and hope given in Jesus but might, after all, amplify it; show us something further on the way that Jesus was pointing to; remind us that no human words or person can ever be the final and definitive word of God?

◆ ◆ ◆

God, Creator of my soul.

God, Creator of all souls, everywhere and always.

26 SEPTEMBER
Last year's terror of going to France – would I collapse so far outside this armoured nest and ruin S's holiday? – is greatly intensified when I contemplate the Spanish holiday which begins on Sunday. For one thing, I start from a far worse state of desuetude: for another, three other people are now involved.

O Mother of Mercy, give me the strength I shall need so badly!

◆ ◆ ◆

Second talk with John R; even better than the first. We reach tentatively towards each other, and surely begin to find that, however different our stages of spiritual development, we are on much the same path; moving in the same direction. Sometimes I can't quite understand what he is saying. Above my head? Rather, above my spirit – but what unbelievable luck for me that he has come here!

◆ ◆ ◆

To combine a real humility towards unbelievers with the *unfailing* recognition that our whole conception of what man is and what he should be is utterly different from theirs.

And immediately, with that marvellous and almost familiar appropriateness, I come on this in Merton's posthumous book.

> Most modern secular humanists are concerned with man in the abstract, with the *human species* . . . For Marx it is man, scientific and objective man, who will one day humanise himself and the earth; but Marx had little patience for the claims of the fallible human person, and no interest whatever in such values as love, compassion, mercy, happiness. Thus it is not difficult for the abstract and scientific doctrines of modern humanism to become means by which the individual person is reduced to subjection to man in the abstract. And, as Gabriel Marcel has pointed out, this vast and awful abstractness hovers over the abyss of mass society to bring forth from it the anti-humanist and irresponsible monstrosity that is mass-man.

> To which must be added, of course, that throughout their history the Churches have also dehumanised and dechristianised man by making him into the miserable abstraction of *a believer*, bound in obedience to their own absolutist conception of what he is and what he ought to be.

◆ ◆ ◆

And now when I pray for 'The Pain of the World' my eyes move from the ingrown and terrified face of Verlaine to Augustus John's beautiful profile of poor Julia, sent us by Lawrence just after her death. Then, in 1935, two years before she became my brief *femme-de-trente-ans*, she had already started on her appalling calvary of a life; her charming, faithless husband dead in her arms after two or three hopeless years of 'marriage'.

5 OCTOBER
Back from Spain – mission more or less accomplished; and oh, the mercy of this bed.

Of course I wouldn't have gone if the choice had been only mine. Which doesn't mean that it wasn't 'good for me', as well as real pleasure to the other three for much of the time (or so I guess) and to me at rare moments in that week of endurance, fear and even acute physical distress. Ah, what a wretch am I!

First the hellish journey from Heathrow to Seville via Barcelona, with all the anticipated delays, irritations and packed people. For this I had prepared by secreting what I had calculated would be enough gin to see me through, without seeing me too far. But a Pernod in the Seville hotel finished me off, and made a disastrous start for one and all. No such trouble afterwards – as indeed I knew there wouldn't be – but hard foot-slogging in hot city streets; hot and cramped car journeys to Cordoba, to Granada and back to Seville. And when the time came for the Alhambra, show-piece and Mecca of the whole expedition, I was writhing in bed the whole of that single scheduled day with a wicked gastritis. My wives were ministering angels; and with the help of fiercely effective antibiotic pills (bought by Anne at the expense of some of her own sightseeing) I was just able to make the journey back to Seville next day. But remained painfully weak and queasy for the whole second half of our packaged week.

As for the sights I did see, the Cordoba mosque with its cathedral inside was certainly striking enough; Seville Cathedral was big; but I suppose the smaller Cordoba churches were the best. Yet I know by now that I cannot make my responses on demand in this way. I doubt if even the Alhambra itself would have moved me deeply – though I was perpetually, if mildly, interested by the strange Moslem-Christian history of that very strange bit of Europe.

My strongest feeling was a painful love for Laura, who had anticipated this holiday with such high expectations, and who often seemed more bewildered and uneasy than really happy. Also great admiration for my first wife's indomitable zest – for seeing things, for swimming, for walking everywhere, for meals, for lively talk. And, of course, my loving respect for S, whose calm and good spirits were never disturbed.

But I fear I was a Jonah throughout; a rotten, and often silent, companion.

The best time for me was an hour alone in the cathedral on our last day in Seville, when I stayed all the time in one of the less crowded chapels and went through my substitute for prayer. At least I was able to be cooled and calmed there. (But did I feel closer to those who were praying around me than to such disbelieving friends as Terry or Robert? Truly hard to say.)

Some good meals, not only for the food and the wine but because I managed to hitch myself up into something close to pleasure for the occasion.

Arrival at the excellent Granada hotel – just before the bug hit me – and a wonderfully cold swim with Laura and Anne in the hotel pool.

Charmingly frivolous card games in hotel bars after dinner, with coffee and liqueurs.

The four of us in a carriage clopping through the gardens of Seville in the warm dusk . . .

I am deeply ashamed by this dreary account of what should have been a delightful occasion. Three people I love, and so much which should at least have excited the mind and raised the heart. But my mind and heart are utterly stultified by journeys, by cities, by hotels; above all, of course, by airports.

But perhaps my pretence of enjoyment was more effective than my present shame has made me believe: I doubt if even S realised how much I was hating so much of it; how hard it was to keep some sort of smile on my face. (And if this passage ever appears, it will be so long after the event that the revelation of my lumpish incapacities will no longer pain or shock.)

In this condition it seems to me that the natural tendency of the human mind, heart and soul is always downwards – no less than the body is pulled down by gravity. Down into greater weakness, sin, weariness, repetition of useless patterns. And God's Sisyphean task is to work against this downward pull; to roll us up the hill again; to renew; to revivify.

◆ ◆ ◆

And now the old horror is added to that strain, weariness and shame. At least in Spain we had no news of the world for six days, but this afternoon I have been reading yesterday's *Observer* and feeling more horrified and disgusted at the turning of every page. This hateful, futile, even frivolous Gulf War continues unabated, Arabs and Persians murdering and mutilating each other for nonsense. Bombs thrown at a synagogue in Paris. The USA swept by idolatrous 'Christian' sects, crying for bigger and better bombs; harsher punishments; more wealth . . . And then a report by American scientists on the predicted effects of nuclear bombs in New York; the horror more nakedly and dreadfully displayed than I've ever seen it before.

First the usual sense of a mad and bad world, whirling faster and faster to an agonising end. The usual loathing of our 'leaders' – and in particular of those two appalling American buffoons, Carter and Reagan, whose minds are so totally filled with their grotesque electoral contest that even a war is seen only through those mad spectacles.

216

But then the usual deflating sequel: do I really think that Carter and Reagan are worse or more foolish men than ordinary people? Worse or more foolish than myself, for example? And this is hard to answer without some form of hypocrisy. As a private man I have no reason to think that I am less selfish or self-centred than either of those candidates: less idiotic in my vanity; less mean-spirited in my reactions to public woe; less blindly enclosed in my own trivial obsessions. Nor have I any sentimental faith in the people. In fact most of us are little Carters and Reagans, not even fiddling but squabbling and scratching at each other while Rome burns.

Yes, but we are not trying to become president of the United States. And that extra degree, that almost insane degree of vanity, does surely distinguish these men from nearly all the rest of us. And this means that the harm we can do is very small compared with the total disaster which the faults they share with us can bring on the whole world.

And of course I must also say that I think the views I hold are wiser and better than theirs. We have to stand away from our own beliefs: *we are not our beliefs*. I trust my Christian faith and my loathing of the arms race as I could never trust myself. I believe with all my heart, mind and soul that the only right policy for any government in the world is to divest itself totally and immediately of all nuclear armaments. This is part of the faith on which I would stake everything.

And if the answer comes, as it must, that the contrary belief is just as passionately held; and think, besides, of all the horrors committed in the name of passionate belief . . . Well, I will not be pushed into a flabby subjectivism on this. I cannot and will not say that the faith in freedom through the nuclear arms race is just as valid, just as worthy, just as rational as my belief that nuclear war is the ultimate crime and horror.

The old, impossible conundrum.

7 OCTOBER

Then all this aching puzzlement, strain, misery blown away by a wonderful walk this afternoon. Great clouds racing over the sky; squalls and sudden bursts of sunlight; and as I walked through this known and loved weather, above this known and loved valley, I was back in my natural habitat again; jubilant; attentive; restored. An acorn fell from high up plum on the bald centre of my head, and bounced out of its cup onto the leaf-strewn road beside me. 'Don't worry about that – or that – or that! Walk and watch! Walk and watch! Look at May Hill on the far northern horizon: at the long fingers of the cedar flapping up and down in the wind; at the hazel, bramble and blackthorn in the hedges. Smell the farmyard! I can even smell the sodden grass of the fields.'

This was a reaction not only from all those contorted thoughts and fears of yesterday, and not only from the tense strain of exile in Spain, but also from a whole summer of forced labour on the new garden, hardly relieved by a single carefree walk. And it might seem grossly frivolous, I suppose, to be so easily relieved of so many heavy and serious cares: to be tossed up into something close to joy immediately after being crushed by the heavy weight of the world's woes and one's own sins. Yet I trust this rare exaltation in the present moment more than I trust any other mood I know. Callous indifference? No, grateful acceptance of what is given and the certain knowledge that happiness is always right – even if unhappiness isn't always wrong. And what use is it to add one's own stultified and stultifying misery to the great misery of this world? Never, never reject or doubt a gleam of heaven's light.

◆ ◆ ◆

To remember, always, that her God and mine are not the same. That any attempt to push my God at her – my partial view of God on her's – can do nothing but harm. Hoping and praying, of course, that our two aspects of God will slide together some time, like two distorted views of the moon sliding together so that the whole full moon will shine on us both.

8 OCTOBER
Jean has just telephoned to tell us that Veronica★ has died, of pneumonia, at eighty-six. Shock and distress, in spite of her age and many years of half-life. But almost at the same instant the base thought of our inheritance. The comfort, the reassurance of having even more money than we have already.

But no forced guilt, please. No bogus wailing either for her death or for the too, too solid humanity of my reaction. *Humani nil a me alienum puto*† should apply as much to one's own human-all-too-human thoughts as to everyone else's.

◆ ◆ ◆

A modern prayer: 'Lord have mercy upon me, a Pharisee.'

★ P T's stepmother.
† 'Nothing human is alien to me.'

11 October

Back from Ganthorpe and the rather dismal funeral; dismal, I mean, rather than really sad, for how much grief did any of us really feel for that awkward old lady? Well, I did feel a tenderness; and a certain reverence simply for the occasion of her death. But my prayer was 'Forgive us, dear Lord, for the inadequacy of our feelings.'

◆ ◆ ◆

And now a nephew of Connie's telephones to tell us that she died suddenly two days ago. I was shocked again – can the sudden news of death ever be accepted without any shock at all? – but also very relieved that she had lived in her Exmoor cottage up to the end.

15 October

Back from Connie's funeral at the Taunton crematorium. Well, I wept a few tears for her when the moment came. But how many for the old lady I'd known, respected and greatly liked during the last four years; how many for the young woman I had passionately loved in 1926?

Absurd moment of pride. Among all those nephews and nieces, great-nephews and great-nieces I was *her only child*. And I think she was more open in saying this when we saw her in August than at any time since our extraordinary reunion in 1976.

◆ ◆ ◆

Re-reading Connie's last letter makes me think again about my evidently unusual readiness to write so frankly – by and large! – about my private life and troubles. After all, I am not particularly irreticent in conversation with friends; and could live quite happily for days on end without any conversation at all.

I suppose I feel that the only interesting things I have to say are the things which have most closely affected me. Certainly I understand much better now why the attempted autobiography which I included in *Part of a Journey* failed so quickly. What interests me are the immediate reactions to daily events, the ideas which come and would otherwise so quickly go, the unexpected and often unsuitable emotions. In other words, I now find the current of any life far more absorbing than the large remembered 'events'; the reconstructed patterns. (And as for 'careers', which dominate so many auto-biographies, they are the most boring topic of all.)

At least I am sure that the best that I have to give now as a writer is in this book. Though I think it is braced and strengthened by the occasional public statements of my reviews. (And yet how difficult I still find it to write as directly as this after that complicated process by which experience was distanced and transmuted when I was writing *Pantaloon*.)

16 OCTOBER
A NEW START. More hope for us now, I think, than for many years. More hope, that is, that our love for each other won't be so constantly blotched and smeared by ugly resentments and ancient anger.

◆ ◆ ◆

No, I didn't love Connie. It was 'Slellins' I loved – my name for her on the farm when she was three-quarters mother to me and, on my part, one-quarter wife. I was very fond of Connie; respected her as much as anyone I know. But I think I have been too ready with the word 'love' these last few years; grabbing at it, insisting on it. I would guess that most of us love very few people indeed. Outside my own family – which always includes Anne – I can think of only five or six people.

The more important love seems, the more chary one should be about throwing the word about.

As for God, my Holy Mother in Heaven, I can't say I know her well enough to love her. And yet, at the best moments, I do believe that I am her beloved child – too childish, still, to return her love.

(Today it was at exactly 2.35 p.m. that this heavenly mother first crossed my conscious mind. O God, how we neglect you in the immense and absorbing triviality of our daily lives. And it seems that we are constructed in such a way that this triviality is our natural state of mind; our habitat. Is it any wonder that you are able to reach us so seldom; or that when you do indeed penetrate and occupy a single person, we marvel at the rare spectacle of holy light, love and hope shining in the drab absurdity of earthly life?)

◆ ◆ ◆

Cold rain sweeping up Monnow Street as I was shopping this morning. And again I rejoiced in our native October weather, as did the other shoppers, loudly exultant in their complaints.

17 OCTOBER
S and Laura have been brought even closer together by music. Now they plan to go to the opera together in Cardiff and Bristol; and the great thing in this is that it is *an equal* passion, an equalising passion. They love and admire the music; they love and respect each other in listening to the music.

◆ ◆ ◆

The Schillebeeckx books are like a huge lump of rock at which he is patiently chipping away, now from this direction, now from that. And gradually I begin to discern the rough outline of a possible Jesus. S's books are clumsily written, cursed with jargon, and he makes the heaviest possible weather of the journey. But the need to struggle with him as he has struggled with his material may well be more helpful than if he himself had been more deft and elegant.

◆ ◆ ◆

This has been a day of maximum doubt. The whole contraption seemed so absurd that I hardly dared to glance at it. Yet I never for a moment doubted that this is what I am landed with for the rest of my life. This great mess of faith and argument is *mine*, now and for ever. If I were deprived of it, I feel as if I should instantly implode with a decisive pop, nature abhorring the total evacuation of a mind and heart.

◆ ◆ ◆

I have never known such a year for acorns: brown and green ones crushed into the wet roads, and many still clustered on the trees. I avoid, without much difficulty, thoughts of death and rebirth; eternal recurrence; the impermanent hills, scarcely more enduring than we are. But I cried for a sign on my walk today; and hoped that the sign would be Connie as she used to be, dressed in khaki breeches (which were very strange for a young woman then), waiting for me at one of the gates into a field of cows.

20 OCTOBER
Now Laura is actually introducing S to music she has never tried to appreciate before – Rossini, Verdi, Puccini. This afternoon as S was playing *Trovatore* in the sitting-room I heard one of those great soprano arias while I was digging in the garden, and suddenly I was in tears. Not happy tears, tears of joy, etc. Tears of ordinary misery, surprisingly triggered off by the deep sadness of the singing.

◆ ◆ ◆

How important is it that we should believe in a God who knows all our thoughts, 'unto whom all hearts are opened, all desires known and from whom no secrets are hid'? We certainly assume that this knowledge is one of the essential attributes of God. In fact that he knows far more about our minds and hearts than we can possibly know ourselves.

I think that if we took this attribute away it would be a great, but not perhaps an *irreparable*, loss. Perhaps God – or the angel – is able to know us fully only when we are able to open ourselves fully to that holy and blessed perception. Perhaps that is the main purpose of prayer – that we should no longer be shut up in the terrible isolation of our hidden secrets.

◆ ◆ ◆

I now feel that the most important difference between Christians is between those who think first and most of God as Father/Mother/ Holy Spirit and those who think first and most of Jesus. Nor do I believe that even the most devout Trinitarian is really able to pray to that strange contraption with equal attention to all its persons. I believe I shall always be a God-man rather than a Jesus-man. (Though the more I read of Schillebeeckx, the more fascinated I become by the work of trying to uncover the reality of Jesus through the NT texts.)

21 OCTOBER

Third meeting with John R; and the best so far. I told him my worries about my still-growing unsociability, and he was immensely reassuring. Not that he is a soft and easy comforter, but he saw at once that this is a real part of my present nature, therefore of God's purpose for me, and that kicking against these particular pricks is useless and therefore wrong. *Acceptance* was his message: do as you are shown. He spoke of St Paul, the Law and the Spirit. When the Law is superseded it doesn't mean, as the orthodox Jews imagined, that man is free to do what he likes. If he is 'faithful' – i.e. as open to God as he can be – then the Spirit has its own perceptible discipline. When I spoke of my letters as a possible 'cop out' from the obligation of actually meeting and talking to the people, John seemed quite sure that, on the contrary, they were part of my proper work.

But we didn't, I'm glad to say, talk only about me. He told me something about the difficulties of his life as a parson; and we found that we are beset by the same kinds of problems. (Though he always shows me, without in the least intending to, that he is far wiser than I am in the ways of the spirit.)

This evening I came on this wonderfully appropriate passage in Tourville: 'Live . . . without ceremony . . . do quite simply what you can, keeping within the limits of what you feel able to do. Do the best you can, simply and promptly, according to your physical strength and the particular bent of your soul. That is all we have to do in this world, wherever or whatever we may be. It is with this that God creates holiness in us without our knowing anything about it.'

◆ ◆ ◆

I note that the scribe who took down Dame Julian's *Revelations* adds a nervous postscript in which he warns us against 'selecting only what you like, and leaving the rest. That is what heretics do.' And that is exactly what this heretic intends to do. I want to excise the loving heart from this wonderful book; and I see nothing wrong whatever in doing so.

22 October

Buber's *Tales of the Hasidim* – so like certain Christian works (e.g. Merton's selections from the Desert Fathers) and yet with a holy charm, humour and wisdom all their own. Here, for example, is a wonderful reassurance for me:

> Imagine a man whose business hounds him through many streets and across the market-place the livelong day. He almosts forgets that there is a Maker of the world. Only when the time comes for the Afternoon Prayer does he remember, 'I must pray.' And then, from the bottom of his heart, he heaves a sigh of regret that he has spent his day on vain and idle matters, and he runs into a by-street and stands there, and prays. God holds him dear, very dear, and his prayer pierces the firmament.

This from the Baal Shem Tov – clearly one of the greatest as well as one of the most engaging saints in modern history.

◆ ◆ ◆

And this morning, as if to reinforce what John R said to me yesterday, comes a letter from one of my correspondents *most unexpectedly* telling me of the good my letters have done him.

◆ ◆ ◆

This evening as I was at my usual prayers I gradually realised that everything was going with a wonderful smoothness; a sense of order, all-right-ness. My prayer seemed, for once, entirely natural and to lead naturally into an outside world where everything was as it should be. Not the ecstasy of Dame Julian's 'All shall be well'; yet a state of what I take to have been absolute faith. It didn't seem extraordinary in the least, but like a proper and ordinary state which I am constantly missing through all my pandemonium of fears, vanities and anxieties. Nothing mystical; no oneness with the bright yellow beech trees, but a sense of being calmly and thoroughly *at ease* on earth and under heaven.

This lasted all the way to Lydney, to meet Laura; and gradually drifted away as the evening passed. I felt that I had seen what the ordinary state of a real believer is like. And I'm sure that this was closely connected with the 'acceptance' that John R was talking about yesterday evening.

23 OCTOBER

And just as Dame Julian's scribe warns us so severely against taking only what we choose from her *Revelations*, so the author of that ghastly work *The Revelation of St John the Divine* ends with a dire threat of the evil which will befall anyone who either adds to his work or reduces it. How vain these prophets are!

(But I'm sure that Dame Julian herself would never have said that we must take every word she wrote as undiluted truth and be damned if we don't.)

◆ ◆ ◆

Discipline of the Spirit. 'In a sense Luther took the matter too lightly. He ought to have made it apparent that the freedom he was fighting for led to making life, the spiritual life, infinitely more exhausting than it had been before.'

It is typical of Kierkegaard to put it in this baleful way. Tourville is saying the same kind of thing, and much better, in this passage:

> We must follow our own path and not worry about the puddles into which we fall; otherwise we should never move on at all . . . I wish so much that you could get hold of what perfection in this world consists of. It is not like going up a great hill from which we see an ever-widening landscape, a greater horizon, a plain receding further and further into the distance. It is more like an overgrown path which we cannot find; we grope about; we are caught by brambles; we lose all sense of the distance covered; we do not know whether we are going round and round or whether we are advancing. We are certain only of one thing; that we desire to go on however worn and tired we are. That is your life and you should rejoice greatly because of it, for it is a true life, serious and real, on which God opens His eyes and His heart.

Wonderful! A passage to read again and again, and particularly when lost in the brambles.

◆ ◆ ◆

The Consecration of the House. A holy rune.

◆ ◆ ◆

'The Work of God.' But as I looked for the four-hundredth time at those furrows (in *The Fall of Icarus*) the grim thought came to me that God is only scratching the shallow surface of our Earth. Most of us live for much of the time in dark caverns several thousand miles into the globe.

◆ ◆ ◆

But, O dear God, this pain is so wretchedly *uninstructive*!
    Who are you to judge?

24 OCTOBER
Schillebeeckx – the excitement of a great detective story.

◆ ◆ ◆

This appalling *Revelation of St John the Divine*: at least 90 per cent hatred to 10 per cent of love. If that.

◆ ◆ ◆

I am sometimes appalled by the apparent weakness of God's activity on this earth.

◆ ◆ ◆

Reading the proofs of *Part of a Journey*. At first I was exhilarated, and thought what a splendid work this is; how much it will mean to many, many people. But after three days' work I had a sense of heavy surfeit; almost disgust.

◆ ◆ ◆

S shouted up to me to look out of my window, and I saw a green woodpecker hopping vigorously across the lawn. S, Laura and I united in happiness at this startlingly cheerful sight.

26 OCTOBER
Martyn and Pinkie.★ We have just parted from them in Monmouth after a visit of the usual delight; and a promise on both sides that they will come again in March. At the moment I feel overwhelmed with melancholy that we see so little of such dear and life-giving friends as these.

◆ ◆ ◆

★ Old and close friends.

225

A brilliant nature programme on TV this evening; the immensely complicated ecology of a giant fig-tree in Central America. Horror. All this self-perpetuating cycle of wasp and tree seems to be everything that God and Heaven and holy man are not – an infinitely ingenious but blind impulsion to survive and perpetuate . . .

27 OCTOBER

It does begin to seem that there has been a real change: that we are both calmer, more quietly loving, more at peace with each other and ourselves.

Heavenly Mother, may this be the seed-bed in which new flowers will slowly germinate, sprout, grow and bloom.

◆ ◆ ◆

Sometimes Schillebeeckx speaks in a loud and true voice of his own: 'The third day, the day of salvation, is already a living reality and unfolds within our history, which continues on its accustomed way (with no apocalyptic transformation of the temporal order of events), a radical newness and a future charged with hope.'

◆ ◆ ◆

A little reassured about this enterprise by a quotation from Thomas Mann, when his wife was complaining about the intimate revelations he had made in his writing: 'The most intimate is at the same time the most universal.'

◆ ◆ ◆

From Tourville:

It has been said that on the battlefield there are defeats more glorious than victories. That is true also of the daily defeats of the soul in the struggle which we begin afresh every day, making new plans to do better and experimenting with new ideas and methods in order to succeed . . . That is really our great merit in the sight of God. Do not be surprised because I say *great*, even though in itself the merit is very small. It is great because we are extremely weak and because God knows the clay of which we are made.

◆ ◆ ◆

The *Gita* speaks of 'Maya, the maker', and then elaborates like this:

Maya makes all things: what moves, what is unmoving.
O Son of Kunti, that is why the world spins,
Turning its wheel through birth
And through destruction.

226

Here the word 'Maya' is being used for what we would call blind necessity; or materialist causation. And Krishna is spoken of as 'standing apart' from this whole process. Which fits very well with the theology of Peterborough!★

◆ ◆ ◆

Jeffrey has just brought the perfected (I hope) typescript of *Pantaloon* from Gloucester station; despatched by Collins two days ago. At least it *looks* very splendid indeed; each volume bound in bright and different coloured plastic covers.

28 OCTOBER

One day I would like to write a short introduction to Dame Julian, presenting her as almost fully emerged from the ecclesiastical bog; paying lip-service to the Church when she feels she has to, but really presenting a new Christianity of pure love. Her *Revelations* is a much purer work of love than any book of the New Testament.

◆ ◆ ◆

'The Hope of God' – up on the mountain top of *Icarus*: then 'The Work of Love', with eyes on the plough and furrows. What is the difference? The Hope is given us by God in order that we may trust in his Work, which is more often than not imperceptible to our earthly eyes.

◆ ◆ ◆

Sudden visit of a sad elderly lady. She revealed, in the course of general talk, that her daughter is (*a*) estranged from her, (*b*) schizophrenic, (*c*) married to an alcoholic. Whenever one penetrates under the surface of a life, one finds such horrors lurking.

◆ ◆ ◆

Rearranging all my books, which have become very untidy again since I did this last. A delightful task; preparing for a winter of hard work.

Also, I've now almost completed the garden shed at the back of the house. *Very* rough carpentry; but how much I prefer working with wood to working with earth or stone. My happiest memories of Rugby; the woodwork shop, and M'Gaulay with his drooping white moustache. Easily my favourite place and favourite member of staff.

◆ ◆ ◆

★'Evensong at Peterborough' – a short article P T wrote for *Encounter* after visiting Peterborough Cathedral, reprinted in *Part of a Journey*, pp. 195–207.

I am very much enjoying Buber's *Tales of the Hasidim*. The (eighteenth-century) Baal Shem Tov became encrusted with fantastic legends almost as soon as he was dead; probably before. But a wonderful and comical saint shines through them. In fact the legends don't distort our vision of him: they are like holy lamps hung all about him, and perhaps showing more of what he is than the literal truth could have done all by itself.

◆ ◆ ◆

Waiting to hear about Nasi, who is giving birth at this very time. Great anxiety. My worst dread on such occasions – that the baby will be deformed. How close we feel to them both!

29 OCTOBER

Jeffrey came round at 8.30 and shouted up at our bedroom windows, 'It's a boy!' Most unlike him; and when we hurried down we found him in a rare state of elation, which immediately affected us as well. Great rejoicing over the coffee.

◆ ◆ ◆

Tom rang up, and we went over to have tea with him at his sister's house in Caldicot. He was transformed. I have never witnessed such a marvellous recovery. For I never saw anyone closer to physical death – without dying – than on our third visit to Cardiff hospital last winter; or nearer to spiritual death on our fourth and last visit. (His bitterness seemed to well up from the very depth of his heart.) But now he has recovered not only his physical health but also his faith. I would describe this as a healing miracle.

On the way over, in the early dusk, I rejoiced that it is still possible for me to be *dazed* by the beauty of this valley at this time of year.

◆ ◆ ◆

'Cleanse *the thoughts of our hearts* . . . ' This was due to the sixteenth-century error of believing that we do indeed use our hearts for thinking with. But now the phrase has acquired a beautiful, metaphorical splendour. '*Le coeur à ses raisons* . . .'

◆ ◆ ◆

Schillebeeckx. In a sense this whole gigantic enterprise – the 1,600 pages of the two volumes – is a monstrosity. And often I feel it so; the turgid, repetitive scholar-thinker chewing and chewing over those short texts; and often coming up with the dreariest of platitudes. But at least it has thoroughly taught me the infinite complexity of NT origins; the virtual impossibility of finding Jesus of Nazareth through the great golden haze of the Risen Christ.

♦ ♦ ♦

Nuclear terrors. And one of the greater ones is the suspicion that they may be largely on my own behalf. But when I imagined myself dying in the greatest agony, but no holocaust, I was delighted to find that my heart lifted at once. That would, after all, be infinitely more bearable to contemplate.

Yes, but I find I am still tempted by the thought of dying before it happens, if it is to happen. A cowardly way out: 'What I don't see . . .'

Of course the prospect of the holocaust ought to have just one quite simple effect on us – to make us all the more determined to live and love well while the world still has time for it.

♦ ♦ ♦

Pinkie gently insisted last weekend that I am not a Christian because I don't believe in the unique Incarnation. Yet I feel more and more of a Christian as the years pass: more and more that this is the tradition in which I am at home; that these are the terms which I can use (even if I sometimes change the sense of them a little); that these are the values I hold; that the *deepest* truth of Christianity is also my deepest truth. (Though I'd be hard put to it to say just what that truth is.)

31 OCTOBER

Drove to Gloucester with Nasi's mother, Pari, to see Nasi and the baby. Pari, who had been a matron in Tehran, complained that the Gloucester hospital wasn't up to her hospital in Persia, which was run entirely on American principles. Another, and even older, atavistic reaction. I said nothing, but felt ruffled indeed.

Splendid baby, with a great thatch of black hair – Edward Thomas. Half-Jeffrey; half-Persian. Nevertheless, I could not help my wretched Bomb-gloom almost driving out the pleasure of looking at him. What sort of a world, etc. Yet we believe that giving birth to children is somehow a good in itself.

But this is often false. Often it is a crime to produce a child – e.g. the eleventh in a starving family of ten. And there should be no mystification about this.

♦ ♦ ♦

' . . . that we perfectly love you and worthily magnify your holy name . . . ' I have repeated this so often, but it only occurs to me this

229

evening that the second phrase offers a second line of defence. If we can't love God – which is a very hard task indeed – we can at least praise him in song and prayer, which is much easier. And which may help us to love him in the end.

♦ ♦ ♦

What is my minimum, least doubted 'act of faith'? That this material realm is neither the only nor the highest level of reality.

In these miseries of doubt I turned to my best-loved Pissarro reproduction – the Pontoise street-scene with the two old people shuffling along the gutter, and the bright winter sunlight streaming between the houses. For the first time I noticed the line of trees at the very far end of the street. And I said to myself, there is an unknown world beyond those trees. Great comfort given, and hope restored.

♦ ♦ ♦

Now I have 'faith'; for most of my life I had little or none.

Does this mean that I look at the same things in a different way?

Does it mean that I simply make a different selection of things which are there to be experienced?

Or does the faith reveal things which are not, in any real sense, there for those without faith?

Does faith actually create experiences proper only to itself?

Certainly life does look and feel very different now: translucent, or at least as if it could become translucent at any moment.

1 NOVEMBER
Dream. I was lying in one of the big rooms under my little one in Peckwater Quad (Christ Church) and was in a state of what I called 'Declination'. This meant that I was getting *positively* weaker and more depleted; spreading this all round, to the extent at last that even Connie was affected by it and brought low.

When I woke, I realised that this had been a theological condition – the exact opposite of that Exaltation which Jesus achieved for himself and others by his raising to the Spirit (Baptism, Transfiguration); raising to the Cross; raising from the Tomb; raising to Heaven . . .

♦ ♦ ♦

Perhaps it is significant that I wrote nothing yesterday about a dreadful event which may have been partly responsible for my extreme doubt and self-questioning in bed. Driving back from Gloucester we were brought to a crawl by a huge lorry grinding up the hill from Mitcheldean. At one point I thought I saw a curve of the road clear

230

ahead, and told S she could pass. But as soon as she pulled out, and forward a little, two cars with headlights shining in the dusk appeared almost on top of us. She braked hard and got back with only about two seconds to spare.

And then I was appalled at the thought that I so nearly killed not only S, Laura and me but also the people in the other car. And all because of my meaningless impatience – meaningless in this case because there was no reason at all for getting home at 5.30 rather than at 6.00.

I immediately thought: 'We have been spared, but this is a lesson from God which I must never, never forget. This was a most drastic warning from heaven about this dreadful fault of mine.'

Is this pure superstition? It led, in any case, to agonised speculations.

2 NOVEMBER
A night with Lu and Bernard in their very pleasant house on a wooded estate near Farnborough. At school most of her great energy and determination was devoted to avoiding work. Now, working for three science A-levels at the local tech – in preparation for medical school – she is not only working with tremendous diligence but obviously with brilliant success as well. This determination, when roused to it, is something which Anne, S and I and all our combined family have in common.

Bernard told me many interesting but deeply depressing things about the horrors of the industrial world. I suppose I would no longer call myself a socialist but an anarchist/distributist. Which means that I hate the system we live in more deeply, and I think more wisely, than in my socialist years.

But I hope and trust that this doesn't involve me in any feelings of moral superiority. God knows, they would be grossly unjustified.

◆ ◆ ◆

Have now struggled to the end of Schillebeeckx's enormous *Jesus*; and am rolling up my sleeve 'to read the stuffing out of' (Wodehouse) his even more enormous *Christ*. What a great tangle of a book that was. I felt, all through, the straining to express himself in the most orthodox terms he could find – straining against a great yearning for greater freedom.

3 NOVEMBER
Merton tries hard to make out a case for Vatican II's long statement about war and peace. But he can't disguise that they completely

funked the issue of nuclear arms; never could bring themselves to say that even to possess them is a fearful crime against true Christianity. Every prelate, priest and professing Christian should be specifically asked: 'Would you in any circumstances press the button yourself, and launch those rockets on Russian cities?'

♦ ♦ ♦

'There is nothing about which we know everything.' Bossuet.

♦ ♦ ♦

Alas, I have got almost nothing from this careful re-reading of the *Gita*. Here are two almost consecutive verses:

> My face is equal
> To all creation.
> Loving no one
> Nor hating any . . .

> Though a man be soiled
> With the sins of a lifetime,
> Let him but love me,
> Rightly resolved,
> In utter devotion:
> I see no sinner,
> That man is holy . . .

So we are to love God/Krishna, but he remains utterly indifferent to us. Perhaps, though, one can detect the concept of a loving God trying to struggle free from all that appalling impassibility.

'They [Liberal Christians] persistently write as though Christianity and other religions claimed to dispel mystery as one might dispel a fog.' Geddes MacGregor. Yes; *that* is where Liberal Christianity went so desperately wrong. The true religious quest should, no doubt, be a series of revelations; but the revelations are of one luminous and pregnant mystery after another.

♦ ♦ ♦

'Morality is not a castle in the air, or, as Huxley conceived it, a precarious and short-lived revolt against the cosmic order. It is life's ultimate meaning or nothing.' John Oman. Yes; but this would be better still if he had used the word 'love' instead of 'morality'. Morality has acquired too many drear and sour connotations.

♦ ♦ ♦

On the telly one of Reagan's last campaign speeches. The usual appalling cant and claptrap; but suddenly he looked up from his text and yelled 'Shut up!' at a persistent heckler. What a relief! What an almost joyful sense of truth breaking through all the lies. For a while I positively liked him.

◆ ◆ ◆

5 NOVEMBER
Never has the suddenly cold and wind-blown outdoors seemed so much an alien, and even frightening, world. But also an enticing and enthralling one. These last few gardening – and shed-building – afternoons have been a marvellous refreshment. The rare boon of *health*: conscious health; an intoxicant of the highest order.

◆ ◆ ◆

'The Grace of God.' A fascinating phrase, which I never seem to use directly. The notion of something given for nothing; of a great reservoir of love.

6 NOVEMBER
Reagan's landslide. Cold shivers, indeed. Not that I feel any strong personal dislike for him – in fact I disliked Carter's ostensible personality rather more. But I think with real terror of the kind of men who are behind him.

'No annihilation without representation' was one of my father's best quips.

◆ ◆ ◆

I lent Pinkie the spare proof of *Part of a Journey*, feeling that she is its ideal reader. Then came her delightful thank-you card to S for their visit, ending, 'Tell Philip that I am savouring every moment of his book – it's unbelievably much the book for me.'

Such warm, brotherly feelings for this only one of my old friends who is plodding and prodding along in the same direction as I am.

◆ ◆ ◆

'And from whom no secrets are hid . . . ' It sometimes sounds as though the intention of this was ominous; even a threat. 'Don't for a moment imagine you can hide your dirty little thoughts from ME.' But if God is as I believe him to be, what a relief to know that he knows it all; and understands the folly and worse far better than I can myself. For even in these very good days – the best for many months – I know what a fair-weather man I am. How beset by unholy fears.

◆ ◆ ◆

233

Father P rather wry in Monmouth about his own spiritual idleness: feeling it very hard to remain spiritually alert against his age and many infirmities. I took it upon myself to give him a small pep-talk; which he didn't take amiss in the least. But I do see that one of the heaviest demands of our faith is that we may never rest in it. Schillebeeckx puts it well: 'Reality is always a surprising revelation for thought, for which thought can only be a witness. In such experiences of what proves completely refractory to all our inventions we shall finally also discover the basis for what we rightly call revelation.'

But how does this square with that Peace of God for which we so fervently pray? How to be at peace and yet restlessly open to constant new *and upsetting* revelations of reality?

Suddenly, tonight, I have again been allowing myself some hopes of a prize in the poetry competition. What a craving I still suffer from for applause and praise and admiration. A gross recidivism.

7 NOVEMBER

'Here is another result of the fundamental mistake: that Christianity is not proclaimed by witnesses but by teachers.' Kierkegaard. Yes, but I doubt if he, in his almost terrifying arrogance, was much of a witness himself.

♦ ♦ ♦

Y's admiration – even to the extent of supposing me to be a saint – makes me horribly uneasy. He hasn't even met me. I feel that I must *make* him see that this is utterly, indeed ludicrously, wrong; or else I am permanently in a false position of the worst kind.

But do I detect a tiny tremble of satisfaction – 'Suppose he were right, after all?' Well, a quick return to the reality of my state promptly knocks *that* on the head.

8 NOVEMBER

All our supplications should be (a) reminders, and (b) celebrations.

Thus, 'Lord have mercy!' should mean 'The Lord has mercy, glory be!'

9 NOVEMBER

Stimulated, perhaps by S and Laura going to Cardiff to see *Tosca*, I listened to some music when I was half-tight yesterday evening. How it *pierced* me again – the Mozart Quintet; *Nuits d'été* . . .

♦ ♦ ♦

Why do we alone in the animal kingdom copulate face to face? Could it be it is only in this position that we can show real love for each other, visible on the face?

♦ ♦ ♦

11 NOVEMBER
To David and Phine in their newly acquired Shropshire farmhouse. Joys of a new establishment; the rebuilding; the beautiful unknown country; the strong sense of life clearing its throat, at the very least, in order to say something interesting and good.

♦ ♦ ♦

A book on the spirit world, by Allan Kardec, first published in France in 1874. Extremely sensible, rational, thoughtful. But suddenly the heart sinks when one of the consulted spirits says that their means of communication with men is 'something like your animal magnetism'. Alas, so many of our 'spirits' seem to pick up the scientific theories of the moment, however false these later prove to be.

♦ ♦ ♦

Reading Dame Julian yet again. I must say that I intensely dislike all the early revelling in the gory details of the Passion. Though I see very well that she regarded these visions as the supreme demonstration of God's love for us.

12 NOVEMBER
This evening I asked John R how he came to be a clergyman. He told me that he had tried several things first – engineering and psychiatric nursing among them – but this was the first pool he had stepped into in which he couldn't feel the bottom. A wonderful answer.

13 NOVEMBER
Liberal theology again. The great contrast is those deep and passionate men – Paul, Augustine, Luther, Pascal, Barth . . . Can we restore their depth and passion without their appalling doctrines of damnation? Why ever not?

♦ ♦ ♦

Fear and the Bomb. If genuine light is given, as I lie upstairs in misery, it *never* takes the form, 'Well, but it may not happen after all.' It always takes the form, 'Yes, but even if it does happen . . . ' (For example,

'Love of God and man will be all the more needed, both before and after – if there is an after.')

14 NOVEMBER
At last I have to face what must surely be the true diagnosis of this recurring – sometimes almost constant – ill-health. It is my depression again, but pushed resolutely down and projected into physical illness. Indeed I can feel it constantly rebelling against that confinement, and darkening the mind as well.

After gloomy newspaper reading – Reagan's horrific rearmament plans – I am oppressed by what I finally recognise as a sense of personal guilt. Foolish and irrational.

Still, now and again, the childish notion that I can escape from all these afflictions by some sudden act of dramatic desperation. There is no such escape.

15 NOVEMBER
Our day in Warwick before the D A committee meeting at Rugby. How I *slogged* my way around that castle; slogged my way up and through breakfast on Sunday morning. Effort and fear.

But the meeting – our first for many months – was splendid. It was a real happiness to see these friends again; and a real comfort to me to know that every one of them knew exactly how I had been feeling.

17 NOVEMBER
I have now finished going through the typescript of *Pantaloon* which Collins sent me. Most of it still seems to me to be very good; but there are far too many horridly bad bits; and the last thirty pages – my *Paradiso* – are unbelievably awful. I realise that I shall have to spend many more months on this work, which I had assumed to be long ago in its perfected form.

This competes with the writing up of my current journal; and I begin to wish that I knew roughly how much time I may expect. Anyway, I couldn't possibly allow *Pantaloon* to be published in its present form; and tend to regard it as an act of grace that all those publishers rejected it and gave me this chance to work on it yet again.

◆ ◆ ◆

Nearly all the way back from Rugby in the dark I was repeating 'Heavenly Mother . . . ' to myself. Like holding back a collapsing dam with a braced back. (Yes, but not a very big dam!)

18 November

Then, out of the long wet grey, a sudden blue and breezy day. I was in just the mood for it; and worked with marvellous crispness; first at the revision of *Pantaloon*, then at constructing a rough-tough wood-bunker just outside the garden gate. (Met Dave Snowdon in St Briavels and, when I told him about my recent 'carpentry', he said, 'Ah, so you're what we call a chain-saw chippy.' Dead right: chain-saw, chopper and mason's hammer.)

◆ ◆ ◆

The word 'idolatrous' must be used with great care, and *not* simply to describe beliefs in God different from one's own. But it does seem to me that all claims to have grasped God firmly, defined him accurately, learned exactly what he wills for us, *do* deserve this disobliging term. Thus all creeds tend to idolatry; so does sectarian salvationism; so does Liberal Christianity in its most crudely explanatory form.

◆ ◆ ◆

Perhaps every genuine act of faith is always rewarded by a revelation. Or rather achieves an insight.

◆ ◆ ◆

O Heavenly Mother, help me to love, and give me the courage to sustain my love and make it effective.

20 November

Bought a large, misshapen but beautifully coloured cooking apple, and put it on the Holy Shelf instead of Susie's glass ball: 'The Life of God' (whatever that may mean).

Also found a single Compton-Burnett in the Monmouth library. Hadn't read one for twenty years or more, and dived into it as if into a refreshing pool. What a joy! And a marvellous repellant of the fear which had been beating its black wings, as so often, at the very edge of my vision.

◆ ◆ ◆

There is this that I thank God for – that I've never been faced with the problem of whether or not I would take an aged relation or dependant into my house. I *believe* that I would have done so if it had been called for: I *know* that I would have found it a heavy trial.

Worked *very* hard all morning on my review of Küng; then went for a windy, leaf-blown walk to try to get it out of my head. Failed. The wretched mind *would* come back to it, thinking up changes, etc., until I actually shouted, 'Oh shut up, *shut up*, SHUT UP!' But instead of looking at trees, valley and so on, I had to stop continually and write down the proposed changes in my notebook.

R.M. wrote to me a few weeks ago and said: 'God must look forward to 5.30 every day, when that busy, restless, enquiring mind leaves him in peace for forty minutes.' I see what he means. In many ways, besides, it is an exhausting affliction to have a mind like mine; which is hardly ever content even to drift aimlessly around. A *grinding* sort of mind; but very little flour emerges from the Heath Robinson contraption inside my head.

I actually do feel overworked today, which would seem grotesque to anyone hearing an account of my normal working week. In fact my time was already well filled by journal, review and letters; so it does seem a problem to fit in what I now find will have to be quite a massive rewriting of *Pantaloon*.

◆ ◆ ◆

Dame Julian's gory vision of Christ's bleeding head and face. I suppose the way to take this is that it is a vivid showing of the intimate relationship between love and suffering. Which is essentially a *Christian* perception; and a very rich one, though capable of the most hideous distortions.

◆ ◆ ◆

The *Gita*. Arjuna to Krishna:

> At the sight of this, your Shape stupendous,
> Full of mouths and eyes, feet, thighs and bellies,
> Terrible with fangs, O mighty master,
> All the worlds are fear-struck, even as I am.

Rather unecumenical reactions to this sort of thing. A bit *too* exotic.

◆ ◆ ◆

All prayers are the same prayer: 'Thy will be done.'
   But if you believe that God's will is always done anyway that prayer must surely have a very different meaning – pure resignation to whatever happens. Whereas belief in a God struggling to do his will, and needing our help to do it, gives the words a much more positive sense.

◆ ◆ ◆

Haunted again by the little Penny boy from Brockweir – swinging out over the river on the rope hanging from a tree, as he'd done many times before, and the rope breaking and dropping him into the water to drown. Also – and even worse – the account I read in some newspaper ages ago of two small boys playing in a goods yard; getting into a wooden container whose lid fell shut on top of them. The oval ring fell back over its projection, so that they couldn't get out. How long did it take them to die?

Morbid thoughts? But such things lie at the very heart of our reality.

◆ ◆ ◆

Is it my new role, then, to be crucified on the cross of all that I write for others? Ugh!

◆ ◆ ◆

R.M.'s letters. I feel more and more affinity with this unmet psychiatrist in Kent. A man of violent longing; as insatiable as I am.

22 NOVEMBER
I sent, rather surreptitiously, for a tiny electronic alarm-clock advertised in the *Observer* colour supplement. It arrived yesterday, and I now try to set it for every successive hour during the day to remind me of prayer. The old folly – trying to get spiritual help from gadgets. On the other hand, it *may* be a help; and God knows help is what I need. (I also recognise a clownish element in such goings-on; and told the tale quite successfully to our Beaufort friends on Thursday.)

Fear breeds self-contempt: self-contempt weakens one in the struggle against fear. A wretched spiral indeed.

◆ ◆ ◆

Reading a book of fourteenth-century history. Vividly reminded of the horror of all periods when studied at all closely – though this one, at least in France, was perhaps a little nastier than most. Saints are freaks; sports; perhaps some sort of mutants.

◆ ◆ ◆

'The man with a passionate sense of the divine milieu cannot bear to find things around him obscure, tepid and empty which should be full and vibrant with God.' Teilhard, quoted by Merton. Merton's comment:

Like so many other key terms in the New Testament, the 'world' is used in two senses. One which is to be 'hated' and the other to be 'loved'. Now it is precisely the 'world' that is 'empty, obscure and without God' that is to be hated. But the difference between the two worlds *depends on us* . . . Hence, it is the duty of the Christian to love the world by doing all in his power, with the help of God's grace and fidelity to the demands of the divine will in his everyday life, to 'redeem' the whole world, to transform and consecrate it to the divinising power of the Spirit of Christ.

Yes, that *is* the task. But even with God's help it seems to be one of inconceivable difficulty.

For example: what is the difference between cigarette manufacturers and hired assassins? They both *knowingly* kill for money; though, of course, all the hired assassins in the history of the world have killed only a fraction of the number killed by the tobacco industry. Yet these mass-murderers are respected members of society.

23 NOVEMBER

A walk to St Briavels in mist and rain. The good, dull Coldharbour countryside where, even without a mist, one would never guess that beautiful and dramatic valleys lie east, west and south. Walking very quietly but firmly, and talking to myself most of the time; trying to quieten my mind and *quietly* awake the spirit. 'Peace. Peace. Peace.' at each fourth step, for a time. And I felt that even 'The Peace of God' or 'Heavenly Mother' would somehow be pressing too hard.

Horror of violence. Yes, but you yourself hold onto a large sum of money which would undoubtedly and rightly be taken from you by those in bitter need if it weren't for the whole apparatus of potential violence which keeps that money in your bank.

And *yet* this very thought is itself violent; and was ill-suited to the purpose of my walk. I wanted to *still* the restless, self-tormenting mind; and finally – after the quiet Sunday village – I did succeed in doing this. For there is a right time for very different mental activities: a time for quiet and a time for self-criticism . . . And my weakness is to indulge in useless tirades against myself when I know that it would be *more use all round* if I could keep quiet.

24 NOVEMBER

Our thirtieth wedding anniversary. My dear love! Yes, it is true that I have never loved you so much as I do now.

We had a very expensive and unspeakably bad meal; but didn't care at all about that. Then back to the George for cheery chat with Roy and Deidre. An excellent celebration.

◆ ◆ ◆

So the Sisters at Tymawr not only attend the offices and do their physical work: they also have to do two hours a day of private prayer! Surely *some* time should be set aside for freely chosen reading – but I expect they know better than I do!

25 NOVEMBER

But a definite hangover this morning. (I've long recognised that hangovers don't depend on whether I have been drunk or not but, more or less strictly, on how much I have drunk.) So it needed firm resolution to work on *The Common Soldier** this morning; and even more to work on laying the bricks at the end of the new lawn extension this afternoon.

The result, though, was a fine recovery and the feeling that, with God's help, I'd saved a day from dilapidation; dissolution; won it for order, work and happiness.

◆ ◆ ◆

S tells me that she has begun to hear my 'tapping' again between bursts of typing. This is my, usually quite unconscious, beating out the rhythm of a line on the top of my desk as I write – in this case rewrite – *Pantaloon*.

In most of my writing years I wrote between bath and drinks (5.00 to 6.30) as well as in the morning. But this is now my prayer-time – or rather it includes my prayer-time which fills up too much of the hour and a half for enough working time to be left over. So I refuse even to look àt my morning's work when I come upstairs with my tea and lie down on my bed. Something of an effort.

◆ ◆ ◆

'Thus it is terrible to have anything to do with God who neither can nor will give one direct certainty or a legal relationship – and yet it is blessed; blessed to be, as it were, nothing in his hand, who is and who ever will be love, however things may go.' Kierkegaard at his wonderful best. (But a page or two later on in the *Journals* he is moaning about the iniquity of a servant who has been so inconsiderate as to leave him in order to be locked up in an asylum. Driven crazy by K's presence?)

◆ ◆ ◆

S's delicious chicken meal tonight, so infinitely better than what we paid £30 for last night.

*Ninth volume of *Pantaloon*.

Work-time and prayer-time. Is prayer to be 'counted' as work, then? For me it is work, and usually fairly easy work. I suppose it should be very hard work indeed, or – and far better – *play*.

◆ ◆ ◆

It is unimaginable that any government would say to the people, 'Look, since we believe in this policy of reducing what you have to spend we will all live like the poorest members of the community.' Or even, 'We will live like the average members of the community.' But how do they dare to go on lecturing the poor on the need for them to become even poorer, while they themselves . . . ?

I suppose those politicians would answer, 'But it wouldn't make any difference to the economy if we did reduce our own personal expenditure.' And this shows how abysmally far they are from understanding the simplest laws of personal conduct and human relations. If Mrs T, or Michael F, were to live like the people they harangue in their different ways (but ultimately the same old way – i.e. 'We' to 'Them'), it would have a miraculous effect on the whole country, so I believe.

But they can no more give up their accustomed luxuries than I can. (My only merit there is that I would never dream of telling other people that they have to live on less than I do *for the good of the country*. Ugh!)

◆ ◆ ◆

Arjuna: 'Some worship you with steadfast love. Others worship God the unmanifest and changeless. Which kind of devotee has the greater understanding of yoga?'

Krishna: 'Those whose minds are fixed on me in steadfast love, worshipping me with absolute faith. I consider them to have the greater understanding of yoga. As for those others, the devotees of God the unmanifest, indefinable and changeless, they worship that which is omnipresent, constant, eternal, beyond thought's com-pass, never to be moved. They hold all the senses in check. They are tranquil-minded, and devoted to the welfare of humanity. They see the Atman in every creature. They also will certainly come to me. But the devotees of the unmanifest have a harder task, because the unmanifest is very difficult for embodied souls to realise.'

Here the *Gita* comes very close to Christianity. And I remember that Ramakrishna also insisted that man can worship God either as a person (or many persons) or as the Unmanifest, etc. But there seems to be an implication even here that it is harder *but better* to worship the abstraction than to worship the person. I cannot feel this. But that may be because I am such an infinity away from the unitive vision, etc.

28 NOVEMBER

Must avoid turning this journal into a hospital chart; or series of daily bulletins on my mental and physical condition.

◆ ◆ ◆

So I continue to clock in for my three minutes of prayer every hour of the morning and afternoon. And I feel almost as if I were *opposing* the will of God by this stilted and mechanical procedure. Yet Father P said yesterday: 'The great thing is never to give up praying; to keep on, however little it seems to mean.'

◆ ◆ ◆

'Perhaps . . . my grief was prayer enough.' Leslie Paul.

◆ ◆ ◆

My proposed New Testament anthology. But alas, it would be just as easy to make an anthology out of the monstrosities in it – particularly from *Revelation* and *St Matthew*: but also, all that envy, self-pity and whining self-righteousness in St Paul's epistles.

◆ ◆ ◆

Is this (habitual) misery a form of wrestling with the angel? I wish I could think so: perhaps I can.

◆ ◆ ◆

'Perfect love casteth out fear.' Yes, but it is also true that nobody could love if he had never known fear. For fear is almost the deepest emotion which we all share. We can love each other in shared fear; we can love even strangers in the knowledge of the fear which they must share with us.

29 NOVEMBER

Finished *The Pilgrim's Progress* at last, after reading about two pages a day as part of my devotions. I cannot honestly say that I liked it at all, or derived any conscious benefit from it whatever. Alas? Sin and Judgement and cruel Self-Righteousness. How little time Christian spends on his journey trying to give real help to others, instead of abusing them for being so wickedly misguided.

◆ ◆ ◆

243

The Fall. Perhaps best to drop the term, so misleading are the biblical and subsequent associations. But *something* extraordinary and dramatic must have happened, at some time; or – much more probably – over a certain period of time. This was the entry into the human mind of (*a*) self-consciousness; (*b*) non-material values; (*c*) yearning for the unknown; (*d*) a sense of responsibility, with all its terrors.

A radical change from animal existence. The animal became a person; the brain became a soul.

♦ ♦ ♦

'The Passion is a symbol for man of the cruel and relentless nature of earthly life.' Leslie Paul, in *First Love*. Yes; but how much greater the Passion seems if it is taken as the presence and bitter suffering in this relentless world of a holy and heavenly soul which was braving a material reality never blessed or created by God.

Leslie Paul is also very good on the difference between the pagan and the Christian virtues. The first – prudence, fortitude, temperance, justice – are all of them defences against harsh reality: a fortress mentality, closing in against all the terrible dangers which surround us. Whereas the Christian virtues – Faith, Hope and Charity – all 'throw out tendrils into the future'. All of them, I would say, bravely expose the heart, body and spirit to the worst the world can do, in the faith that the transforming light of God can be found in even the most appalling aspect of this world.

♦ ♦ ♦

Perhaps it may be true that the fear/pain/misery which I experience now is a little more on others' behalf; a little less exclusively for myself.

♦ ♦ ♦

And on that walk through the mist to St Briavels I was also suddenly accosted with the words: 'Now is part of Always.' And I felt that this was not to be translated into high terms of Time and Eternity, but simply left to simmer on its own.

30 NOVEMBER
Reverend Mother seemed tired and sad at mass this morning. My monstrous feeling that she has *no right* to be so: as our mother she must wear an eternal smile of loving strength. A childish, not a childlike, reaction.

♦ ♦ ♦

The Italian earthquakes resurrect memories of the Lisbon earthquake in the eighteenth century. This time 'God' has followed up his first action by a series of unseasonable snowstorms, just to show what 'He' can do!

Odd how few orthodox Christians will ever quite face this *unavoidable* conclusion from their premises.

◆ ◆ ◆

I try to avoid the debilitating stabs of nostalgia: 'Be Here Now' and so on. But sudden uninvited memories of playing with Jason and Lucy on that castle mound in Suffolk; and then of those Ponham games* with Phine and Poll in the garden of Cob Cottage. In fact those were bad years; worse than these in many, many ways. But how strangely *all* lost time has the power to wound our present!

◆ ◆ ◆

We must not consider that which comes from our natural impulses as being part of our real selves. We are not responsible for our feelings but for our decisions. What does it matter if our sensible nature feels upset? If we act rightly, then all is well. You would probably rather not experience those perpetual contradictions in yourself of which St Paul also complained. But you will remember that our Lord did not agree with him and left him as he was. 'Unhappy man that I am! The good that I would I do not and the evil that I would not, that I do!'

In other words, we have not the characters we should like to have and we have those we should like not to have. What are we to do?

Instead of chasing after them, we must simply do without them and be satisfied with acting rightly, without wanting to feel inclined to such action.

Tourville again. And how often, lately, from him and others, I have been receiving the same sort of message!

◆ ◆ ◆

Revelation. The Christian revelation did not lessen the horrors of the world, but it added to them an enigmatic but capable-of-saving light.

◆ ◆ ◆

Buber's *Tales of the Hasidim* are a real marvel and eye-opener. They are very non-Christian: very funny: moving: holy: wise-innocent . . .

---

*Games based on 'Ponham', a mythical country invented by P T when himself a child (see *Part of a Journey*, pp. 93–4). Cob Cottage – S and P T's earlier home in Suffolk.

1 DECEMBER

Is there weeping in heaven for the poor victims of the Italian earth-quake? Surely there must be: and yet heaven is supposed to be a PLACE OF JOY!

Really, there are times when all this sort of thing seems so puzzling and contradictory that I wonder whether it mightn't be better to think no more about it. (As if I could!)

◆ ◆ ◆

Docility. A very good Christian word.

◆ ◆ ◆

I got *New Seeds of Contemplation* out of Tymawr library again. Perhaps Merton's supreme achievement. Depth after depth.

◆ ◆ ◆

Here are two intelligent and well-intentioned people who genuinely *love each other*. Yet they cannot live together in the same house without about one row every two weeks. What hopes, then, for those furious worlds of conglomerated strangers – such as America and Russia?

◆ ◆ ◆

This, from Pascal, quoted by Charles Williams in a splendid little book of daily prayers etc., sent me by R.M., entitled *The New Christian Year*: 'From all bodies together, we cannot obtain one single little thought; this is impossible, and of another order. From all bodies and minds, we cannot produce a feeling of true charity; this is impossible, and of another and supernatural order.'

I had quite forgotten this, though I read the *Pensées* so assiduously at one time. Of course it says better and far more concisely much that I have been stammering about in these journals. With his brilliant succinctness Pascal presents the whole compelling argument for belief in a higher order of reality.

2 DECEMBER

A Trip to Bristol. S dropped me near George's to do my shopping, drove on by herself to the new shopping centre. I got exactly the two presents I wanted in two different shops; then found exactly the two (rare) Oman books I wanted in George's second-hand department. As I was paying for these, and several other good finds, I asked the young man whether he knew the names of any bookshops in the country which specialised in second-hand religious books. He didn't; but a man just behind me immediately told me two, and also of a directory in which I could look for the names of others. Himself a bookseller, no doubt; but wore a faintly angelic guise to me.

Settling in the pub where we'd agreed to meet, I felt that my angel, if not the Heavenly Mother herself, had indeed done a wonderful job for me that morning.

Then in came poor S with a harried, almost agonised, face to tell me that she'd had to spend an hour parking the car; then been rebuffed in M & S trying to get a refund on a dress. Also believed the jack, etc. had been stolen . . . Worse was to follow. In the Queen's Street car park, where she'd left the car, we couldn't find it for twenty minutes. Mild horror on my part; but she was now in tears, which I understood all too well. The nightmare of the city as Xmas approaches, for bumpkins like she and me.

Thank God for a very soothing Chinese meal after that; and much love between us.

◆ ◆ ◆

Listening entranced to Verdi's *Otello* I suddenly thought that tragedy is, after all, no better than a monstrous hoax. For human misery is never in the least like this: splendour is the last thing we associate with the reality of suffering.

A sanctification of our misery, then?

I don't know. I am in the mood, these days, of feeling that I don't know anything at all.

◆ ◆ ◆

In George's I picked out a book and read a sentence which read something like this: 'The mind contains the actual object of its own worshipful desire; not the knowledge that the object exists outside itself.' Here lies the start of a major folly. The human mind, unable to bear the continued faith that God exists far outside and beyond it, and enters it only in the small degree that the mind can apprehend it, takes possession of God and appropriates him; makes him merely a deep element within itself. The ultimate bullfrog-expansion of the swollen ego.

◆ ◆ ◆

A friend in need to lunch. I'd planned to do some more earth-shifting after he'd gone; but he stayed till it was dark. I managed to remember that I had done far better work staying with S and him and talking than I could ever have done in the garden. Bravo!

◆ ◆ ◆

247

At one point Kierkegaard does manage to face the fact that he, like other failing Christians, cannot bring himself to give all – or even much – to the poor. But how spitefully, even self-righteously, he wriggles around even here.

◆ ◆ ◆

A terrible passage of virulent hatred and contempt about the villeins written by some nobleman or other. Even then the hatred of the rich for the poor was even greater than the other way round. Interesting, too, that it accuses these poor wretches of eating goose and drinking wine, etc. 'They *all* have colour TV, you know. And the woman who comes in for me has a much better washing-machine than *I* could possibly afford.' Ugh!

And on Radio Bristol the other day, a woman protesting that prisons seem to be like 'luxury hotels' these days. My furious impulse was to say, 'Put the bitch in one of those crowded cells for a month or two!' Unchristian!

◆ ◆ ◆

I have washed and polished the beautiful bit of quartz which Phine gave me long ago. And once again it serves as a marvellous object for the most detailed and scrupulous attention.

3 DECEMBER

Ah, how very good *Pantaloon* is in nearly all its parts. And how clearly, now, I can see which bits are weak and how they can be strengthened. Thank God those publishers refused it – though I doubt if any of them read far enough to reach the bad bits; or would have known, if they had.

◆ ◆ ◆

Speaking aloud to oneself with a very deliberate simplicity. I find this actually induces the simplicity, like artificial respiration. A refreshment of the mind.

4 DECEMBER

Monmouth. In a shop door, a woman and I stepped back smiling to let the other go through. I thought that I recognised the same propitiatory desire to please which I knew was on my own face; and which appears only on those faces which have displeased greatly in their time. In my case, I was not only feeling the old yellow bones of the past showing through my skin: I was also feeling guilty about my renewed fears; the *sickness* of constant brooding on horror, brought on this time by the armies of the Warsaw Pact gathering around Poland's frontiers.

Looking at the fields and woods on our way to Monmouth, at the faces and houses as I was shopping, I felt again as I used to in the late fifties. How normal; how everyday; how 'eternal' the valley, etc. But I look at them all as if I were visiting a friend in hospital who is on the point of death, but hasn't the least idea of it. Yes, and somehow there is indeed something sickening about this inextricable mixture of terror and pity.

Most of us, in any case, are hopelessly ill-equipped for even the normal conditions of life in this world. How we blunder along on this obstacle course; falling down and falling down . . .

5 DECEMBER
'Religion is the sign of the oppressed creature, the heart of a heartless world, just as it is the spirit of a spiritless situation.' So far this might be a profoundly melancholy observation by a profoundly religious man consciously enduring the dark night of his soul. Only after this moving preliminary does Marx add: 'It is the opium of the people.'

6 DECEMBER
I am now becoming quite attached to this little clock, with its hourly angelus of shrill pips. At least it forces me away from over-concentrated work or reading, and makes me take three minutes off to be as quiet and attentive as I can.

◆ ◆ ◆

In so many R C books they write about 'Catholic' this, 'Catholic' that; and some of them hardly use the word 'Christian' at all. In fact the more extreme of them sometimes seem as if they belonged to some weird semi-pagan rite of their own. This appears all too often in an otherwise fascinating life of that weird near-saint of fifty years ago, Vincent McNabb.

◆ ◆ ◆

'God' has now followed his Italian earthquake and subsequent winter storms with typhoid and typhus. He has *so many* things up his sleeve for his human victims: an infinite ingenuity.

But I came on this passage in late Merton which strongly suggests that he too was finding Almighty-God-the-Creator-of-All-Things a useless or worse than useless concept: 'The mercy of God in Christ . . . is the epiphany of hidden truth and of God's redeeming

249

Love for man. It is the revelation of God Himself, *not as infinite nature, as a "Supreme Being", and as ultimate, absolute power*, but as Love, as Creator and Father, as Son and Saviour, as Life-giving Spirit.' (My italics.) Though he uses the word 'Creator' here it seems in the context to mean Creator of Man through the entry of the 'Life-giving Spirit', in sharp distinction to any God of the Earthquakes.

◆ ◆ ◆

Oman's marvellous suggestion that we breathe the supernatural on earth as inevitably, and usually as unconsciously, as fish breathe air in water.

But alas, that great book *The Natural and the Supernatural*, which I found so triumphantly in George's, has the same fault as the new Küng, though scattered with better illuminations, so I think. It belongs to that now very old-fashioned order of careful and plodding religious apologetics which seems strangely irrelevant in our present situation.

Much more to the point is this little paperback called *The Gospel Without Compromise* by Catherine de Hueck Doherty. This is a passionate cry from the heart for genuine Christian witness – real brotherhood, fellowship, love – which means nothing less than those who have giving all except their own barest means of subsistence to those who have not. Not just giving money or goods, but giving themselves. Nothing less can save the modern world from destruction.

Yes; I believe this too. I do believe this too. But I am like the rich young man in the Gospels; I turn away sorrowful, knowing that I cannot do what is required of me.

But that doesn't mean that I can't do *anything*, surely.

8 DECEMBER
I have also evolved a prayer to be said in the car – though not for drivers. 'Heavenly Mother' – looking at a tree or hill or even the living edge of a motorway; 'Light of the World' – looking up at the sky; 'Have Mercy on Us' – looking down and closing the eyes.

10 DECEMBER
I've taken again to careful examination of the beautiful piece of quartz which Phine gave me years ago. I could go on examining it for a lifetime and never see all that is there to see; let alone memorise its marvellous facets – and great sudden heads of rhinos or old men. An

apparent object of love. But this is a metaphor, of course, and mustn't be sentimentalised into something else.

◆ ◆ ◆

Epigenesis is the word preferred by Waddington for what is usually called embryology. It stresses the fact that every embryological step is an act of *becoming* (Gk. *genesis*) which must be built upon (Gk. *epi*) the immediate *status quo ante* . . . In contrast with epigenesis and tautology, which constitute the worlds of replication, there is the whole realm of creativity, art, learning and evolution, in which the ongoing processes of change *feed on the random.* The essence of epigenesis is predictable repetition; the essence of learning and evolution is exploration and change.

This, from Gregory Bateson's fascinating *Mind and Nature*, is the beginning of wisdom for all scientists who are still down in the waste of materialist determinism.

◆ ◆ ◆

'You lucky cat,' said I to Bubbles lying on my bed, 'you never have to make decisions.' Yes, but perhaps we need to make, ought to make, far fewer than we usually suppose. Perhaps man is too proud of the image of himself as a decision-making animal.

◆ ◆ ◆

Who would dare to describe anyone else as a nonentity, if they thought for a moment what the word means? Even without working out its meaning the contempt behind the word is a terrible thing. Just as nobody is a nonentity, nobody is 'mediocre' or – somehow most terrible of all – 'second-rate'.

11 DECEMBER
Ah, how rationally, kindly and decently we talked across the kitchen table this morning. Then I read her a fine passage from Merton about rebirth – or rather about all the things that it is not. But at the end we both felt: 'Fine, but please send the instructions: we don't know how to play this game: where do we start . . . ?'

Well, I have my own idea of moves we could make; but that is a game which she will not, cannot, play. I mean some form of meditation together – the candle on the table . . . So I must be barking up the wrong tree: the Tree of Faith, perhaps, instead of the Tree of Love.

And at once I find this in Merton: 'If you regard contemplation principally as a means to escape from the miseries of human life, as

251

a withdrawal from the anguish and the suffering of this struggle for reunion with other men in the charity of Christ, you do not know what contemplation is and you will never find God in your contemplation.'

Should we, then, try to meet in the contemplation of our own love for each other? Why does that seem absurd: even disgusting? Perhaps because two turned so fixedly in on themselves is really no better than one. And because this 'love' which we talk and write so much about is something which can show itself only in action – best of all in quiet, unselfconscious, everyday, cohabitation. For 'love', prefer the moderate word 'consideration'.

12 DECEMBER
Cricked my back again, just like last year but much more mildly, and with what almost flagrant relief I retired to bed in total exemption of guilt. Or if there was any left – thinking of S and her almost desperate Christmas preparations – this was soon erased by starting further work on the revision of *Pantaloon*. (Possible *to make notes*, in bed, on what will need to be done. Exhilaration *both* in the long passages of splendid stuff *and* in the recognition of changes which must be made.)

13 DECEMBER
But out of this deep content up here in my own room, in my own bed, in my own mind, comes this frightening thought: 'Is it possible that in the end I shan't want to see *anyone, ever*?'

♦ ♦ ♦

Sometimes a parable or fable which presents an extreme hypothetical situation can suddenly and brightly illuminate a truth which is hard to see clearly by ordinary daylight.

Imagine, then, that the missiles have all been fired; that everyone on earth has either been killed or is bound to die by radiation, etc., except for ten young men and ten young women in a single perfectly constructed fall-out shelter. Imagine that they have everything they need, and that they are as sure as they can be that they will be able to stay alive in the shelter until it is safe to emerge. Imagine that they are qualified to create a tolerable life for themselves in the devastated world, and thus begin to repopulate the world again. They know that they represent the only surviving hope for the continuation of the human race.

Now imagine that a dying old woman staggers up to the shelter and starts frantically beating her fists on the perspex door, obviously imploring those inside to let her in as well. They know that if they open the door they will die as surely as she will; that the very act of opening the door will condemn the human race to extinction. They also know, of course, that this particular old woman is only one among thousands of millions who are dying in the world outside.

What do they do?

Surely the humanist answer must be that they keep the door firmly sealed and let the old woman die. And surely the Christian answer must be that they open the door, welcome the old lady in with love, and do all they can to comfort her in dying before they have to begin offering the same comfort to each other.

In other words, either the human race continues, at the cost of an act of cruel and conscious rejection; or it ends, in an act of pure love.

I felt greatly exhilarated by this, until I thought that perhaps I heard, in the second case, the golden sound of softly applauding angels. Which would spoil the whole grand affair, of course; not because the angels would applaud – as I'm sure they would – but because if that was in the minds of the twenty holy young people their action would be hopelessly contaminated.

So one must assume that they perform their act of love and mercy purely for its own sake and not at all because they hope to win heavenly approval for it. Yet – how desperately complex these wily hypotheticals can become! – *we* know that such an act of pure and racially-suicidal love could be performed only by people in whom the Holy Spirit was working.

◆ ◆ ◆

God is a strange person indeed – the only one I know who never answers when I address him.

◆ ◆ ◆

I have always known that most of my praying must be to a pattern, just as true art always contains a pattern. But just as the good artist knows how and when to break his pattern, so I must learn – have begun to learn – how to break the pattern of my prayer. Usually by very simple and direct talking.

14 DECEMBER
Well then, what would you really desire most from God if you could get what you asked for? 'To live with my wife in holy and loving happiness until we die.'

◆ ◆ ◆

To Bubbles, lying on my bed as I prepare to begin my evening prayer:
'All right then; you're welcome to stay and partake of this meal, such
as it is: my spiritual Kattomeat. And though you would certainly
prefer the real stuff, it is *possible* that you may share something of this
with me too.'

◆ ◆ ◆

The harpooning and cutting up of a whale, on TV. These were the
traditional whalers from the Azores and the note of the programme
was regret for the passing of their way of life, ousted by the great
factory-whalers of the Antarctic. But I felt, 'Yes of course, this is what
we are really like' – and *deeply, deeply*. What hope is there for man
when this sort of thing is deep in his nature?

Yes, and I have spent some of the most joyful hours of my life
fly-fishing for trout – i.e. killing not out of necessity but for pleasure.
Alas! And would do so again if it was offered. I gave up at the time of
the BH community not because of any true revulsion but because it
seemed a wrongful waste of time and petrol to make those summer
expeditions to the Monnow.

15 DECEMBER

Violent depressive tears again. It is not that one really *believes* at such
times that the horror will last for ever, but that it is impossible to
envisage or conceive of any other condition.

But now, in my recovery, I suddenly think of that encounter group
in 1972. Why have I put it so much out of my mind that I didn't even
mention it in the review of my past religious life which I was asked to
write as a preface to *Part of a Journey*? Partly, perhaps, because S hated
that experience as much as I was deeply moved and changed by it. I
was in frequent tears *of love* for at least a month afterwards; and it was,
I'm sure, the closest I've ever come to a true religious experience.

No, there was nothing false about it – certainly nothing sentimental. *That* was the time – years before I usually reckon it – when
my heart and mind were at least partially opened.

◆ ◆ ◆

We are the prisoners of, among so many things, our *scale*; both of time
and space. Imagine a being for whom our universe is an atom; a
million of our years, a second. Why not? Limited by our scale, by our
five senses, by our small minds, how do we ever *dare* to forget the
enormity of our ignorance!

◆ ◆ ◆

At times the very highest intent is to get through the day somehow, using every available means of support. And there is real heroism in this – absurd though it must sound to the young, the stable, the strong, the healthy, the good.

◆ ◆ ◆

One of the great blasphemies of our time has been committed against children and childhood. How I used to pride myself on seeing them as naturally savage creatures who have to be tamed, as kindly as possible, into the rigours of adult life. But there is a special holiness in childhood, as I understand now, perhaps for the first time. And for the first time the famous NT quotations have come startlingly alive to me. 'Except you become as a little child . . . '
 What a task!
 In fact, 'Oh why hadn't I realised before . . . ' is about the best of all our wails: or can be. And in very small things too; for example, the positive pleasure to be found in lighting the fire each day in our wood-burning stove, instead of treating it as a dull chore. And this will be granted me almost every single day from October to May.

◆ ◆ ◆

Nearly every definitive promise of salvation in the NT is balanced by a threat of damnation. It must be accepted – but how few Christians do – that the *biblical* Jesus told us to love our enemies but constantly damned his own to hell.

◆ ◆ ◆

Read Schweitzer's autobiography for the first time; and without any strong feeling except a sort of bewilderment that he could have done so much. 'Reverence for life' seems to me to be one of those catchphrases which solve nothing – say nothing which hasn't been better said long ago.

◆ ◆ ◆

It still seems to me that the only true rebellion of my lifetime was the counter-culture and hippies of the late sixties and early seventies. There were plenty of follies there, of course, some of which I joined in myself. But this movement rebelled against the right things in the right way. All forms of violence and deliberate ugliness simply take the current values of adult society and carry them a stage further: a strange form of denial.

16 December

I have never seen so clearly before that all arguments for or against the existence of God are useless and ridiculous. To think of Freddie and that Jesuit going through all their clever gymnastics on the wireless in the forties and fifties! How could that Father X not have seen that there is nothing to be said; only things to be done.

◆ ◆ ◆

Sudden very vivid memory of ordering beautiful and expensive photographic equipment about ten years ago. I used to include with my order a request for instant dispatch, pretending that I was just about to go away somewhere. This was because I *couldn't wait* to get the new enlarger or zoom lens. And I can't deny that the pleasure of the parcel arriving was very great.

◆ ◆ ◆

A new spoken-aloud recollection of the day at the 11 p.m. angelus. At the end I said, 'And you are helping me to understand what has happened today.

'Well, but do I really *feel* that this is so; that you are present and listening? No, not quite; but I certainly feel this more than I feel that it is not so.'

17 December

Walked 'the wrong way' round the loop, which I haven't done for years: it is quite a different walk, of course; and perhaps a better one. But it means steep climbing at the start, which is why I usually choose the other way.

An absurd conversation with my mother: 'You didn't really do so badly – in some ways, quite well. But of course you see now that I haven't done too badly either. Or say, that both of us have done equally badly. But do I really believe this? No, I'm afraid I don't – I *really* think that I've done quite a lot better than you did, though I know perfectly well that it is not at all correct to say such things . . . '
Then I thought of myself sobbing at her death-bed and wondered, genuinely wondered, whether she had seen me there. Then I thought that if, as we somehow always assume, the dead can read our minds and hearts, she would have known that although it may have been partly the drink that was doing the sobbing there was also a seed of truth and love in my grief. Has it flowered since then? Well, it has certainly germinated and grown a little.

Apples on the bare trees, looking as if someone had hung them there.

But soon my mind was off on an all-too-familiar fantasy – that when I got back from my walk S would tell me, after tantalising me first with a little guessing, what had happened while I'd been away. Yes, a telegram from Philip Larkin to 'Theodore Philips' to say that he has won the poetry competition . . .

Caught myself at this too; and immediately, rather guiltily, began staring hard at the valley and making appreciative comments – 'Yes, yes, it's such a *soft* light, isn't it? Really great.'

So much of my life has been lived as if it were being witnessed that it would seem even more absurd if there is none.

◆ ◆ ◆

By now I am well aware of certain downward spirals which one must not enter – e.g. the real shame inspired by this book, *The Gospel Without Compromise*. Yes, I am a rotten Christian hanging on to my money as I do. But perhaps there is a certain creditable humility in admitting this. Perhaps it is my proper role to suffer this guilt. But such complacency is intolerable . . . etc., etc.

Or, in the case of my mother: 'I know that I shouldn't think that I've done better than her. But it is better to say that I do think this than to pretend that I don't. Perhaps; but it is quite wrong to be satisfied with *that* . . .'

I present these as examples of spirals which I do not, in fact, any longer enter: or rather I withdraw the instant I feel myself being sucked down into one of those futile vortices.

In fact altogether, on this walk, a fairly high level of enjoyable fatuity.

◆ ◆ ◆

But suppose that, instead of these anthologies of joyful 'religious experience', one were to make a collection of *saisons* – or moments – *en enfer*?

The result would not, I think, be *an equivalent* to the others. What would be lacking would be that sense of a deeper and more abundant reality. In fact, what is felt is emptiness, not fullness.

◆ ◆ ◆

As for religious experience in general, I feel that I am like an enthralled spectator at a play; and it seems less and less likely that I shall ever be given a part to play on the stage. And am quite content with this.

◆ ◆ ◆

Nature mysticism. Always a bit of a bother to me, though I suppose it's the only kind I've ever come near to experiencing. I believe it

257

should be described as high aesthetic emotion, rather than true religious experience.

◆ ◆ ◆

One very important point . . . is that you can't see the demonic unless you are fortified by divine power. The demonic seen as demonic is a divine revelation of what is against spiritual goodness and wisdom. This revelation of the 'againstness' of something is a tremendous good as a protection; it is the revelation of evil in its true, its proper nature. First of all in human life, we are immersed in those evils of fixation, wrong tendencies that drag us down or impede progress . . .

This – from Michael Whiteman, whom I greatly respect as the most hard-headed modern mystic I know of – is very tempting. But does it account for people who play around with black masses, etc. and thoroughly enjoy whatever it is they experience?

18 December
Nature mysticism again. However powerful the impression of the whole universe as 'one great harmony', etc., we know in our non-mystical minds that this simply is not the case. Nature is full of conflict, confusion, disaster, cruelty . . . Therefore it may be that the person who believes that he is experiencing the natural world in this way is really penetrating the appearances and having a direct experience of another realm altogether. In fact he/she may be glimpsing Heaven through and by means of earthly objects, yet failing to recognise that this is what is happening.

◆ ◆ ◆

Another Matthew Manning book. Demonstration after demonstration of quite amazing psychic powers, amply confirmed by many witnesses. And Pinkie, who has heard him address the Society for Psychical Research, is quite convinced of his sincerity.

But the scientists often almost flee at his approach; so terrified are they of the stubbornly inexplicable.

20 December
Gifts of God and Love. S's sudden idea, when Laura was in great distress, that Jean M might be able to help her more than either of her parents can. So we took Laura over to Ross and left her with Jean for an hour; and the effect was wonderfully good. Such occasions –

beginning with the idea 'occurring' to S – come as much-needed confirmations of faith.

◆ ◆ ◆

My angelus-alarm nearly always surprises me, even if I have seen only a minute or two before that the hands of the clock are just approaching a quarter past. But sometimes those absurd little pips sound almost like a heavenly voice gently recalling me to a welcome and needed activity.

21 DECEMBER

To Tymawr on the darkest day of the year. Immense refreshment after two weeks of fairly severe trials. A good, quiet sermon by John R about waiting in the wilderness of Advent for the great event. And a particularly warm talk with Mother and Sister P. They were telling me about making alterations upstairs to hold two new postulants; and I asked them not to forget that I would be applying before very long. Rather more than a joke: a longing.

As I was the only guest, I was given my breakfast on a tray in the library; and felt this a great privilege. Sun was up as I drove home, ten times happier than I'd been on the dark drive over there.

◆ ◆ ◆

I really must stop puzzling about 'Why?': not 'Why am I here?', etc., but 'How should I be?', etc.

22 DECEMBER

Finally tried to tell John R the whole story of our married life, with all the honesty I could command (and with S's permission). He could not have been better, or wiser. By our apparently endlessly repeated misery we may be doing what God is inviting us to do; may have to endure it for the sake of something of which we ourselves can never be fully aware.

He ended by saying that, having twice been with us together, he could hardly believe that we'd been married thirty years – ' . . . there seemed to be something so sweet and simple in your relationship.' For me this is the final confirmation that we do, together, somehow unconsciously reflect the love of God. Too many people have now said this; and all people I greatly respect.

So out of hammer-and-tongs comes the quiet glow from the hearth. After the fur has been flying fiercely all over the place, it evidently settles down into an extra smoothness of the two pelts. Amazing!

Wisdom. Can always be detected by the fact that it reveals something to one of which one was almost, or half, aware before. Even that it confirms the momentary illuminations which, without confirmation, we might so easily dismiss as fantasies.

◆ ◆ ◆

I have taken to making much more thorough recollections of the day when my 10.15 angelus sounds. One good effect of this is to make me realise that the days, far from following each other in a greyish-black sequence, are all quite distinct; unique and variegated. Lights suddenly shine in forgotten places – lights of love and happiness just as often as those corrective lights which make me aware of many a minor perfidy or ignobility, usually in the mind, but often in word or action too.

◆ ◆ ◆

From Lev Gillet:

> Don't quantify God. Don't quantify the love of God. The love of God is a kind of atmospheric pressure which is bearing on everybody equally. The only difference is that there are people who open themselves up to this pressure, while others close themselves. But it is the same undivided, total, divine, absolute love surrounding everybody, speaking to everybody, acting on everybody.

Beautiful! Better than my model – in 'Evensong at Peterborough' – of a dark globe surrounded by divine light pressing to enter it. But entirely the same idea.

Or this, from an anonymous contributor to one of the Religious Experience Research Unit books, *Living the Questions*:

> It's rather like being in a room with a hydraulic ceiling. When you have such an experience as this the ceiling is raised. There are so many ways in which the outer, conscious person can be enriched. He has to fill up this area, this volume that is left when the ceiling is raised . . . For when the ceiling is raised that new space is quite hollow. You are invited to fill it up – in fact you have to do so. And each time it is as though a list were given to you. Further potential of character, of evolution, is shown to you, to fill the newly created space: what you have it in you to become. And the consequence is that you do feel in part a new person, with a greater capacity than before.

Yes; *I know what is being said.*

23 DECEMBER
Jeffrey came over this morning to tell us that Edward has cataracts on

260

both his eyes. Horror and pity, mitigated by love, and by gratitude to him and Nasi for feeling that we are people who ought to be told.

He came again after they'd taken the baby to a specialist in Cheltenham; and it seems most likely that an operation can be performed and that the only bad effect is that he'll have to wear glasses at least for much of his childhood.

I was sharply reminded of Phine's birth; my first sight of my first child in her oxygen tent. Also, of all poor Laura's multiple woes in infancy. Perhaps because parental love is the most natural, in fact the easiest, it is also true that nearly all parents suffer more with the afflictions of their children than with the afflictions even of each other. (Of course, extreme vulnerability and dependence come into this as well.)

◆ ◆ ◆

Jase telling me about helping to organise a CND group in Coventry. He will do far better at this than I did in the late fifties – but I find a certain pathos in his determination to see even this as a means towards 'revolution'. How hard that old illusion dies! 'A really new under-standing of socialism,' he said; and I realised that I am no longer a socialist at all, if that still implies a belief that social rearrangements – however drastic – will eventually create the Good Society. (And yet how despairing, and somehow unctuous, it sounds to say that 'only a change of heart . . . ' and so on.)

24 DECEMBER
And P, who was a complete stranger a year ago and whom we've only seen two or three times since then, writes: 'Meeting you and Sally is the best thing that has happened in 1980.' I cannot resist writing down these testimonials, coming as they always do as such a strange reminder that we do not *seem* like people who spend so much of their time in one kind of torment or another.

I have even wondered whether the prayer we say together every night and morning may, perhaps, have enabled God . . . It often seems so weary and perfunctory, but it is a real prayer for love, trust and honour between us. And, of course, I know that these are far deeper than the anger.

◆ ◆ ◆

This book by Baroness de Hueck Doherty called *The Gospel Without Compromise* has the same kind of extreme but entirely sane passion which I find in Merton. (Re-reading *New Seeds of Contemplation*.) And now that I'm reading Monica Furlong's life of Merton I learn that they were close friends when Merton was a young man, torn between becoming a monk and joining Baroness de Hueck's first Madonna Friendship House in Harlem.

The Gospel Without Compromise is a noble and anguished cry that Christians should live their faith instead of endlessly talking about it. And 'Yes,' I say, 'yes, how very true, how very true!', knowing as I say it that I shall never live in the way that she rightly demands.

◆ ◆ ◆

As for Merton, I often feel that I strangely resemble him – but rather in the way that a slow-worm resembles a python. (Or is this false modesty? No, I don't think so, for Merton was a great *man*, and I shall never be that. On the other hand, it still seems to me possible – likely? – that *Pantaloon* is a queer sort of great book.)

◆ ◆ ◆

At least I am certain of this – that I shall never abandon this search as long as I live. By which I mean that I shall never despair.

28 DECEMBER
Evening prayer on the rosary: The Hope of God followed by The Work of God. The first is the prayer of a man caught in a mine disaster and praying for the rescuers to reach him in time. The second is the digging, picking and shovelling of the rescuers, which the trapped man may not hear at all for many hours or days. (Yes; and perhaps he may die before they reach him. But even this doesn't mean that they weren't trying with all their might to reach him.)

◆ ◆ ◆

Weeping in the bathroom in a state of very grim depletion, I suddenly seemed to be presented with a picture of myself at twenty-five, as if seen from the outside. And I was enabled to say, well, at least I am closer to being a human person than he was. What an *automaton* he seems to me now: a wild automaton, but none the less driven by compelling and scarcely examined inner forces.

◆ ◆ ◆

Lucky indeed to be reading this fine life of Merton during this bad time.

◆ ◆ ◆

The Incarnation. For me the value of this idea lies in the way it anchors man to God; can save him from the terrible vaporisings of theological abstraction. What is God? Well, he showed a great deal of himself in Jesus: showed, perhaps, as much as we would be able to see.

◆ ◆ ◆

There is a kind of love which suffers constant erosion from the acid of repeated and repeated conflict. But there is another kind of love which is able to see each bout as a shared and not a separating pain. It is at least possible that we have been blessed with this second kind of love.

◆ ◆ ◆

Much worried, too, about my relationship with Terry and the *Observer*. It seems to me that I am being steadily pushed out, as if in preparation for my retirement next year. But what I'd hoped, and T had spoken of, was that I would be on contract after that to write, say, twenty-five reviews a year. It's only lately that I've come to realise how desperately I would miss reviewing if I were altogether deprived of it. This journal is no substitute for that particular kind of pulpiteering!

29 DECEMBER
How hard it is for religious writers not to have too much or too little common sense. How fatal an excess of it – the deadness, the dreariness: how fatal an insufficiency – the phoniness, the false extravagance and 'poetics'.

30 DECEMBER
The Incarnation. We certainly need the idea of *a* person in whom God and Man were exceptionally united.

◆ ◆ ◆

Tuchman – *A Distant Mirror: The Calamitous Fourteenth Century*. I can only bear twenty or thirty pages at a time, so desolating is this history of that frightful century. The darkness is almost unrelieved; and when I came on one man who at least refused to recant on the scaffold, died bravely and with a humble prayer, I almost burst into tears.

◆ ◆ ◆

The human existent is redeemed and delivered into the full freedom of the Christian person when it is liberated from the demonic and futile project of self-redemption – the self-contradictory and self-defeating enterprise of establishing itself in unassailable security as if its existence were identical with being, and as if it were completely autonomous . . . This implies a constant wearying effort at deception, with eager thrusts of passion and power, constantly frustrated and falling back into the cunning futility of trying to outwit reality itself.

Very late Merton: he has obviously been reading existentialists – but what good use he makes of them.

◆ ◆ ◆

I got into a state of mild rage and desperation in the garden today – failing to make a wall stand up. But this made me pleasantly aware of how rare this is nowadays; how dreadfully common it used to be. (Watch out for a blow from the Great Smugness-Punisher Above!)

◆ ◆ ◆

Pantaloon. What a joy it is to be working at it again; to find that nearly all of it is so very good, and that when there are changes to be made I can easily and fluently return to that idiom and posture.

I was so emphatic, at the end of the first published volume, that this was not to be in any sense a *Bildungsroman*; not a progression towards any Great Light, but a constellation of equal lights. Yet how plain it is to me now that the book is a journey towards the light of God – though never, of course, into it.

◆ ◆ ◆

Anne's angel fell from my Holy Shelf and broke on the floor. No superstitious feelings whatever, I'm happy to say; and it can easily be mended.

◆ ◆ ◆

There is always something at least faintly ridiculous about 'doing' theology; and describing oneself as 'a theologian'. I am reminded of Rajneesh's very proper mockery of the title 'Doctor of Divinity'. Also, of the fact that our dreary scripture lessons at school were known as 'Div'. I don't recall that any of us ever had a single revelation of God.

◆ ◆ ◆

So 1981 begins for me with one of those constant upsurges of deep shame. What are you doing for *them*, for the afflicted of the earth; the starved, the tortured, the oppressed? What can anything you write do compared with that minimal act of *giving money*?

1 JANUARY

Can't bear to read Tuchman any longer. (Hard to remember that this was the century not only of Dame Julian but of all the great Rhineland and English mystics.)

♦ ♦ ♦

My afternoon's work – levelling the far end of the lawn – was as good as yesterday's attempt to build the wall was bad. The beautiful action of digging directly out of one place and throwing the earth onto another; both operations being essential parts of the work. As one side sinks, the other rises. Very satisfying.

And I was thinking of the much-improved bowls we shall play in the summer; thinking of all these domestic games and their great value. S and I at draughts or chess are not in real conflict; we are in a state of communion over the chess-board. Or on the bowling green.

♦ ♦ ♦

'We cannot know whether we love God, although there may be strong reasons for thinking so, but there can be no doubt about whether we love our neighbour or not.' St Theresa.

It may be a slight sign of grace that I now take almost as much pleasure in finding a good quotation for this journal as I do in thinking or experiencing something apparently on my own. (In both cases I like to think – and almost do think – that the Spirit has blown into my mind.)

♦ ♦ ♦

The film of *Papillon* on TV. The three of us were strangely drawn together – S, Laura and I – as we watched it far beyond my usual bedtime. Love in the frightful darkness of Devil's Island and French Guyana. A more highbrow fashion of the last twenty years has been to produce works of total, unrelieved horror and despair. This is thought to be both 'honest' and 'deep'. In fact it is an act of vulgar wickedness: a slick, unearned despair.

I was going to write that no great work of art can be morally odious – however skilfully evil minor works may be. Then I thought: 'But what about the *Inferno*?' A very great work, I take it (have read it only in translation); yet the whole theme is not only physical torture but punitive physical torture. What's more, the victims are often Dante's personal enemies.

Surely it is an outrageous operation, however magnificent the language, etc.

◆ ◆ ◆

I keep on trying to write a creed; and failing. Its only function would be to establish a provisional liberation within a new order: a new opening towards the future, and therefore towards its own super-session. In fact it would have exactly the same function as a new scientific theory.

◆ ◆ ◆

Christian prophetic hope assumes that all existing societies are evil and can be improved. It utterly denies that a perfect society can ever be created. The very idea of a perfect earthly society is a sort of insult to the human person – for every utopia reduces individual men and women to Man, or Human Nature. Real men and women must always be too awkward and strangely shaped to be fitted neatly together like toy bricks in their box by a social engineer.

Also, of course, the Christian faith assumes that we must always, while on earth, be in a state of tension, at the least; constantly disturbed by the difference between what we are and what we might be.

◆ ◆ ◆

And I immediately find Schillebeeckx saying this much better than I have: 'For men who believe in God, any socio-political liberation is only partial; indeed if it claims to be *total*, it essentially becomes a new form of servitude and slavery.'

(But how strange that Merton's name doesn't appear in the index of either of Schillebeeckx's great books on the NT. That world of Christian scholarship is a world of its own. It seems that they write almost entirely for each other.)

2 JANUARY

There is, of course, the possibility that some – the more 'deserving' – survive death and continue to move forward in another realm; while others are snuffed out, having failed to qualify. I find this idea deeply offensive, whether I imagine myself to be in the first group or in the second.

◆ ◆ ◆

The Hasidim. I love Buber's tales, and love these strange holy men through those pages. But reading their history is another matter. Alas, they were rent with personal feuds and envy. And what about this: 'The Besht believed that there was a spark of divinity in every Jew. Jacob Issac went further and maintained . . . that every Jew could be a Moses and should be satisfied with nothing less.' Of course what one expected from Jacob Issac's going further was that even a very few *gentiles* might, on occasions . . . The absolute inward-turning of those people can't be explained by persecution. They were saintly, deeply ingrown men and women.

But then how very few holy persons have combined deep spiritual passion with openness of mind and heart. *We must try to do both.*

3 JANUARY
Carol service at Tymawr this afternoon. I found that I was in a bad humour as I drove over there; and my uneasiness was increased by the fact that I was put in the front row, and at the end nearest the altar. This meant that when some danced, to my right, and some sang, to my left, I felt that I ought to be constantly looking from one lot of Sisters to the others. What's more, I could see the dancers only by awkwardly twisting my neck round to the right.

I began to feel the absurdity of the situation; and also the endearing absurdity of the whole performance. And this put me in a much better humour. I had indeed prayed that this would happen, but had supposed that it would be granted, if at all, by some access of serious devotion. Not at all. And how much more than we guess – I guess – God acts through our sense of the absurd.

In fact, I did feel afterwards that the Sisters had gone too far in this affair; that it was altogether too much of a performance, and that the invited guests were an audience rather than fellow-participants.

But what has stayed most vividly in the mind was a glimpse of Father L's face as he was praying; a simplicity of trust and goodness which I had never seen in him before. *There* was a true reflection of God's holy light.

4 JANUARY
A *zooming* afternoon. The work went with a satisfying rhythm, and the new prayer, found on the back of a pamphlet about Worcester Cathedral, sang up into the sky as if it was bound to reach expectant and gratified ears there.

'Grant, O Lord, that we, following in the steps of those who have loved and served thee here, may be so guided by the Holy Spirit that we may think those things that are right, speak those things that are true and ever follow thy calling; through Jesus Christ our Lord.'

It was at the word 'calling' that my spirit seemed to soar up into that wonderfully clear and receptive blue-green winter sky.

(But I have now changed it around a little – ' . . . think those things that are true, speak those things that are right . . . ' I do feel that this is much better, for we should always think as truthfully as we can, but there are many, many occasions when we should think, or write letters, rightly but not truthfully.)

5 JANUARY

S has gone off to spend two nights with Lucy and Bernard, so I am in the very unusual situation of being alone here. None of the craving for company I've felt when left alone before. Even a certain fatuous self-satisfaction at my self-sufficiency, as I fry my own sausages and settle down with them in front of the telly.

♦ ♦ ♦

'And the darkness comprehendeth it not.' I know this really means 'the darkness has not overcome it'; but I like the apparent meaning better. We, in the dark of the world, simply cannot understand the light of God, however much we may blindly grope towards it.

♦ ♦ ♦

I may repeat 'The Pain of the World' ten times at every evening prayer, trying to understand the phrase by staring at either Verlaine or Julia. But I know, of course, that if the whole pain of the world really flowed into any single human mind and heart they would be utterly and instantly burnt out, like a fused wire. I don't believe that even the greatest and most loving saint could survive such an experience. The anguish of individual human beings – past, present and, perhaps most terrifying, future – is as inconceivable as the love of God.

And alas, the love of God 'cannot withstand it'.

♦ ♦ ♦

A multiple sclerosis victim on TV: 'You've got to believe in something.' My ears prick up at once. 'And I believe in the non-animal-fat diet.' The joke is on me; not on her.

♦ ♦ ♦

These from Gabriel Marcel's *Problematic Man*:

To the extent that he learns to speak in an atmosphere of love, the child participates in a kind of re-creation of the world.

There is perhaps no one, even outside of all religious practice or conviction, who has not had the direct experience of this influx of being which can emanate for each of us from a word heard, sometimes even from a smile or a gesture. We are here beyond all psychology, for this word or this gesture are essentially bearers of something else, which can certainly not be contained in a formula or a concept. What is significant is that he who has addressed this word or smile to us appears to us, without any such intention or even awareness, as the witness of a certain transcendent reality.

(*Cp.* Father L at Tymawr, whose expression of utter trust was not even directed at me. Yes, and it even seems that there are times when S and I *together* reflect the light of God's love without being in the least aware of it.)

The main point of Marcel's noble little book is that Christians must accept the 'inquietude' in themselves which too many of them suppose to be a peculiar attribute of modern, irreligious man. Not just because we feel for them (the irreligious), but because we share their experience of tension, doubt, dissociation . . . Unless we do so, we become like the Pharisee praising himself for not being as other men.

◆ ◆ ◆

'My Lord and God, take this myself from me and give it as thine own to thee.'

I have been saying this prayer lately with great vigour and *empressement*. But today I suddenly thought: 'Yes, but do I really mean this when I say it? In fact what does *it* mean, anyway?' Well, I half-know what it means; and half-mean what I half-know that it means. This kind of ambiguity seems to be an essential part of the whole business.

8 JANUARY
The old apple on my shelf had begun to lose its colour, so instead of it I started arranging four small Cox's in a pyramid. It took me about twenty minutes to get them as I wanted – in the right state of disorder under control: or order broken in just the right way and to the right extent. Which is what all art is aiming at. And which life itself ought also to be like. (I am more and more amazed, as my recollections improve, by the total individuality of each day, within such an obvious framework of apparent monotony and repetition.)

◆ ◆ ◆

Father P today: 'You are lucky, you know, to have started so late in life. Things come freshly to you which those of us who have been believers all our life find all too familiar.'

When I told him about my reviewing worries, he said: 'I imagine that you now feel it is a vocation.' Well, I hadn't quite got to that point; but how eagerly I agreed. And an essential part of that vocation is, in a sense, *not to let it show*. I do sometimes feel that many of my readers must be saying, 'There he goes again,' as soon as I turn pious on them.

What a difficult craft this reviewing has now become: to be as honest a Christian witness as I can be, while remaining a lively *general* reviewer.

◆ ◆ ◆

Praying tonight, I suddenly said: 'You who are there!' For often, now, I envisage a close, friendly, attentive and *limited* intermediary spirit. Less limited than I am, but by no means the Great I AM, Ultimate Being, etc.

◆ ◆ ◆

I always knew that *Pantaloon* would not be a tragic work; and indeed it is not. The old question remains of whether Christian tragedy is possible. Only in the sense, I suppose, of a believer losing his faith; for so long as there is Hope there can't be genuine tragedy.

◆ ◆ ◆

Contrition. I never can feel, when reflecting on my lurid past, that I ought to apologise to God for it – though perhaps I should indeed apologise to some people whom I injured. But the real point of the operation now seems to be this: that we use the sins, errors, follies of our past – right up to yesterday – to make a kind of compost out of which present and future flowers may grow. A rasher metaphor would be that the past, rotting down as it should, gives off a gas which we can light and see by; see better by.

◆ ◆ ◆

Extraordinary how much there is in the OT, and in the NT also, about 'my enemies'. Some of the psalm-writers, for example, seem to be constantly surrounded by wicked men whose whole object is to harm or destroy the psalmist. An odd conception of life.

◆ ◆ ◆

S gave me a magnificent reproduction of Seurat's *La Grande Jatte* for Xmas, and I took it to Monmouth yesterday to be framed. I used that picture a great deal in *Views From a Lake*,* to represent the middle-

---

* Seventh section of earlier version of *Pantaloon*, published by Chatto & Windus in 1968.

bourgeois course against the revolutionary course (Delacroix's barricade) and the aristocratic (Watteau's *Departure for Cythera*). But of course the picture means far more to me than that. It is one of the most *mysterious* pictures I know. Ominous, perhaps: but perhaps also *expectant*. The stiff figures might suddenly burst into weird but radiant life and movement.

Meanwhile, my prayers across the Bruegel continue to provide sudden small revelations. For example, that 'The Hope of God' is attached to the towering white cliff in the left-hand top corner: 'The Work of God' to the ploughman and his furrows. And I thought – for the first time – that perhaps our hopes of God are too high, too sublime, while his work is really going on at a much lower level.

◆ ◆ ◆

High Noon for the third or fourth time. *Good* old Gary Cooper! Good for him, goodness me!

◆ ◆ ◆

Meditation. At best a successful walk along a tightrope; *not* falling off on either side into mental wandering, *but always* aware of the balancing feat which is being performed. In other words the mind may avoid wandering, but only by concentrating attention on this act of avoidance. Whereas, of course, the mind ought not to be clenched in that way, but gloriously open, still and free.

How hard are Thy ways, O Lord!

10 JANUARY
Dying We Live. Perhaps it is easier for God to reach people when they are in a really extreme situation. (How few people, whether believers or not, die 'badly'; even in appalling circumstances.)

11 JANUARY
A simple but very useful form of instruction: the sudden recognition that we ourselves are reacting in exactly the same way we recently found inexplicable, or even blameworthy, in somebody else.

◆ ◆ ◆

Strange resemblance between much of the *Gita* and Stoicism. The notion of being 'cold, unmoving and to temptation slow'. I find this ideal wholly wrong: a form of iron complacency.

◆ ◆ ◆

How much are you worried *about the Poles*?

Alas, I am much more worried about the dangers *for us* of a Russian invasion.

◆ ◆ ◆

Prayer in the garden, resting from digging:

> Heavenly Mother,
> Light of the World . . .

And as I looked up at the sky a flock of gulls was glinting and gliding just overhead. Very satisfactory.

◆ ◆ ◆

More splendid Merton from this posthumous collection (*Love and Living*). 'A demonic existence is one which insistently diagnoses what it cannot cure, what it has no desire to cure, what it seeks only to bring to full potency in order that it may cause the death of its victim.' (Sartre, etc.)

◆ ◆ ◆

The one thing which seems to have *slightly* disturbed Kierkegaard's almost unbroken self-righteousness was his occasional recognition that he was not living as Christ told us to live – i.e. giving all to the poor, etc. But he used this awareness to praise himself for his honesty, as against all those awful parsons!

◆ ◆ ◆

Evening prayer, through *Fall of Icarus*. It is at 'The Work of God' (ploughman, plough and furrows) that I feel my ignorance is greatest. We simply cannot know what he is doing in the world. On the other hand, we can be sure of our Hope of God; and even fairly sure of our Peace of God, when it descends. 'The Love of God' is simply our fundamental act of faith. 'The Light of God' is mysterious, because it must include much more than we recognise as being this.

◆ ◆ ◆

I used to have bitten and perhaps dirty finger nails. During the last two or three years I have let them grow, and I am almost obsessed about keeping them clean. As so often – from one foolish extreme to the other, though fully knowing that wisdom lies between.

◆ ◆ ◆

Resolution to study the Old Testament. In a way it is more obviously interesting than the New Testament; so much and such extraordinary history involved.

The great pleasure of walking in rain or snow is that I feel myself so thoroughly *in* the weather; and to be fully sharing it with trees, fields, hedges, etc. If this is nature mysticism it is only the very mildest form of it. My affection – if it is that – for non-human forms of life seems to me to be based simply on our having shared such a long heritage of evolution: you coming all that way to be here, at this moment, with me who have travelled a different but contemporary journey.

On the same walk I was saying my outdoor prayer (or car prayer) and had fixed on a single tree for 'Heavenly Mother'. But then I saw that there was another tree half-hidden behind it; so I immediately switched to 'Mothers', and with a sense of increased delight. Next time I embraced a whole row of trees; and found the plural address even more satisfying. The more the better. '*All* the company of Heaven.' Why so much pride in the Unitive Way, etc.? Even if God is 'One', she must surely be many as well.

♦ ♦ ♦

Finished evening re-readings of the *Gita* tonight. No, it hardly speaks to me at all – except in the passages where it comes close to Christianity.

♦ ♦ ♦

I've now finished all the corrections to *Pantaloon* up to the end of the last volume but one, *Malcontenta*. I am *very* pleased with this work, and feel sure that I have now got several things right which were badly wrong before. Also, I greatly enjoy the scissors-and-paste work which is involved – or rather scissors-Sellotape-and-stapler. Somehow, those quite complicated mechanical operations give a sort of endorsement to the alterations.

But now that I've arrived at the last volume, *The Return*, I have suddenly got myself into a panic. So much of it is so very badly wrong. Will I ever see how to get it right?

The fact is that I simply didn't know how to achieve that non-tragic (and, by implication, godly) ending at the time I was first attempting it (1975). Now I know much better what it's all about; but that very knowledge makes me very doubtful about my ability to express it.

Prayed almost violently for help; and my eye was immediately caught by Buber's *Between Man and Man*, which had been prominent but unnoticed on my shelves for a long time. Took it down, and rediscovered there *exactly* what I needed. Many, many problems remain; but I'm sure that I can see the way forward now.

I would *like* to get it done by April, when *Part of a Journey* comes out. In the possible glow of that book's success I might, after all, get some response for *Pantaloon*. But this isn't something that really matters. What does matter is that the last volume, by far the most important, should be absolutely as good as I can make it – trenchant, crafty and *true*.

♦ ♦ ♦

How much I had dreaded these elderly years. Even in my fifties, the thought of being SIXTY appalled me. What's more, I doubt if I'd be able to make much of these years now that I've reached them if it weren't for my faith and all the passionate interests which surround it.

Easy to say, then, that I reached for this whole apparatus in order to keep myself going; a piece of what used to be called 'wishful-thinking'. Yes, but just as easy to say that God could not/would not show me this way forward until I really needed it.

15 JANUARY

Not to talk in terms of illumination, etc., but simply to try *to see the point*. For I do believe by now that every object, person, event speaks to us if we have ears to hear. Recollecting my bad waking this morning, dragging myself out of bed and downstairs to the stove, etc., I thought: 'But that, too, is a usable situation.' That was also speaking to me, if I had been willing to hear it.

Thus 'responsible' can perhaps be best understood as meaning much the same as 'responsive'. The only truly responsible person is one who is constantly responsive. (For how can one be responsible *for* a person unless one is responsive *to* him/her?)

16 JANUARY

And on *this* walk it was the wind which gave me satisfaction. A strong wind in my face as I was coming down the hill to the Bennetts': a thoroughly benevolent opposition – Buber's 'Adversarius' and not his (detestable) 'Inimicus'.

This time 'Heavenly Mother' coincided first with a house; then with the bus-shelter. Just as good as trees.

♦ ♦ ♦

Such heavy work on my Kafka review this morning. Amazing how lightly I used to toss off my reviews in the old days – in fact, almost until last year. Now they seem to me – for the most part – like mighty and formidable tasks. This doesn't mean the present reviews are either better or worse than the earlier ones; but it does mean that I am much more concerned about them. My vocation?

♦ ♦ ♦

Of course there is no plateau for S and me to reach; but at least we are now on one of the pleasantest slopes of the mountain that I can remember. There is conscious, but unspoken, love in so many of our actions and reactions.

◆ ◆ ◆

I now realise that all this talk about monism and dualism has never made any sense to me at all. It seems to me that we have – in the mineral, vegetable, animal and human 'kingdoms' – four distinct levels of reality for all eyes to see. So an open-minded *pluralism* is surely the wisest attitude to adopt – with the willingness to accept that there may be millions of unimaginable levels beyond and above our own.

Why this craving for the *Unitive* way, etc.? Why so much pride at having arrived at a *monotheistic* faith? For me the more levels the merrier: a glorious succession of wider and wider rainbows.

◆ ◆ ◆

Sharp tingling pains in kidney (or bladder) induced mild thoughts of mortality. Most contemptible of these was: 'Well, at least I won't be here for the Great Horror!' – momentarily forgetting all who will.

If I were told that I am indeed going to die very soon (it's much more likely to be a kidney stone!), one of the things I'd say to S is this: 'I really believe that we have, in a sense, up to a point, according to our lights, *made it together*.' (But how rash and asking-for-it this sounds as soon as I remove the anticipation of death just ahead!)

◆ ◆ ◆

We need much more Yin in our society and much less Yang: much more intuition and feeling, much less celebration and activity. More of the Female; less of the Male. The danger of Women's Lib (with which I'm, generally speaking, in great sympathy) is that they may simply be reducing the total of Yin by themselves becoming more Yangish. Perhaps what's really required is that women should be a bit more male; men a great deal more female.

◆ ◆ ◆

Merton continues to delight and astonish me:

At no time can the mystery of mercy be understood if we become obsessed with finding out who is the creditor and who is the debtor. [S and me, over so many years!] The climate of mercy becomes life-giving and creative when men realise that they are all debtors, and that the debt is unpayable . . . There can be no question of a

275

limit to pardon – a pardon that becomes meaningless and ineffectual after 'seven times'. We seek that divine mercy which, enduring for ever, and dynamically active as a leaven in history, has entirely changed the aspect of human existence, delivering it from its forfeiture to a syndrome of accusation, projection, resentment, and ultimate despair. We seek it not only in our hearts and minds but in man's world, his common life on earth.

(I like the way he takes 'their' jargon and uses it so neatly against them.)

◆ ◆ ◆

We should pray not just that we may reflect the same light which Jesus first shone into the world but that, however minutely, we may increase it. Otherwise, what is the point of us? Parable of the talents.

◆ ◆ ◆

I can understand all the zest and refreshment of that whole process of getting rid of faith which lasted from the eighteenth century until half-way through the twentieth. But I cannot see that 'humanism' has anything at all to offer *now*. OK, God is dead. Great! So what do we do next?

One cannot live for ever on a certain historical act of negation. And, of course, the Heroic Age of theism, rationalism, humanism is long past. So what are you going *to do with* that huge gap you have given us?

17 JANUARY
England *v*. Wales at Cardiff. That ding-dong was nail-biting enough, though I no longer bite my nails. Took the result with melancholy rather than the old rage; and this absurdly persisted through the rest of the day.

18 JANUARY
And even today the picture of Dusty Hare missing that last vital penalty still haunts my mind.

19 JANUARY
Dreamt of a (strictly) Earthly Paradise. A sunny slope on which a collection of booths had been set up with wide passageways between them. Atmosphere of bright colours; great affection; amusement; sex, drink and drugs (but all harmless, unpunished pleasure). Bookshops

and wise men, from both of which one could gain knowledge, understanding, wisdom; all of which would involve a new kind of experience of a new kind of reality.

Not insipid at all, as most utopias are. Perhaps a sort of gateway to heaven and the Beatific Vision.

◆ ◆ ◆

A slight rivalry for space is developing at the top of the garden between the St Francis shrine (under the yew trees) and the furthest extension of the bowling green. I don't really find one any holier than the other.

◆ ◆ ◆

'Deliver us from all our fears', etc. But what about those fears for our loved ones which seem *inseparable* from our love? 'Teach us to care and not to care.' The simplest interpretation is teach us to care about others and not to care about ourselves; though I know this isn't what Eliot meant.

◆ ◆ ◆

'The Hope of God.' A dual but interlocking meaning – 'The Hope which God gives us of Himself.' And 'The Love of God' must mean 'The Love which God has for us and which should be responded to by our love for him.'

22 JANUARY

Those two are very close to us: we love them both. Yet in their present trouble they seem incomprehensibly far away; and neither S nor I feel that there is anything we can do for them.

Told John R about this, and said I suspected that in most questions of whether to interfere or not he would favour not. He laughed at this, but didn't deny it.

He also said this evening that he found it very hard to make friends with someone who hadn't 'made a Christian commitment'. I know exactly what he means; there is, alas, a sort of vague but limiting barrier.

◆ ◆ ◆

The more I read of modern theology the more convinced I become that the word 'myth' has become much too capacious a portmanteau. It casts a semi-transparent haze over everything we try to say.

◆ ◆ ◆

As I was praying aloud on my bed today, Bubbles suddenly began a loud and spontaneous purring – which is most unlike her. Was she, I wondered, aware (as I was not) of You Who Are There? How I hope so!

◆ ◆ ◆

'The Kingdom of God is manifestly not of this world (all forms of millennial and messianic Christian optimism to the contrary), but it demands to be typified and prepared by such forms of heroic social witness that make Christian mercy plain and evident in the world.' Merton. And how loudly and clearly he still speaks from the grave. How better could one put the whole bitterly vexed question of Christianity and Politics!

◆ ◆ ◆

'At the time of sinning sin has the power of self-preservation in a man, and gives him a certain strength, physical strength, the strength of despair, not to remain with the thought of guilt.'
    Kierkegaard at his best. What an armour of sin I used to walk about in forty years ago; and even made the armour shine. (So I would probably do again, if my passions were as vigorous now as they were then. Would I? Would I, though? How can I ever tell!)

24 JANUARY
Very foolishly I expressed regret tinged with resentment when S again decided not to come to Tymawr with me. She and Laura attacked me strongly for this, and with good reason. But I was quick to say I was sorry, and even to carry it off as a joke.

◆ ◆ ◆

I wonder why no group of Jews since the first century has had the idea of accepting Jesus, simply as one of the major Jewish prophets? I feel sure that he himself would have understood this role far better than all the complexities of our Christology.

◆ ◆ ◆

It is disturbing to get up in the morning assuming oneself to be in a reasonable state of temper, only to find oneself quite unexpectedly snapping at a loved one almost at first sight. A case where 'I' might have been all right without the stimulus of a 'Thou'.

◆ ◆ ◆

Birds singing loudly in the garden today, to greet this astonishingly mild weather. How much it affects one, such a sudden bursting of one season into a very different one.

◆ ◆ ◆

The shared devotion to opera of S and Laura is a delightful and extraordinary thing. For the first time Laura is S's equal; in fact, so far as Rossini and Verdi go, her superior. I feel a bit boorish upstairs in my bedroom while those marvellous arias come floating up the stairs. But alas, for me, for the time being, music does not speak at all clearly to my condition.

25 JANUARY

I find that I have three books by Buber and two about him. Devouring these, I see more and more clearly just what was so dreadfully wrong with the present end of *Pantaloon* – and just what is needed to put it right. Much more astringency, for one thing. The reminder that nobody 'lives happily ever after'.

◆ ◆ ◆

Reading Keith Thomas's excellent history book, *Religion and the Decline of Magic*, is a sad reminder of how truly appalling most ordinary Christianity has been for most of its existence – narrow, superstitious, hating, bullying, full of fear . . .

◆ ◆ ◆

Usually, after lunch my mind and body tell me to go to bed. But I have to defy that here-and-now message in the acquired knowledge that what is needed is, on the contrary, some hard work in the garden; or at the least a short, sharp walk or run.

◆ ◆ ◆

For a long time now I have been marking each day in my diary every evening with increasingly complicated figures. No. 3, on the left, for depression; No. 4 being average; No. 5 quite common; a very rare No. 6. In the middle of the page a large number for days passed without a depressive No. 3; and on the right a number for days without smoking; another for days without a row.

A bit dotty, perhaps. But at bad times it is often encouraging to look back and see how often times have not been bad.

◆ ◆ ◆

Once upon a time a man – call him Adam – called to God to come down into the world to help him. This was a call which God couldn't refuse, although he knew how much new pain and evil he was bringing to this man and all his descendants by giving them the Knowledge of Good and Evil.

◆ ◆ ◆

Those diary numbers show how much of my life is grindingly *preventative* rather than openly *responsive*. I concentrate on trying to avoid pain and sin much more than on welcoming joy and love. Alas!

26 JANUARY

John E's surgery this morning (bladder pain). How humble and abashed people look there; as if this were the ante-room to the Last Judgement.

Then, when I took my specimen to Lydney hospital, I found a young man idly writing a letter at the reception desk, and an old lady patiently waiting for him to attend to her. I walked straight past through forbidden doors and handed my bottle to a perfectly willing nurse. When I came out, I suggested to the old lady that she should do as I'd done: but she didn't dare to. This has little to do with differences of character between us; almost everything to do with a sharp difference of class. I have the confidence of my richly 'U' voice; she the timidity of her poverty and Forest accent.

◆ ◆ ◆

So *fearfully* wet and false, that last part of the last part of *Pantaloon*. I simply hadn't the knowledge then; and know that I have at least acquired some of the knowledge needed during the very eventful last six or seven years. Thank God!

◆ ◆ ◆

The thought that we shall all be totally forgotten on earth a very few years after our deaths no longer worries me in the least. I have no very great desire to buttonhole posterity.

◆ ◆ ◆

The true light of Jesus – which I long to see – is not to be found in all that he said; still less in all that is written that he said. It is in that part of what he said, or was written that he said, which was spoken or written when God was speaking through him. The idea that any man could be speaking for God all the time seems quite inconceivable; even absurd. How much that Jesus said must have been utterly mundane and everyday – e.g. 'I wonder what there'll be for supper?', or 'I'm feeling a bit tired this morning . . . '

◆ ◆ ◆

'In the last analysis . . . ' – one of the worst cant phrases of our time. Analysis is such a very O K word. 'In the last *comprehension* . . . ' wouldn't suit at all.

◆ ◆ ◆

But this time when Bubbles was lying on my bed as I prayed, I made a special 'intention' towards her and she never stirred from her deep sleep . . . let alone purred her holy appreciation.

◆ ◆ ◆

More and more drawn towards a smaller god; or even smaller gods. There is something deeply right – as well as obviously wrong – about the tribal god of Israel. An intimate, sometimes almost comical relationship. 'The Lord' is a pleasing relic of this attitude. Rather this than Brahma any day.

◆ ◆ ◆

Fears about *Pantaloon* ever seeing the light of day remind me of the best thing my father ever said to me. He was staying with us at Barn House when the shattering news arrived that Chatto were going to halt publication of *Pantaloon* half-way through. 'Try to think', he said, 'that it is the workshop which matters much more than the shop-window.' This has been a real help to me ever since.

◆ ◆ ◆

Do not move on to the next object until the single breath for the one before has been fully completed. (Similarly, do not pull the plug before you have completed your peeing. Still the same silly haste pursues me.)

27 JANUARY

'Please don't worry!' (because I love you); 'Please don't worry!' (because your worrying is a burden to me).

How close these can be, or seem to be; but they are miles apart.

Buber writes: 'If you wish to believe, love.' But this seems to me to be one of the rare occasions when he wrote without thinking hard enough. For it is at least as hard to love as it is to believe. I rather think I find it harder. Perhaps the hardest thing in the world.

◆ ◆ ◆

The Problem of Evil. This is *not* a mystery – a word which must be very carefully and sparingly used: it is a plain and intolerable contradiction.

◆ ◆ ◆

The point about the superstitious form of Christianity described by Keith Thomas is that it is profoundly and basely materialistic. Virtue (i.e. correct beliefs and practices) rewarded by prosperity; and vice versa.

28 JANUARY
Yes, my little angelus-clock really does ensure that I pray more often – however cursorily – throughout the waking day. (But this morning I found that I had devoted the whole two minutes to wondering whether or not I would be justified in hiring a cement-mixer!)

◆ ◆ ◆

Benign ritual of a Monmouth Thursday:
1) Driving into Monmouth with S along the valley.
2) Parting from her at the C A B office.
3) Shopping.
4) The warm library.
5) With Father P in the Swan – a single Coke.
6) Talking with Bill in the Punch-house – strong pints of beer.
7) S joining us there.
8) Wilson benignantly presiding in the Beaufort; and a variety of other friends.

◆ ◆ ◆

But things have been a bit too good to be true these last few weeks.
    Well, and why should I still expect (demand?) that everything should be *nice*? For most people life isn't nice at all.

◆ ◆ ◆

Chinese playing mah-jong on the telly. One of those quick shafts of happiness taking me back to a childhood which was *not*, after all, nearly so bad as I often think and say. Those delightful family games in the drawing-room at Melina Place.★
    And Alex 'Hurricane' Higgins playing such delightful snooker that

★The Toynbee family's London home.

282

order and beauty seemed to be re-established in spite of our wretched condition.

But at lunch-time, talking of Schubert, looking at a Rembrandt self-portrait, we were suddenly as close as ever we've been. (The fact that this didn't last can't alter it in the least.)

'Whosoever seeketh from God ought besides God, doth not seek God chastely.' St Augustine.

Chastely. Best possible word.

2 FEBRUARY

Brailsford's fine book – his last – *The Levellers and the English Revolution*. Another sharp reminder of how appalling the ordinary Christian record is; the almost universal desire to persecute all who disagreed with one's own version of the Truth. Levellers – and still more, Diggers – are like bright candles in that naughty world.

◆ ◆ ◆

Laura now wants to leave her flat in Gloucester and commute to her work from here. This seems a good idea: *reculer pour mieux sauter*. At the moment her jumping has been a little erratic, and therefore disturbing. And it will be very good for S and me to have her around again.

4 FEBRUARY

John R to dinner. He must have enjoyed himself because he stayed till midnight. Laura, who had never met him, and S, who had scarcely talked to him, both felt as I do – that he is a remarkable man. And his remarkableness is remarkably unremarkable. A wise man, and a funny one.

5 FEBRUARY

Awake from about 5.00 to about 6.45. Then a quick but sweet dream before Laura woke me at 7.10 to take her to Lydney station. We put on the car radio – a new and splendid acquisition of S's – and were immediately carried off into one of the late Mozart piano concertos. And a fine, delicate sunrise over the Severn; over the Cotswolds. This was a 'Moment'; though nothing very grand or great.

◆ ◆ ◆

Brought back the beautiful reproduction of *La Grande Jatte* from the framers in Monmouth today. I have taken down the Bruegel, after

283

more than a year, and hung the Seurat there instead. For the moment I find this quite disturbing. This is partly because I have loved, and prayed across, the *Icarus* for so long; partly because the Seurat is far larger – indeed only just fits into the wall of my 'shrine' – and therefore looms at me and dwarfs the apples, the angel and the bust of Verlaine.

But there is something else. Although I love this picture too – and used it all through one volume of *Pantaloon* – there is something almost sinister about those ninepin figures in the brilliant light and sharply divided shade. How that great bustle in the foreground dominates everything!

But I shall try hard to make this change.

6 FEBRUARY

When we went back to Ganthorpe last month we brought back the brass two-humped camel which Tony won as first prize in the Peking gymkhana camel race – forty-five years ago. It was very black, but S has begun to make it shine as bright as gold. Certainly a sacred object.

◆ ◆ ◆

Tension! *Tension!* TENSION! How to stop and turn back this horrible crescendo? Have faith in faith. Yes; but I am in fear of Fear.

7 FEBRUARY

But a short walk in the wind-blown woods suddenly relieved the tension which had been tightening inside me during the last three days. How well I know, though, that it may come back as suddenly as it went away.

◆ ◆ ◆

McKeating's excellent book, *Studying the Old Testament*. Was it Buber who led me to this? Anyway, I begin to see much more in the O T and in Judaism than I did. A splendid *earthiness*; and it's just that holy earthiness which I need for the last section of *Pantaloon*.

Strange echoes of all those 'Div' lessons at school, year after boring year. But as far as I remember, we never did anything but *Kings* I and II.

◆ ◆ ◆

Thinking of Father Philip's suggestion that I have a 'vocation' to write my reviews, I suddenly wondered whether I am indeed being 'called' to live this extraordinary life of reclusion in which I spend so much of

284

my time reading and writing. (All my reading, now, is more or less directly for the sake of my writing.) Am I a hermit devoted to the search for God, upon instruction?

I know how dangerous it is to think like this. But perhaps we are *all* called. Certainly it is no sign of exceptional worthiness.

♦ ♦ ♦

How deeply touched I was that when I telephoned Phine in my utter desperation she came at once. An act of unquestioning love: and how much good she was able to do us both!

8 FEBRUARY

A very good mass at Tymawr, and a wonderful sermon on the Beatitudes by John R; his usual holy common sense. I tried to pay more attention than usual to the words of the liturgy; and was rewarded by finding how many of them do, after all, 'speak to my condition'.

♦ ♦ ♦

A day can suddenly *go bad*; like an apparently healthy fruit which turns rotten in a period of a few minutes. Well, I suppose the appropriate quotation for this is 'Except the seed die . . . ' Tiny growths of new life from every rotten day?

♦ ♦ ♦

If to be a conservative means being even moderately satisfied with the way things are – in *any* society – then indeed I do not believe that this is compatible with being a Christian.

♦ ♦ ♦

Much uneasiness with my review of Mary Kenny's book, *Why Christianity Works*. I attack her for her facile attack on others: I judge her for being so free with her own judgements. 'Judge not, that ye be not judged.' (But when I said this to Father P on Thursday, he reminded me that the Devil is very good at quoting scripture: and suggested instead: 'The truth shall make you free.' Much relieved.)

9 FEBRUARY

This crazy idea we have when contemplating our messy lives that if we do something kind and loving one day, but something selfish and unconsidering the next, the later failure cancels out the earlier success. In fact what is done well is done well for ever; and what is done badly can be *redeemed*; used for good. Perhaps *that* is the heart of Christian hope.

◆ ◆ ◆

Meeting Guy Farrer* at the George this evening, after many months. How much I like and *trust* him. Trustworthiness: a great quality to which, perhaps, we don't pay enough attention.

I told him what John R had said about S and me – the 'sweetness and simplicity' he'd sensed in our relationship. As Guy knows us much better than John does, I expected him to smile at this; but he gravely endorsed it. (Perhaps I should not note such things down here; yet they are not acts of self-satisfaction but of very necessary reassurance. It is to them we must cling when our encounters seem to be all complexity and bitterness.)

◆ ◆ ◆

'At the end of my tether!' I thought. Then I remembered how I had said this in company once, during the terrible years just after Anne left me, and how my old friend Robin Mount said, 'But the trouble with Philip is that he hasn't got a tether.' Yes, but I have got one now, though I dare say it stretches much further than I sometimes fear.

And I also remember that ghastly moment on Galway station during the same period, and how I said to myself before the Dublin train came in, 'I just can't go on any longer!' Then, 'All right, so what do you *do* about that? How exactly do you *stop* going on?' And the answer was that I could lie down on the platform, which would simply have landed me in a local hospital, and in an unchanged condition of incapacity to go on: or I could kill myself, which I've never had the least serious intention of doing.

So I came back to the Isle of Wight, developed a lung abcess, presumably in a last desperate attempt to get Anne back; spent many unpleasant weeks in various hospitals, but emerged with just enough strength to go on living my abominably painful life. So it goes.

◆ ◆ ◆

No, I am not the Lamb of God. I cannot take on my frail shoulders the sins of someone else. I have plenty of my own, thank you. Nor has this ever been a Christian demand, that we should fancy ourselves in any such atoning role.

◆ ◆ ◆

* A Monmouth friend.

286

'Faith appears to be the first inclination towards salvation: then follow fear and hope and repentance, which growing up together with temperance and patience, lead us on to love and knowledge.' St Clement.

Yes, that sounds like the right order. But in my case I suspect that fear came first; and that hope was then my way to such faith as I now have.

♦ ♦ ♦

'For anger does not only make one's soul impure; it transfers impurity to the souls of those with whom one is angry.' Rabbi Pinhas of Koretz, in Buber's *Tales of the Hasidim*.
    Yes!

♦ ♦ ♦

Merton on the Virgin Birth. Making a show of great firmness and decisiveness, but in fact quite uncharacteristically woolly and evasive.

And my thoughts have also been turned towards Mary by reading a short, but very well-documented, life of Bernadette. Her B V M had blue eyes, a huge rosary at her belt, a blue girdle . . . in fact all the *bondieuserie* of the age. What's more, her seemingly most important words – 'I am the Immaculate Conception' – were pronounced only a few years after that weird doctrine had been promulgated by Pius IX. So the whole thing might seem to smell very fishy indeed.

Yet Bernadette was certainly a most genuine saint, with something of Joan of Arc's amazing directness, simplicity, and sometimes sharpness, under interrogation.

I am as totally convinced that the doctrine of the Immaculate Conception is a piece of complex doctrinal nonsense as I am that Bernadette *really* saw and heard exactly what she reported. So where does that leave me?

12 FEBRUARY

I value more and more – as I become more and more 'enclosed'? – my Thursday morning talks, first with Father P and then with Bill. I think I can honestly say that I love and respect both these extraordinarily different men.

The perfect culmination, of course, would be Wilson and the Beaufort. But alas, for the time being we simply are not *up to* this prolongation.

However, this time we did see Wilson for a few minutes; enough time for me to be reminded of his ever-enduring decency, even nobility. I was trying to explain to him my difficult, tortuous relationship with our common friend X; and had reached a point where I didn't want to go on; didn't want to say something about X which would have been painfully harsh. Wilson immediately said, 'Don't say it.' He is the very opposite of a gossip. Though I disagree deeply with many of his views, I always know that he is an honourable man and that there is no malice in him at all.

◆ ◆ ◆

So S and Laura have gone off to London, to see *La Cenerentola*, and I have been alone here now for nearly five hours, feeling rather cheerful in my solitude, full of thoughts about beer, TV and pork pie. Then came the sudden, almost devastating thought of S's unhappiness; and the difficulty she might be having in putting a brave face on things in London. Love, pity, deep sympathy and shame.

A shaft of light from God? It seemed like that.

◆ ◆ ◆

There is to be a TV programme about aircraft-carriers, and we were given a foretaste of this by an enthusiastic admiral: 'The most powerful, lethal and destructive weapon ever devised in its time.'

Jesus, it is *hopeless*! Hopeless that any man should speak such words; still more hopeless that he should be encouraged to speak them to the widest possible audience.

13 FEBRUARY
It is right to defend oneself against monstrous and absurd charges. But how easily that vigorous and proper reaction can turn into self-righteousness or self-pity, or both.

◆ ◆ ◆

Bernadette. What they call her 'passion' – i.e. the appalling suffering of her last year, in which her whole body seems to have been raw, inside and out. I can't pretend that I really understand why saints should be submitted to such horrors: none of the given explanations makes much sense to me.

◆ ◆ ◆

What a fearful, platitudinous old bore Gurdjieff seems when one reads his quoted words. Either that or a purveyor of opaque and pretentious nonsense. So one must simply assume that it was his personality alone which did the trick; which convinced so many very intelligent and open-minded people that he was a great spiritual leader.

15 FEBRUARY

S away with Lu for two nights. For the first time that I can remember I've felt it a blessing for us to be apart. In fact we both believe now that the way to get closer is to do more things separately – e.g. even our summer holidays this year.

♦ ♦ ♦

So no poetry prize for me. And certainly no great surprise or shock either. It was a wry consolation that it was I who first helped the winning poet, Andrew Motion, to get his work published. Ah, you Suffering Servant, you!

In the evening three of the judges – Heaney, Causley and Hughes – talked about the process of reducing 35,000 entrants to twenty-one prize-winners. To my mind they are all good poets; and they spoke very shrewdly about the whole affair. No hard feelings; but I still think that three of my four poems were at least as good as the winner. Clever, conscientious judges; but sadly misguided.

Well, I did feel that though they are different from each other, all three are more like each other as poets than any of them is like me. I doubt if *Pantaloon* is in any sort of swing; or ever was.

♦ ♦ ♦

The purpose of meditation is to try to disappear into the condition itself. No longer to be in a special place of one's own but to be in *that* place, where many others have been, and still go. Or rather into which many others temporarily disappear. If I can achieve this only to a very small degree, it is a real refreshment of mind and spirit.

16 FEBRUARY

I keep thinking of John R's instant recognition of Bim's stone figure as a holy object. This has made it even holier for me than it was before.

♦ ♦ ♦

'Without biological evolution which produced the brain, there would be no sanctified souls.' Teilhard.

At first sight this might seem *either* too obvious to be worth saying *or* a piece of crude materialism. In fact, it is a simple and important truth which is too often forgotten by the spiritually-minded.

18 FEBRUARY

If you love and help those who have come your way (been sent you?) to love and help, be loved and helped by, then you are doing all that is required of you.

But is this really so? What about social/political action?

This must depend, I suppose, on where one is and what sort of person one is. Some are certainly called to this; others, just as certainly, are not.

◆ ◆ ◆

Brailsford's book on the Levellers is always interesting, often very moving, because he gives credit, and often affection too, to almost everyone. Even the most arrogant, jeering Cavaliers are respected for their courage. And he is wonderfully shrewd and just on Cromwell, one of the most difficult historical figures to penetrate, appreciate, and criticise justly.

◆ ◆ ◆

A letter from Mary Kenny which overwhelms me with a humble respect which I certainly failed to show her in my review. A good move by her, in every sense. In fact it would be a fine thing if Christians could start competing on these lines.

21 FEBRUARY

I see that Penguin are bringing out a book called *Maternal Deprivation Reassessed*. Wouldn't it be one in the eye for S and me and so many others who have blamed Mummy for their faults if it were now shown that awkward mothers should have been good for us!

◆ ◆ ◆

A certain old man used to say, 'It is right for a man to take up the burden for those who are near to him, whatsoever it may be, and, so to speak, to put his own soul in the place of that of his neighbour, and to become, if it were possible, a double man; and he must suffer, and weep, and mourn with him, and finally the matter must be accounted by him as if he himself had put on the actual body of his neighbour, and as if he had acquired his countenance and soul, and he must suffer for him as he would for himself. For thus it is written: We are all one body.' (From *The Paradise of the Fathers*, in *The New Christian Year*.)

Yes; but is it possible in this extraordinary and holy process to take *the sins* of the neighbour as well? Somehow, it should be; but then what should the neighbour be doing?

Anyway, this is one of those great passages which clearly show the immense difference between Christianity and humanism.

◆ ◆ ◆

290

Cromwell. His conviction that God is with him is both wonderful and appalling. I cannot believe that the light he believed himself to receive was simply a false light; yet he so terribly misinterpreted it that he was able to justify all his actions by it, even Drogheda.

Seventeenth-century history. Again, the horror of being reminded how frightful Christian practice has been in the past. How could such as C. S. Lewis have talked about 'living in a post-Christian society'? There never was a Christian one: only, at any time, a tiny number of true Christians working against the general current of their churches.

◆ ◆ ◆

D A had become a burden and a worry; I knew that I had to give up this last attempt at a genuinely social work: that I am not fitted even for this much of it. But how much I shall miss the individual people.

◆ ◆ ◆

Thick snow and dead-still air. How beautifully muffled we are here.

◆ ◆ ◆

Bladder pains worse than ever, and further thoughts of cancer. Hardly any qualms. O death, where is thy sting? Well, I'm nearly there, now. (But if John E told me the worst possible news, I'd probably be deeply dismayed, to put it mildly.)

23 FEBRUARY

Now, when the words 'May I live in the Knowledge and Love of God' bring my eyes to the window, the snow on that overgrown hedge reveals a clear gap through which I can see the snow-weighted hedge at the far side of the field – A Way Through. And I imagine another gap in that hedge, and so on and on and on – recession after recession, bringing the eye at last to a glimpse of heaven. 'Recession of birdsong' (*Pantaloon*) – and this word has always meant a great deal to me; the ever further reaching on and on towards God.

In *La Grande Jatte*, too. When I come to these words after dark, my eye follows the receding trees and figures with much the same excitement.

◆ ◆ ◆

It seems that the phrase 'the love of God' is much more common in the Old Testament than in the New Testament; in fact, that it occurs in the NT only in quotation from the OT. Faith is far more prominent than Love in the NT.

Well, wherever one starts among the great virtues one comes

immediately to all the others. 'Justification by faith alone' is a dangerous slogan only because it implies that faith can be isolated from Love,
Hope, Humility, etc. But faith without those *as part of the faith* is a
terribly false kind of faith.

♦ ♦ ♦

S calling from her bedroom, wanting me to help her move her bed.
'What?' I called back from my own room; and immediately heard the
harsh irritation in my voice, as it were without expecting it. A real
shock!

♦ ♦ ♦

This unusually heavy snow has broken three branches of the lilac. S
and I were out shovelling in the road together for half an hour; very
exhilarating and companionable.

♦ ♦ ♦

More friendly thoughts of death – or should I say cowardly thoughts?
And yet I'm very well aware of how desperately incomplete my life is
now: of how much there is to be done here still.

♦ ♦ ♦

The narrow physical space into which I've squeezed my life. But I
know that there's no horizontal, spacial escape; no sudden going off
somewhere in different company. I can only escape upwards and
inwards – towards transcendent God and towards God within.

♦ ♦ ♦

Sudden sense of vertiginous emptiness; an inner vacuum-pit into
which my whole self might fall. The usual way to fill this pit is by the
acquisitions of vanity – praise, applause, prizes . . . And they still do
quite a good job when they come my way; but not such a good one as
they used to do.

24 FEBRUARY

I hate breast-beating. A little joke of mine has been that you have to
puff out your chest a long way before you can beat your breast to real
effect – i.e. resoundingly. But one must nevertheless face this recurring sense of abysmal futility; shallowness; even fatuity. Face it yet try
to reach through it, and hold onto the firm assurance that *this is not the
whole truth*.

♦ ♦ ♦

But out in the snow again, and the sun too today, I walked very happily round the loop-road, strongly refreshed by the beauty of this world.

◆ ◆ ◆

'You are under the power of no other enemy, are held in no other captivity and want no other deliverance but from the power of your own earthly self.' William Law.

◆ ◆ ◆

I recognise more and more that there is a lot to be said for *conversational* prayer; an easy meandering, recalled gently to the point from time to time, as if God – or at least the angel – were indeed really here; not only to listen but also to answer. I do have faith in such a presence, though never awareness of it.

25 FEBRUARY
Three days of hard work on the (totally reconstructed) end of *Pantaloon*. Utterly frustrated. One bit of bad writing after another. The old lesson – that nearly always when this happens it is because there is something wrong – false or simply insufficiently seen – about what I am trying to say. (Occasionally, though, repeated failure may simply mean that I am trying to say the right thing but that it's very difficult to say it properly.)

In this case I realise that I *still* haven't made Daisy into a real person, hard though I've tried. She is still mainly WIFE – not a person but a role.

26 FEBRUARY
Father P. Bill. Lunch with Jean H, and the Hope-Simpsons. Then who should we find at home but Bim and Bim's Rose! Though quite exhausted by so much very enjoyable company already, we were delighted to see them. Towards both I have something close to fatherly feelings. Listened in amazed admiration to Bim's account of how he clowned his way through Europe and much of Asia. Took him up to look at where I'd put his little stone figure – and even he looked at it with amazement and said, 'It's beautiful, isn't it?' I asked him what was in his mind when he was carving it and he said chiefly the technical problem of how to give it the right shape without weakening any part of that soft limestone.

That's the way things go. If he had *set out* to make a sacred object he might have utterly failed.

28 February
Suddenly I see, for a flash or two, that the evidence of God is everywhere, and overwhelming.

1 March
Met Kerry, Mary, Bim, Rose, Dave and Michele in the George for Sunday drinks. The really joyful reunion of a Barn House nucleus. What a good community it was at its best!

◆ ◆ ◆

By what strange compulsion do I so continually lose my false teeth? Is it some deeply unconscious refusal to admit that I am disintegrating with age?

◆ ◆ ◆

S and Laura to Cardiff to see *Marriage of Figaro*. Laura off to the Coliseum for *La Cenerentola* again, this time with her cousin Celia and husband Jeremy, who is one of the directors. She had a wonderful time; was even taken backstage to meet the prima donna.

And now S is going up with Lu to a concert at the Royal Festival Hall. What a splendid opening up for all three! And makes me realise how much my reluctance has prevented S from going to concerts and operas; which she did constantly when she lived in New York in the forties.

Did I feel a tiny qualm of exclusion? Well, very tiny; and quickly blown away by real happiness at this development.

◆ ◆ ◆

The way Dame Julian hastily adds 'and Holy Church, of course' every now and again is almost funny. Best example so far: 'Here too we can see that we have no great need to go out in search of different varieties. No further than Holy Church, in fact, our Mother's breast. Or, *in other words*, our own soul, the home of our Lord.' (My italics.) But the words are other indeed!

◆ ◆ ◆

Mrs T in the USA. She seems almost manic in her total and loud-mouthed confidence that her appalling policies – both her domestic and, even worse, her belligerent foreign policies – are indisputably right. Must not hate her.

3 March
Now, after what seemed an eerily early spring, we are in the real dead

of the year again. But I walked very cheerfully through that grim, cold and wet day.

✦ ✦ ✦

Only when you really try to let your mind be free and open, as in prayer, can you realise how closed it is; how narrow, and how tightly packed with preconceptions. But this is a most *liberating* recognition! For it makes one guess at all the empyreans of supernatural reality that lie outside our possible understanding. Well, some of which can perhaps just be glimpsed by this very process of humbling the mind.

✦ ✦ ✦

I've never gone in much for prayers of thanksgiving. A great lack. I now see how much my evening recollection can be enriched by making it an occasion for thanking as well as regretting/repenting.

✦ ✦ ✦

How very simple the truth that a person cannot possibly be at home in a universe which is thought of as quite impersonal.

4 MARCH
Dreamt of building a stone spiral staircase. And when I woke up I realised that I'd learned exactly how this could be done; how the steps should be cut. A very fine image, too, of our slow plod up the spiral, mostly in the dark but arriving periodically at a tiny slit of a window in the thick wall of the tower. Each successive window *should* give us a slightly wider view of land, sea and sky.

✦ ✦ ✦

Oh that Mrs T! What a torment she is. In the pulpit of a City church she pronounces that 'the creation of wealth is a Christian obligation'. Unbelievable!

✦ ✦ ✦

As I work on *Pantaloon* I constantly reflect that the whole work may be utterly destroyed for ever in the holocaust. An infinitesimally trivial loss, of course, in that context. But not to me.

Yet I did begin to feel today that I could think of doing this (very hard) work as an offering to God even if man (poor man!) is to be deprived of it.

✦ ✦ ✦

When and where a person accepts himself in the totality of his existence and so experiences himself as one, confronted with the incomprehensible mystery embracing his existence and letting him submerge himself more and more deeply in this mystery in knowledge and freedom, he is living out what prayer really is and means, and he experiences what is meant by God . . . One must have courage to speak into the darkness in hope and trust.

Karl Rahner – quoted in an excellent new book, *The Human Potential*, by Peter Hinchcliff and David Young.

This is the best invitation to Christian faith that I have read for a long time; must surely speak, as it is meant to, to a great many suffering non-believers of our time.

6 March
Rashly accepted a telephone invitation to join in a BBC radio discussion in Cardiff. Since S does all the driving when we're together, and since she couldn't come with me this time, I had to do thirty miles each way on that ghastly motorway. Scared stiff – literally, for I found that my whole body was tense with the strain, particularly coming back in dark and belting rain. A bumpkin's nightmare. And never, never again, I swore to myself.

Nightmare even after arrival, since I couldn't find my way to the entrance of that enormous and ghastly complex.

The talk, with Mary Kenny and Peter Hinchcliff in London, was a bit strange in the physical absence of the other two, but pleasant enough once we got going. At least some sort of a plug for *Part of a Journey*, which is due to come out in only six weeks' time. (But how many potential readers will be reached in Wales at 8.10 on a Sunday morning?)

Stopping for a drink at the Moon and Sixpence in Tintern I found the lavatories had been renamed 'Colts' and 'Fillies'. Seldom felt less coltish as I peed there after my harrowing drive.

So the outside world really does seem just as horrifying as I always assume it to be. Blessed nest here!

7 March
Very, very cheerful today. But by hard thinking through those pink and flossy clouds I did recognise that if I were always in this delightful condition I really would miss a great deal. Most of what I am looking for, in fact.

◆ ◆ ◆

Still very tired this morning, but the obligation to write a review was a wonderful restorative, as nearly always. Strained away at the first half page, then suddenly released and writing with superb ease. (Hard not to believe that someone up/out there is lending a hand.)

♦ ♦ ♦

Whenever one starts chasing after what looks as if it might be a coat-tail of the Lord there is almost immediate danger (*a*) of exaggeration and (*b*) of exclusion.

♦ ♦ ♦

Why this maddening current piece of jargon 'on-going'? Why not either 'continuous' or 'progressive', whichever is appropriate?

♦ ♦ ♦

Laura and I to dinner with Jeffrey and Nasi. I am amazed at how much more at ease she is socially now than even three or four months ago. And therefore how much more interestingly she joins in the conversation. How much are Rossini and Verdi responsible for this very beneficial change? Who can tell! An opening out to music could easily mean an opening out to other people as well.

8 MARCH
'Say what you like, but be careful.' John Wisdom, whom I always considered to be indeed the wisest of all those Oxford and Cambridge philosophers who were connected with the linguistic schools. Thus he removes the harsh and ridiculous censorship on the use of language which some of them tried to impose on us all.

♦ ♦ ♦

Rain! Rain! Rain! And for two weeks now I have been unable to do any work on the lawn extensions. Bad for morale. (But it's absurd, of course, that I should be dependent on that daily physical work to keep up my spirits.)

♦ ♦ ♦

The words 'intersect' and 'traverse' are packed with meaning for me. Earth traversed by heaven, as a three-dimensional pencil can be pushed through a two-dimensional sheet of paper. (And it is an old question to ask what the two-dimensional inhabitants of the paper would make of this.) The pencil itself may be intersected by a four-dimensional reality . . . and so on *ad infinitum*. So that through our next-realm-up, as it were, we may receive distant echoes and hints of still higher and more inconceivable levels of being. Heady speculations indeed!

◆ ◆ ◆

The Peace of God. I have never known it; probably never will. But the words have a vital meaning for me none the less.

◆ ◆ ◆

S had been away, staying with Lucy, for twenty-four hours before I even thought to say a prayer for her. Thus, changing the one I use most of all:

> Heavenly Mother,
> Light of the World,
> Bless her and keep her.

◆ ◆ ◆

'Spiritual gluttony.' A very good phrase by Emma Shackle, for those who are constantly trying to engulf more and more religious traditions and cook up a vast steaming pudding of eclectic faith and practice.

◆ ◆ ◆

Listened to a film of *Figaro* on TV with Laura. It was wonderfully good; yet all the time I was itching to get away and upstairs to bed. Sat it out partly for Laura's sake, who loved it so much and loved to talk about it too.

Today we met John Morgan in the George, a great and expert opera-lover, and she was in rapture at his insider's talk.

Is it by some sort of unconscious response to all this music around me that I have suddenly moved a whole stage further in my growing fascination with the visual arts? I hope to move from the ordinary biographical history which I'm reading now – and what a relief after years of that unrelieved diet of holy books! – to an immersion in the *Pelican History of Art*. For the first time I see the splendour of Ben's life-work; to see history through art. Though in his case it was more a case of bringing history in to understand art better.

◆ ◆ ◆

Potatoes instead of apples now on the Holy Shelf. I start with them now, instead of with Verlaine, for 'The Pain of the World'. The pain of those multitudes all through recorded human history who have had to slave for a living. Later in that prayer I return to a faint gleam on the topmost potato for 'The Light of God' – which can redeem even the most heartbreaking and mind-crushing labour.

Yes, it *can*: but how very seldom it does. And in most cases if any hope shone into those brutalised lives it could only be the cause of sharp pain. Is it better, then, that they should be left in their normal state, numbed by unrelieved exhaustion?

◆ ◆ ◆

All intense emotions – joy, terror, fury, anguish – devour the present moment and look neither back nor forward.

9 MARCH
Real trepidation as I come to the last few pages of *The Return*.[*] I know that the long passage about Daisy as a full and fleshly human being is utterly right; that he has to confront his wife as a real person, yet – as in the previous version – as a sort of angel. But the very last pages present enormous problems and possibilities.

'Don't try any tricks!' I said to myself. 'Keep it simple!' As if simplicity weren't the most crafty trick of the lot!

◆ ◆ ◆

My increasing bladder pains. I tell S that I certainly won't jump the queue; must wait till the Bristol hospital communicates with me. She insists that if they don't do so soon I should go privately; points out that I would be taking her line if she was in my situation.

Morally dubious either way – nobly standing out against wife and children for the sake of one's principles: or graciously giving in to pleas of family . . .

◆ ◆ ◆

Holding hands with S for our evening prayer I felt for the first time in perhaps three years that something was alive and tingling between us. Asked if she felt it too. Alas, no.

11 MARCH
As always a wonderfully easy but enlightening talk with John R. We never discuss doctrine, but talk about all sorts of things within the understanding of our common faith. This is how it should be – that faith comes in, however indirectly, as a whole new element; a new dimension of the ordinary world.

[*] Twelfth and final volume of *Pantaloon*.

I was very flattered that he told me about his sudden inability to pray; the real pain of this; the need to start thinking about the whole thing afresh . . . And I knew that I could talk to him about this with understanding – even helpfully: which I never could have done four years ago. (So something does change, then?)

13 MARCH

Bladder and bowel pains getting worse – therefore death in the offing, of course. Strong feeling now, under this nonsense-threat, that I must finish what is demanded of me, at least as far as writing is concerned. This means the last volume of *Pantaloon* and this continuation of *Part of a Journey*.

(But as for what is demanded of me as man, brother, husband, father – I don't know what this is and never will know. Except that it must surely be more than I've achieved so far.)

◆ ◆ ◆

Meanwhile, our next-door neighbour, Betty J, is dying of her cancer, and hasn't more than three weeks at the most. I pray for her; but how very weakly that prayer emerges from my own comparatively trivial distress.

Betty's extraordinary desire to hush up her condition; as if it were something to be ashamed of.

◆ ◆ ◆

The Miner's Arms just outside Bream has now been renamed 'Ye Olde Wynding Wheele'. So it goes.

◆ ◆ ◆

A really bad bit of writing while trying to do this horribly difficult end of *Pantaloon*. Clever-clever. Yes, but what is needed is not a retreat from that but an advance to clever-clever-*clever* – which will look like genuine simplicity. (I have no other route to the appearance of simplicity.)

◆ ◆ ◆

Began re-reading my 1941 novel, *The Barricades*, which I have scarcely looked at since it appeared. Very pleased at first by many good things in it. But revolted in the end by its ignorance and false sophistication. The glamour of rich life thinly disguised as satire.

◆ ◆ ◆

' "Man goeth to his long home." Short preparation will not fit so long a journey. O let me not put it off to the last, to have my oil to buy when I am to burn it, but let me so dispose of myself, that when I am to die I may have nothing to do but die.' Thomas Fuller.

17 MARCH

It has seemed to me, and very strongly, that I've received help for *Pantaloon*. And that I must allow myself to be more and more in Heavenly Mother's hands for doing this part right – the most important section of the whole work.

◆ ◆ ◆

I tend to think that I have never had any powerful religious experience. But what about the counsel I get in the course of what seem to be my own thoughts? And what about the joyful recognition I get when reading other people's books? For example, from this extraordinary and passionate work called *Poustinia* by Catherine de Hueck Doherty. Perhaps I receive no spiritual passion directly from Heavenly Mother, but I certainly catch it from a book like this. Real joy in bed tonight. In fact it became an almost visionary evening as I lay there in a half-doze, seeing one curious image after another behind my closed lids. Once, for example, a passage with a box standing in it. Nothing special, except that everything about it was special; extraordinary; as if leading me on to the unimaginable kingdom.

21 MARCH

Terry tells me that Malcolm Muggeridge has actually rung up and asked to review *Part of a Journey*. This is very flattering, and could be very useful. I don't feel that he and I see eye to eye about religion – far from it; but I immediately began re-reading the book as if through his eyes. What will he think of this? Will he write about that? A childish obsession. But I do very much want this book to be widely read; unlike all the other books I've ever written, it has no real point except that. It is my first attempt at direct communication with as many people as possible.

22 MARCH

Tea with Dave and Michele. They were kind and affectionate, but I gather from something they said and from Bim's recent letter that all the rest of the Barn House group are agreed on a view of how and why the community came to an end which is miles apart from the view S and I have formed of those months. They really do believe that we ruthlessly kicked them out simply to satisfy our greed. This is a shocking as well as an angering discovery. My impulse is to write to them all and say, 'Hey, stop it! It wasn't like that at all.' But what good would that do? And in any case it may have been rather more like that than S and I can bear to admit.

◆ ◆ ◆

Jeffrey came to Tymawr with us after many months of staying away. I was absurdly anxious that he should enjoy it and benefit from it; so when he told me that he didn't like some of the new chants I felt most uneasy. This is really a form of suppressed bossiness on my part. The question of whether Jeffrey goes or doesn't go to mass is entirely for him to decide; not my business at all.

23 MARCH
On this beautiful fast train from Parkway to Paddington. No real anxiety about the Collins lunch; in fact I am even looking forward to it.

◆ ◆ ◆

And indeed all seemed to go very well. Taxi to Duke Street pub; two quick barley wines (shorts to avoid having to pee in the middle of lunch); good talk with about eight assorted religious journalists and Collins managers. They seemed to have really liked the book; and even to like me through it. I did my best not to change this excellent state of affairs.

    Then taxi straight back to Paddington – one drink on that train – and into S's arms in perfect condition. I was very aware that prudence was now controlling me as seldom, if ever, in the past.

◆ ◆ ◆

There is no end to the sun and sunlight image for God and divine light. Even by night the sun is still shining around the world. Even on the darkest and greyest day the light is percolating through that seemingly solid layer of rain and cloud. Sunlight, on a windy day, falling now here, now there . . . The sun itself known to be utterly different in kind from that shining disk we see. And yet the disk is an admirable sign of the sun's inconceivable reality . . .

◆ ◆ ◆

Reading about the life and works of Charles Williams. Obviously a great soul; yet almost all his writing seems to me to be not only bad but pretentiously and affectedly bad. How can this be? If God could shine through his person so clearly that others were nearly always aware of this, how could this God-enlightened man have failed to recognise the deathly falsity of what he was writing? I don't mean, of course, that he wrote lies; but that his chosen words utterly perverted the truth of what he had seen because they were so *ill*-chosen; so pompous; so grandiloquent . . .

24 MARCH
Changed window-prayer. 'Heavenly Mother' – palms together, eyes closed, face raised; 'Light of the World' – face a little lowered, eyes open on the light which filters through the densest trees; 'Have mercy on us' – head lowered, eyes closed, hands crossed on breast. (Gathering and keeping the filtered light of God.)

◆ ◆ ◆

So many Christians still insist that we are the highest of God's creatures; made in his image, etc. It really seems most unlikely, not only because there may well be beings on other planets who are much closer to God than we are; but also because there may well be beings in other realms who shine much more brightly in heaven's light than even the brightest saint – e.g. angels.

◆ ◆ ◆

> The peace of God, the peace of men,
> The peace of Columba kindly,
> The peace of Mary mild, the loving,
> The peace of Christ, King of tenderness,
>   The peace of Christ, King of tenderness.
>
> Be upon each window, upon each door,
> Upon each hole that lets in light,
> Upon the four corners of my house,
> Upon the four corners of my bed,
>   Upon the four corners of my bed.
>
> Upon each thing my eye takes in,
> Upon each thing my mouth takes in,
> Upon my body that is of earth
> And upon my soul that came from on high,
>   Upon my body that is of earth
>   And upon my soul that came from on high.

303

Gaelic prayer from *God of a Hundred Names*. And how the heart *aches* for that lost directness, simplicity, perfection. Earth understood in the light of heaven; and how easy and natural the move from that to the 'soul that came from on high'. Since then we have made so hard and harsh a distinction between them, whatever our intentions.

26 MARCH
I had taken Laura to Lydney and was back in bed again, half-asleep, when S came in to tell me that Betty J had died in the night. Even after so much preparation it is a shock – to S, of course, far more than to me. The event itself is always a mystery.

But alas, my renewed and racking internal pains kept my mind from Betty for most of the day.

◆ ◆ ◆

Guardian review of a new William Burroughs book. The reviewer describes in some detail Burroughs's gloating and loathsome inventions of sci-fi evil; brutality; infinitely cunning degradation and horror. But he refrains from making any comment whatever. Was he afraid either to denounce such a book or to praise it? I fear so.

◆ ◆ ◆

'There are always three degrees of consciousness, all infinitely divisible: (*i*) the old self on the old way; (*ii*) the old self on the new way; (*iii*) the new self on the new way.' Charles Williams.

Very shrewd and useful. I feel that I am bang in the middle of the second category, and unlikely to move much further towards the third. If so, so be it. That may well be the *right* place for me.

27 MARCH★
Poland looming again. I pray for peace. I can't tell whether such prayer can in any way affect what happens; but I strongly believe that any effect it might have would be vitiated according to how much personal fear enters into it.

Remember this: nothing in this world is too bad to happen.

Anyway, I think such general prayer – that all of 'them' be given wisdom – is almost certainly meaningless.

28 MARCH
This almost continuous ill-health is craftily horrible in that it seems to

★PT's unrevised manuscript begins at this point.

have no cause or label. But getting through what should be such a delightful family evening as this was painfully hard work from 6.30 to 10.00.

Why is this? Is there some purpose in this too? Is it, in fact, the old bloody depression forced under by pills and taking a mainly physical form?

Am I, O Heavenly Mother, to be the representative of the many who have to fight through life in this wretched way?

29 MARCH

'We seek truth in ourselves, in our neighbours, and in its own nature: in ourselves, judging ourselves; in our neighbours, sympathising with their ills; in its own nature, contemplating with a pure heart.' St Bernard.

30 MARCH

Looking at the crucifix at the end of my rosary today, as I do every day, I suddenly realised that I don't really understand the heart of Christianity at all.

I can give a reasonable explanation of the Crucifixion; but it is, of course, a true mystery and I cannot even see it as that.

31 MARCH

Out of bed to Betty's funeral – no self-congratulation, thank God! (Or is that it?)

Sad, of course, but a real sense of community; the end of the loop-road mostly there: our neck of the woods, quite literally.

◆ ◆ ◆

What I see in Charles Williams – more and more – is that it is not so much his believing more of orthodox Christianity than I can believe but of his knowing how to use this vehicle much more fully than I do. He filled it more full of lived life and meaning. I wish I could do this too, but – as yet – I can't.

(Yet there is something about his work which is deeply alien to me; even repugnant. What?)

I APRIL

No alcohol. Spoils day considerably, but don't mind the ginger beer regime when it actually arrives at 6.30.

But still it is *appalling* that my whole day can be so upset by this small change of regime – one pint of ginger beer instead of two pints of Guinness.

Grey day (though in fact it is perhaps the first of spring and very beautiful) – all pleasure extracted from it by the 6.30 privation ahead.

Oh for the liberty of the Sons of God!

◆ ◆ ◆

How plain it is that a weak man is a dependent man and a dependent man is imprisoned by his dependences.

Even John R arriving late for a brief visit completely threw me. In fact I am as dependent on my regime as ever I was; perhaps more so.

And I read a book (at Tymawr) about Christian endurance in a Japanese POW camp. Fearful *dysentery* for months on end, four to a cage. Just the reminder I needed!

◆ ◆ ◆

Suddenly, thinking of *the* Adoration, I found that I was adoring: or at least knowing what it meant.

A great moment!

◆ ◆ ◆

Jack vividly describing how his priest at Cwmbran celebrated mass – 'so that each word and movement had real meaning'.

◆ ◆ ◆

'We must grant absolution to ourselves and to all men each night, and begin each new day with a clean sheet.' Stevenson.

2 April

Now – on a minute item in the news about the unspeakable 'Tony' Benn – it seems almost certain that Poland will be invaded.

If it concerned myself alone, I would be *glad* to learn that I have an incurable cancer.

◆ ◆ ◆

TV programme on Ethelred the Unready, and the fearful fate of the Saxons under the Danish invasions of the late tenth century. Time after time it has been the end of the world for some community or other. Why not us?

◆ ◆ ◆

I do not believe in Original Sin, but nor do I believe in 'the basic soundness and goodness of ordinary people'. (Bishop Wilson of Birmingham.) Most of us are not wicked, but we are meagre, inadequate and desperately self-centred. We certainly cannot do without the grace of God.

◆ ◆ ◆

What is the deepest unifying factor? PAIN.

3 APRIL
I think I've now at last got the accompaniment to the mantra right:

'Heavenly Mother' – shut eyes to the full light of the sky.

'Light of the World' – eyes opened on some small, dim filter of light coming through a thick tangle of branches.

'Have mercy on us' – eyes down and shut again.

4 APRIL
The immense gap between (e.g.) Küng and Catherine de Hueck Doherty.

◆ ◆ ◆

'Though the Three Persons of the Trinity are all essentially equal, my soul most readily understood love. Yes, it is his will that we see and enjoy everything in love.' Dame Julian.

◆ ◆ ◆

S's real worry about my stomach. For the first time in my life I felt my death more strongly as a grief to others than as loss and horror for myself. That for *her* – and the children, to a lesser extent – I must try to live longer than this.

◆ ◆ ◆

'Someone has said that it is possible "to listen a person's soul into existence".' Catherine de Hueck Doherty.

5 APRIL

Categories

1) Things that matter a great deal, which I constantly worry about, but about which I can do nothing. (E.g., US and Russian foreign policy.)

2) Things which matter a great deal, which I worry about spas-modically, and about which I can do something. (E.g., my own communion with God and my loved ones.)

3) Things which matter very little, which I constantly worry about and should put out of my mind altogether. (E.g., whether *Part of a Journey* will be praised and widely read.)

4) Things which matter scarcely at all, which I can do nothing about and which I worry about considerably. (E.g., getting the garden mown and ready for spring planting of flowers, in spite of my confinement to bed. The lawn can be got back into order later by hand, the flowers can wait.)

So the only legitimate worry is No. 2. For this is both very important and within God's power and mine to do much about.

6 APRIL
And what would Jesus of Nazareth have said if someone had asked him: 'Are you the Second Person of the Trinity?'

◆ ◆ ◆

There is only one way *for me* to deal with (e.g.) the horror-fear of nuclear war, and that is to try to make every occasion of com-munication valuable and valued.
  Tonight, with this in mind, I did speak much better to Laura about her problem than I would have done without this thought.

◆ ◆ ◆

Is it my vocation to write? Certainly, but my *primary* vocation is the same as that of every other Christian – to love God and my neighbour.

◆ ◆ ◆

My Recollection of the Day at 10.15 – which includes Adoration (usually the hardest), Contrition, Thanksgiving, Supplication and Intercession – usually lasts till 10.45 or later. So it is now at least as long (and much more fruitful, surely) as the regulation readings, meditation and fixed prayer at 6.00.

7 APRIL
S in her wretchedness, having given me so much loving help through these rotten days. I was able to give something back to her in her distress, though weak and sick with my debility. The help of God.

308

8 April

I doubt if I ever got so much solid work done on *Pantaloon* as I've done in this bed this last week – not in any week since I began work on it in 1953. (Almost as if I'd been given this hateful disease in order to get the work done in time!)

◆ ◆ ◆

Shame, humiliation and self-disgust are never an adequate motive for real change. Only positive hope, strength, love, courage . . . (I would say, only the grace of God, but many receive it without being the least aware of it.)

Just as it is hopeless to make 'you must not' part of your proselytising. They will find and impose the necessary prohibitions for themselves once they have made the great joyful and liberating acceptance.

In fact, the not doing certain things is part of the freedom which accompanies the much more important doing and the still more important being.

9 April

Having struggled all day, suddenly let fly at S – who responded, of course. But at least I had my heartfelt apology ready by the time she came back from fetching Laura.

Also this event gave me the audacious satisfaction of realising how rare such outbursts are.

◆ ◆ ◆

If all the spiritual force exercised on and in the world were suddenly nullified . . . what would be left except a dead husk of humanity in a world without hope or meaning?

◆ ◆ ◆

Important to distinguish between pride or cockiness and a useful reminder in bad times that one can be – has sometimes been – strong, helpful and loving, when this was called for.

◆ ◆ ◆

'Man is matter and spirit, both real and both good.' Eric Gill. This is, of course, the 'sane' Christian attitude; but I'm not at all sure that I wholly share it. For many people – sick, crippled, aged, tormented by impossible desire, hideous – the matter of their bodies is a horrible affliction. They may endure this well; they may even make good out of the bad, but this doesn't alter the baldness of the bad.

309

10 April

So wretchedly weak this morning. And through the windows the spring is rushing ahead.

◆ ◆ ◆

A good dream. Little old Russian lady who had been giving talks. Isaiah (Berlin) comes up to her and they greet each other with Russian warmth.

Now there is a little group of us all round her: we take each other's hands, but hold our hands low, though sloping slightly upwards. She says, 'May there be a blessing,' and I feel a surge of happiness and adoration.

When I woke, I added the words: 'And may each of us pass this blessing on to others.' If only such things could be done in England now!

◆ ◆ ◆

'What I am does not satisfy me and has become me without my consent; what I am I endure.' Simone Weil.

Re-reading Jacques Cabaud's life of S.W., in real physical distress, I realise that the great heroes and heroines are no use to us weaklings in our hour of need. How far away they seem!

◆ ◆ ◆

The worst day so far. A feeling of deep, almost perpetual physical distress. Not much actual pain but debility like a positive and malign invader of the whole mind and body. Prayers reduced to a helpless opening of the palms; groans; vain repetitions . . .

Desperate thoughts of hospital: how could I bear it now that I've become so room-bound? Death better.

11 April

Sudden relief. Recovery obviously beginning. Letters from Mary Craig and Father Pippin. Boundless joy, looking out of the window at the spring and longing to be out there again – miles away!

And surely at last – what a morning! – I've got the end of *Pantaloon* right!

◆ ◆ ◆

The horrid fact is that very often when we are called upon to do our best we are at our worst – e.g. in pain and great discomfort while dying.

◆ ◆ ◆

The less one is capable of heroic virtue the more one should honour it and love it in others (such as S.W.). This, at least, I never fail to do. But it must be said that such figures also evoke the hatred, mockery and contempt of the envious.

◆ ◆ ◆

Simone Weil's life shows again that in our time a thorough and thoughtful search through the whole spectrum of the Left is an absolutely necessary stage in the progression of an honourable human being. The impulse – to love and honour your fellows – should never die or weaken. The familiar progression from Left to Right is simply a collapse into cynicism, barbarism and gross self-interest.

For however full of hate too many left-wingers may be, the cause is the cause of love. The Right, by total contrast, is meaningless without hatred and contempt.

◆ ◆ ◆

S.W. – I had forgotten that her period of religious passion covered only the last five years of her life.

12 APRIL
It is extraordinary how one act of heroic virtue seems able to counterbalance a vast mass of brutish wrong-doing. 'A candle in a naughty world.'

◆ ◆ ◆

S.W., a very pretty small girl, 'chose' to be physically ugly and in pain, just as many saints have chosen to be physically ill and in pain.

13 APRIL
Well, if I had been content with a mild and safe ending I would have betrayed my faith. Better to fail, but make the intention plain.

14 APRIL
Bristol hospital – and All Well! S now reveals she had seriously thought that I was going to die.

◆ ◆ ◆

'They do not know that it is the chase, and not the quarry, which they seek.' Pascal. And is this also true of our chase after God?

◆ ◆ ◆

311

How *stupid* to pray for peace when it is in the very nature of our lives that we shall never have it.

The amazing thing is, I suppose, that the horrors that happen never coincide with total incapacity to deal with them. Into the small interval a beastly situation is inserted.

◆ ◆ ◆

Pantaloon – FINISHED, and sick of it: 1953–81, RIP.

How I pray that I shall never have to alter another word of it.

15 APRIL
In certain situations the attempt to say 'I, too, am to blame' is a form of sanctimonious self-indulgence. There is plenty of real self-blame to be practised without these exotic acts of false atonement for others.

17 APRIL
Two good copies of *Pantaloon* now completed. My self-poisoning nearly over. But utterly whacked I lie in bed and read Wodehouse. What perfect refreshment!

18 APRIL
Easter Saturday. Between death and resurrection. And so it feels.

◆ ◆ ◆

There is, of course, a truth about myself behind all those self-revelations in *Part of a Journey*.

◆ ◆ ◆

LU!
&
LAURA!

19 APRIL   EASTER DAY
But my attention, of course, has been diverted to Malcolm Muggeridge's review of *Part of a Journey* in the *Observer*; and the excerpts from the book which they've published on the front page of the Review. M.M. considers me to be torn between Roman Catholicism

312

and humanism; also, 'still entrenched' in scepticism. How can he think either of those things after reading the book!

This absurdity is heavily underlined by the fact that they've put a huge full-column photograph of *me* at the top of the excerpts – and a tiny single-column reproduction of Piero's Christ (resurrected) near the bottom of the page! Jesus!

◆ ◆ ◆

Now for Easter musings – if I can rise to any.

◆ ◆ ◆

This is in every way the season of hope. And I do believe there is real hope – suddenly – for S and me. For the renewal we have needed so badly and for so long.

◆ ◆ ◆

No wife. No beer. No cigarettes. Semolina and Complan my only food. These deprivations seem almost unbearable. But how trivial they are – and how temporary!

◆ ◆ ◆

That great melancholy mug in the *Observer*! How it oppresses me now!

◆ ◆ ◆

Unable to digest either food or books, I lie writhing on my bed, and often in tears. The worst day for many months.

20 APRIL
Kept down a breakfast egg. Bravo! Hope!

◆ ◆ ◆

Jesus of Nazareth: that scarcely visible young man; but from whom light streams forward into the New Testament, into the early Church, into all later history . . .

◆ ◆ ◆

It could be said that my near-intolerable pain threshold is very low. Or it could be said that near-intolerable pain is simply *that*, for everyone who experiences it; and that the ostensible cause is of no real significance.

◆ ◆ ◆

313

Forcing down well-chewed bread and gulps of milk, my immediate objective is to get myself back into a condition in which I can drink without harm or relapse. For, until I can regain the immense comfort of moderate beer, I simply exist against pain.

◆ ◆ ◆

Beloved Laura!

◆ ◆ ◆

Suddenly through the window that I constantly stare through from my bed I see the beautiful pale trunks of beeches faintly shining in the evening sun. How *could* I have never noticed them before?

And what a joy they give, even in the middle of these bloody stomach cramps.

◆ ◆ ◆

No beer or meal to look forward to now in the evening – but there seems to be a relief of pain somewhere between 8.00 and 9.00. This does just as well as the positive pleasures: perhaps better.

Remember that the body, which causes so much suffering, is a self-healing instrument.

◆ ◆ ◆

Now (at least) I am suffering directly *for her*. There is a point in it.

21 APRIL
Laura and I have managed alone here together for six days now; but I see very clearly that we wouldn't make a viable couple. Each day, we each feel the need of S more and more.

22 APRIL
Have decided that by now this wretched physical condition is nearly all psychosomatic. This is a great relief – though it doesn't actually make me feel physically better.

These days are for *nothing* except endurance. Pure time = pure hell (as S.W. wrote).

Now the nights are threatened too – and this is perhaps more than I can bear. (And how do you *not* bear it, then?) O Heavenly Mother, heal me; guide me; save me! Ativan no longer working. Nothing but time and time and time . . .

23 APRIL

The corner turned? Certainly I was *in* the spring for the first time as I drove Laura to Lydney. And driving to Monmouth through the new larches and the wild cherry, moments of near-adoration.

◆ ◆ ◆

Dr John E rings up to tell me (*a*) that the specialist can again find nothing wrong with me (as I've now suspected for many days); (*b*) that John's wife, Betty, died the day before yesterday. This grim news at once throws my precariously regained health into disarray. Betty E's death and P. Toynbee's health loom at least as large as J's fearful loss. Are there no limits to the depths of my paralytic self-concern? (What it amounts to is that a sick, unhappy, frightened man – or *this* one anyway – is a machine into which every impinging event is fed.)

◆ ◆ ◆

But the real *healing* value of resolutely doing the next thing.

26 APRIL

Snow falling, thicker than we've ever known it here. I can hardly get to the shed in my gum-boots. No electricity.

Reading, because I must write my review tomorrow, a desperately trivial book. Thank God S is with me now; but this is a gloomy Sunday indeed – boxed in by snow after so many weeks of being boxed in by illness.

Inner resources? For all my prayers, meditation, etc., they remain wretchedly meagre.

◆ ◆ ◆

So I have to be taught, over and over again: (*a*) that I am a desperately weak man, thrown into distraction and misery by the least upset in his carefully constructed regime; and (*b*) that I have never given full recognition to another human being.

◆ ◆ ◆

YES, it *is* depression – almost a relief?

◆ ◆ ◆

These fourteen hours (so far) without electricity become an appalling, an almost insupportable affliction.

27 APRIL

The appalling devastation to the trees – including that yew at the end of the garden to which all my work of the last two years has been meant to lead the eye.

◆ ◆ ◆

'Be here now' only at these times of horror; clenched in the present moment, and no way out.

◆ ◆ ◆

Snow-walk to St Briavels with S. Exhilarating, but utterly exhausting. (Five days ago I could only manage the 800 yards to Birchfield and back.)

Detestable nervousness passing the house of just-bereaved J.E.

◆ ◆ ◆

Today I got up from my review twice, going out to talk in the snow (a) to Jeffrey and Simon, and (b) to our neighbour Chris Morgan.

Could this be the beginning of a real turning outward at last?

◆ ◆ ◆

'Sorrow is ever making channels for joy.' (From *Christ in You*.)

28 APRIL
How I am *forced* back on the bare reality of this house and its needs: ultimately, of whether my faith is strong enough to sustain me here, now, with S, with love of children and friends . . .

◆ ◆ ◆

But this passed – was overcome – more quickly than ever before – under God.

◆ ◆ ◆

Saw the Bennetts walking across their field towards us, and actually leant on the gate to wait for them and discuss how the snow had hit the farm. A wonder! 'It's all sent to try us!' said he at the end. Well now!

◆ ◆ ◆

' . . . from whom all holy desires, all good counsels, and all just works do proceed . . . ' I have more holy desires, S has more good counsels: perhaps we share our little helping of just works.

◆ ◆ ◆

Heavenly Mother, help me to will to be well.

◆ ◆ ◆

Perhaps a better way to pray would be something much more *casual*. 'Here I am, and there are you . . . ' The more complete our acceptance of the second part, the more direct and easy the approach should be. That I may be more aware!

◆ ◆ ◆

I once almost believed that permanent confinement to this bedroom would be no great hardship. But now, after two months, off and on, I feel terribly confined and stifled here. I would not do so, of course, if my spirit were free; were more free.

◆ ◆ ◆

Assuming that each of us is a point of intersection where the spiritual plane 'crosses' this material plane, then it would be misleading to say that angelic powers are 'here'; are 'in this room'. Better, perhaps, to imagine them equally close but situated (we have to use such words) on that spiritual plane which most of us can only *consciously* inhabit (we have to use such words) on rare occasions.

So angels or spirits of the beloved dead may always be close, but very seldom accessible.

◆ ◆ ◆

If this is indeed the return of depression, am I any better equipped to deal with it now than I was five years ago? *Possibly* – but I am very doubtful. The one thing which I do feel even more than I did before is horror at S having this dreadful lump to support.

And won't that, then, increase the whole burden to be borne – for both of us? Not if I use my concern for her in the right way – which would be (perhaps) one way out of the depression.

◆ ◆ ◆

S in Monmouth. I ate a very careful meal; got the wood and the coal; swept the floor; laid the stove; changed my clothes; shaved; walked 200 yards along the road and back. By this meticulous behaviour I may have warded it off.

◆ ◆ ◆

Began my prayer of thanksgiving: 'Heavenly Mother, if it was you who helped me out of that . . . ' But do I really believe that it is like that? Or is the help endemic within me? Always there if I can draw on it?

◆ ◆ ◆

The abysmally selfish thought: 'I would be only too happy to die out of this.' Then the memory of S's tearful face when I waved goodbye to her in 1951.

◆ ◆ ◆

S's friend K at the C A B has a husband who was operated on for cancer of the prostate gland six months ago. There are now secondaries in both his shoulders and both his hips. He is a practising doctor, fifty-six years old.

But this only makes one's own lesser condition of misery and fear all the worse, adding to the total.

◆ ◆ ◆

When at my lowest physical, mental, spiritual condition, I re-read one of my books which assures me that death is an experience of holy and unmitigated bliss.

30 APRIL

> By your strength,
> And by your love,
> O Heavenly Mother,
> I shall be healed of my sickness;
> I shall be made whole
> In body, mind and spirit.

◆ ◆ ◆

If devils, demons, etc., have any reality at all I can only conceive them to be the spirits of dead human beings who have lost their way over there, but who are *temporarily* beyond all heavenly power of recovery. Heaven/God would undoubtedly recover them if It/He/She could.

An alarming idea – that even in that realm the power of love is not absolute.

The existence of devils, demons, etc., would be a fearful affront to God.

◆ ◆ ◆

The only 'other reality' with which we are all familiar is that of dreams. This is a great disadvantage to us if we ever try to conceive of a higher realm; an afterlife; paradise or heaven. For dreaming is a much lower level of experience than waking life, whatever instructive symbols it may contain for us. It is lower because we have virtually no volition: we are simply submitted to various sights, sounds and emotions.

◆ ◆ ◆

Light (continued). It is all too easily blocked out.

◆ ◆ ◆

Decided that this journal must be very different from *Part of a Journey* – far more succinct; precise; sharp . . .

◆ ◆ ◆

What folly and brutish conceit, all this talk about being 'born-again Christians'. (All three US presidential candidates, to start with!) Genuine rebirth must be the rarest, strangest, most wonderful, most *changing* of all human experiences.

◆ ◆ ◆

So now, sated with death-consolation books, I hope to embark on a great course of art history – largely through the *Pelican History of Art*. This, under the threat of being ill for many months – which seems a possibility.

'But I shall forget every page as soon as I've read it!' – I thought with horror and experience.

Very well then: this reading will not be acquisitive: it will be more like that *lectio sacra* of which the Sisters speak. It will be holy reading, and looking, valued for itself alone and not for anything that may stay in the conscious mind.

(Thus I can turn a failing into a joyful benefit.)

◆ ◆ ◆

Temptation to send brief identical notes of apologetic thanks to my dozen correspondents re. *Observer* extracts from *Part of a Journey*.

Resisted. (If I am not even a proper letter-writer, what personal contact have I left with strangers?)

1 MAY
Decided to start a resolute US campaign for *Pantaloon*. So hunted up old reviews and letters in the big black trunk, in order to compose some sort of prospectus for agents, grant-dispensers, publishers, Texan universities, etc.

In the course of this ransacking of papers decided to get rid of a huge stack of letters – a bitterly painful separation. Letters from Giles, Ben, Connie, David, Paddy, Lyall, Patrick, Julia, my parents . . . even an old diary of Tony's. So many dead, so many not seen for years and years . . . But who cares except for me, and why should they!

Found a familiar photograph of Tony and put it up on my wardrobe between my (laughing) father and the Augustus John drawing of Julia. Tony's death, forty-two years ago, is still the most painful I have known. (Three Icons of Pain – four, with Verlaine on the shelf.)

◆ ◆ ◆

Death by radiation is even worse (perhaps) than crucifixion. Should he have waited for this, then?

2 MAY
When you think of it like this, daily life seems scrappy, pointless, futile: but if you could only think of it *like that*, every moment is a chance of new light and better love. The empty or the ample moment.

◆ ◆ ◆

I cannot think there is any way forward for me now except, somehow, through the image of Christ. Yet how impenetrable it still looks, the little crucifix at the end of my rosary.

3 MAY
So what is the Christian story, in my own simplest terms? That a young man filled with the light of God teaches rebirth through love of God and Man; dies in order to free men for this new abundance of life; appears after his death in order to confirm and reassure those who have believed in him.

This is too *thin*, somehow.

To think of *Christ* now – rather than, or beyond, Jesus of Nazareth.

◆ ◆ ◆

That his coming is the supreme and final transforming event in the whole history of the universe – or even of this earth – that I shall never believe. That it is a still living, holy, transforming event for me I more and more believe.

At its very crudest: since Jesus Christ/New Testament/Fathers/Saints . . . are all *there*, why not use them as fully as you can?

◆ ◆ ◆

Neville Ward's *The Use of Praying* – the best devotional book of our time? At least as good as the best of Merton.

◆ ◆ ◆

320

I read the phrase 'a loving openness to experience' and recognise how very few of us achieve this. What Scrooges we are, unable to open our hearts and minds; frightened to risk the little security we think we already possess.

◆ ◆ ◆

Return of the Courbet – and a bright, chaste lemon instead of that dim pile of half-rotting potatoes.

The Seurat is a really *oppressive* picture – and no doubt meant to be.

◆ ◆ ◆

Looking at Tony's photograph and then, traversing forty-four years, at the recession of pelting rain and green hedge and trees through the window, it seemed for a moment that this seeing with the eyes is a metaphor for true vision, and not the other way round.

◆ ◆ ◆

Through Jesus Christ, God flowed into the world and the whole potential of humankind was raised, including the potential for suffering. The Crucifixion was at least this – a promise of pain to come.

◆ ◆ ◆

At bad times, like this sick and fearful afternoon, all the surrounding substance of the world is nothing but a blockage; a thick, impenetrable *stuff*.

At good times (if I remember), there are half-opening lights all over the place.

◆ ◆ ◆

How much of this familiar pain is utterly negative – fear of more pain; deprivation; loss; death? And how much, if any, is due to thwarted longing – an insatiable hunger for more light, more love . . . ?

◆ ◆ ◆

To look for perfection in a book is as foolish as to look for it anywhere else. Who are we to say that God herself is perfect?

◆ ◆ ◆

The family I belonged to as a child was not, I suppose, a very happy one. But it seems to me this morning that this cannot be something over and done with; decided and abandoned for ever. Somehow, somewhere, some-non-time, we shall all five be glorified in the love we brought when we were together.

I do not believe in time. (Except nearly always.)

◆ ◆ ◆

Jesus Christ: the hallowing of pain.

◆ ◆ ◆

Thinking some of the time that I *may*, after all, have an inoperable cancer of the stomach or colon, I realised that the notion of the quantitative value of the time left me has become meaningless. And this is a great mercy. Sixty days or twenty days, why should I care? What I do care about is using each moment as properly as possible. And I recognise that this should be my only care, whether I have a terminal disease or not.

(On the other hand, sixty days or, say, fifteen years would make a lot of difference to my outlook.)

5 MAY
One of the weakest mornings yet. Real feeling that this may well be the terminal decline. S and I talk openly of cancer, which is right, but *God*, how I fail in courage. What a misery of a man, when strength is needed most! And how utterly different *she* would be!

◆ ◆ ◆

This message came on the morning I needed it most. Once Christ is separated from Jesus, then this figure of the holiest man must change as we change; must grow and develop – yet Jesus of Nazareth should never be obliterated by the growing and evolving Christ. He legitimises it: he keeps it tied to earth and history; prevents it floating away like a balloon.

◆ ◆ ◆

Yes, there was today a real moment of literal adoration. I closed my eyes and was kneeling behind some children, on the edge of the Magdalen meadow. I was there, and I was rapt for a few seconds into a joyful ecstasy of worship.

If only one could keep such rare, rare moments fresh! (But *something* remains.)

◆ ◆ ◆

I look sadly through my much-valued shelves of biography for something to read. But why should I want to know about Hemingway or Pound or Trotsky or Freud? Because they are fellow human beings is the proper retort. Yes, but how much of God's light did any of them see, or search for? Each of these lives was lived in darkness, and even in the cause of darkness. (This sounds abysmally narrow; but I cannot help it.)

So, I shall read Troyat's *Tolstoy* again.

◆ ◆ ◆

Sometimes I feel almost sure that death is working fast inside me. At other times no such feeling whatever, weak and ill though I still am.

◆ ◆ ◆

I am an apostle to the spiritual dolts.

◆ ◆ ◆

Prayer for a Dying Man (or one who fears that he may be dying):

> Heavenly Mother,
> Help me to receive
> Your strength and your love,
> So that I may think less of myself,
> Feel more love for others
> And ever follow thy calling
> In this time.
> Through Jesus Christ who brought us
>   new light and love from God.
>   Amen.

◆ ◆ ◆

Only a year ago I recognised, with horror, that I would have been more appalled to hear that I had a terminal illness than that S had one. Now I feel just the opposite. But this is still fearsome selfishness; better to will that she should die first, so that I may take the far worse portion of bitter, desolating bereavement.

◆ ◆ ◆

A rather grim afternoon visit to the surgery, though John E was his usual wonderfully conscientious self. He has found a lump in the right (ascending) colon: thinks it probably isn't cancer, but may be. Sixty to forty against; and might well be successfully cut out in any case. But perhaps my life has contracted and contracted these last six years in order to bring me to the last contraction of all.

◆ ◆ ◆

One of the great unsolved Christian problems: what are we to do with the will? Submit it wholly to God? Does that mean, for example, that I

323

shouldn't strive and resolve to get well? (Perhaps the supreme effort to be made is the effort to stop making any effort at all.)

♦ ♦ ♦

The notion that S and I 'need' more time – say another ten years – to work our way to a real communion of heart and spirit is absurd. We could do this in two days . . . two hours . . . perhaps two minutes. The desire for more time is absurd. In fact hateful bereavement is the *only* really fearsome enemy.

No, painful death is also fearsome enough. God knows.

♦ ♦ ♦

If I could choose between dying in my sleep tonight or living another six months of badly borne pain and fear, I would *of course* choose death tonight. For all our sakes.

But best would be those six months of pain and misery transcended; witnessing to my faith through the strength and love of my God.

♦ ♦ ♦

This, of course – whatever the outcome – is a supreme test of my faith. My worst fear is that I am, *seemingly*, far more ready for death than I thought I ever could be, simply because my life has petered out into futility and repetition.

♦ ♦ ♦

Square my trial to my proportioned strength. (And the best way would be not to diminish the trial – for which one cannot pray – but to increase the strength.)

6 May
Pastor Wurmbrand and the martyrs.* Fourteen years of gaol and torture. What about *that*, then!

♦ ♦ ♦

But this morning, feeling better and far more cheerful, it does seem to me that there is much more for me to do here; real Christian explorations to be made.

♦ ♦ ♦

*Persecuted for his faith, Richard Wurmbrand spent fourteen years in a Communist prison in Rumania – including three in solitary confinement in a cell thirty feet below ground. He recounts his experience, and that of other Eastern-bloc Christians, in his books *In God's Underground* and *Tortured for Christ*.

Arrival of Allchin's book *The Dynamic of Tradition* – just what I need? I would always prefer to read a writer who has penetrated more deeply into the Christian tradition than I have: crudely, one who believes more than I do, if he has thought and felt his way to those beliefs. Those who believe less than I do are useless to me, since I have passed through all those stages – whether towards greater truth or greater nonsense.

✦ ✦ ✦

If I have had any experience of God I would find it in the way my life has been *guided*. Certainly not into happiness; not into virtue; but into a greater freedom of heart and mind in spite of all the constrictions and repetitions.

✦ ✦ ✦

Before these pains (11.30 a.m.) – sure enough over in the right-hand colon as John E diagnosed – I'd begun to feel cheerful for quite the wrong reason for this stage. That is, a conviction that all will be physically well; that I have no cancer; that I'll soon be up and about again . . .

   If this is shown to be so, I shall legitimately rejoice. But in the present state of total uncertainty I must find a deeper source of happiness. Nothing less than Dame Julian's.

   All shall be well *whatever happens*.

✦ ✦ ✦

One tin of Newcastle Brown – after eight days' total abstinence. Delicious: the sheer delight of *the taste*!

✦ ✦ ✦

Not the *amount* of time, but the *quality*. This seems so obvious, but under this threat I do have to remind myself of it from time to time.

✦ ✦ ✦

I still worry a bit about getting the new lawn sown!

✦ ✦ ✦

Allchin (very good). If Christian orthodoxy is deepened *enough*, a universal and marvellous truth begins to shine. (But there may be other shaft-heads too.)

✦ ✦ ✦

My prayer – that I may have the strength and love to cause S a minimum of pain. But this is inextricably bound up with the prayer

325

that I may not suffer the kind of pain which reduces me to a whining wreck of a man.

◆ ◆ ◆

Lack of fibre, alas, and soon, perhaps, lack of guts in the most literal sense.

◆ ◆ ◆

Astonishingly bitchy *Guardian* review – but I hardly care at all.

Amazing to think that the review I most minded about in *Tea with Mrs Goodman** days was the *New Statesman and Nation*. I wrote *only* for its readers! Now, with this book, I want it to be read widely much more – well, *rather* more – than I want to be publicly praised for it.

◆ ◆ ◆

My usual end to certain regular prayers – 'Through Jesus Christ, our Brother and Bringer of Light.' But he wasn't just a bringer of light: he *was* a light. If I can understand this, I will have got a great deal further.

◆ ◆ ◆

Bim's little man suddenly had 'The Pain of the World' to bear. And why not? For how could he repeat 'The Love of God' without being able to bear pain as well!

◆ ◆ ◆

A man so ludicrously spoilt that any disturbance of his normal, protected life seems almost unbearable. (Threat of hospital.)

8 MAY
Fear all day yesterday. Very drear on way to Gloucester and hospital. Worse still when plonked down in the first waiting-room. 'Here begins the great pain-machine' which will drag me away from my own house, my own room, push me into a ward, where none of my 'properties' (e.g. holy shelf and spit bowl) can go with me; where I shall be sliced up and left in worse pain than ever, only to die a little later for all those intervening horrors.

But everything was so efficient, everyone so pleasant, that the virtual confirmation that I have cancer seemed to matter less than this. I was X-rayed by sound and light, and am to have a barium enema on Monday – this astonishing speed suggesting all the more forcefully that they believe it to be little old C.

* An experimental novel by P T, published in 1947.

Driving back we both felt oddly cheerful, partly because I am now being taken in charge, after all these weeks, kindly and very competently. But also because people simply do adjust, and we have come to this knowledge (near-certainty) by fairly merciful stages.

Certainly it isn't at all as I imagined: nothing like so grim. And watching the much-loved Severn Valley on the way home I had *no* feelings of 'Ah me! So soon I shall see you no more!' etc. Nor any particular intensity of regard: more or less the usual pleasure that it is there.

If the worst comes to the worst, I am certain of one thing at least – that she will make a far better job of widowhood than I would have done of widowerhood.

A splendid letter and review from David H – '*Courage!*' (just what I most needed to be told) – and a splendid review in the *Tablet*.

Absolutely no sense of indifference about what happens here after I'm 'gone': on the contrary, a sense of real continuity – and perfectly conceivable without my being there to endorse it.

I do indeed thank God for this day. Yesterday, from lunch-time on, was pretty bad – partly, at least, because of fears of today's fearsome labour. But today – *whatever follows* – is good in itself and for itself.

◆ ◆ ◆

And just now we made love, vigorously and beautifully – the first time I've been able to do that for at least six weeks of this growing debility.

◆ ◆ ◆

When I feel ill and miserable I would like, for myself, to die at once.

When I feel well and happy I would prefer to live a bit longer; but, for myself, death seems quite O K too. (This can't last!)

Why do I *wish* Lu, Anne, Pinkie . . . to know? Partly, I suppose, for the bad old motive – to be playing a dramatic role. But more because I really do feel that I can benefit from their loving concern. (Is this true? I certainly hope so.)

Of course the proper re-completion of *Pantaloon* makes an enormous difference. So does the publication of *Part of a Journey*. And as for all the accumulated pages of the present journal, they might be better edited – and drastically cut – by someone else, rather than by me.

Faith? In the form, today, of utter thankfulness to God or Angel for having made so good a day out of one which threatened to be so terrible. Do I mean that God is responsible for the speed, kindness and efficiency of that hospital? I see that I can't quite mean that, though I almost do. I must mean thanksgiving for enabling S and me to come through the day with enhanced happiness and love. *So far.*

Oh, but I do become more and more horrified by modern 'human-ism'. More and more convinced that only death and despair lie there.

◆ ◆ ◆

Of the three dead on my cupboard, my father had a stroke which gave him fourteen months of terminal hell; Julia was lapsing into senility for years; Tony shot himself at twenty-four. If I should die of cancer at sixty-five, it won't be pleasant; but I would choose this, for myself alone, gladly, rather than living to my father's age (eighty-four) and then having his ghastly death.

But talking to Jase and Lu on the telephone I did come close to tears. How much better, though, that we should all share this as a family: nothing to be either hidden or meandered and mulled over.

I would have made a dreadful very old man.

◆ ◆ ◆

For me, not nearly so bad as depression. (But the danger is that the illness – rather than the threat – tends to bring depression back.)

◆ ◆ ◆

Belief in survival not very strong these days. But at least it is an intriguing possibility, which it certainly wouldn't have been even up to four years ago.

◆ ◆ ◆

Millions and millions of people go through this, with all the anxiety, pain, sorrow. The Community of Pain – which is the only way for most of us to come anywhere near the Community of Love.

◆ ◆ ◆

Can it be seen, all that lies ahead, as a fruitful, even rewarding, experience? It *should* be seen like that, but I doubt if I shall manage it.

◆ ◆ ◆

Perhaps if I do come out of this with more time ahead, I shall be changed; taken out of this wretched state of constriction and insane privacy. That would be a joyful effect.

◆ ◆ ◆

Conversation with Anne: 'But we do want you to stay longer . . . ' Very touched.

9 MAY

The morning prayer (taken from Bella Bown) becomes very important: always should have been far more important than I've made it. 'A quiet time in which I ask God to guide my footsteps through the hours ahead, to guard my tongue, and show me what to do in every encounter or situation throughout the day.'

I sometimes suppose that I have received virtually no communication from God, angel or spirit throughout my life. But I now believe that we all receive communications if we know where to look for them; and that in my case it is by direction of my life and mind when this is most needed, rather than by illuminations of spiritual truths or heavenly reality. My surest prayer, perhaps, is simply to 'You who know me, love me, and help me'.

◆ ◆ ◆

I woke up with scarcely any surprise or dismay – as if the Fact had settled deeply and almost comfortably down into my mind. (Into my heart? My soul?)

◆ ◆ ◆

Through my window a thrush singing, new leaves swaying in a small breeze . . . And *this* is not eternal or anything of that sort – but the joy of that which I receive does seem to be indestructible. Somewhere or in no place, some time or in no time, that joy, small vision, is part of the eternal reality.

◆ ◆ ◆

'You are brave,' said sweet Phine on the telephone. But there isn't an atom of bravery in it: this is given, if ever anything was.

◆ ◆ ◆

Without any doubt what I had always imagined, on getting such threatening news as this, was not only panic, horror, misery, etc., but also a total lack of interest in continuing to do any work for possible reading after my death. But I feel none of these things. (And who knows that in some strange way the depression years weren't preparing me for this? Showing me life at its almost unendurable and frightful, so that death seems little in comparison.)

What I should most like to do now – but doubt whether I can – is to write a book, however short, for others in my condition. There are no such books that I know of; except strictly Christian books on holy dying, and strictly non-Christian books on the sociology of dying. But I would write if I could for the confused and uncertain: in fact for exactly the people I wrote *Part of a Journey* for.

329

Since it was always going to end, the only question was how and when. Perhaps the when seems a bit early, since most of my friends who survived war and suicide in youth seem likely to survive at least into their seventies. But the only question that matters is 'Was there *essentially* more to do – first in my human and divine love, and second in my work?' Well, there is always more to do in both. But I believe we can do the first – S and me, the children, Anne . . . – in whatever time is left. And I believe that I can get this, and the great bulk of rough work between it and the end of *Part of a Journey*, into *editable* form, at least, in the next few weeks or months.

◆ ◆ ◆

No cigarettes for three weeks; and no difficulty either. But Guinness this morning, with real enjoyment – even if punishing pain should follow and teach me the ancient lesson in a new form.

◆ ◆ ◆

As for nuclear war, I don't *believe* that my probable escape from it does much, if anything, to diminish my horror. It is still the thought of my children which appals me worst.

◆ ◆ ◆

It becomes plainer and plainer to me that the hard and simple truth is probably this: that I can face dying gently out of health into mere weakness without any personal distress – except for the separations. But that if I am ill and in pain I shall die in querulous misery; even black depression. And that, after all, is the way most people die.

◆ ◆ ◆

Watching Cup Final – quite keen Spurs should beat Manchester City, for Jason's sake. An exciting draw and replay; but I wasn't much excited, only very tired. One's mind *is* coloured, though – e.g., how many of those twenty-two young men will die of cancer? And thank God they never give more than a passing thought to that.

Oh yes, death does lie across everything, but not morbidly so, most of the time: simply as a way of looking.

Certainly I still bother about cutting the old cherry away at the bottom of the garden – and how I am to get the grass sown.

Never, never have I had a better excuse for tumbling exhausted back into bed. Even with good excuses before, I have constantly felt strong twinges of guilt.

John R, on becoming a parson: 'I wanted a job where I couldn't feel the bottom.' Dying would be that sort of job too.

But of course it is always present in my mind that this whole affair may turn out to be some clownish false-alarm. That would be in keeping, of course.

Would it be a good idea to write a great list of all the ways of dying which I shall escape? E.g., no brutal car smash; no stroke; no lung cancer; no interminable senility; no Parkinson's . . .

I believe that I feel closer to those I love than I ever did; not in the least because separation may be fairly close, but because death is something to be shared. A dying man can offer his death and, by sharing it, his survivors can partake of death fruitfully before their time.

Twenty-five years ago when Julia (Mount) was dying of cancer, aged about forty-two, she said to me: 'Never forget there's nothing one can't get used to.' And what a difference between her age then and mine now! More or less the fullness of my days.

How much of my whole present attitude is bravado and self-deception?

◆ ◆ ◆

Reading an excellent Penguin, *Care of the Dying* by Richard Lamerton – not morbidly but to inform myself of very necessary facts. *There is no need for pain*, simply if *enough* analgesic, anti-emetic and laxative drugs are given.

◆ ◆ ◆

'They that love beyond the world cannot be separated by it. Death cannot kill what never dies. Nor can spirits ever be divided, they love and live in the same divine principle; the root and record of their friendship.' William Penn, quoted by Richard Lamerton.

But I would say more than 'the root and record of their friendship'; somehow – God knows how, where, when – they love and live forward as well as backward.

Lamerton writes: 'A man can make a positive achievement of dying, a great final step forward.' Important to avoid dire self-consciousness about this – a 'Roman death' (or, for that matter, a clownish one) – but certainly the dying *should* go forward: with the living.

◆ ◆ ◆

How would I like to die if I could? Kindly; quietly; if possible, usefully.

◆ ◆ ◆

I hope that other subjects creep in soon. God forbid that death should be my only thought – until death.

331

It may well be, of course, that I can't go any further on this journey here; that I simply haven't the equipment – moral, mental, spiritual – to find more light or feel more love. In which case, I would like to reduce this great mass of post-October 1979 material to some sort of sense and order. Then it might be the proper time to die.

(If it weren't for S – but for her too, in some strange and painful way – my death might be the best thing. A liberation. Not in any bitter sense at all. Perhaps we have *together* come to the point where death is as right for me as continued life is for her. And somehow we shall still be together in that apparently harsh and total separation.)

◆ ◆ ◆

And all my children are grown-up.

All my grandchildren seem to be growing up very well.

I have no longing to go anywhere I haven't been – except to many more English churches, and perhaps a few French cathedrals.

◆ ◆ ◆

Phine and David to lunch. How good that he should ask me: 'What did you feel when you were told?' In fact there was no single moment of dramatic annunciation, but the point is that this was an interesting subject for discussion like any other – like: 'What did it feel like when you first published a book – or when you had your first baby?'

◆ ◆ ◆

'It is easy to suppose that, having mastered psychology, one has understood Man; but there is much more to see than these paintings on his shell.' Lamerton.

◆ ◆ ◆

Perhaps if I could more fully plumb the depths of *this* moment, looking out of the window at the new leaves . . .

Talking alone to Phine up here. Such simple directness of her love, to which I could at once respond in the same way.

◆ ◆ ◆

So now I set forth on a book called *Conquering Cancer*, by a French doctor. Too much? Certainly not: I want to know as much as I possibly can about my condition. I am properly and deeply interested – a new subject. But what made me order these two books from Penguin months ago – well before I was first ill? They are not at all the kind of books I usually order or read.

◆ ◆ ◆

Bereavement. Perhaps there seems a certain fatuity in thinking too much about that – but this is absurd, indeed itself fatuous. For it seems to me more and more that *everything* will be worse for S, at least for a year or two. First the hard slog of nursing – then the grief of being alone. My part (assuming pain is kept decently down) is easy. And what about the children? Anne? All beloved friends? Yes, they will suffer. They will suffer, when I shan't be suffering any more, whatever my state.

♦ ♦ ♦

Sometimes it does seem as if death were churning away down there in the bowels – spreading a sort of hollow weakness outwards and through the whole body.

♦ ♦ ♦

Thinking of S and her likely, or possible, scenario, I realise what an immense work I have to do on myself for her. Well, the work is one we must do together as much as we can.

♦ ♦ ♦

As soon as you start thinking, I might have 5 years . . . 2 years . . . 6 months . . . 6 weeks . . . , these different times immediately take on strangely different aspects. And in some ways the shortest seems the most beguiling, the most magical; not simply more precious.

No, this is wrong. The contemplation of the shortest period enhances all the longer ones as well. Enhances and deepens.

♦ ♦ ♦

When I feel very stupid, even ashamed, at having been blind and deaf to so much that is offered in this world and out from it, I must remind myself that I too have been given a way. Though I have very little idea of what it is.

♦ ♦ ♦

In the afterlife, they say, we associate not with those we loved here but with our natural spiritual associates. I want none of those, thanks, whoever they might be. I want my own dead, and later my own to-be-dead.

11 MAY
Hospital waiting-room. Without all that long slog at prayer, devotion, conduct, thought – which nearly always seems utterly fruitless – I would not be sitting quietly here waiting for my barium

X-ray, not greatly caring how long I wait either here or in this world.

♦ ♦ ♦

Home again, having learned that the growth (still unspecified) is outside the colon, pressing in on it. 'Is this better or worse than being inside?' I asked the doctor. He paused; then said, 'It's different.' Not much change there! There is also diverticulitis on the *descending* colon – so no wonder my whole abdomen has been feeling a mess.

We are to see the surgeon on Friday – four more days of nothing, lying on this bed. Well, of *something* let's hope; but this afternoon I feel unbelievably sluggish in mind and body.

♦ ♦ ♦

A slight abrasion between S and me in the car on the way home – our first since John E first discovered 'the lump' five days ago. Well, it can't all be sweetness and light till death us do part. But it will be – it must be – a time of growth; new light; new love . . . communion.

♦ ♦ ♦

I must say the idea of a malignant tumour is very repulsive – shooting its dreadful little secondaries through the bloodstream to lodge God knows where.

♦ ♦ ♦

I never for a moment forget that if our roles were reversed, S would die at least as well as I can hope to do – whereas I would be a clumsy, uneasy, miserable, even perhaps an irritable attendant.

But just now I went down to the kitchen to comfort her in her tiredness and low spirits. There should be real reciprocity right up to the end. Why not?

♦ ♦ ♦

Deathbed scenes of the utmost beauty and nobility will keep floating into my mind. They are no joke: real poisoners of truth, simplicity and love.

♦ ♦ ♦

When I told Bun the (tentative) news on the telephone he began crying at once, and it was hard not for me to do so too. Of course the news came to him like a sudden blow, which it never did for us. But there is also a special relationship between brothers – *blood*-brothers – and he and I are the only survivors of that family.

♦ ♦ ♦

To take my mind away from unprofitable, perhaps noxious, speculations about the afterlife:

'Attend to *this*!' Pause to look, and hold.

'Attend to this!' Pause to look and hold.

'Attend to this! . . . '

♦ ♦ ♦

Jase on the telephone: 'I really can't take it seriously.' And I know just
what he means. (But still, death does come in the end to even the most
unsuitable recipients.)

♦ ♦ ♦

I am distressed at the thought of not seeing those I love any more, or
being seen by them. But otherwise there are no old experiences which
I long to repeat, and no new ones which I long to try.

♦ ♦ ♦

These pains tonight are more tolerable than earlier ones, because they
are legitimised. Though not very sharp, they are *the real thing*.

12 May
One temptation for the dying is to exert a sort of blackmail on their
survivors: for example, I am tempted to ask S to think and feel harder
about religion.

Avoid this. But remember that it's also possible that I may be given
a message to pass on.

♦ ♦ ♦

The Courbet apples play a bigger and bigger part in my life. This is the
picture I would gladly die with: as holy a picture as any that I know
well – though Courbet wouldn't have liked that word, I imagine. A
quiet radiance: the light of my angel, who will lead me safely through
all these days and nights.

♦ ♦ ♦

Just as S and I are finishing our morning readings (rather intermittent)
of *Dying We Live*, I begin it again from the beginning. They were
martyrs, of course, which I am far from being; but it is possible for me
to share their joy in dying.

♦ ♦ ♦

335

Certain permissible pleasures – e.g. Guinness again at lunch-time, as well as in the evening. The last-cigarette principle.

◆ ◆ ◆

Pascal's wager is a monstrosity, of course. But it can be drastically restated like this: 'If you make no assumption of faith, however tentative, you will remain blocked and hemmed in; make an assumption of faith and see whether it doesn't offer you a way forward, a light in the dark, *an intelligibility.*' *Credo ut intelligam.*

◆ ◆ ◆

S ringing up a neighbour downstairs, mainly to tell him the news of my plight. I was *extremely annoyed* that he spoke so much about his own affairs that she couldn't get a word in about me for about fifteen minutes. Damn it all! I mean to say!

◆ ◆ ◆

Tolstoy's *Death of Ivan Ilyich*. Perhaps the really hard decision for the dying man is to know when to make his penultimate bolt for the odour of sanctity. Too soon, and you may make a blot in the interval: too late, and you die shaking your fist.

◆ ◆ ◆

Clowning still at one's own funeral – e.g. to arrange with a sprightly undertaker for a cannonade of rockets to burst out of the coffin between hearse and church. (But that, I suppose, would be thought a bit Dada and old hat. Still, it would be *my* notion of keeping the flag flying to the very end.)

No, this is not amiable self-deflation. It is the old, rash ego-production. 'Funny, funny me!' bursting into the middle of a ceremony which is not really my business at all, but hers; and theirs.

◆ ◆ ◆

Seeing Guy in the George. A real joy, and perhaps a keener appreciation of him even than before. But also, since I was feeling very rusty and clanking, a certain sad sense of going through the very, very familiar motions of meeting a friend in a pub.

◆ ◆ ◆

Tom Sawyer-like funeral fantasies buzz round my head like wasps which I keep trying to swat.

◆ ◆ ◆

336

I write down here a great many foolish, even ostentatious, perhaps utterly meretricious, ideas. But I do have a sense that the dead-weight of my illness is somehow sinking down and leaving all these ideas fluttering and floating above it like paper streamers. (Yet I do wish to record the follies, for they are a necessary part of the true record.)

◆ ◆ ◆

Contemplate the sublime joy of receiving music, art, poetry. Treble it. Well, you may say that no human mind could contain such adoration. Perhaps not, but other minds (hearts, souls) might; and ours might, after some great rebirth. The point is that *nothing prohibits the possibility*.

13 MAY
The natural process of dying is a slow diminution of life until the last thread to be cut is scarcely perceptible. Or one is travelling further and further into a tunnel with the light fading behind one. And perhaps, at the point of total darkness, the light from the other end of the tunnel suddenly shines ahead.

◆ ◆ ◆

Nothing in my whole life has done more to persuade me of the love of heaven than the calmness, even, at times, the real happiness which has followed the news of a week ago.

◆ ◆ ◆

Patrick O'Donovan finds *Part of a Journey* 'fascinating' – high praise from him – and writes that Bishop Butler, late of Downside, 'thinks it terrific'. Such praise from a Roman Catholic theologian! I do some-times believe that it will be a really useful book – an effective book.

◆ ◆ ◆

There have been more martyrs to the Christianity of Hate and the Christianity of Self-Righteousness than there have been to the Christianity of Love.

◆ ◆ ◆

Looking at my hands and reflecting that perhaps in a few months they will be rotting in a grave gives me not even the slightest *frisson* of dismay. Though I have greatly enjoyed physical activities, from rugby football to sex and drinking beer, from gardening to swimming in lakes, rivers and sea, I have never felt particularly attached to my body; certainly never felt that I *am*, in any important sense, my body.

My hunger for newspapers, which has been abating over many years, is now declining even more steeply. Not that I am becoming remote from 'the world', but that the earthly spectrum which absorbs my attention moves further and further away from public affairs. It is not that I feel disdainful of public affairs, but they cannot concern me here and now as the Courbet apples or the trees outside my window persistently, increasingly, speakingly concern me. 'Poignant' is exactly the wrong word. No sense of future loss, but of gain up to the very end; and perhaps beyond it.

◆ ◆ ◆

I wept my first tears just now: at the memory of how, when I was leaving London airport for Tehran in 1952, a year after our marriage, and turned to wave a last goodbye, I saw to my amazement that my young wife was crying.

So now I wept for her love. I wept for her abandonment again. I wept for all the love we've never been able to show each other. All the love which has been blocked, distorted, turned aside by our own inability to give and receive all that each of us had to give and receive.

It isn't too late. (A very much needed illumination.)

◆ ◆ ◆

A quick backward stare at my life suggests that it has definitely *not* been a happy one. There have been ostensibly happy times, but I've never been satisfied enough to rest in them; always pushing on to the next thing, restless and hungry and anxious and discontented. But I now take it that this was what I had to be, to my great cost and to the cost of others – particularly of Anne and S. Even these last years of self-imprisonment have been just as frantic as all the years of chasing about in the world. And I couldn't have done my work – *Pantaloon, Part of a Journey* – without that temperament. (Or without the patience and endurance which run parallel with and underneath all the frenzied rushing and scrabbling.)

◆ ◆ ◆

And *God*, how I pray for some *real* shucking off of the scaly old self before I die! Will these new conditions be enough to enable me to do that? Or will I perhaps be given better ego-stripping conditions after death? What a job still utterly undone! Like the inside of a 500-year-old pigeon-loft.

Ugly frivolities, buzzing about in my head like bluebottles.

◆ ◆ ◆

338

Holy Angel,
Help me to cleanse my mind
And free my spirit.

♦ ♦ ♦

But now a whole constellation of small, bright and happy memories of childhood. Blessings. 'Don't take things so heavily,' says my angel.

♦ ♦ ♦

Best excuse ever for staying in my room and in my bed: 'Terribly sorry! A spot of cancer!'

♦ ♦ ♦

Why write? To try to give people support, hope, comfort and light *towards* the truth of heaven.

♦ ♦ ♦

The superscription of *Pantaloon* is from Villon's *Grand Testament*: '*Qui meurt a ses lois de tout dire.*' But I now begin to doubt whether this condition gives us any such privileges.

Just now S expressed more or less total disbelief in survival, as she's often done before: and for a moment I felt as if I had a better right than her to make a declaration about this. 'Damn it, I ought to know better than you; I'm nearly there!' But not only have I no extra information; it's also the case that my situation gives me no special right to pontificate about anything, *except* on the emotions, reactions, etc. which a man may have in the face of death. This is my only special knowledge *vis-à-vis* those who have not yet had this experience. What's more, nothing is to say that when they do have it they will have any of the same experiences as I am having.

♦ ♦ ♦

The Pope shot. After the first absurd sense of extra-sacrilege it simply falls back into the general horror of our age. The horror of every age. The horror.

♦ ♦ ♦

It might be said that if ever there was a time when a person is justified in thinking about himself it's when he knows that he's soon going to die. It seems to me that the opposite is true. This immediate contemplation of one's own evaporation (at least from *this* scene) should be the greatest possible help in the task of reducing and seeing beyond the self.

♦ ♦ ♦

All thought of posterity, enduring fame, etc. is pompous rubbish.
Thank God I don't give a damn for that. (But *do* mind a great deal, of
course, that the job should have been done.)

♦ ♦ ♦

Of course I shall be interested in the doctor's diagnosis on Friday. But
what I find hard to understand is that I am not *very* interested. (Still, if I
was told – after all this – 'You have a tiresome cyst, which we can
easily remove, and there's no reason why you shouldn't live another
ten years,' the prospect would be daunting, without a doubt!)

Then what about my love for S and others? Well, it isn't in the
nature of love that the more *time* it has the better.

♦ ♦ ♦

The angelic order is superior to the human order; and this is demon-
strated by the fact that guardian angels do not, presumably, get bored
with their charges.

♦ ♦ ♦

But there is something badly wrong – for my mind seems to be
trivialising the whole affair. At least it should be a serious business,
even if never a pompous one. The dignity of dying . . . Perhaps too
much of my acceptance is simply a readiness to scurry away before
various ills of old age can overtake me.

O Lord help me to understand!

The answer that seemed to come was that this is my due time: that I
have earned my death now. (But haven't the tragic eighty-to-ninety-
year-old wrecks in those ghastly 'homes' earned *their* quietus long
before?)

14 May

> Holy Angel,
> Help me to clear my mind,
> To calm it,
> And to freshen it,
> So as to receive your light.

I find the word 'Heaven' far more amenable now than the word 'God'.
An order, a realm, a company rather than a single Great Being or
Power. And if a single being, then my angel is far more accessible; far
more credibly *here* and listening than any High God could be. (How
well I understand praying to little local saints in little local shrines.

Somehow we must regain this intimacy, this beauty of smallness in the other world no less than in this one.)

◆ ◆ ◆

I love the way Christianity cuts right through history. The N T, the Fathers, Augustine, Anselm . . . Great Christian perceptions spring up to us from every age – and we can add to them. The river flows on as strongly as ever: perhaps more strongly and truly now for being pressed into such a narrow channel.

◆ ◆ ◆

Perhaps the main reason why the modern world seems more terrible than any earlier one is not that the means of destruction are greater than before, but that sensitivity to evil is sharper and wider than ever. We are, after all, a self-disgusted civilisation: the first in history? What about the O T? Not really – only a few individual prophets raged against Israel's sins. But in England or America now there is a deep malaise, passionately articulate at one level, dumbly felt (and perhaps resented) at most other levels. Most people in the U K now are aware, and would admit if gently pressed, that there is something deeply rotten, cruel and obtuse about the society they inhabit and sustain. In spite of obvious appearances, this may be the *humblest* historical epoch so far. It is certainly the humblest Christian epoch.

That is why a true Christianity, of love and hope and humble, exploratory faith, could spread a great light; win many souls.

◆ ◆ ◆

Beer; enlightening book; Courbet apples; sun on trees through the window . . .

At last comes the recognition that whether, or how often, this happiness is ever to recur has nothing at all to do with its strength and reality now.

◆ ◆ ◆

Before she left for the C A B we were tussling a little about whether my drinking beer could have any effect on my colon. Just now she rang up to smooth it sweetly over. How glad I was! Then Laura rang up from Gloucester to ask how I was feeling. Then Ann H rang up to thank me for *Part of a Journey*, and to speak so warmly about it, and particularly about S. Also loving letters from Guy, Reverend Mother and Pinkie. I feel this morning that I am surrounded by love and concern.

◆ ◆ ◆

341

The perpetual incarnation is God's unceasing mercy and salvation poured into earth from heaven. Why do people find it so hard to accept the wonderful sacred drama of a realm of hard, spiritless necessity *invaded* by the saving spirit of God – his weapons being love and truth, hope and beauty, and (above all) that holiness which is for us his very essence? In this drama *the* incarnation was perhaps the greatest victory of invading heaven over the stubborn inertia of earth.

Why is there also such stern avoidance of the notion that heaven (i.e. the next realm up from earth) is also capable of change, of evolution, of more abundant life springing from less abundance, of love growing in strength, wisdom and craft? And who knows how the change from Neanderthal to Jesus, and *beyond*, was not somehow related to an equivalent (though for us unimaginably different) change in heaven?

Keep the Eternal, the Absolute, etc., if you wish – far further above heaven than heaven is above earth. (Though I do not see how it can help us much from where we are now.)

◆ ◆ ◆

Surely for most of us straight Love of God is utterly beyond our capacity. We must love him through his works (*not* his creation). We love him through the people he has made lovable; through the works of art he has made possible; through the holiness of his saints; through the beauty he has enabled us to see in trees, rivers, skies, seas . . .

◆ ◆ ◆

Have begun to eat bran for the good of my lesser evil – diverticulitis. I notice on the carton that this is also a good preventative of bowel cancer. Locking the stable door . . .

◆ ◆ ◆

Assuming that they operate and that the cancer might break out irrepressibly again any month, any day, in that situation there are two possible and opposite attitudes: to go about in perpetual fear of the worst; or to go about in perpetual blessing for each day without it. I really believe that I shall be given the second attitude.

◆ ◆ ◆

The absolute minimum spark of faith: 'There must be more than this.'

◆ ◆ ◆

A sudden, startlingly beautiful glimpse of sycamores in the sun.

'Yes, it's good *now*! It's good now and always – not this time and next time and next time and next time . . .' Not a hoarding of future occasions, but the assurance of an everlasting occasion.

342

Worse pains than for many days, but not the real thing yet, as I very well know.

◆ ◆ ◆

Watched Spurs win the replay, while S and Laura were at *La Traviata* in Bristol. Then rang up Jase to congratulate him.

◆ ◆ ◆

It is another blessing that Laura is moving back to Gloucester on Saturday – so that if it has to happen here she won't be coming back each evening to see it.

15 MAY

The final diagnosis, from a very pleasant and frank surgeon in Gloucester. Yes, it is cancer of the colon, and the colon itself is in a wildly disorganised state – as he showed us on the X-rays. The complication may be attachment to the right kidney – in which case that kidney would have to go, too. In any case, I am to have the operation as soon as possible. S, for the second time, speeding things up by pleading urgency. What a guardian-wife she is!

No shock, of course, by this time; though S did have some lingering hope that it would prove to be benign. How close we are!

◆ ◆ ◆

'Les maladies sont les voyages des pauvres.' Also, it seems, of obsessive stay-at-homes like myself. A fairly keen interest in the passing scenery.

◆ ◆ ◆

Why have I been always assuming death within six months? Because it was *convenient* to do so. But after this operation I suppose I shall start to live indefinitely – which is what we all do anyway.

◆ ◆ ◆

More and more my prayer is of thanksgiving that I am being guided along a way; that the way is prepared for me; that I am under direction and given perpetual support.

◆ ◆ ◆

Flowers from Nancy Bell, my longest-lasting, sweetest and most undaunted depressive friend from Cumbria. In a vase on my window-sill, a bright and vigorous symbol of love across years and miles and probably great differences of temperament.

◆ ◆ ◆

343

But tonight the glow has gone out. Things seem cold, flat, unworthy . . .

And talking to Poll on the telephone this evening I was too breezy: there was a rather tinny bravado . . .

16 MAY

He talked about 'a growth' yesterday – until I asked 'malignant?' and he said yes, in a pleasantly matter-of-fact way. Of course I almost knew the answer, and felt no shock whatever. But did I feel a certain *relief*? Did I feel that after all this fuss and bother and letting so many people know, it would have been a bit *too* characteristically bathetic if I'd had nothing but a polyp? (Ludicrous word!)

Did I even feel that having prepared for at least a large possibility of death I might as well have it? Or rather – and more respectably – that I had been moved up to a new level of grace and holy concern so that I should be able to deal with this situation; and that I have no wish to be brought down again? (As I seemed, all the same, to be brought down last night.)

◆ ◆ ◆

But this morning is beautifully calm again; trusting; *full*.

◆ ◆ ◆

Wet leaves of may and sycamore after a heavy shower, and the sun glittering on them as the wind shakes them. Such things I now look at with renewed intensity and happiness – not because I may not see them for much longer, but because they are of immediate significance: almost direct manifestations of heavenly light.

◆ ◆ ◆

Just now two tickets for *Don Giovanni* at Covent Garden arrived for S and Laura. As the envelope was opened by my bed I couldn't but hear the price – £31 each! Before I could stop myself I was expressing shocked amazement – much regretted almost as soon as spoken. I got a proper drubbing from both of them, and well deserved it since S never complained in the days of my far wilder extravagance – cameras and dinghy and records and caravan and hi-fi and bikes . . .

And if money is to be spent, how better than on opera for those two – a new life for them both; a new life shared by them both. Still I am puritanical about free spending by others: a shameful meanness, particularly in present circumstances.

That was no part of the way.

344

No, but whenever I look at the Courbet I feel the utmost reassurance. It is almost as if my angel lived in that picture, always ready to say: 'Yes, but in spite of your follies and shames, which are real enough, you are blessed with grace and guidance. You will be led back to your way. You will not fall. You will reach . . . what we cannot describe to you but the state which is right for you.'

♦ ♦ ♦

A most affectionate letter from Steve who has read *Part of a Journey* and says that it has made him feel much closer to me. I do indeed feel close to him, and all the Barn House old-timers, though I shared so little of their life. We didn't come together for nothing.

♦ ♦ ♦

It sounds dangerously canting and unctuous to say so, but I really do feel more thankful now than I did before I knew that I had cancer. The blessings shine all round me.

♦ ♦ ♦

For the last two or three weeks I have been writing these notes in the hope that someone (David Edwards?) might take away all the material I've assembled since the end of *Part of a Journey* and edit it into a posthumous book of some kind or other. But now I begin to think that I shall probably at least have time to do this myself – to make at least one more good and useful book before I die. I'm sure there *is* such a book concealed in the great heap of wheat and chaff – but what sort of book it would be I can't yet see at all clearly. A continuation of *Part of a Journey*, in much the same manner? Or something much sharper, clearer, tidier, more concentrated?

♦ ♦ ♦

Looking up at the window through the lower halves of my spectacles I see not much more than a blur of green, with vague recessions here and there. Pushing the spectacles down on my nose a marvellous clarity is provided, and many details of perspective. Imagine another and equivalent clarification, and then another, and another . . . Working towards the Beatific Vision.

♦ ♦ ♦

What a dominating figure that tall, handsome, courteous surgeon has become in mind! How bitterly ashamed I would have been if I'd shown the least tremor of dismay when he confirmed the bad news!

♦ ♦ ♦

345

S has quite rightly decided that I shall hobble as far as Birchfield with her every afternoon, so as not to become hopelessly bed-ridden.

By way of mild revenge, I raised my stick to my forehead just before we reached a lady walking her dogs and said: 'Arternoon, ma'am! Cancer of the right bowel, ma'am.' (Not *quite* within earshot.)

◆ ◆ ◆

There is no bottom to the depths of my false thinking – e.g. that the Way for me would be more or less comfortable, whereas the only promise is that I will survive even the worst without abandoning my faith.

◆ ◆ ◆

It is important to have the best possible thoughts, but even more important not to pretend to be having better thoughts than one is.

17 MAY

The Family.

Joy in the Face of Death!!

◆ ◆ ◆

Hateful puerility of posthumous rewards and punishments – as opposed to posthumous revelation, work and learning for all. Not reward, but the joy of unimaginably greater fulfilment.

◆ ◆ ◆

Of a sinful *condottiere* the famous couplet sounds superb:

> Betwixt the stirrup and the ground
> Mercy I asked, Mercy I found.

But what about this:

> As from his horse the saint was tossed
> He heaven cursed; he heaven lost.

◆ ◆ ◆

Start with LOVE, HOPE and OPENNESS TO FAITH. Or put it that Hope and Love are the motive forces for an ever-expanding faith. Love and Hope with no progression into Faith may be true and effective, but must surely be incomplete; deprived; forever working against the grain.

346

LOVE. HOPE. Then, using these two together, you must find your own way towards FAITH (using all possible help). The more Hope and Love you achieve, the more you will be compelled outward from the apparent world towards the intersecting realm of the spirit.

◆ ◆ ◆

Lu rang up the hospital and found that it will be at least another ten days before they take me in. How curious that I feel no anxiety or impatience; though presumably my little black ball (on the X-ray) is swelling all the time.

◆ ◆ ◆

The purely disinterested man, who acts only for others and not at all for himself, would be a monstrosity: a giver who refuses to receive. Real love is exchange of love, and it is just as blessed to receive as it is to give.

◆ ◆ ◆

I am not a man of heroic virtue, and it would be grotesque folly to try to live as though I were.

But my capacity for love, hope and faith is far greater than my achievement, and it would be wretched sloth and cowardice to resign myself to my present condition.

◆ ◆ ◆

How much is my apparent readiness for death due to weariness with this life and what it has become for me here; and how much to a moderately holy acceptance of the way on which I believe that I'm being led? Very hard to say. Probably much of both. And how I hate the thought of dying to be rid of life.

◆ ◆ ◆

John Lampen's review of *Part of a Journey* in *The Friend*. It takes the form of a letter written to me by, indeed, a friend. And at first, because it does not appear in an important place and because it criticises me for being over-cerebral, I was irritated by this; perhaps even scornful. It took S to show me that this was in some ways the best – because the most direct, affectionate and helpful – review that I have had. After all, that is the kind of response I hoped for, isn't it? Or was I really looking for straightforward and maximum praise, both of myself and my writing? And even if this is so, what better praise than this:

Almost every day there's something provocative or consoling, some encapsulation of what many of us must have reached towards

347

at some time, or something fresh and startling. . . . Over the two years' journey, you recognisably become a truer, wiser, more loving man. That looks horribly patronising, written down; but I have to write it because I need to respond to all you have shared with me.★

19 MAY

Amended morning prayer of May 9th: 'Holy angel, keep my thoughts loving, truthful and faithful through this day; help me to guard my tongue, and show me what to do in every situation or encounter during the hours ahead.'

◆ ◆ ◆

To apply 'small is beautiful' to prayer and all religious thinking. Not Father, Son or Holy Spirit. The single angel – who may, for all we know, be a part or aspect of the whole God but who is also a person attached to me. To see the large through the small; the public through the private.

◆ ◆ ◆

What a pity that it was Wesley and not George Fox who led the great revival. Love, in Wesley, was blackened by damnation and exclusion; whereas Fox, for all his faults, preached openness of faith; love and light for all.

◆ ◆ ◆

'That was the true light that lighteth every man that cometh into the world.' *John* 1.9. *Every* man.

◆ ◆ ◆

The jay which constantly perches on a branch in the far hedge which falls exactly in the middle of the gap in the near hedge. Obliging.

◆ ◆ ◆

I read in one of our medical books that cancer doesn't kill by destroying vital organs; or even by taking away vital energy in order to feed itself. It kills quite mysteriously by an inexplicable process of depletion.

And that is just how it seems – almost as if I could feel that little dark ball radiating weakness through all the rest of my body.

◆ ◆ ◆

★ Excerpt supplied by editor.

If I am to die, I should like to be able to *use* my dying and death to good purpose. And this should be possible; by receiving and diffusing that extra grace which is surely given to us in this process of completion.

Such fine sentiments; but, after a recent maelstrom, any talk between us sadly trundles back into the old familiar niggling and nagging. My everlasting mistake is to be too damned high-minded; even sentimentally dishonest; trying not to look down at the real trash, its cinders, gravel, dog-shit; trying to imagine that we are walking on the Milky Way.

And perhaps I will have anything but a fancy death. Perhaps I will die – as so many do – too full of my own physical miseries either to receive love or to spread it.

◆ ◆ ◆

And now I vividly remember how my father had that heart attack about five years before his death, and how dismayed I was when I visited him in bed and found him all set for a holy death. He told me that he had been reading Plato again, and St Paul's epistles – and the whole performance seemed to me to be utterly false and contrived. And instead of that graceful and exemplary death, he was to spend fourteen months dying of a stroke, transformed into a savage child and semi-idiot. How ruthlessly life and death destroy our hypocrisies; or any momentary forgetfulness of the unspeakable bloodiness of life on earth. For life is not a mixture of light and dark, but darkness redeemed – for some, at some times – by the marvel of heavenly light.

◆ ◆ ◆

For most people:

All illness demoralises.
Absolute illness demoralises absolutely.

But there is a minority whose morals, and virtue, rise to meet their illness. I very much doubt that I shall be one of them. (For example, I do not conceal the pains, discomforts and exhaustions which I feel.)

20 MAY
Massively complicated papers from the solicitors about my father's estate. Morning prayer with light switched onto the shrine. Then that light out, bedside light on, to read these documents – i.e. God switched off, Mammon switched on.

◆ ◆ ◆

349

'To the Zapotek Indian time is not something behind and in front of him, but around him.' Helen Auger, quoted by John-Francis Phipps. Just as I read this I looked up at the photograph of Tony, and it made the most illuminating sense to me. I have never really been able to feel that he is simply over and done with. (Though neither have I ever felt his actual presence at any time since his death.)

◆ ◆ ◆

It is the injurer who needs to feel injured: so the injured is obliged to defend himself against the charge of being an injurer. In so doing he quite forgets that he is not only the injurer but the injured.

◆ ◆ ◆

To take too much blame is as wrong and as harmful as to refuse to take enough. The proper task is always to try, with our very limited means, to see a situation justly.

◆ ◆ ◆

To leave one's money to the starving millions and away from one's family would be an act of gross hypocrisy. This is strange, in a way, for there is no question about where the greater need lies; and yet I have no doubt of it whatever.

◆ ◆ ◆

Going into hospital in six days' time. Just as well, for the days get heavier and heavier here. And yet I do rather dread being yanked out of this burrow.

21 MAY
I think it was right and necessary for me to read almost nothing except religious books for the last four years. This has been an important part of my search, and a continual stimulus for my journal. But there has also been a hectic and grasping element in it: something too narrowly acquisitive: an inability to recognise that holy truth (all truth is holy) can be found in many different kinds of book. I *hope* that I'm now launched into what must be my third reading of *The Idiot* – no very sharp departure from my previous fare, but a true novel, all the same, and by no means exclusively holy.

◆ ◆ ◆

I see with extraordinary clarity now that one of my worst faults in life has been a cowardly optimism – something very different from Christian hope. Yes, things *must* be all right now: that horror *can't* happen again: now there is *real* and *growing* love: now there *is* happiness ahead . . .

I have failed in truthfulness, because truth is so often harsh and painful. But there can be no real love, happiness or anything else without truthfulness first of all.

◆ ◆ ◆

A very good *strong* review in the *Telegraph* – with a posthumous remnant of poor Jamesie's★ tacked on the end. I am the ant to his grasshopper, and praised for it. This evoked a smug acceptance – and the thought of how widely our paths had diverged: his to the flashiest high society, mine to penitence in the woodcutter's cottage. He to being murdered in his own flat, and I, with luck, to a quiet death from cancer.

But I caught myself out almost at once in these odious reflections. Didn't J have, perhaps, a certain simplicity, even sweetness, under all the panache, of a kind which I have never had? And which of us can ever presume . . .

But wait a minute, no hypocrisy either! I know perfectly well that there are worse people than myself; and, being no saint, I am not so overwhelmed with love for all and humility before God that such distinctions never cross my mind.

◆ ◆ ◆

I had forgotten how funny Dostoevsky is; and how skilful a story-teller. *The Idiot* begins much better than *The Possessed*, which I tried and failed with a year or two ago. Yet I seem to remember that the climax of *The Possessed* is as appallingly good as anything he wrote. Nobody else could have created Myshkin – or Alyosha. And what makes him a supremely great writer, of course, is the constant force of his passion for the true, the loving and the holy; his deeply perceptive loathing of falseness, baseness and frivolity.

◆ ◆ ◆

'I think you are being very staunch,' said Jason to me this evening – a kindness which gave me immense pleasure, since this has never been one of my qualities. Yet I am as sure as I can be that this has not been won by me, but given to me.

A good evening altogether. Wonderful sense of life's abundance.

★James Pope-Hennessy.

22 May

No, this process of getting steadily weaker every day is not altogether unpleasant, except when I make myself get up and do something. When I do that, I get very breathless and various parts of my abdomen complain a bit.

If I were to have no operation I would probably glide off into quite a pleasant death, hoping to keep my wits about me more or less to the end. The worst thing, and not unlikely, would be all the pain and discomfort of the operation followed by a fairly quick and painful outbreak of secondaries. But even that, provided I can die at home and properly 'analgesicsed', is a perfectly tolerable prospect.

On the other hand, this whole experience might lead to some sort of mental, spiritual and physical revival. Very badly needed if life is to go on, for S and I have been getting into a deep and painful rut here: two ruts, over which we peer, frown, grin, stare at each other in a terrible mixture of boredom and growing incomprehension.

◆ ◆ ◆

A terrified young Bulgarian escapee has come to Monmouth from London to seek my help against those he believes are out to murder him. S and Jase have gone to the Beaufort to meet him.

I can do nothing except pray – which seems, in fact, nothing. The strangest thing about it is that, even if I were well, I would probably have been very little help to him; whereas he couldn't have found two better people than my wife and my son.

◆ ◆ ◆

It is strange that I know of no book on Christian dying – and can't even imagine one – which would be the very least use to me. No *certitude* of an afterlife, however attractive or persuasive, would help. The point is to be able to die in the hope of one, but also with an absolute readiness to suppose that (as Robert Graves said to me) 'there are no second helpings'; that, in some sense I don't at all understand, we are already in another and perhaps timeless realm as well as this one in which time creeps so slowly past as I lie in bed.

◆ ◆ ◆

Very, very tired this morning. Trying to think of Jesus puts me into a total weariness of the spirit. That whole topic simply seems too difficult; too remote; too obscure; too rubbed and scraped and battered.

◆ ◆ ◆

'The Holy and Blessed Ones.' A new address, and one which is lit up brightly for me just now. Saints and angels; God knows what loving spirits in this world and in many others, or moving between them.

◆ ◆ ◆

My illness prevents any hectic making hay, but I have the strongest conviction that I wouldn't be in that mood even if I were healthy (but condemned). A quiet intensity, perhaps: hardly that. No sense whatever that each minute, hour or day is more precious because there may be so many fewer left than I'd expected.

23 MAY

How gamely our neighbour, Mrs J, died of cancer about six weeks ago! She was eight years older than me; was still moving about her house a week before she died; had no nurse, but only an amiable friend whose help she nearly always refused. It was her pride to be self-sufficient almost to the end.

I have no such pride; but her example does urge me at least to cause as little trouble as possible. But I am not good at concealing my pains – and don't feel sure that I want to create that sort of stoical barrier between me and S. There should be a happy medium between that and the barrier created by whining self-pity and collapse.

◆ ◆ ◆

The first spoken words in St Luke (the angel to Zacharias) are 'Fear not'. A little later the angel says 'Fear not' to Mary; then 'Fear not' to the shepherds. It would be twisting this myth to make it a message against the terrible ravages of human fear, since it was obviously meant simply as a reassurance against awe at angelic splendour. But I would make 'Fear not' the primal message of the whole N T.

◆ ◆ ◆

The Idiot. When all the rabble assemble and Dostoevsky revels in their nastiness, my heart sinks. How well I know that art and truth require that Myshkin be set against these evil lunatics – but I know all about them already and I can't bear to be told it again.

◆ ◆ ◆

Does one think of prayer as a penetration of the holy mystery by the one who prays; or as a penetration of the one who prays by the holy mystery? I have tried both, and seldom – perhaps never – experienced either. (But the second seems the better bet these days.)

◆ ◆ ◆

353

John Austin Baker's reconstruction of Jesus and the Resurrection, in *The Foolishness of God*, is as good as any I have read. But when it comes to the Incarnation/Atonement, he falls into such an almost childishly naive argument that I had to give up my re-reading of his book. God wouldn't be so mean as to send anyone but himself to do this horrible job! As if the horrible/glorious job of suffering for the redemption of others hadn't been done on God's behalf by millions of men and women. It may make sense to say that Jesus 'did the job' more completely than anybody else – but I can no more take the scandal of particularity than I ever could.

And yet . . . and yet . . . I cannot think it only a fluke of history that the life and death of Jesus were so much more momentous in their results than, say, Mohammed. And can any non-Muslim really feel that *he* was one of the three or four sublime figures of history? (I would put him on about the same level as Luther – a high level, but lower than that of St Francis or St Theresa: a human-all-too-human level, after all.)

So we can't simply say that Jesus must have been sublime because of his enormous historical effect . . . Oh damn it! Why can I never get anywhere *near* him!

◆ ◆ ◆

Slinking back to life-after-death books again. This latest one – all sweet little cottages and flowers that don't need weeding or watering – makes me pray for oblivion.

◆ ◆ ◆

There are times, such as this evening, when the world seems irredeemably horrible, the apparent alleviations only a means of making the dominant horror more apparent. A very ordinary film about the Battle of Crete provoked this mood, together with pains in my belly all afternoon. And now I feel that I want nothing more than to be out of it once and for all.

As for Isaiah (Berlin) on BBC 2, his dear familiar face only added to my melancholy. I haven't seen him for at least eight years – and even if I live another eight, my chained-up life here makes it most unlikely that I'll ever see him again. So many old friends this life has lost me. What sort of life is this to lose!

(But two nights ago I was rhapsodising about life's 'abundance'. Yet these see-saws are old hat, and probably nothing whatever to do with my condition.)

◆ ◆ ◆

I write great quantities of stuff in this big loose-leaf notebook, assuming that my condition will give me rich material, fertile ideas. But death is the oldest topic in the world, and why should I think that I shall find anything new to say about it?

(Well, my topic is not really death but dying, and that has not, I think, been much written about by those who are experiencing it.)

◆ ◆ ◆

The nightingale, as usual at this hour. 'Jug-jug to dirty ears.'

But he has *pierced* these ears, if not with the beauty of his song, with the richness and poignancy of its associations.

◆ ◆ ◆

Every time I read anything about God's nature or his will I vow that I'll never write another word on those impossible topics. Or simply repeat almost the last words of Dame Julian's *Revelations*: 'You would know Our Lord's meaning in this thing? Know it well. Love was his meaning.'

So when even the excellent Neville Ward writes that God willed 'that war should be permitted to break out in September 1939 and last six years' I feel that his impertinence is gross: a blasphemous presumption.

◆ ◆ ◆

'Heavenly Mother, give us both as much truth about ourselves as we can bear. Then a little more: and a little more. May each of us help the other into the pain of truth, with love to make the pain bearable; faceable.'

◆ ◆ ◆

In this household, in these days, love seems to have taken a terrible beating. But it is struggling upwards again, like water pushing up through densely packed stones. And this will be a better, more truthful love or it won't be love at all.

◆ ◆ ◆

Amended prayer of Basil the Great: 'Thou, O Heavenly Mother, who art the help of the helpless, the hope of the hopeless, the calmer of those who are wild with fear and anger, the comforter of the sick and the sad.'

◆ ◆ ◆

'To reject experience is one of the most common ways of rejecting God.' Neville Ward. Splendid. But to accept every experience as God-given is one of the most terrible ways of maligning God. (Or

355

rather one might, with heroic virtue, accept all one's own experience as sent by God; but to accept the crushing afflictions of others in this way seems insufferably complacent.)

24 MAY
But in spite of the few occasions when Neville Ward slides into orthodoxy with a little too much facility (too little prepared) I still think his *The Use of Praying* one of the three or four best devotional books I have ever read: now for the third time. What a mass of this kind of literature there is; how little of it I find any use to me at all. But at its best it is the most valuable of all Christian writing.

We keep on gnawing and nagging away at theology – but perhaps the whole gigantic operation has been nothing but a great children's game. Blow hard at it, and it will float off like thistle-down.

◆ ◆ ◆

Anne coming to lunch, saying goodbye in my room afterwards. We were able to say that we love each other as much as ever, and that our marriage had much good in it, as well as so much that was wild and desperate.

A sad, sad feeling of what I'd destroyed in those years by my frantic, grasping, insatiable temperament. But it is very good that so much has survived – revived – over the thirty-three years since that marriage collapsed.

◆ ◆ ◆

This strong desire to end 'well' has a certain amount of play-acting in it. But not much. The main wish is to end well *with* S and the children, Anne . . . not to perform on my own. *Anything but* to perform on my own.

◆ ◆ ◆

'There being a message of beginning or deepening in every ending, their sufferings are worth working through with considerable care.' Neville Ward.

◆ ◆ ◆

This rough and grinding struggle to meet Jesus Christ; to see and hear him; to understand something of what he means . . . It can only be by some flight of true poetry – and it is a long time since I inhabited that world (in spite of twenty-eight years writing *Pantaloon*). Perhaps I lived in poetry only between the ages of about sixteen and twenty. Can I get back there now? Why not?

                      Redeem
      The unread vision in the higher dream . . .

                          ◆ ◆ ◆

            Suffer us not to be separated
            And let my cry come unto thee.

And this evening the nightingale sings to me almost directly, clearly
and without the miserable muffling of self-consciousness.

25 MAY

Up till now I've been very averse to using 'poetical' language when
trying to write about religion. I've seen too many dishonest evasions
made that way. But now I do feel that unless I can get away from this
prosaic scrabbling at the figure of Jesus Christ – which becomes more
and more elusive the more I scrabble – I shall never grasp him at all. It
is not a question of mythologising him, which has been done, God
knows, time and time again, but of seeing the real man in the kind of
terms which alone might bring him to his own extraordinary life.

  I *don't* mean to write poetry about him, an idea which fills me not
only with dread but a kind of nausea. I suppose I mean find and
contemplate individual words and phrases, some of them so ancient
and well-worn that I've always brushed irritably past them until now.

                          ◆ ◆ ◆

Jesus of Nazareth:

    Total forgiveness by God if (*a*) you yourself forgive, (*b*) you repent.
    Healing, forgiving, etc., by direct authority of God.
    'Abba'.
    Associating with tax-collectors and sinners.
    Sabbath made for man, etc. LAW TRANSCENDED.
    Love and *respect* for children.
    Irony, wit, humour.
    Love your enemies: go to the gentiles.
    JC inseparable from his message. 'Verily, verily, *I* say unto
        you . . . '
    Self-identification with poor and oppressed.

  A distinct, distinctive and religiously revolutionary individual. *Yet*
(or therefore) very much of his time and race. No Superman or
Everyman or Culture Hero.

  I ADD: he had his faults – went to John the Baptist for remission of
sins; very hot-tempered; sometimes arrogant . . .

                          357

A very, very, very great MAN, and no nonsense about it. START FROM THERE. All the miracles perfectly acceptable – also *Transfiguration* (see many saints).

Resurrection. In form so contrary to all expectation – i.e. no glorification but re-emphasising the shaming wounds of the crucifixion. On all the evidence seems very likely indeed. *But not foreseen by the living Jesus.* Last words surely as in *Matthew* and *Mark* – 'My God, My God . . . ' Died close to despair. Learned of his special role (beyond mere Messiah) between Friday evening and Sunday morning.

But after the last resurrection appearance – WHAT?

God knows! (And *we* do not. *None* of us does.)

Was he, perhaps, taken up into God, in such a way that God himself was changed by this conjunction? Was the all-loving aspect of God enormously strengthened by its work in the life and resurrection and absorption of Jesus Christ?

Oh, what idiocy, to speculate like this!

Take off! Take off! *Die* into more of the truth: it seems you can live only into greater and greater nonsense.

◆ ◆ ◆

Having gone through the hell of depression and emerged into the flickering light of *Part of a Journey*, that would seem to be a very proper and even holy progression, with a well-accepted death as the perfect climax. But this was to forget that *other people* are also engaged on their own progressions, and that these may bash into one's own and completely buckle it.

◆ ◆ ◆

Or was the life, death and resurrection of J C a *pattern* for us all? Not an *example*, which is absurd, but a sacred version of what we must all do in much less sacred terms – live, die, be born again . . . And has some new element of grace entered *me* during these last few weeks? If so its hardest task will be to shed itself on S – who is strongly resistant to anything which might emanate from me. That grace will have to use real craft to bring us together in love reborn. (Less than that would be nothing – worse than nothing.)

◆ ◆ ◆

If I had to die in hospital, then I would much prefer to be in a terminal ward where we all know our situation and can talk about it as much or as little as we choose. Where comfort can be given and received.

◆ ◆ ◆

Hospital tomorrow, in any case. My hermit crab dreads being winkled out of his shell: my sensible man looks forward to getting in and out again as soon as possible. But there are also some stirrings from that moribund enquirer who used to look forward to every experience, both for its own sake and as possible material to be written about.

♦ ♦ ♦

Jason very enthusiastic about *Part of a Journey*. (And Phine and Laura also.) What great pleasure it gives me that my children like it. Perhaps there is some deep sense in which one is writing for them; as a continuation of telling them stories when they were little.

♦ ♦ ♦

The concept of a man without sin is not only self-contradictory: it is repulsive. We shall never know whether Jesus really raged so violently against the Scribes and Pharisees: we can be quite sure that there were occasions when he lost his temper; behaved selfishly; gave way to fear . . .

♦ ♦ ♦

Self-consciousness of the worst sort keeps breaking in. But I *observe* that I conduct myself sensibly in front of others, talking about my illness only when it crops up, and then quite naturally and easily. In this there is no calculation at all: it is a pure gift.

♦ ♦ ♦

The Holy Child – or rather, Baby. An astonishing and wonderful idea. Thus JC has *drawn to himself* so many rich and beautiful conceptions.

♦ ♦ ♦

'I want to strive for one thing – to fall into the earth at least as a fruitful and healthy seed.' Alfred Delp, sj (from *Dying We Live*). I get much comfort from reading this book again; but never forget (*a*) that they were martyrs, and (*b*) their conditions were a hundred times worse than mine. But still I too would like to die as some sort of Christian witness – which doesn't necessarily mean saying a single word about my faith.

♦ ♦ ♦

To be able to see one's death as both very unimportant and very important. Very unimportant socially, historically, etc.; very important – like every other death – in this small group around me and also *sub specie aeternitatis*. (How much this phrase is misused, to mean 'in the light of all historical time', or something of that sort.)

◆ ◆ ◆

Now, on this last night before hospital, apprehension is certainly stronger than curiosity. Also the lack I shall feel without my books or my sacred objects. And no nightingale either.

But the greatest loss by far will be S, of course, on whom I depend enormously without, I hope, making any very heavy use of her dependability. To know that she is in the house, or will soon be home. And now, after his week here, Jase has also become a solid and a needed figure.

Still, I have a long and delightful experience of hospital nurses, one of whom, from forty years ago, is still the object of certain charming fantasies.

◆ ◆ ◆

Astonishing to think of that large team about to go into action with the object of keeping me alive. Such an *intimate* transaction! After all, they don't know me from Adam. Why do they assume that it's right to work hard to prevent me from dying?

26 MAY
A very pleasant ward – but when S said goodbye I found myself in tears, to my surprise and dismay. Memories of being left at a new school by my mother. But the other boys – mostly a little older – are very friendly.

Young doctor has just been to see and examine me. Also very nice, but says I'm unlikely to have the op this week. Likely to be sent home for the weekend after the kidney X-ray, etc. Oh God, another week of waiting! But I must be 'staunch', as Jase told me I was; 'brave', as Anne, Phine and Poll have all said. (Only I know how far I am from any sort of secure fortitude.)

◆ ◆ ◆

The tricky thing about forgiveness is this. If A has wronged B, it is unlikely that A will have accepted that this is so. Therefore any ostensible *act* of forgiveness on B's part will seem as nothing but a counter-attack; will almost certainly *be* nothing but a counter-attack.

Therefore B's forgiveness must be disguised; or, better still, genuinely enveloped in simple love. Best of all is that A and B should see themselves sharing in that love of God which obliterates all the trivialities of the usual injuries we do each other.

360

As for the major injuries – Nazi/Jew – forgiveness is probably impossible for all but a tiny minority. And an equally tiny minority is capable of being forgiven.

♦ ♦ ♦

Back into the delightful mild kidding between the nurses and the elderly male patients.

♦ ♦ ♦

Heavenly Mother,
Light of the World,
Have Mercy on us

– now refers to me and the four other members of my ward.

♦ ♦ ♦

Talking to Mr C, a man of about my age. Very nervous and talkative; his longing for his own bed at home; first time ever in hospital; first time separated from his wife for thirty-three years; admits he weeps at the end of each of her visits. Compared symptoms. Felt strong affinity with him – with all of them.

♦ ♦ ♦

Imagine if I were to 'bring the Word' to this ward, what insufferable presumption that would seem! Yet a strong evangelical would feel that he was grossly neglecting his duty *to them* if he said nothing.

Strange. I agree that it is of great importance that everyone in our sort of peril should get closer to God. But deeper than all that faith is my deeply engrained respect for other people's right to be whatever they've chosen to be. We are all elderly men (not that I'd preach at young ones), and why should I suppose that my truths have the right to take the ascendance over theirs?

(Bristol hospital! Young seminarists coming round. Ugh! – just as much now as then.)

♦ ♦ ♦

But what also comes wearily back to me is the extreme length of the hospital day – and sometimes night as well. The only way to deal with this is to think as little as possible of time passing; as much as possible of each bit simply happening to be there. And to be prayed through as much as possible, either by reading, by repetition, or (far the hardest) by free meditation.

♦ ♦ ♦

A nurse coming suddenly to take someone else's temperature and pulse is a notable event, of course. And this shouldn't be thought of as a sad sign of how boring our life is, but, on the contrary, of how attentive we become to events which would repay such attention in *any* circumstances. (But this is aspiring talk.)

◆ ◆ ◆

'All life in awareness is a blessing, and we show this by blessing those around us.' Neville Ward.

◆ ◆ ◆

Learn to THINK SLOWLY; but not lethargically.

◆ ◆ ◆

Now an old man of about ninety has been put in the bed opposite mine. He has what might be a cheery, even a cocky look; but he is *very* frail and wheezes all the time. Return of that rather base thought that since I've started dying while still in reasonably good order I might as well finish the job. What a swiz to have to go through all this again, but by then much worse, in say fifteen years' time!

And as for the fifteen years, I simply don't feel that I shall be able to fill them with further growth. (Unfortunate word!)

This is just as cowardly an emotional preference as a desperate fear of death would be. What I long for, and do sometimes feel, is an equal and glad acceptance either of life or of death.

Never, never forget that whatever happens during this stage you will have got to a different place, and – if you live this part rightly – a better one. With your help, dear Mother; blessed Angel.

Faith in these terms is not a comfort but an invigorating work.

◆ ◆ ◆

If I sit forward in my bed, I can see the cathedral and the incredibly ubiquitous May Hill immediately behind it. If only my bed were by the window, instead of the furthest away from it.

◆ ◆ ◆

One man now has *ten* visitors, including three small children. What a Scrooge it makes me to say that I wouldn't at all care for such a congregation. (But greatly valued S, Jase, Laura and Chrissie at 3.30.)

Yet these tremendous family gatherings – eight at another bed now – are really a very fine sight. *Yes!*

◆ ◆ ◆

One blessing is that my expectations of *possessing* have never in my life been so low. Can I say that my expectations of being, of changing, of growing have never been so high? *Try* to be able to say that.

◆ ◆ ◆

The pretty nurse sticking suppositories up my arse. No satisfaction whatever: that, of course, would be asking altogether too much. Though not necessarily 'the wrong thing'.

◆ ◆ ◆

The threat of appalling gloom. Remember, though, that nothing can be worse than the worst of 1974–7. Nothing of *this* sort – i.e. distress of circumstance – can be so bad.

◆ ◆ ◆

In an important sense I have now joined *my kind*.

◆ ◆ ◆

For many weeks my life has been very restricted, but still, to a large extent, within my own control. Now I have been taken over completely by this benign organisation.

◆ ◆ ◆

Looking back as clearly as I can, it seems to me that my life has truly been one long unhappiness, relieved by rare occasions of *joy*, mostly before I was twenty; and many moments of bright pleasure scattered from start to finish. Think of the century's decades – the twenties to seventies – all hellish in their different ways. And now:

1974–7   Depression.

1977–81   Desperate withdrawal: constant battering.

1981   CANCER.

Wow! And yet I don't feel that things could, or perhaps should, have been otherwise.

◆ ◆ ◆

As night falls I hear grislier and grislier descriptions of the post-operation horrors which are in store for me. This will be, of course, the worst physical misery I shall ever have known. They have a great advantage over me, even the worst sufferers among them, in having their operations well behind them.

27 May

The old man looks very appreciatively at the nurses; even manages a charming leer.

Mr C is a compulsive talker: a rather childish man indeed, and his garrulity sometimes gets tiresome. But it is impossible to dislike him.

✦ ✦ ✦

They talk a great deal about their past troubles, and about an entirely rosy future, getting back to their previous lives. Nobody has yet mentioned the possibility of secondaries and death.

✦ ✦ ✦

Just spent several half-hours waiting outside various X-ray rooms. No impatience, of course, for what was there to be impatient *for*, except being returned to Ward 10. But I doubt if I'd be impatient in any circumstances nowadays. Except perhaps to catch a train or – dim and distant prospect – to get into a pub before closing-time.

✦ ✦ ✦

Listened to Dvořák's Violin Concerto on my earphone. Not a great work, but a very charming one, and just suited to my incredibly rusty state of musical appreciation. This must be the first complete piece of music I've listened to for eighteen months. Very strange, and certainly something to do with that weird tension between S and me.

✦ ✦ ✦

A sudden setback for poor Mr C; his third; and the wound may have to be opened again. Of all the ward (perhaps excepting me), the man least able to bear such a misfortune.

I take it as a warning to me, as well as a cause of sympathy. I must expect the worst at every stage – even the possibility (always in mind) that my trouble will be inoperable.

✦ ✦ ✦

Took about twenty minutes shaving this morning. So it goes.

✦ ✦ ✦

'It's no use worrying' – sardonic little Mr K to sad Mr C. 'What will be will be – and we're totally in their hands anyway.'

This is the sensible, dour, humanist attitude. And how rash of Christians to think they can say much more than this: to think they can say that out of every new setback may come a *transfiguration*. At the least, a gain in the wisdom of active love.

In fact these are not similar reactions to grim experiences, but opposite ones. The stoic becomes tougher; the Christian tenderer. Or so he *should*.

◆ ◆ ◆

S and Jase came bringing wonderful letters about *Part of a Journey*. I have never had such letters after any earlier book, not even *Pantaloon* Vol. I.★

It has spoken to certain people in ways which I can't, of course, understand; but which I had certainly hoped for.

All it is really saying, I suspect, is 'Never give up!'

◆ ◆ ◆

Ah, my wife and my son! Both so dearly loved, though the son so much more simply; the wife so much more costingly and creatively.

◆ ◆ ◆

Now that pain in my left eye has suddenly got much worse; and I've asked to see the doctor about it. Of course the (probably absurd) notion of a secondary comes to mind. Also a Job-like sense of multiple afflictions, what with X and Y and the bowel cancer and now this.

A small-time Job, of course.

A poor man's Job. It is precisely my function to be a severely minor version of any great role; and this is a function which seems to meet a real need. More a vocation than a function, though a very strange one.

◆ ◆ ◆

We tend to nag away at trying to make distinctions between the afflictions which are our own fault, and those which are somebody else's fault; or nobody's. But pain is pain, and the uses of pain are there in all cases. We are deprived of them only if we lie to ourselves about the causes, *either* way:

'Well, it's not my fault.'
'It's all my fault for being the sort of person I am.'

Self-deception is the hardest crust of all for God to pierce.

◆ ◆ ◆

Mr C in a bad way; but the awful thing is that I find it very hard not to feel a certain contempt for his endless, repetitive self-pity.

★ The first four sections of *Pantaloon*, published as one volume in 1961 by Chatto & Windus and later extensively revised by P T.

This is odious on anyone's part, in any circumstances; but it is particularly odious from someone generally renowned for his lack of fortitude, stamina, etc.

◆ ◆ ◆

Liverpool beat Real Madrid in the room next door to our bay. About eight of us from Ward 10 were taken clean out of our troubles mainly by that harsh criticism of the play which gives most people so much more satisfaction than praise.

◆ ◆ ◆

All the offerings that are given to us throughout the day (in the form of pills, cups of tea, thermometers, plastic bottles to pee into, meals, cheerful and consoling words, injections, dressings, clean sheets . . .) are gratefully received as constantly renewed tokens of 'their' concern; and even esteem.

In this hospital I have no feeling of the cold superiority which can vitiate all this munificence, but more of the genuine tribute paid by health to sickness; the service paid by knowledge to ignorance.

◆ ◆ ◆

Today has ended as a remarkably faithful day. Partly with the help of Neville Ward's *Friday Afternoon*, I have seen the *sense* of my condition more clearly than ever before. I mean the use which God can make of it if I can keep my heart and mind open to him.

I wouldn't dare to say, even now, that God is responsible for my cancer, but certainly these last very harsh seven years of my life (both by my own 'fault' and not) reveal a remarkable, utterly benign and fruitful meaning to me now as I look back on them. And this culminating affliction seems entirely apt and right whether it ends in renewed life for S and me, or death for me and renewed life for her alone. Or rather for her with me in some sense still with her, but no longer too oppressively so.

I really can imagine, without the least bitterness, that she might live a genuinely refreshed and renewed life, with me present to her only in some more remote and *manageable* way. Either from another world, or through memory, or both.

28 MAY
Between 6.30 a.m. and 10.30 p.m. there are sixteen hours. And this is my first day in which absolutely nothing is to be done to me. (I have to stay in hospital to be seen by Mr T on his rounds tomorrow afternoon: then home for the weekend and back next week – presumably – for

the operation.) But I don't find these hours particularly oppressive: I shall again do my long, rather desultory prayers to the rosary:

50 'The Hope of God' – to one bead and breath each
50 'The Work of God' – to one bead and breath each
50 'The Light of God' – to one bead and breath each
50 'The Peace of God' – to one bead and breath each
50 'The Love of God' – to one bead and breath each

– and 'Thy Will be Done' on each intermediary breath.

Much lying back with very little going on in the mind. Occasional ten to twenty pages of Troyat's *Tolstoy*. At least one piece of music on the earphone. By evening, occasional four or five pages of Neville Ward – fairly concentrated attention.

And, of course, desultory conversation with fellow-patients, and constant attention to every event in the ward – from Mr K carrying his bag along to the lavatory, to old Mr W having his plastic nose-bag applied and oxygen administered through a bottle of bright-blue liquid.

The fact is that if it weren't for the absence of S and Jase this would make a much better day than the many, many I'd spent in my bed at home. I even feel that I've partially joined the world again.

◆ ◆ ◆

And now a telegram from Pauline and Tony (Rumbold): 'Praying for good operation and quick recovery.' They *will* be praying, too, and so will many others. And many more will be thinking of me and hoping for me. A real support and comfort.

◆ ◆ ◆

Mr J's unfailing kindness and encouragement to Mr C. (Yet he talks with violent hatred of 'yobbos' and gypsies: was quite convinced yesterday that Real Madrid played dirty because they were foreigners, while Liverpool were always penalised only by the monstrosity of the referee.)

◆ ◆ ◆

Mr C was shivering in bed this morning. The young doctor, a sister and two nurses all came and sat on his bed – not just to comfort him, we decided afterwards, but to warm him up as well. A charming piece of primitivism – near-bodily contact – in this super-technological institution. The human warmth here is not in the least frozen out by the high technology.

◆ ◆ ◆

367

Splendid letters from Patrick (Rivers) and Father Philip: the last more emphatic than I would now be (strangely enough) that the cancer wasn't sent by God, but can be used by him. (I am as sure as ever that God does not send the savage and dehumanising afflictions which crush so many millions – and would, of course, crush me. But I do find it hard not to feel that *some* hardships do have a holy purpose, and not only a holy effect.

◆ ◆ ◆

A little talk about God's will with Mr N – multiple stones and gall-bladder – in the television room. Agreed on total acceptance of death in the hands of God. Two practising Christians out of six!

◆ ◆ ◆

First act of aggression against me – by a very fat blonde staff nurse. 'Get up, Mr Toynbee. We don't like our patients to lie in bed all day.' Benign aggression, of course, but a disturbance to my complacency. Alas, I *much* prefer bed to sitting in this chair beside it.

◆ ◆ ◆

Now the American doctor brings me good news – that both my kidneys are in good order, and that the operation will definitely be on Wednesday.

But he too has added a disturbing element – by saying that I can stay here until Wednesday if I wish, instead of going home for the weekend. Well, which *do* I wish? On the whole to go home, for the company of S and Jase. But to stay on here, without the upheavals of going and coming back again, does have its attractions.

This question, of course, is far more in my mind than the good kidney news. Or than God's mysterious ways. And next in importance comes my faint disgruntlement at not being allowed back into my bed.

◆ ◆ ◆

Mr C giving a much worse impression to his wife than I'd heard him given by the doctors. This infuriated me – but it is the weak man's natural revenge on life for ill-treating him. I have felt that temptation myself in the past – *not* during any of this trouble so far – and must have given way to it at times. (And I have a disturbing premonition that I shall pay heavily for this harshness towards poor Mr C: that when I am in real physical distress I, too, shall fall into wretched self-pity, and inflict this all too readily on S.)

◆ ◆ ◆

368

So now it seems that Mr T will want to keep me here over the weekend; which means that I shall have done eight days in hospital before the operation. I simply must not think of these days as cumulative; in which case, why not stay here?

It's not as if that beloved room at home is much of a joy when I'm in such poor condition as this.

There is a certain pleasure, too, in accepting 'their' decisions about me with the utmost confidence and goodwill. A sort of anti-Kafka state of mind.

◆ ◆ ◆

Eye hurting worse than ever this evening. And Job a far less attractive role than yesterday.

This discontent intensified by the dear guests just departed – including Phine who drove two hours each way to see me.

◆ ◆ ◆

Powerful fears of actually going blind. And how would this Job stand up to being (a) blind, and (b) in constant expectation of recurring cancer?

I'm strongly inclined to say better (a) and (b) than (a) alone.

Could I – would I – learn Braille in such conditions?

O blessed angel, how deep into gloom I've fallen from your grace.

And prayers have been no help at all, as usual.

◆ ◆ ◆

'We can live with dignity only if we live on a few things, chosen for the way they speak deeply to us. We cannot live at all if we do not select from the plenitude of possible experience. We are simply distracted by the meaningless shouts, whispers, pulls, wounds, nudges that time is if human reason and spirituality fail to get to work on it.' Neville Ward.

◆ ◆ ◆

So Mr W fought at the Somme and Passchendaele; was wounded and captured in 1918; went to Dunkirk as a Territorial; advanced into Germany in 1945.

When I expressed conventional horror at the worst battles of the First War, he said, 'They were a bit of a do.' And then, after some reflection, 'We lost some good boys.' And now, almost helpless with arthritis and bronchitis, he wonders whether any of it was worth it. But in what sense?

'These young hooligans wouldn't fight now.'

I feel sadly sure that they would, but couldn't possibly argue with such a veteran as this. And one who bears his unbearable condition with absolute courtesy and not a word of complaint.

♦ ♦ ♦

A newcomer just brought in, his face writhing with pain from his wound. And Mr C still in the operating-room after nearly two hours.

Dread! Dread! Dread!

How did I *dare* to think a single uncharitable thought about fellow-sufferers!

♦ ♦ ♦

Now this is hell, nor are we out of it.

♦ ♦ ♦

About five years ago Lu had her gall-bladder removed. How little I really remember of visiting her in that great hospital at Abergavenny. But my dearly loved daughter was in the sort of pain that I am going to experience next week.

♦ ♦ ♦

A miniature Job is all very well; but haven't I at certain moments over the last two or three weeks seen myself as an almost Christ-like figure – Jesus with a grin? But here in this ward Mr W is a man of more decency, dignity and courage than me: Mr J, who left today, was far kinder to Mr C, and far more concerned with him than I was. As for Mr C, he had the sweetness of his weaknesses. (I saw him just now being wheeled back after two and a half hours of his second operation, his beaky, unconscious face fixed in a mask of misery.)

♦ ♦ ♦

But some relief comes from the absurdity of my chosen last words. They are: 'It is difficult to avoid making noble remarks.' Or, for that matter, facetious ones.

But I know perfectly well that I shall be guilty of no such puerile self-consciousness. God will provide sense and decency: perhaps even the things that most need to be said.

Always, *always*, on this journey any assurance and sense of gain (last night) is followed by a bitter self-perception which almost destroys it. But it must not be allowed to destroy it altogether. If there is any real gain it can only come from holding onto the original assurance in its new state of being tattered and corroded by self-contempt. And so it goes on. And there is no other way for it to go on.

♦ ♦ ♦

'There is a better and a worse way of living with disaster. However great the good of which life has been robbed by it, new good immediately begins to be made if we choose the better way. There are powerful kinds of good that can come into life only where something has gone terribly wrong. That does not justify even the smallest area of life going wrong; it just happens to be one aspect of the composition of things.' Neville Ward, *Friday Afternoon*.

29 MAY
This morning a slow, quite cheerful coming awake, as usual, from 6.30 to 8.00. But I found that the old worry about my post-retirement age future on the *Observer* had lodged in my mind like a piece of grit. A future with no reviewing at all is a worrying prospect. You can't teach an old dog to stop doing old tricks. But worry was quickly cushioned away by the slow and regular palpitations of this womb-hospital.

I learn from one of the nurses that Mr W was a sergeant-major. He didn't mention this yesterday.

◆ ◆ ◆

Am I becoming institutionalised – after three days? Certainly I positively enjoyed my first two or three hospitals, and took violently against them only when I had two in quick succession twelve years ago – Achilles tendon, then appendicitis. The ordered and well-regulated life does have a strong appeal for me: also the company, not too much enforced but pleasantly *there* for each of us to join in as much or as little as we choose.

◆ ◆ ◆

Tomorrow's menu to be chosen from at about 8.45. The choice is hardly exciting, of course, but it deserves to be pondered.

◆ ◆ ◆

When reading *Christ in You* – the only flagrantly religious title so far, here in hospital – I bend the book over so as to conceal it. This is not in the least due to shame; to not daring to be a Christian witness, etc., but simply to a (perhaps ludicrous) notion of good manners. Even to this extent one should not thrust one's faith at others.

It is not as if any of the others, observing that I read holy books, would be the slightest bit inclined to look with more favour on religion. And I think that what 'the times' need is far more quietness about our beliefs; far less hectoring; far less wearing of our faith on our sleeves.

Then what about *Part of a Journey*?

371

That is quite different; a deliberate vocational act. Besides, nobody has to read it unless he wants to.

◆ ◆ ◆

For the first time this morning a real desire to eat as much as I can get down and to walk 300 paces up and down the passage. I dare say the good news about my kidneys has freshened up my optimism in the ordinary sense of the word: the hope that I shall get well and stay well.

But as soon as this occurred to me I immediately tested for death reactions. All serene! I foresee no danger at all that a healthy and increasing desire to live longer will produce any new fear of failing to do so. God holds me so firmly in the trust that either outcome will be good.

◆ ◆ ◆

Yesterday Jason and I were talking with approval about the anti-nuclear power movement in Europe. Just now Mr K brought over to me the house journal of the company he worked for until retirement. They make switches and circuit-breakers for nuclear power stations!

I did make a nervous remark or two about radiation and disposal of nuclear waste: but he dismissed all that with total confidence. And what ignorant protester would dare to argue with such an expert? Any more than I dared to discuss war and peace with Sergeant-Major W. Or care to make a parade of my faith before any of them.

Still, at least I now keep my beads on top of the bedclothes when I tell them, instead of under the sheets as I did on my first day, very uncomfortably.

◆ ◆ ◆

An hour ago I talked to Mr C in his recuperation room, much tubed-up but far more cheery than he was yesterday before the operation. Just now there has been a scurrying of nurses down the passage, and we are told that 'Mr C is not very well.'

How can one do anything *but* pray fervently for him and his wife – however useless one knows that such prayers have proved to be, over and over and over again.

◆ ◆ ◆

And now a nurse comes into the bay and I ask how he is. 'He died,' she says; and we – Mr N, Mr K, Mr W and I – are stricken. We speak of his wife, but then say nothing else.

Of course, I think with more horror than ever of how uncharitably I wrote about him two days ago.

What prayer can I offer now which won't seem futile or worse? That she, the childless widow, shall derive good from this appalling harm? That seems true and sound enough in a book (Neville Ward), but it is hard to cling onto when you are so close to a real case in all its unspeakable emptiness; vacuity. (Seeing Mrs C led into the secretary's office.)

And Mr W? What does he feel, who saw so many thousands killed when he was a boy, and many of those his friends? He looks too old and worn to care. Perhaps that can happen; I don't know.

Yesterday S gave me the news of an old friend's death in Monmouth. It was a shock – but not, to be frank, a very great one, for he had been ill off and on for years. And now this virtual stranger's death appals me.

I have been so glib about my own death, and S's widowing!

◆ ◆ ◆

And now a hearty, puce-faced Scotsman of seventy is being settled in Mr C's bed. He can't possibly know how his jollity grates on the ward, but I hope he won't be too ebullient for too much of the time. (I would hope that, of course, in any circumstances.)

◆ ◆ ◆

Now Mr T has done his rounds; and this time he seemed much more godly and aloof. I had expected him to know all about my case, the results of my tests, etc. But no, the other two doctors had to explain everything to him; and, when I said (which I'd said twice before to others) that my last shot of penicillin had very nearly killed me with an anaphylactic shock, they all seemed surprised–and Mr T ordered this to be written in large red letters across my papers.

That would have been a particularly foolish sort of death.

And now I am more or less told to go home after all – till Tuesday. Upsetting.

◆ ◆ ◆

One thing I become more and more convinced of – that Christians make a terrible error if they base even the slightest part of their faith on any form of survival. Our faith must stand or fall on this that we know – in all its misery, horror, apparent hopelessness. Unless it can make its harsh but saving sense out of what we experience here and now, it is a useless fairy-tale.

Not that we can now *know* there is nothing after death, any more than we can *know* there is something. But even if we knew that we would survive, the faith would still have to depend on *this* reality of matter and spirit for its justification. There is something demeaning and vacuous about the assurance that ultimately we needn't care what

happens to us here because all will be wonderfully well afterwards.

Treat death as a blank of ignorance; treat life as something which
must be hallowed here and now. Every here: every now.

◆ ◆ ◆

How incurably corrupt our reactions are! Inextricably tangled with
my horror at Mr C's death is a sense of drama – even of it being a
valuable item for this notebook.

Don't exaggerate, though!

◆ ◆ ◆

Woodroyd. Back in the old bed again for four more nights. Many
solicitous telephone calls. But a strange sense of existing between two
worlds. I *really* still belong in the hospital, and will do so until the
operation is over and they give me my order of release. So the house
and the room seem almost alien; certainly a bit unreal.

◆ ◆ ◆

Perhaps our situation is something like this:

> P feels: 'I have had extraordinary experiences, even made extra-
> ordinary discoveries, which I want to tell her about. But when I try
> to do this I am reduced to stuttering confusion by the thick blanket
> of her resistance.'

> S feels: 'He is constantly trying to impose himself and his beliefs on
> me, so I must resist him in order to survive as an autonomous
> person. He does not really respect my autonomy, but sees me
> chiefly in the light of his own personality.'

For example, tonight we started to talk about death. The topic simply
evaporated between us.

She is unwilling to think in terms of loving and creative change,
partly because he talks about it far more than he achieves it.

She is very suspicious of his talk: he is hurt, perhaps angered, by her
suspicion.

She does not grant enough to the genuineness of his talk: he does not
grant enough to the justification of her suspicions.

30 MAY
But a very good talk with S in the kitchen this morning. We were able
to discuss (*a*) ourselves and (*b*) our religious attitudes without once
raising our voices or even interrupting each other.

374

I see how close we can come if only we allow ourselves to approach each other quietly.

◆ ◆ ◆

Amazing! I drove into St Briavels this morning and had a pint in the George!

My outward health is certainly far better now than before I went into hospital. This must be largely because I was worried before about a whole number of things which have now been cleared up. A sense that all my insides were a convoluted mess; a dread of the hospital; fears about S.

Now I know exactly what is wrong with my body, when and how it will be dealt with; I know and like the hospital; S and I are closer than for a long time, and clearer.

◆ ◆ ◆

Letters of loving condolence about my illness mingle with letters of loving communication about my book. I find that by now I don't distinguish very sharply between them.

◆ ◆ ◆

Reading a new book, by Pamela Vermes, on Buber – who became (with Simone Weil) one of the two guiding lights at the end of *Pantaloon* – I suddenly realise that I no longer think of mysticism as the primary and essential witness to the reality of God. I don't understand how any thoughtful believer could be *hostile* to the great mystics; but nor do I any longer believe that the single test of religious advance is how near you can get to the 'Unitive Way'.

Nor do I now think that prayer can be tested by experience or non-experience of God. For I now understand that God works in us in ways of which we are quite unaware until, perhaps, we are looking back instead of staring with great fixity into the present moment.

Or better, perhaps, to say that as we are trying to live in the present moment we may become quite suddenly aware that its quality is different now from what it was one year, two years, three years ago.

Just as the scientists now believe that evolution occurred by sudden mutations rather than by gradual change, so it may be that our spiritual growth is of the same kind.

◆ ◆ ◆

What did Buber mean by 'God's everlasting birth'? It is a phrase which fills me with excitement, hope and half-understanding.

◆ ◆ ◆

375

Is it possible that somebody generally recognised as a great saint, in action, in prayer, in being, might say on his death-bed: 'I have never had a single moment's experience which I would confidently describe as an experience of God'?

I think it quite possible – and also that he lived and died in the most ardent faith, hope and love.

◆ ◆ ◆

This lady (Pamela Vermes) tells us that total doubt of God's existence is an integral element in *I and Thou*. I found no such thing in that book. To me it would be a disastrous rift, utterly destroying the book's value.

Thoughtful believers rightly make a great deal of doubt in our time, but it should never be other than a necessary form of suffering, and a falling away from truth. Never to have doubted may mean never to have fully believed. To incorporate doubt into one's abiding faith is an act of sheer nihilism: the faith is instantly exploded and nothing is left but hollow words.

Oh the terrible sophistications of our age!

◆ ◆ ◆

Without being fully aware of it, S might say something like this to herself: 'Always *him*! First the Noisy Boozing; then the Community; then the Depression; then the Pious Withdrawal; then the Book; then the Cancer . . . Then the Death?'

◆ ◆ ◆

Praying for my brother, Bun, this evening, as I often do, I found these words: 'Heavenly Mother, give him the *freedom* in which his goodness of heart may grow: let him have enough *space* for his soul to swell and shine in.' (We are all so fearfully cramped by the faults and weaknesses which have themselves swollen within us, and so much against our will.)

◆ ◆ ◆

Thanking God each night for keeping me in strength – and for some growth in my understanding. Though not in ways that I could put into words.

This is one of the simplest and most natural prayers I have ever prayed.

◆ ◆ ◆

I don't think there is much pride in my fairly calm acceptance of death as a real possibility. But I do get a certain satisfaction from the occasional evidence of surprise which I observe in my loved ones. The non-believers among them will probably say, his *religion* gave him a strength he would never have had without it. Alas, they are very unlikely to say, his *God* (and therefore ours too) must have given him this strength.

◆ ◆ ◆

'At one time the work of this stage of life was mistakenly described as preparation for death. The Christian life is not a preparation for anything; it is a learning how to live here and now in freedom from fear and self-concern, in open faith and hope and love.' Neville Ward, in *Friday Afternoon*.

31 MAY
Spent part of this Sunday morning typing some quite complicated information for Collins's reapplication to the Arts Council for a grant.

They seem very optimistic about getting at least a token, and this will greatly help in trying to interest some rich Texan university in sponsoring *Pantaloon*. I don't care overmuch by now, but it would be very nice if *Pantaloon* were published during my lifetime.

But it now seems more important to me that I should get this journal into a publishable state.

◆ ◆ ◆

John Silverlight (of the *Observer*) offers the consolation that Moshe Dayan had just my operation three years ago – and look at him still! If my eye gets any worse, I might resemble him in more ways than one.

◆ ◆ ◆

A beautiful afternoon for a change, and as I half-drowsed up here I heard S working in the little bed outside my open window to make herself a herb garden. Also the *Rosenkavalier* on the radio, and suddenly that wonderful tenor aria, opening the way towards heaven. (How atrocious that would be as a metaphor, but I mean it quite literally – if that is a word one can ever use in this domain. Degrees of the metaphorical?)

◆ ◆ ◆

Mind and heart both working badly this evening; death seeming a simple relief from a life here which has become intolerable: unlivable. Sudden bitter resentment against S. This will pass, of course; and even now I know how wrong and *hopeless* it is.

The appalling thought even came to me – a thought *only*, *not* a

377

possibility or a temptation – that my last word might be one of savage abuse. Hell indeed!

Praying for this to pass . . . It begins to pass . . .

I wish I could honestly say that the nightingale is helping it to pass. Not perceptibly – but perhaps imperceptibly.

The Imperceptible Effect. I do believe more and more that this is the deeper and the more enduring.

◆ ◆ ◆

But when I leant out of the window just now I was a *little* transported by the extraordinary clarity and resonance of his song, as if the whole valley below his tree were acting as a sound-box.

◆ ◆ ◆

No more prayers or readings together now. Well, I dare say they never amounted to much – and perhaps I should have realised that I was imposing them on her.

Premature? Or just an error, and always would be? God knows.

1 JUNE

But, thanks be to God, another marvellously quiet, undramatic but genuinely exploratory talk this morning. I think we really *learned* from each other – about each other and about ourselves and about the thirty-one years of complex tensions between us.

If, which is very unlikely indeed, I should go the way of poor Mr C when I am back in hospital, then this weekend will have been a great mercy. A crowning mercy.

◆ ◆ ◆

Just as we certainly keep our greatest love for each other, so we also inflict our different aggressions almost exclusively on each other.

I suppose that in a sense we have both known this before, but never before with such clarity and such mutual understanding.

Buber's responsiveness – which is the only true responsibility.

◆ ◆ ◆

Buber translates the formula YHWH not as I AM THAT I AM but as I WILL BE THERE SUCH AS I WILL BE THERE – i.e. it contains 'a conspicuous theme of unpredictability and novelty' (Pamela Vermes).

This is a further development of 'God's everlasting birth'. Something tremendous is emerging here.

◆ ◆ ◆

John R has just been round for a talk and then lunch. He agrees with me that Christian faith should not be *based* on any doctrine of an afterlife; but he firmly believes that we do continue as individuals after death. I liked to hear him say that, but feel that my own mind must remain entirely open.

◆ ◆ ◆

And this afternoon, the voices of my wife and my son gardening outside to the indefatigable cuckoo.

Disturbed at the prospect of my quickly approaching operation. But if I can think of my mind as *essentially* a receiver and not a manufacturer (of, for example, anxious anticipations of pain) then I know that what I shall receive will be strength and unspoken understanding. Peace, in fact: that peace which the world cannot give.

◆ ◆ ◆

The more I think about Jesus of Nazareth the more heart-breaking it seems that so very few people were able to know him. All we have of his ministry is a jumble of corrupted words: but he himself must have been so much more wonderful than even the best of his words.

◆ ◆ ◆

Well, the last day of the hols has been pretty good, after all; an energetic walk to the usual corner, stopping for a chat with Jeffrey, Nasi and Simon; then a large meal of lamb, kedgeree and broccoli; cheerful talk with S and Jase . . .

S said that my quite cheerful feelings about going back to the hospital are a complete contrast to my terror and tears each of the six times I had to go back to Bristol for my E C T. All that is more or less a blank to me now – but this I do know, from many other sources as well as my own experience, that bad depression is the most total horror and desolation that a human being can know. The prospect of death by cancer is child's play in comparison.

◆ ◆ ◆

I have to understand that S's more or less irreligious temperament is not just her right but perhaps right, *tout court*. That (in my terms) God perceives that the loving co-existence of religious man and irreligious wife can be a great good. (Anyway, 'irreligious' is perhaps too strong a word: she would say – has said – that her Way is through people. I might presume to say that she moves towards God best by not even considering God. The Imperceptible Effect – as in me!

◆ ◆ ◆

The Incarnation. Believing that God could be seen with *extraordinary* clarity in Jesus, we recognise all the better that God can be seen with *ordinary but perpetually surprising* clarity in our wife, our friend, our ward-mate in hospital.

◆ ◆ ◆

I must say the thought of death under the anaesthetic is extremely repellent to me. That would be to die like a dog being put down: there would be no *dying*, and if I don't have to face an utterly reducing process of dehumanisation I don't want to be deprived of the proper stages. I want to learn all I can from it; and I know there is far more to learn than I've learned so far.

2 JUNE
Back in hospital. New young houseman around to explain all details of the operation. What emerges is that if there has been no spread my chances are 'good' (whatever that means), but that if it has spread they are virtually non-existent – i.e. neither radiotherapy nor chemo-therapy would be any use.

This seems rather more formidable than I'd supposed; but I must not let it lower my spirits, which are reasonably high just now. Slipping very easily back into my 'other' bed and the ways of the ward – but only Mr K is left of my old comrades. (What a *long* time it seems since I was here before!)

◆ ◆ ◆

Spoke to a man of about forty in one of the single rooms who has a growth on a kidney. How much worse his state than mine – in his trouble but, still more in his wretchedly young age.

Also, Mr K has just been over to my bed for a long and very complex talk about his domestic worries – chiefly his wife's vague-ness and tendency to leave money lying about. He seems more concerned about this than about his own condition.

◆ ◆ ◆

They have now begun clearing out my bowels – which must, says the staff-nurse, be 'crystal clear' for the operation.

Painful spasms; violent diarrhoea.

Drip attached to mobile stand, so that I can take it with me on my constant visits to the lavatory.

It has begun now – the discomfort which must get much worse before it gets better.

◆ ◆ ◆

Suddenly and inexplicably we are wheeled into the other bay of Ward 10 (male) in quick succession. Now indeed I am on the assembly-line – a grim feeling: the honeymoon well and truly over.

I wouldn't wish to live in *this* present moment, let alone the ones that are coming!

Helpful nurse to dry-shave my belly and cock – very disagreeable, particularly with shooting pains from that monstrous purge. Then yet another X-ray, with an enema to follow . . .

But I try to tell myself that all this is given a certain grandeur by the high level of my operation: it is on the grand scale, surely.

◆ ◆ ◆

From little remarks made to me or overheard I feel sure that nearly all of us are apprehensive; even frightened. And we are brought tentatively close in our anxiety.

◆ ◆ ◆

The Work of God. An alarming image came to me this evening of us all as miners, each cut off in his own shaft; the company of heaven working towards us from outside; working to free us into the unimaginable sunlight.

◆ ◆ ◆

How bright and *strange* these visitors already begin to seem. The world of positive health, after all, is already about four months away from me.

And how desperate the conversation with this probably dying old man in the next bed. Either, 'You look so much better . . . you'll soon be home,' etc., or detailed talk about what people are doing in the outside world in which nobody even *hopes* that the inmate takes the faintest interest.

◆ ◆ ◆

Oh keep us in *hope*, dear God!

◆ ◆ ◆

'I haven't given up hope,' says the old man's dear wife, 'and *you* mustn't give up hope. If we both pull together we'll be all right, the way we always have been.'

'No, I haven't been watching the telly. We neither of us ever did, did we, when the other one wasn't there? We only like to watch the telly together, Tom.' No self-pity. No falsity. The *quietness* of love. Everything she says is perfect: the holy common sense of long, long married love.

And as she was leaving she smiled down at me and tickled my bare toes!

♦ ♦ ♦

I cannot get over the wry, comical, *good* face of that old lady, as she looked at my face to see whether tickling my toes would be all right. How delighted I am that she instantly saw that it would be!

♦ ♦ ♦

This is the bay for those awaiting an operation; my old one – except for me – for those who've had one. Veterans there; rookies here, just about to go over the top.

♦ ♦ ♦

As soon as any writer speaks of the Eucharist as 'the central and fundamental act of Christian worship' and so on, my heart sinks a mile and I either abandon the book or make a hop, skip and jump. Alas, this rite means *nothing whatever to me* – except, I suppose, a concentration of shared worship.

♦ ♦ ♦

It is certainly *not* true that this most recent of many hospital experiences has led me – after my long seclusion – to marvel at 'the goodness of ordinary folk' or any nauseating rubbish of that sort. After all, I have been well acquainted with ordinary people at many periods of my life; and it would show an astonishing previous blindness if this old slush suddenly flashed on my mind like light from heaven.

I was never a misanthropist, in any case.

But still I have been more impressed by kindness here than by any other human quality. It is a place in which kindness can flourish.

3 JUNE DERBY DAY
7.00 So I am fifth and last on the list: therefore may be put off until tomorrow. This fills me with dismay, anxiety, etc. But let it not get worse than that! After all the very unpleasant preparations yesterday, and the disappointment last week, a further postponement would be a real blow.

8.20 'The Peace of God . . . The Peace of God . . . The Peace of God . . . ' on the rosary, 500 times. This seems to have done a little good. But the best is simply to assume that there will be another postponement.

No doubt I am much better at accepting this sort of thing than I used to be. But I don't find it easy.

So now I dread the operation being put off far more than I've ever dreaded the operation.

10.05   Four hours of lying flat since they got me up: 1,000 beads and 'Peace of God's. How would I have borne this boredom before I began to pray and meditate? Much boredom; considerable anxiety (about postponement); slight fear.

But also a certain satisfaction in taking it without even inner complaint.

11.00   Courage, patience, fortitude – the three qualities I have most obviously lacked are just the ones I am going to need most for the next three weeks.

Be here now – which means, make the most of the hours before zero hour. (And will mean, make the most of the long, long hours after the operation, but as I well know there are degrees of pain and discomfort which almost prohibit wise thoughts, prayers, meditation, etc.)

12.00   I think it is the total emptiness of these hours which is the most afflicting element. And it would be foolish not to say that those with more equable and easy-going temperaments find this sort of thing much easier than even my amended self.

Heavenly Mother, give me the strength to be peaceful.

♦ ♦ ♦

'In a major experience of adversity . . . the struggle is not "about" *enduring* the suffering but *serving God in it*.' Neville Ward.

Yes, yes! I think he is right but it is hard indeed to understand what it means for me here and now. No physical pain or discomfort, but this is the worst so far (except for that dreadful day at Woodroyd). If I *knew* that I was to be done today, three-quarters of the wretchedness would go.

I think I exaggerate a little, though.

Everything is tolerable.

♦ ♦ ♦

Think of S and Jase at home. Think *hard* of them – what they are doing now; thinking; saying; feeling – and thus try to keep the mind off this wretched centre of the universe here in this bed.

♦ ♦ ♦

Seems better now: calm being given.

◆ ◆ ◆

My opposite neighbour, a rather pompous and querulous man, has just been making a great fuss about his *barium enema*! (Nothing!) This makes me feel better, though no doubt it shouldn't.

◆ ◆ ◆

How one genuinely longs to enter a temporary torment. Now, every minute takes me towards the worst: then every moment will take me away from it.

As for DEATH, except for my usual assumption that I shall die under the anaesthetic, there are too many other things to think about.

4 JUNE

The most terrifying physical experience of my life. Coming to from the anaesthetic I was completely paralysed, though hearing everything they were saying with perfect clarity. And I was being throttled by a breathing-tube deep into my lungs. *At last* they took it out and I could breathe again.

About two hours later S, Jase, Laura and Phine were there, and I could tell at once that the news was severe. S was very, very gentle and a little tearful; had spoken to Dr P and learned that the cancer had spread so widely that they'd simply sewn me straight up again without taking anything out at all.

'They say,' she told me, stroking my cheek, tears shining in her eyes, 'that it will be weeks rather than months.' The last blow – and not *really* unexpected. It does make a strange and appropriate pattern.

Anyway, they filled me full of analgesics and I spent a weird night, dopey but increasingly aware of the situation. Moments of horror, but longer periods of acceptance. Grief for S, but what a joy these children are being and will be to both of us. The love of my family is a wonderful sustenance.

The nurses take care of me as if I were an eight year old. And this particular one, in the Intensive Care Unit, is really an angel of loving-kindness.

◆ ◆ ◆

CANCER – a galloping crab.

◆ ◆ ◆

Dreadful afternoon of vomiting, stomach cramps and implacable coughing. At last they gave me yet a fourth type of analgesic, which does seem to do the trick – i.e. stop the pain without muffling my mind. This is supremely important, for however many weeks there are to be.

Then they got me out of bed and into the chair for the first time since the operation. I had dreaded this; but in fact it was positively refreshing. I stumped out 400 steps from my chair – and one of the sisters said I might even get home this weekend. I now really do have this firm resolution *to get as well as I can for as long as I can*.

When S and Lu came this morning, they said they needed these visits as much as I do. A beautiful and heartening idea – and we have promised not to tell white lies. This is our way now.

◆ ◆ ◆

The little woman in her sixties coming into my room to tell me about her friend who had just been brought in with what must have seemed like a serious cancer. She started talking about prayer, and we found that we agreed exactly about what it should and shouldn't be. 'Thanks for the help you've given me,' she said as she left, and I thanked her back, and both of us were speaking the truth.

◆ ◆ ◆

Reverend Mother just rang up to send her love. And Guy. And Paul. And Anne and Anne Charles and Ann Horne. And Bill. And Terry. And Jack. And Pinkie and Martyn . . .

Also more letters about *Journey* – better letters than I'd dared to hope for.

I don't see why it shouldn't be a far better ending than I'd ever expected.

◆ ◆ ◆

'Flo', whom I hear but never see, is driving the other ladies mad with her whining, artfully-offensive, self-pitying selfishness. And if I were in her bay, I'd probably have been fairly rude to her long ago.

But the worst I've ever heard from the other women was a slight inflection of weariness.

5 JUNE
Very hard work washing and shaving entirely on my own. This immediate objective of regaining all the health that I can is absolutely essential to me.

Mr T is coming round this morning, and I suppose I *would* rather like a word of praise from that handsome fellow. But I am not in the least dependent on it. What means much the most to me is Lu, S, J, J

385

and Laura all saying that their visits to me were not by any means pure charity: that they benefit from them as I do (though not *as much* as I do, of course, I add to myself).

◆ ◆ ◆

But now (10.30) that Mr T and his cortège have been and gone without a single pat on the back, I do realise how very inappropriate that would have been.

◆ ◆ ◆

I don't believe that at the moment any of us have passed into a deep sense of grief for ourselves. There is so much to be done, thought through, felt through: to be raised by, rather than to be sunk by.

(But as always in a close circle it is surely the leaver who is the lucky one. And, in the case of S and me, how far worse for the children if S had been 'taken' first!)

◆ ◆ ◆

In discourse now, compliments get thinned out of our love. There's no need for them to pick the currants in the spotted dog.

◆ ◆ ◆

Also it is still an immense mercy that we do not know the hour, the day, the week. When other men enter into this decision – e.g., planned execution – the intolerable has happened.

6 JUNE

Sunday? Not even sure of the day and frighteningly disorientated, I realise that I've adopted one policy far, far beyond usual excess – i.e. that of taking tablets, injections, etc., whenever offered. At this rate I'll simply fade away before ever getting back to Woodroyd.

Must concentrate on *next* move, to give impression of being manageable there. A tricky manoeuvre, because underneath it all I am – at least temporarily – very disorientated.

◆ ◆ ◆

A very amiable perpetual battle between the small plain nurse and me about whether I am to get out and wash myself.

In a sense, I have *all* the cards – but she knows I can't claim the privileges of the dying unless I really *am* dying, and she knows I don't want this to happen *nearly* yet. I also know that I can't keep going that much longer unless I do really attempt her strength through my campaign. Another of those interminable *divine catches*!

386

How clearly sentimentality differentiates itself at this time. How closely and directly, for example, Phine and I were able to talk last night. And each revelation of divine love is a revelation of shared feeling.

◆ ◆ ◆

Though far, far from completion, the process of purifying my feelings does go on. For example, a certain tender drama attaches to me seeing Anne this afternoon: but much more an honest longing for simple words of assurance and love.

◆ ◆ ◆

Now the nurses are practising turns and reverses as they *chassé* down the passage together. There is no tension or even contrast between the serious and the frivolous sides of their art.

◆ ◆ ◆

11.58 The night-long dreams (suddenly come back) of the military hospital after Balaclava.

Other waves of memory: that we are all honoured and elevated to the ranks of the military dying. But I was aware that this was made more real by the fact that many of the *patients* were female; and one tremendous R S M was a very grand nurse.

In fact at *this* hospital level there is not much distinction between the tragic and the frivolous. Everything can be either; more 'either' than at most times.

◆ ◆ ◆

A last visit from Mr K who is going out today, cured physically but up to now still domestically discontented as he has been for the last forty-nine years! Whereas I go home to a few weeks of great family happiness.

I remember I put a problem of this sort to myself in *Part of a Journey* – and decided in favour of the (then hypothetical) second case. Very glad to find I now do – in fact.

◆ ◆ ◆

There may be several last-minute shocks still to come, but it still seems that the usual impurifying old self-consciousness really has blown away at last. How can we best show our love, most truthfully? For nothing else matters in the least.

◆ ◆ ◆

387

Running on the Walberswick Marshes; mud between the toes, geese overhead, etc. Fine, but no loss of any significance.

Clearing the way, clearing the way, clearing the way – so that S and I can move forward into that supreme stage of *this* way.

◆ ◆ ◆

Palpitating pieces of information float to and fro; flotsam from time past . . .

Is there recompense still to be made? For how much? For how long?

7 JUNE

No fear of death – except that I terribly want to see them again: *must* see S again, though certainly not to say anything specific to her.

I live, am nursed and helped now only because I belong to a society which doesn't believe in putting its old, useless and suffering people out of the way. And so long as I can write I don't want to be scrapped.

MERCY!

◆ ◆ ◆

Fading quickly down again in body and in mind. If only they didn't seem to *have* to go together.

Everything falls off the bed, gets moved, mislaid, taken away. Utter despairing querulousness: on point of tears or screams.

PRAY??!!??

◆ ◆ ◆

Talked and cried separately with Jase, S, Laura and Lu. A very good and very necessary stage. To each a special relationship, and a full one. Most to S, of course, and not just because we are husband and wife, but because she normally finds it so hard to think and feel and speak in these terms.

Such a simplicity of love underneath it all.

◆ ◆ ◆

How rare and wonderful when an aspiration becomes a fact. 'Love is indivisible' is a thought which has constantly and hopefully come back to my mind so many times. Now I know unless I love S, I love *nobody* truthfully and wholly. She is the gauge of my true love of all others.

◆ ◆ ◆

Praying and trying to pray are so very different from each other that perhaps they should be undertaken with the different ambitions always in mind:

388

'Now I am going to try-to-pray.'

'Now I am going to try to pray.'

Perhaps it is equally hard to do both, but I'm sure that the first should be attempted more often; that the second sometimes springs out of the first, the first very seldom out of the second. For true trying-to-pray *is* perhaps praying; something rare, spontaneous and given.

(Any sense in any of this? There is to me, but alas what a muddle to the posthumous reader!)

◆ ◆ ◆

The deep sadness and weariness on young X's face (expecting death) as he passes my door. But because this is a purely fanciful and romantic notion, I put it down here only to illustrate the kind of kitsch I might once have written but no longer have the energy to manage.

◆ ◆ ◆

The twenty-year-old nurse with whom I have a special affinity. The tale of her life and longings. A quiet and self-sufficient girl. In my situation these are the qualities I most respect.

◆ ◆ ◆

First grope to the television room since op. My God, how doddering and senile the ward has become during the last fortnight!

◆ ◆ ◆

Mr T has explained the situation very clearly and well to me since post-op: in fact strangely amended it: now I am to have not 'weeks' but 'months' – two or three months rather than two or three weeks. I was a little worried by the notion that a *severe* burden of two weeks can be borne with more natural heroic virtue (i.e. love) than two months.

They were all reassuring – but this is a two-way game to be played. I must not take the faintest advantage of my wretchedness. Not that it's a matter of calculation but of give-and-take in love, even at its most extreme.

I love her.
He loves him.
She loves him.
I love him . . .

◆ ◆ ◆

389

9.45 Have just dreamed that they, our visitors, are being treated here, and that I've been searching all over the ward for S. I *think* I found her, but woke to the immediate sadness of her not being here.

But then I remember all our quiet words to each other; the sense that we have been shelled like peas, aware of our previous friendly pod but also that we lie open in it to the world.

Great joy is very close!

They seem so genuinely pleased that I shall be back home with them – their rightful property – after Mr T's examination on Friday afternoon. (But it won't be unbearable if I have to stay still longer.)

9 JUNE
Sick, tired, rattled, longing for home . . . 'Nor seems it sweeter ever than it did to die.'

But *shriven*! Shriven! At peace with God and loving all of you the most I ever have.

◆ ◆ ◆

At the present moment the chief horror seems the total deprivation of these scrawled, desultory notes here, probably indecipherable even to myself.

But they are my only life-line.

◆ ◆ ◆

The real test will be this afternoon when they come to see us. My strong temptation will be to 'reveal all', and confess that I'm as low as can be – not even yet (quite) depressed, but tight-drawn and might *go* with a huge *crash* at any time and either way.

Positive antipathies now against several of the nurses, etc.

Oh dear!

◆ ◆ ◆

Luck. For example, Ben would have hated to have talked about his death, and didn't have to, since there was always something vague and uncertain about it. Whereas to me the topic is fascinating, and I must try to guard against being a bore about it.

◆ ◆ ◆

An instant of tension, anguished contradiction. Phine's flowers in bright sunlight on the window-sill: sharp pain across upper abdomen . . .

But a holy meaning is here if you can find it. Further discoveries *must* be made . . .

What is happening, I do now believe, is that the world is now being gradually withdrawn – the senseless collapse is like a slowly advancing tide: twelve hours of familiarity with the dry world is now to be replaced by the strange shapes, ripples and denizens of water.

◆ ◆ ◆

There are now five men in this ward – one young one recovering from a stab-wound in the kidney; the four old ones probably dying of cancer. Not the least sense of 'barricades' between us: gentle goodwill as the sun goes down behind the cathedral. A mellow evening for a county cricket match – what pleasanter fantasy to fade away into!

No, to fade into the reality *between*?

◆ ◆ ◆

We shall share this death more fully and fruitfully than we've shared our lives. (But nothing the least flamboyant.)

◆ ◆ ◆

Now my opposite neighbour has taken to answering questions aloud which I put to him without a spoken word, and at least ten minutes earlier.

Nor do I remember these questions until I hear the answers – *though then I do*.

10 JUNE
I am right up against the window at last, and looking up now into one of the little green valleys of north Herefordshire; a church-tower, a clump on a hillside . . . Is it because I am so tightly co-opted into the world of plain statements and simple things that I want everything to be simple and plain? It isn't as if that valley were winding away into imbecility, but as if the next stage is clear as the first morning again.

◆ ◆ ◆

Never was all work so essentially prayer as it is now: never was it so remote from 'prayer'.

◆ ◆ ◆

That silly bastard W reveals that he's been drinking water all night before his operation. Except for minor pill delinquencies I have been a model of obedience, not only for reasons of common sense but because we suckle this obedience like milk from a kid's mother.

◆ ◆ ◆

391

How we love, and wish to be loved.

◆ ◆ ◆

Ponderous and monumental deliberation of every single thought, word and action.

◆ ◆ ◆

And Sister Lorna writes to tell us that Professor Zich had *just* completed his memorial chapel at the bottom of our hill when the stroke 'took' again. He would have built something else down there, of course, though eighty-three years old, for nobody's work is ever done – but, like mine, it was *substantially* done.

◆ ◆ ◆

Sister L writes to S of the need to 'accept with thanksgiving even if it be so hard to acquiesce with our weak wills . . . I need say no more now – except that I also believe there *is* a right moment and Philip's life-offering seems to have been accepted too *at the right moment*, for all is in God's hands . . . '

◆ ◆ ◆

I read so very little these days – not more than three to four pages a day – that every word takes on an extraordinary significance. These words of love from the Sisters will be my only reading today, and the best I could possibly have.

Sister Karen Joy treating it as *our* book – which is what I would have wanted most of all.

Everything seems to have brought our souls together here and now.

So these letters seem to be not only guiding me and ushering me to heaven, but also drawing S and me closer and closer in the mystery of our closer love.

◆ ◆ ◆

The recognisable faces of the Old Soldiers, not embittered or resigned, but wary, alert . . . as well as seasoned.

◆ ◆ ◆

The 'spiritual', someone said, is the *meaning* of the 'material'.

◆ ◆ ◆

Sister Gillian Mary: 'We are holy ground. Yes, he sows his light in us.'

◆ ◆ ◆

One advantage of this place is that I can stagger from side to side of the passage without it being assumed that I am drunk!

◆ ◆ ◆

Now all six of us are old, gentle and quietly well-disposed towards each other. As if a few ancient opium-eaters had settled down to die in the same den but not exactly *together*. Less fancifully, like a few old logs that have been shifted about at the bottom of a pond and then left to settle to their own devices.

I feel reasonably sure that sudden news of a year's postponement would be good, but news of three months' prevarication, bad. We could much more easily make the larger adjustment than the smaller one.

◆ ◆ ◆

I try to join in the general gossip – half macabre, half concerned and affectionate. But I am too earnest nowadays, or, in flight, too free-flying.

◆ ◆ ◆

Sudden bright aching shafts of TONY are shone through the whole scenario – the real thing. *His* truth.

◆ ◆ ◆

Grief . . . Walking and walking . . . The happiness of nearly understanding.

◆ ◆ ◆

I'm afraid this innocent, inane chattering young man will drive me nuts.

Or does he really help to keep me sane by his Shakespearian-fool-like pitter-patter?

11 JUNE

The first weird gropings of 'dawn', as I sit up and see around me the inexplicable forms of four more or less sleeping old men and one disturbed young one. I puzzle – mildly alarmed – over this scene for perhaps as much as half an hour, receiving more and more hints and suggestions that something is *really* wrong. Now at last, and quite suddenly, I accept the fact that I am soon going to be dead.

Then the detailed gambits come back – e.g., what deployment of pills seems most likely to get me back to Woodroyd quickest?

Also, this whole place has changed its fundamental appearance, and *feel*, several times in the past ten days since I've been back. Just as the people have changed, too – not so much in character as in that *flavour* which is really a much deeper form of apprehension. (This sounds like a supremely – abysmally – literary remark; but it is the opposite. The 'flavour' I mean is pre-literary; even pre-verbal.) And I believe that if I could follow this lead towards the divine centre I would get closer to it than ever before. When I think of S and the others in *these* terms I feel as if I were almost fainting at the possibility of closer communication; even unification. Also, that true *adoration* comes in here.

All stale news, of course, at the Annual Mystics' Convention – 1981 or 1381.

◆ ◆ ◆

Must admit that Steve's absorbed but imbecile staring whenever I am doing anything at all does irritate me rather.

◆ ◆ ◆

It is about one hour till I see Laura, four hours till Phine, six hours till S and Lu (though I always get these things wrong). But none of this time means very much to me. The time which means the most to me is present time – always – thus this is the preparation (*cp. Pantaloon!*).★ Or it could be the slow, rackety latching up of the roller-coaster to its topmost point – its topmost point *so far* – from which . . . It would be foolish even to guess – and on the whole I very seldom do so.

I foresee *a great glory* and I think it would be impossible for me not to do that. (But what form will such a glory take?)

And intervening miseries, deserts, tensions? Simply no point even in wondering.

◆ ◆ ◆

Always new points of genuine interest emerging from one or other of the others. Why never from *me*? It's not that I'm secretive.

◆ ◆ ◆

This seems to be one of those days when you pick on any tag-end anywhere, knowing that it will lead you straight inward to the heart of the flower or outward to the most distant circumference of the universe.

◆ ◆ ◆

★ The final title chosen by P T was *Pantaloon, or The Preparation*, reflecting the central theme of the work.

So many faces of persons forming and blurring away again. Ideal preparation for *calm*, attentive meetings with loved ones.

◆ ◆ ◆

'Ah well, you've got to *laugh!*' says Steve after a particularly long and irritating hinnying. 'You can't keep on crying *all* the time.'

No; but a little more crying now and again might be an improvement.

◆ ◆ ◆

The blurring in my mind of so many different patients and visitors, doctors and nurses is already a sort of unifying process – not THEM and US but THEM-AND-US. And still less do I feel THEM and ME with myself and the rest of the family . . . WE . . . WE.

◆ ◆ ◆

Shifted into a gear of greater simplicity. It does seem as if I have come at least partially out of my hiding – which not only makes it a real pleasure to be suddenly visited by (e.g.) Reverend Crago and Gina, but also makes every small contact the possibility of a little new light.

◆ ◆ ◆

Visited so intensely by so many of the loved-dead. They have been passing *by*, but not in any sense passing *away*, and the message I received (or concocted) was that I would be passing *by* my living friends in the same sort of way. The particular image is of myself at a carriage window, waving to a line of loved ones on the platform as I take a train a few days before they do. And after those few days I shall be on that celestial platform down the line, waiting to greet them one by one; in threes or in dozens as *they* arrive.

(Not to mention the hundreds of beloved dead who arrived long, long before me and were already waiting to greet *me* on my arrival.)

Happy thoughts. And not to be dismissed for that.

◆ ◆ ◆

Then the dismaying idea that I might stay too long in the end; stay beyond our capacity for good conduct continued towards each other.

Only to be written down for the absurdity of the obvious. For the 'good conduct' is not *there* at all, but spread out through every simple and easy manifestation of a love which is being made more and more obvious all the time. By our being together; without drama; certainly without careful consideration of *conduct*. We are being shown; all the time; it is being done.

395

(Perhaps there is some whistling in the dark here. At other times the whistling easily pipes all the dark away.)

◆ ◆ ◆

Appalling Polish news again tonight. So, is our lovable little Garden-of-Future-Memory to be smashed down and churned up by the cruel tanks?

No, not quite so crude as that – but a harsh warning, all the same, against:

> Our metaphysical distress;
> Our kindness to ten persons.

What a weakness of Auden's that he couldn't pay homage first to Martha without abusing Mary; and then vice versa!

◆ ◆ ◆

Growing and nagging dislike of 'irrepressible' young Steve. The rest are fascinated by him, and don't know whether to be appalled or charmed. (Though he wears earphones, he manages to make his music felt by tapping it out with fingers and toes.)

How glad I shall be to get back to wife and daughter – and two nurses! (Must be *very* careful how I treat them in *that* role, though.) Must *fully* co-operate in their efforts to get me as well as I can be, for the long (physical) descent to follow. (Physical descent; spiritual ascent?)

Fight, as I used to fight so hard against all my old physical afflictions.

◆ ◆ ◆

Mr E (cancer, diabetes, Parkinson's, angina . . .) was struggling, and I suddenly realised that with Steve watching the telly I was the most mobile person in the bay (the nurses' bells are not always answered). So I brought over a pillow of my own, and dossed him down in the nearest we could get him to comfort. He looked at me with warm affection out of his heavy, melancholy face.

◆ ◆ ◆

Three nineteenth-century – but just released – Chinese prose writers (very drab covers) sent me, via the *Observer*, to be reviewed. Terry now wanted them back, but I suddenly saw this as my climactic review. There was something I had to dig out of those books, an essential jewel. But there was also something to be robustly refuted; deflated. To let the air out of all that pompous gas bag of the Middle-Kingdom – and yet the whole operation to be seemly in the good old Chinese sense. Something new and extraordinary would emerge from this ceremonial act.

I was becoming aware of all this by about 2.00 a.m. – but it was certainly not a dream. More like one of the old 'hypnagogics'. At 4.00 a.m. I got firmly out of bed with the intention of ringing Terry and *ensuring* that I could review these books, calculating (rightly) that I might just be able to get the review done for the Sunday after next (June 21st). But will he still be *there* – seeing his extreme haggardness in a lavatory mirror? And why 'he'? Why 'there'? Am I already beginning to belong somewhere else?

I was trying to unlock a telephone, but couldn't. Not much caring either.

Finally decided to tell S and Lu about this in the morning. Quite untroubled, back to bed – though the physical effort of doing such things does seem to get greater. (I am hoping for another month at least.)

◆ ◆ ◆

In no sense whatever do I have the feeling of moving *above* the world – but perhaps of reaching out, with feet still firmly planted, and groping outwards like a blind, clumsy, half-mad giant.

◆ ◆ ◆

Sad little stings. S and I drinking at a great mill–pub in Norfolk, after a hard day's riding. Peace and love.

(On the other hand, neither of us would surely envisage an indefinite extension of such occasions without horror.)

◆ ◆ ◆

Physical Descent/Spiritual Ascent: certainly a very common pattern for *holy* dying – Catherine of Siena; Bernadette; Theresa of Lisieux . . . But perhaps the rest of us are given the best physical conditions to match our spiritual state.

◆ ◆ ◆

Ever since Phine was a small child I've had a continuous joke with all my children that they would be taking it in turns to wheel me along the front at Brighton in a Bath chair.

Now S and Lu have hired a wheelchair, and I can be pushed at least as far as Birchfield and back. I shall enjoy this a lot. The irrefutable argument for getting a lift.

◆ ◆ ◆

I could go on lying here, looking at the sky or the ceiling, drowsing, jotting down notes . . . for days, weeks, even months. But I very

397

much doubt whether that would be the deliberate tranquillisation and deceleration which I've been working towards for so long. More like a surrender to Simone's natural force of gravity. *Not* depression, but the torpor of all bovine creatures.

Now – bringing out my beads again – I mean to try at least to make some order out of my heaviness. Even to PRAY again, after so many days.

◆ ◆ ◆

The Last Round-Up

Mr T   Mr B
Dr P
Two staff nurses
Assorted SENS.

The four other old men all have diseased prostate glands and will be in for anything from three weeks to two months; Steve will be out in time for his holiday. I certainly don't feel more unlucky than the others – all of whom have good chances of recovery. But they are all seventy or over, and most of them have more than one mechanical defect.

So, for drab but perfectly respectable hedonistic reasons, I would choose, for myself alone, to die now rather than to linger on rustily and painfully for another five or ten years.

For reasons of love, hope and the spirit I would undoubtedly choose our 'weeks rather than months', in which I do absolutely believe that much that is strange and new will hatch out. If we do only what it seems natural to each of us to do. (As we shall, of course.)

'It is difficult to express the wonder, joy and more with which I feel overwhelmed, watching the way in which Philip's life is being consummated, through so much suffering. How right he is that his way to God is through loving you.' Reverend Mother, in a letter to S last week. I found this rather strong meat at the time, but mean to live up to it – mean to have it lived up to in me.

◆ ◆ ◆

As I left, Mr T came out of his office and said: 'He has been an inspiration to the whole ward – to all of us, doctors and staff as well . . .'

I wanted to say, 'Go on! Go on!', in case any of the family had missed it!

398

S, Jase and Lu brought me home – a rather rough journey – and some emotional apprehensions. The sight of my room, almost completely redecorated in beautiful browns and buffs, new-curtained, new-carpeted . . . was too much of a homecoming surprise for me, and I wept for the first time since S hugged me and gave me the true news after the operation. A short, healthy outburst.

Settled very uneasily into bed, so much the same yet not the same . . . But I was more than touched by all the new equipment, and Lu's delightful little pharmacy. The King's Death Chamber! Bright summer evening on the lawn where bowls will never, alas, be played by the chief instigator . . . (But checked such thoughts, which are always debilitating; never inspiriting.)

◆ ◆ ◆

Sandwich, Complan, pain-killers, laxatives, Ativan . . . They tip-toed away as I trundled quite pleasantly off to sleep . . .

Woken by violent pains across the top of the stomach (5.30), took two more pain-killers; quickly followed by violent and prolonged vomiting.

Really felt death-like when back in bed. How to keep the pain away without the almost equally ferocious 'indigestion'? (How to distinguish them in any case?)

Vision of sweet sinking away, yet in full consciousness of life, death now seems much more remote. Must find some way of dying:

a) not too fast,
b) as alertly as possible,
c) as free of indigestion as possible,
d) as free of pain as possible.

(Order of importance inverse to this.)

Already, alas, no reference whatever to 'holy dying', etc. No good saying, 'Ah, but that's so deeply engrained, you know . . . ' No; prayer must be brought to the front again. God must fill the *whole* mind again! Not, of course, in the sense of being actively thought about all the time – or even on more than very rare and appropriate occasions. But I have learned better than ever in these last few weeks how God can be truly in the mind, suffusing it and colouring all one's thoughts, hopes and actions – or grimly, bleakly absent.

◆ ◆ ◆

399

So we sit up here, Jase and I, talking about various curious aspects of physical pain, quite easily and naturally referring to the present situation. It is poignant, but not unbearably; a little sharper and deeper for the immediate reality.

◆ ◆ ◆

John E swears that he will be able to alleviate physical pain easily enough for my mind and heart to be working fully and properly well before death. *I count on that.*

But there is nothing *to be said*!

(Or do I mean only that there *should* be nothing to be said? Are the necessary things being said, with no great sense of their significance, as the hours pass?)

◆ ◆ ◆

Now whatever we sing in this place, whatever we sing, praise or rejoice here, that we shall glorify a hundred times when we are there.

◆ ◆ ◆

And I am again being pushed and pulled into this world without words, neither dreaming nor awake, neither moving towards God nor away from him . . .

Appendix

Four Extracts from *Pantaloon*

A SERVANT CAVALIER

Watch him now, do,
Our Admiral of the Blue;
Billy the Boy,
Pert master of a convoy;
His fleet the steam-yacht *Lady Maud*;
A cutter; a speed-boat with an outboard.

Here's Billy on his bridge,
A trusty liege;
True friend; loyal servant;
New-baked nautical gallant;
Playmate and counsellor;
Attendant voyager
Through the long courtesies
Of loping summer seas.

On deck below him
Many a tanned or scarlet limb
Of old and young
Simmers in this Aegean sun.
   And there's my honorary mamma,
   Sea-deep in her siesta,
   The toadied queen
   Of all this despicable scene . . .
   Pitifully lank and lean;
   Folds and creases in her flesh;
   Not *altogether* fresh.

But still, but still,
You can surely see, as well,

A certain lizard beauty there,
Dried as a spiced and churring cedar?
    Remember that a queen
    Is her own self but also her demesne.
    And so my affluent lady
    Is her own white Caddy;
    All her boats and scents;
    Gold, myrrh and frankincense.

And if this be a tomb, why
Our spicy tomb is lidded with the sky;
The roof is an eternal blue . . .
    'But *naturally* I love you!'

At which our Billy,
Dreaming of antiquity,
Calls up many a courtly friend
At some royal journey's end:
Those who basked beside
Cleopatra at full tide;
Theodora mummified;
Coarsening Semiramis
In her sepulchral artifice
Of odorous paste and powder,
Growing each year lewder
In the desperation
Of her dissolution.

◆ ◆ ◆

But now Queen Peg has gone
And left her Blue Boy all alone.
She and her party
Have noisily departed
In a snow-white spray
For that clove-and-honey bay.
    So Billy's sprawled on deck,
    Hot wood to cheek,
    Wearing the brief white shorts
    Of all such summer consorts.
    But the rest of Billy
    Is dark as any Gippy;
    Sinewed arm and swelling thigh
    Under the beaming sky.
        And now as he lies half-asleep

He takes a drowsy peep
And sees his gold-haired legs
Shudder like a dreaming dog's,
As if he were trying to run
Out, *out* of this sun;
Or to knee aside
In a great double-bed
Some thin, unwanted mate
Importunate.

Oh but this head is full, is full
Of sun, green sea and gull
All squashed together by the pull
Downwards of the rocking hull.
Here lies a sheerest hulk,
Poor Tom Bowling's bulk . . .

Aye, aye, 'tis absolute,
Billy's moment of truth;
So complete
There's nothing to be said of it.
Of sun and sun-oil all compound;
All-found
And sempiternal
Sun-hatched animal.

Nowt am I now
But a field fallow;
A glug; a glut;
Warm is, and sweet, my gut;
A fuzz; this fuzzing . . .
I hear at last the eternal buzzing
Of Heaven's hive
Where sleepy bees
Zigzag over honied seas . . .

◆ ◆ ◆

Yes, but at Tangiers
Peggy wept dry tears;
And on Bermuda
Billy was even ruder.
Alas, alas,
He was cruel to his lass
From Jamaica to Caracas.

403

Yet on Trinidad
I wasn't so bad.
  (That's where her man ate
  A great pomegranate
  And laughed out all the pips
  From his blood-red-dripping lips.)

At Teneriffe
He climbed a sky-blue cliff,
Being high on kief,
And knew, as all immortals know,
Naught could kill so great a hero.

And ah,
Off Casablanca
You'd have seen these lovers spoon
Like Endymion and the moon.
  (But when we turned back
  To that agglutinated pack
  They stopped their dancing to applaud
  Their lady and her lord,
  As if we two had been
  Playing some great lover's scene
  Just to entertain
  Her parasitic train.)

Only in Gibraltar
Was he a brief defaulter;
Had swum down to the deep sand
And felt the pull of a mermaid's hand,
Cool, cool as algae
Awave in the deep sea,
Awash in his memory,
Stirring some fragment
Of an old lament . . .

  But suddenly he apes
  The apes,
  Their leaps
  And dirty japes.
  Reconstituted clown
  He scampers down
  From the upper town
  And greets his petulant Peg
  With a gorilla's hug.

Yes, now Bill's himself again
All through the Balearic main;
   'Isn't he a brilliant talker!'
   Twixt Majorca and Minorca;
   And in Toulon . . . Oh let it pass,
   For the *Lady Maud* at last
   Has steamed into divine San' Trop,
   The Mecca and the final stop
   Of every summer beau and belle.
      Drôle de lune-de-miel!

◆ ◆ ◆

Now one by one
Fly down into the sun
A swarm – but soon to be a shoal –
Of TONIES grave and droll.
For this is the summer migration
Of the whole denomination;
Tonies lustrous and celestial;
Tonies sturdily terrestrial;
Tonies innocently bestial.

Grave Tony Willoughby,
He's our chief glory;
Nothing of the lackey;
Princely, princely inclined
To kiss an ancient hand.
   Jolly Tony Montague;
   Tony Macdonald-Frazer too . . .
   Each husky man with olive face
   Beautifully knows his place;
   Faint redolence of jungle beast
   Behind the ministering priest:
   A serving knight – and served to taste
   At his lady's midnight feast.

(Now all these Tonies, so I've heard,
Were bred and reared
On a great estancia in
The back-bush of the Argentine.
The genetic plan
Was to produce the perfect man;
The eugenically perfecto
Anglo–dago

Amorous yet sportive hero.
    Therefore the sire in every case
    Was chosen from the Island Race;
    Perhaps a baronet;
    At least a young cadet
    Out of some proud county set.
    The dam, by contrast,
    Was a lovely half-caste
    Señorita;
    Some Pepita
    From the demi-monde of Rio
    Or of Montevideo;
    One of those little monkey-girls,
    Black eyes and curls,
    Tiny hands like paws
    Which discover tiny claws
    Whenever Milord displays
    His icy-hearted ways.)

Well, in no time Billy
Is of that sodality.
Yes, our burnished roamer,
Far-from-homer,
Has found at last his happy niche.
No discomfort, not an itch
As he takes his place amid
These dark heroes of the bed.

And now this credulous young beau
Becomes an honest gigolo,
Daily reciting that great credo
Of the male seraglio:
    'I believe in the golden sun
    'Who shines his light on everyone.
    'O bountiful sun,
    'Your gold light is spun
    'On that celestial spinning-wheel
    'And changes every cad or heel
    'Into a true cavalier
    'Without reproach or fear.'

    What should Billy fear?

Now every tall attentive consort
Is superb on the tennis-court;

High-diver;
Fast but never reckless driver;
At bridge a delicate imparter
Of goodies to his happy partner.
   Opening bottles of champagne
   In the Hôtel de la Reine
   Tony – this is Montague –
   Hums a meridian billet-doux
   As he neatly bends
   His supple trunk, and lends
   Something – oh, *imperial*;
   Prodigal,
   To the morning festival.

But Billy with his dander up
Swears no half-Peruvian tup
Shall outdo his own finesse
In serving an enchantress.
   Watch my overhead smash!
   Look! There's hardly a splash
   As my body, burnt mulatto,
   Cleaves the blue water of the grotto.
      See him suddenly peck
      Gaily at her lacquered cheek;
      Plant a deftly passing kiss
      On the plucked chin of his mistress.

'Darling!' Peggy gulps to Bill,
'I'll get rid of them all
'Just as soon as ever I can.
'Then we'll scram,
'Just my Billy-Boy and me,
'To my simply heavenly
'Little farm in Normandy.'
   O you passing Tony, *stay*!
   All you of the noon levée,
   Never, never go away!
   Dear Princesse d'Armagnac,
   Quack on forever, quack
   Your Indiana monotone.
   And you, old Colonel Groan,
   I'll stand to attention here
   And lend my willing ear
   To every woe
   Inflicted by your feckless matelot!

'But Peggy Hon,
'This is *such* fun!
'Surely you won't forsake
'All these lovely folk?'

   To be alone, alone,
   And bone to bone,
   With none to mitigate
   Our close-coupled state
   Of she and me
   Bound in our beggary.
      How shall I, all winter long,
      Keep on singing my sweet summer song,
      My falsehearted song
      All the winter long,
      All winter long?

AN INVITATION TO THE SHADE OF
WILLIAM BUTLER YEATS

Midwinter, even on my dead domain,
Stirs underground, and you can almost hear
The first, faint swelling of the crocus bulbs.
But suddenly – listen! Listen now! – below them
The rustle of that unquiet poet turning;
Twisting and elbowing against the turf
They piled above him in the windy churchyard.

And it's conceivable – well, *I've* conceived it –
That he could rise again and celebrate,
As best such poor dead fellows ever can,
The ancient pagan rite of the winter solstice.
   For wasn't he much given in his lifetime
   To dallying with unholy lore and legend?

So now he's up; and now I'll have him stride
Along the westward skyline of Ben Bulben,
Lifting his eagle beak and his white mane
Against the breezes and the swelling seas
Which rise to greet him from the Rosses
And off the stony cape of Knocknarea.

But tell me, ladies of the darkened room,
How shall we *accost* their Honours;
Those dead magnificoes whom we revive
From time to time for our illumination?
Better not catch their noble malady;
Better to keep our voices *down*,
Our language *not too much* exalted
By the infection of their stateliness,
Their ceremonial magniloquence.
I'll aim at something honourably respectful
But not so wilfully everyday
That this itself becomes a sort of bluff
Iago-like deceit and affectation.

Well then, I'll tell him as I trot beside him
That I want nothing half so much this Christmas
As the plain dignity of a discipleship;
Pride in the honest service of a master.
For now that I've taken this great liberty –
Stopping to raise him from the tomb instead
Of riding past with cold eye on the sea –
How can I make it up to him except by swearing
Total allegiance; asking nothing back
Except one flash or glimpse
Of that hermetic light he shed and saw by?

But though a Lazarus restored he'll surely
Put on the same old masks he used to wear
Of scholar and mage; of bard and hunting squire.
Or he might wear the maddened mask of Swift
And match, once more, the savage dean's
Urbanely horrible eviscerations.
Or else with Burke's gold tongue
Praise the ancestral wisdom of the tribe
And send all rancorous Whigs to their perdition.

For, in the manner of such impudent poets,
He got the best of every world in sight.
Think how commandingly he took possession
Of ancient Sligo with its misty rout
Of kings and heroes
Dreamed by those goat-herds of the Iron Age.

Yes, but he also commandeered
That masterful and mastering race of gentry
Who always treated so despisingly
The dark Iberian aborigines.
So, to begin with, he could make his own
The myths and legends of the oldest Ireland
And all that grey-blue twilight of Queen Maeve.
But coming of age his greedy eye began
To range much further, took into its orbit
Squire and peasant; merchant, tinker, hunchback
And even the wildest drunkard of Coolaney.

Later he cast a covetous eye
Southwards towards the Galway plain, and upward
To that old landed aristocracy
Whose patrons, gracious as their ageless swans,
Lament for those consummate sons who die
In battle, and whose ordinary death
Is raised at once to that Parnassus where
All the fortuitously immortalised
Glow in some poet's elegiac sunset.
    What *predatory* birds these poets are!

That's how I'll get him! though his falcon-spirit
Soar up the winds from Inishmurray
And doubtless, if I left him flying free,
Would find a gyre or two to pern in.
I'll bring him down from those great skies of the west
By booming, till they boomerang all round me,
All the rich titles won by our seadog marquis.
And when he hears them sounding back and forth
Along these cobwebbed galleries and chambers
Then surely he'll come swooping from those skies
At my old palace in its grave decline.

I'll fetch him with these blue-green copper tritons
Blowing their crumbling shells at Father Neptune;
With leaden statues lurching from their struts,
And those escutcheoned doors he bowed the knee to
Which surely please him better for being cracked
And half their gilt flaked off, the moulding broken.

Our dear-loved poet dearly loved a lord
And must, by the honour of his calling, honour
A fallen lordship in its dignity
More than the vulgar, bright excess
Of *modern* power and pomp; such as that beast Sir . . .

Oh but he'll come for this Nativity
If only so that he can hymn again
Whatever brute or baby might be born
This time, to rise and swell for the next half-year
Until its apogee and mortal solstice.

See how I take him by the arm and lead him
To where the terrace and its arc of statues
Curls round a hill of snow and icicles,
I'll show him the Temple of Diana there,
The Temple of the Four Winds lower down
In that white valley of black trees and fences.
And further off the mausoleum itself
Wearing that snowy crown on its cupola.

'You were a poet, sir,
'Who gave our earthly passions dignity
'Without embellishing their origins:
'You loved the earth, and could as easily
'Be simple, rabelaisian or bucolic
'As solemnly, prophetically entowered
'Among that lucent swarm of stars and angels.
'You had the fierce and humourless gaiety
'Of children, and could play a dozen parts,
'Assuming each for its particular
'New setting of the eyes; cast up or down;
'Sideways; or so obliquely that they'd catch
'Some stone or tree or creature unawares
'And free the corked-up and indignant spirit
'To range about the world forever after.
'And this would lead you far from Ireland's rose-tree,
'And all the Easter blood that watered it,
'To the dead city of Byzantium.
'A country of the mind, I think you meant,
'Where the great spirit of Lucifer descended
'In a fine blend of his angelic light
'Both after and before the Misadventure.
'This spirit fell on certain goldsmiths there

411

'And lent them such a power of artifice
'That they could make a golden singing-bird
'Which sang the same unearthly-earthy song
'To emperor, beggar, clown and drunken soldier.'

And now we're coming back from that sedate
Perambulation of my lawns and temples.
Now I'm a step in front, and southward,
Not talking any longer; what's the use
When not a single word comes back to me
From that impassive ghost and guest of mine?
But looking out of the corner of my eye
I can still see his elegant body move
In tweeds the colour of September wheat;
A dark green shirt and matching handkerchief
Which makes a tidy triangle of olive
Above the heart – I mean if ghosts *had* hearts –
And at the top a finely-crumpled crest
As white as all these snowy garden-paths.
The glasses dangle on their wide black ribbon
And though his eyes are blinking in this snowlight
They seem as prescient as the golden eyes
Of owls at dusk.
        And now he mounts the steps
To pass into the hall ahead of me,
But when I follow I can hear no footsteps
Except my own, bounced to the dome and back.

IN MEMORIAM: ENGLAND 1946

Stucco on Sunday
And roller-skates in an empty street:
A shrill and gritty echo
Passing the hollow cavern of St Luke's.

Hop-pickers high on their ladders among the vines
Stare derisively down
As the Norwood Ramblers' Club
Stride the weald below them.

The Captain, in her frayed blue bonnet
And the red ribbon of her Army,
Is loved from end to end of Moston.

She homed like an old grey pigeon
To every grieving family
Between the Rochdale and the Oldham Roads.

Through dusty glass,
Wired to plaster rock and water-weed,
The Duke of Grafton's pike
Sheds another silent scale.
> *23 lbs and 12 oz*
> *Caught by Robert Symes esq*
> *In Nuneaton Reservoir*
> *November 10th*
> *1908.*

Claret at Candlemas.
  'Thank you for the gracious thought,
  'Your Lordship,
  'But we Fortescues
  'Have seldom made old bones.'

Holy this hay-land
At pitchfork time
    But all the land-girls are gone
    With their sweet pungency on summer evenings.

The Boys' Brigade marches
Down a dockland street,
Jaunty pill-boxes above
The bloated cheeks of twelve buglers.

Slatted garden gates
Under Wimbledon's acacias.
    The motor-hearse
    And the beribboned wedding Daimler.

David with his pen in his mouth
Staring through the office window,
Peppers the rolling sky again
With bandits at ten thousand.
    And all the clouds begin to throb
    With that old confiscated joy
    Of a single summer.

A black umbrella raised
Against the soft rain from Ireland
Along the Blackpool promenade

A punch-and-judy show;
A blaring steam roundabout;
Khaki pullovers and mufflers.

At Nursehill Farm
We watched the Suffolk Punches plough the skyline.

A half-hunter gold watch
Has been smoothed to flash in the sun
By forty years of friction
With the distended waistcoat pocket
Of Alderman Jaggers, Licensed Victualler.

The vet in his MG;
Hacking-jacket and fox-head stock.
    'Poodles are out; boxers are coming in.
    'The budgie is ousting the canary.'

When the local train pants
Up this soft green valley
Not a cow lifts her head.

General Manders,
Veteran of Bloemfontein and Kimberley,
Stirs the duckweed on Little Chadworth pond
With his burnished cavalry switch.

A thatched cottage,
Mauve and pink,
Half-hidden by purple hollyhocks,
On the winter pavement
Outside the National Portrait Gallery.

Chapped and bony knees
Of November hikers
Over Ullswater.
    'Do I belabour my point too much,
    'Gilbert?'

In the lane behind Wells Cathedral
I bought for a shilling each
Canon Fowler's seven-volume
Coleoptera of the British Islands.

The velvet plop
Of horsedung into Rotten Row.
   Mr Edward Bright of Croydon
   Hurries out with sack and shovel.

Now they're queuing for the Odeon
On a warm mauve evening.

What is the rain dropping,
Blown through Leamington Spa?
Who can tell
What this heavy wind is blowing?

Cook has procured
A leg of lamb for the servants' hall,
And all the trimmings.
   But Fanny scrubs the step.

'Mother, Mother, my phantom-leg
'Is giving me hell again this morning.'
   Where is it buried?
   Soused to the bone in a salty swamp
   Off the Irrawaddy.

'What did you buy at Rudge's?'
   'Half-a-pound of mousetrap
   And a tin of pilchards.'
     (What did I nearly buy
     Under the counter at Fothergill's?
      A blouse of yellow roses
      And a sky-blue slip.)

The postman bought seven Anderson shelters
From his neighbours in Alma Row
To make an underground bed
For the pale spore of mushrooms.
   Now the beam of his torch is moving
   Through these tombs of white, emerging buttons
   In the mouldering dark.

In Memoriam
Lt K. M. ('Kenny') Birkshaw:
Oxford and Bucks Light Infantry:
Loos 1915.
   Gillian
   Madge
   Ronald.

Look, the sails are moving again
Through the plover fields of Norfolk.

Scarlet and sounding brass
Of fire-engines along the Strand.
   But in our Number 9 tram,
   Swaying down the Embankment,
   We hear a softer warning-chime
   As we round the bend at Blackfriars.

Tugs in the Mersey:
A bell-buoy tolling for drowned sailors.

I heard the Wolves howling again
At Molyneux,
And all the Spurs were rattling,
Louder than ever
At White Hart Lane.

'The Inshore Parson'
Has donned sou'wester and oil-skins
To wave for Pathé News
Out of a sea-sprayed lifeboat.

Couples entwined,
Serge over nylon leg,
On the worn grass beside the Serpentine.
   'Shall we join them, Rosie,
   'As we used to do
   'Ages ago?'
      But Rosie flings my hand away
      As if to hurl it
      Over the Cumberland Hotel.

At the bus-stop
A satchel-stuka zooms and stutters.
Mavis gives a cry.

The Lambeth Walk is loudly trumpeted
By five bemedalled ex-servicemen
Along the north gutter of Oxford Street.
   Passing in a west-bound taxi
   Colonel Bagley assaults his wife
   With furious doubts of their credentials.

Half-fallen from its rotting pole.
　　But the hard words have been softened
　　Into a ghostly warning
　　By seven seasons of rain and sun.

And we who have come back to Milly's,
Half-past-three men, but long and harshly compelled
By the twenty-four hour clock,
Have been quick to restore
Our old companionable dereliction.

POSSESSION

To Jenny in Asolo

Possessed by that old hunger for possession
I was the shameless snatcher-up of Jenny
Who, in her untransfigured monkeyhood,
Was claimed by the whole bitching banderlog
Which ate each other's fleas in the Piazza.

But you possessed me too, the turtle's phoenix,
Filling my body with your body of light
Till I was lighter than that sodden air
And rose with you above the rancid city
And all that vapouring stewpot of the sun.

Light as the mountain moonlight, you and I
Levitated like two saints possessed
By the transfiguring angel of Mount Carmel.
And as we flew we shed our monkey-hides
And dropped them into the furnace-fires of Mestre.

Naked as Eve restored to naked Adam
We reached the grace of the forgiving moon.
Absolved by snowlight from those mountains
We were possessed by the sudden holy clatter
Which rose from the campanile of San Bruno.

　　And listen now, my love, my human sister:
　　The clock has stopped tonight in the campanile,
　　And time which once possessed us till we roared,
　　Madder than prisoners, up to the Leads and back,
　　Is now our own to keep our silence in.

And now, being dispossessed of shame and penance,
We'll do whatever we choose because we know
That what we choose to do will be as holy
As if we'd never known that painted
Bride of a swollen and corrupted sea.

In these arcades we join the blessed schism
Of silent lovers walking hand in hand.
We're freed at last from that conventicle
Of Dispossessed in the Palazzo Buggins
Who killed the Word by talking; lost their minds
In a thick trance of matter and dreaming flesh.

Blind to the spirit, deaf to the silent lovers,
How could they ever pierce this holy bubble
In which we float, with other rainbow-breathers,
So self-possessed – each other's self possessing –
A foot above those terraced olive trees.

I who have never known another I
See for the first time through the eye of another.
With your ears I hear the mole in the earth;
With your nose I smell the dung and roses;
Possessed by me you taste the quince I taste.

But O my girl of the attracting moon,
By our possession of each other's spirit
We drew the burning dove to hover here
And stoop at the bright conjunction of our spirits
Till two were three, and three were one entire.

And now I'll change you even for the wiser,
And you, within the cool fire of the Lord,
Shall bless me with a further dispossession
Of our conjoined but flayed and sick baboon.
Feel how he shrinks and shivers from the light
Of our own moonrise in the single heart.

Angelic apes, but patiently inclined
Towards the silent music of the angels,
Over the mountains and the sleeping birds
We shall be dispossessed at last, dear angel,
Of everything except this vacant moonlight.

Bibliography

(Works which Philip Toynbee quotes from or refers to in the text.)

Works by Philip Toynbee
The Barricades, Putnam, London, 1943.
Tea with Mrs Goodman, Horizon, London, 1947.
Pantaloon or The Valediction, Chatto & Windus, London, 1961.
   (An earlier version of the first four sections of *Pantaloon*.)
Views From a Lake, Chatto & Windus, London, 1968.
   (An earlier version of the seventh section of *Pantaloon*.)
Friends Apart, MacGibbon & Kee, London, 1954; second edition, Sidgwick & Jackson, London, 1980.
Part of a Journey: An Autobiographical Journal 1977–1979, Collins, London, 1981; Fount Paperbacks, London, 1982.

Works by other authors
AULÉN, GUSTAF *The Drama and the Symbols*, SPCK, London, 1970.
ALLCHIN, A. M. *The Dynamic of Tradition*, Darton, Longman & Todd, London, 1981.
BACKHOUSE, WILLIAM and JANSON, JAMES (eds) *A Guide to True Peace or the Excellency of Inward and Spiritual Prayer*, Christopher & Jarrett, Stockton, 1813; second edition (corrected and enlarged), W. Alexander, York, 1815; reissued by Harper Bros., London and New York, in association with Pendle Hill Publications, 1946.
BAKER, JOHN AUSTIN *The Foolishness of God*, Darton, Longman & Todd, London, 1970.
BANNISTER, D. and FRANSELLA, F. *Inquiring Man*, second edition, Penguin Books, Harmondsworth, 1980.
BATESON, GREGORY *Mind and Nature*, Collins, London, 1979.
BELLAH, ROBERT N. *Beyond Belief*, Harper & Row, New York, 1970.
BLYTHE, RONALD *The View in Winter*, Allen Lane, London, 1979.
BRAILSFORD, H. N. *The Levellers and the English Revolution*, Cresset Press, London, 1961; Spokesman Books, Nottingham, 1976.

BUBER, MARTIN *Between Man and Man*, translated by Robert Gregor Smith, Fontana Library, London, 1961.
   I and Thou, translated by Walter Kaufmann, T. & T. Clark, Edinburgh, 1970.
   Tales of the Hasidim: The Early Masters, translated by Olga Marx, Schocken Books, New York, 1975.
BUTTERFIELD, HERBERT *Christianity and History*, Fontana Books, London, 1957.
CABAUD, JACQUES *Simone Weil: A Fellowship in Love*, Harvill Press, London, 1964.
CASSIDY, SHEILA *Prayer for Pilgrims*, Fount Paperbacks, London, 1980.
CAUSSADE, JEAN-PIERRE DE *The Sacrament of the Present Moment*, translated by Kitty Muggeridge, Fount Paperbacks, London, 1981.
CHAPMAN, JOHN *Spiritual Letters*, Sheed & Ward, London, 1976.
CUPITT, DON *Taking Leave of God*, SCM Press, London, 1980.
DODD, C. H. *The Founder of Christianity*, Collins, London, 1971.
DOHERTY, CATHERINE DE HUECK *Poustinia*, Fount Paperbacks, London, 1977.
   The Gospel Without Compromise, Fount Paperbacks, London, 1979.
DRURY, JOHN *The Pot and the Knife*, SCM Press, London, 1979.
DUNNE, JOHN S. *A Search for God in Time and Memory*, Sheldon Press, London, 1969.
EDWARDS, DAVID L. *Religion and Change*, second edition, Hodder & Stoughton, London, 1970.
   Leaders of the Church of England 1828–1978, second edition, Hodder & Stoughton, London, 1978.
FARADAY, ANN *The Dream Game*, Temple Smith, London, 1975.
FURLONG, MONICA *Merton: A Biography*, Collins, London, 1980.
GOLLWITZER, H., KUHN, K. and SCHNEIDER, R. (eds) *Dying We Live*, Harvill Press, London, 1956; Fontana Books, London, 1958.
GÖRRES, IDA FRIEDERIKE *Broken Lights: Diaries and Letters 1951–59*, Burns & Oates, London, 1964.
GREENE, BARBARA and GOLLANCZ, VICTOR (eds) *God of a Hundred Names*, Gollancz, London, 1962.
HADFIELD, A. M. *An Introduction to Charles Williams*, Robert Hale, London, 1959.
HAMMARSKJÖLD, DAG *Markings*, translated by Leif Sjöberg and W. H. Auden, Faber & Faber, London, 1964.
HAMPE, JOHANN CHRISTOPH *To Die is Gain*, Darton, Longman & Todd, London, 1979.
HAPPOLD, F. C. *The Journey Inwards*, Darton, Longman & Todd, London, 1968.
HAYNES, RENÉE *The Seeing Eye, the Seeing I*, Hutchinson, London, 1976.
HEYWOOD, ROSALIND *The Infinite Hive*, Chatto & Windus, London, 1964.
HINCHCLIFF, PETER and YOUNG, DAVID *The Human Potential*, Darton, Longman & Todd, London, 1981.
INGLIS, BRIAN *The Natural and the Supernatural*, Hodder & Stoughton, London, 1977.

ISHERWOOD, CHRISTOPHER *Ramakrishna and his Disciples*, Simon & Schuster, New York, 1964; Methuen, London, 1965.
My Guru and his Disciple, Eyre Methuen, London, 1980.
JOFFROY, PIERRE *A Spy for God*, Collins, London, 1970.
JULIAN OF NORWICH *Revelations of Divine Love*, Penguin Books, Harmondsworth, 1966.
KENNY, MARY *Why Christianity Works*, Michael Joseph, London, 1981.
KIERKEGAARD, SØREN *The Journals*, edited and translated by Alexander Dru, Oxford University Press, 1938.
KÜNG, HANS *Does God Exist?*, Collins, London, 1980.
LAMERTON, RICHARD *Care of the Dying*, Penguin Books, Harmondsworth, 1980.
LEECH, KENNETH *True Prayer: An Introduction to Christian Spirituality*, Sheldon Press, London, 1980.
LEWIS, C. S. *Christian Reflections*, Fount Paperbacks, London, 1981.
McKEATING, HENRY *Studying the Old Testament*, Epworth Press, London, 1979.
MACAULAY, ROSE *Letters to a Friend 1950–52*, Collins, London, 1961.
MARCEL, GABRIEL *Problematic Man*, translated by Brian Thompson, Herder & Herder, New York, 1967.
MERTON, THOMAS *New Seeds of Contemplation*, Burns & Oates, London, 1962.
Love and Living, Sheldon Press, London, 1979.
MILES, T. R. *Religion and the Scientific Outlook*, Allen & Unwin, London, 1959.
MOODY, RAYMOND A. *Life after Life*, Bantam Books, New York, 1976.
OMAN, JOHN *Grace and Personality*, Cambridge University Press, 1917 (second edition revised, 1919); Fontana Library, London, 1960.
PAGELS, ELAINE *The Gnostic Gospels*, Weidenfeld & Nicolson, London, 1980.
PASCAL, BLAISE *Pensées*, translated by W. F. Trotter, Dent (Everyman's Library), London, 1908.
PAUL, LESLIE *First Love: An Autobiography*, SPCK, London, 1977.
PERRY, MICHAEL 'The Spiritual Implications of Survival' in Michael Perry, *Psychic Studies: A Christian's View*, Aquarian Press, Wellingborough, 1984.
PETRE, M. D. *Autobiography and Life of George Tyrrell* (2 vols), Edward Arnold, London, 1912.
ROBINSON, EDWARD (ed.) *This Time-Bound Ladder*, Religious Experience Research Unit, Manchester College, Oxford, 1977.
Living the Questions, RERU, Oxford, 1979.
SAGAN, CARL *The Dragons of Eden: Speculations on the Evolution of Human Intelligence*, Hodder & Stoughton, London, 1977.
SCHILLEBEECKX, EDWARD *Jesus: An Experiment in Christology*, Collins, London, 1979.
Christ: The Christian Experience in the Modern World, SCM Press, London, 1980.
SCHUMACHER, E. F. *A Guide for the Perplexed*, Jonathan Cape, London, 1977.
Good Work, Jonathan Cape, London, 1979.

SCHWEITZER, ALBERT *My Life and Thought: An Autobiography*, Allen & Unwin, London, 1933.

SOUTHERN, R. W. *St Anselm and his Biographer*, Cambridge University Press, 1963.

STANLEY, A. P. *Lectures on the History of the Eastern Church*, John Murray, London, 1861; third edition, 1864.

TAYLOR, JOHN V. *The Primal Vision*, SCM Press, London, 1963.

THOMAS, KEITH *Religion and the Decline of Magic*, Weidenfeld & Nicolson, London, 1971; Penguin Books, Harmondsworth, 1973.

THORNTON, MARTIN *Prayer: A New Encounter*, Mowbray, Oxford, 1974.

TOURVILLE, ABBÉ DE *Letters of Direction*, Dacre Press, London, 1939.

TUCHMAN, BARBARA *A Distant Mirror: The Calamitous 14th Century*, Macmillan, London, 1979.

UNDERHILL, EVELYN *The Life of the Spirit and the Life of Today*, Methuen, London, 1922.

Man and the Supernatural, Methuen, London, 1927.

The Letters, edited by Charles Williams, Longman, London, 1943.

VASTO, LANZA DEL *Return to the Source*, translated by Jean Sidgwick, Rider, London, 1971.

VERMES, PAMELA *Buber on God and the Perfect Man*, Scolar Press, London, 1981.

WARD, MAISIE *Caryll Houselander*, Sheed & Ward, London, 1962.

WARD, NEVILLE *The Use of Praying*, Epworth Press, London, 1967.

Friday Afternoon, Epworth Press, London, 1976.

WILLIAMS, CHARLES (ed.) *The New Christian Year*, Oxford University Press, 1941.

WILLIAMS, H. A. *The True Wilderness*, Constable, London, 1965; Penguin Books, Harmondsworth, 1968.

Anonymous
Christ in You, Watkins, London, 1918.